THE WALLFLOWER
YAMATONADESHIKO SHICHIHENGE

28

Tomoko Hayakawa

Translated and adapted by
Andria Cheng

Lettered by
Karl Felton

KC
KODANSHA
COMICS

A Note from the Author

It's been six months since I moved, but things are still a mess in my new place! The worst is that I don't have room for all my clothes so I've had to give a bunch away (while crying!). My sweet cat Ten ♡ has finally adjusted and always lazes around in the warm living room. ♡

Seeing her happy makes me happy! ♡
—Tomoko Hayakawa

THE wallflower

YAMATONADESHIKO SHICHIHENGE

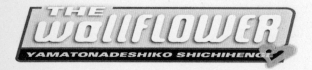

CONTENTS

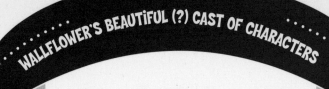

WALLFLOWER'S BEAUTIFUL (?) CAST OF CHARACTERS

SUNAKO IS A DARK LONER WHO LOVES HORROR MOVIES. WHEN HER AUNT, THE LANDLADY OF A BOARDING HOUSE, LEAVES TOWN WITH HER BOYFRIEND, SUNAKO IS FORCED TO LIVE WITH FOUR HANDSOME GUYS. SUNAKO'S AUNT MAKES A DEAL WITH THE BOYS, WHICH CAUSES NOTHING BUT HEADACHES FOR SUNAKO: "MAKE SUNAKO INTO A LADY, AND YOU CAN LIVE RENT-FREE FOR THREE YEARS."

BUT THE ROAD TO BECOMING A LADY ISN'T EASY, AND HER ROMANCE WITH KYOHEI ISN'T PROGRESSING MUCH.

SUDDENLY THE SHOPPING DISTRICT SUNAKO FREQUENTS IS IN TROUBLE! WILL THE FOUR PRETTY BOYS BE HER SAVIOR? ALSO A BONUS PERIOD MANGA SPECIAL! WHAT WILL HAPPEN TO SUNAKO AND KYŌHEI IN EDO?!

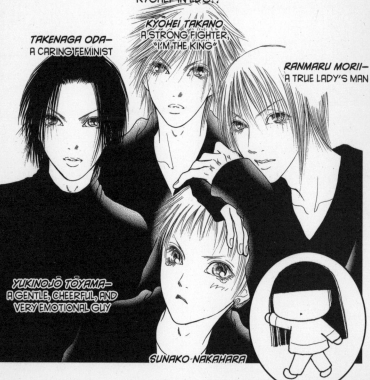

RANMARU MORII—
A TRUE LADY'S MAN
KYŌHEI TAKANO
A STRONG FIGHTER, "I'M THE KING"
TAKENAGA ODA—
A CARING FEMINIST
SUNAKO NAKAHARA
YUKINOJŌ TŌYAMA—
A GENTLE, CHEERFUL, AND VERY EMOTIONAL GUY

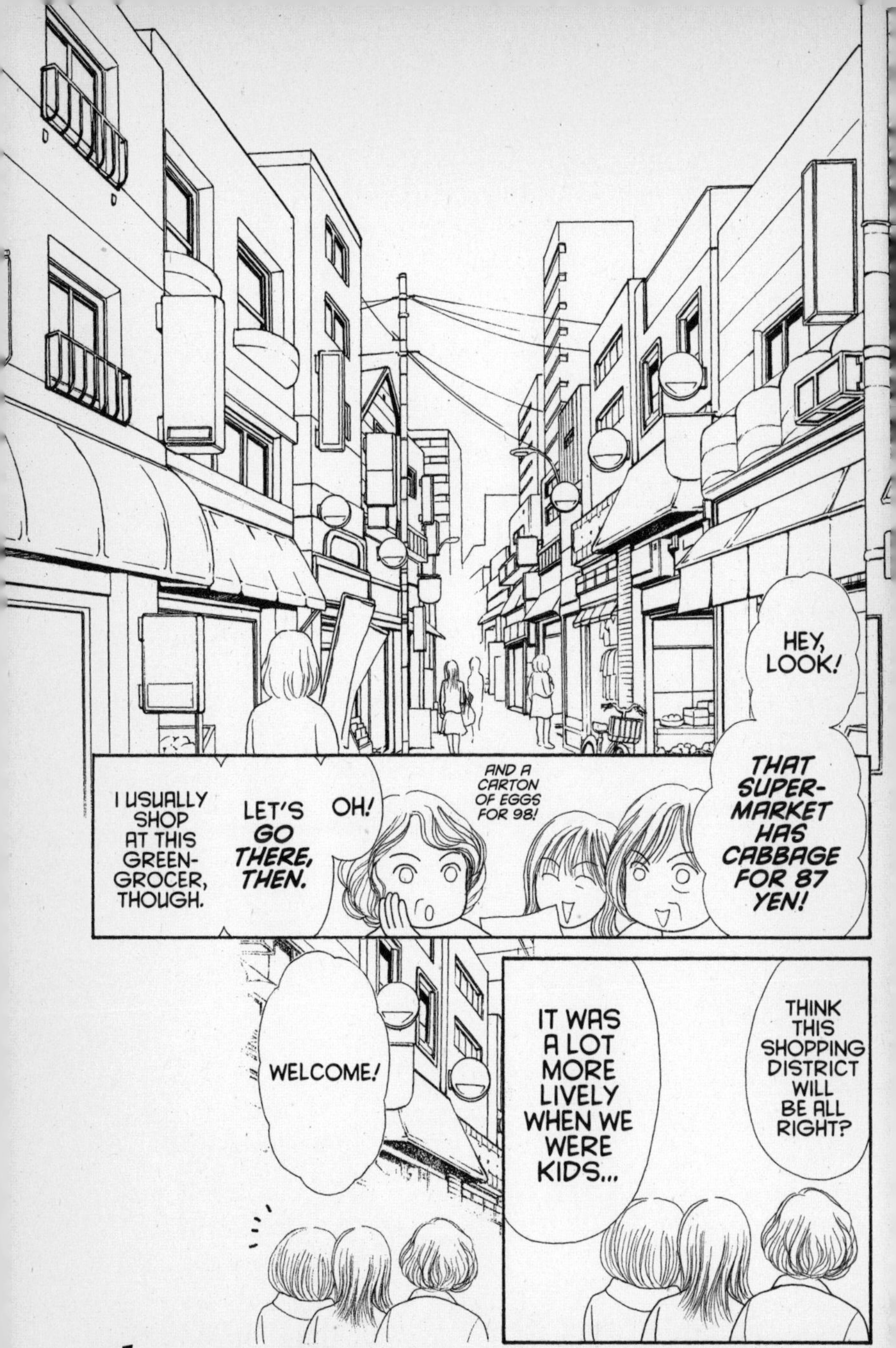
HEY, LOOK!
THAT SUPER-MARKET HAS CABBAGE FOR 87 YEN!
AND A CARTON OF EGGS FOR 98!
OH!
LET'S GO THERE, THEN.
I USUALLY SHOP AT THIS GREEN-GROCER, THOUGH.
THINK THIS SHOPPING DISTRICT WILL BE ALL RIGHT?
IT WAS A LOT MORE LIVELY WHEN WE WERE KIDS...
WELCOME!

Chapter 112: Save the Shopping District!

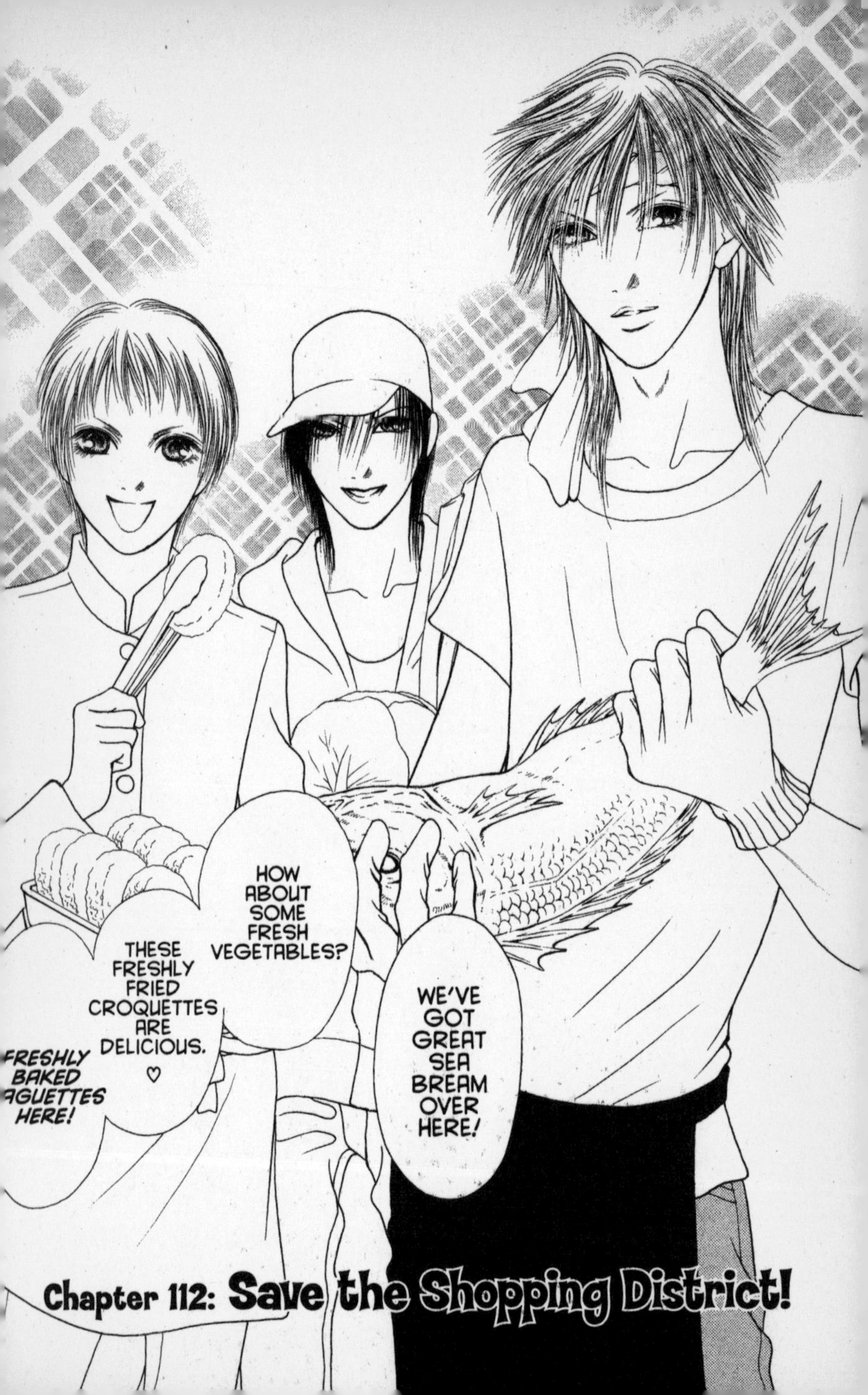
WE'VE GOT GREAT SEA BREAM OVER HERE!
HOW ABOUT SOME FRESH VEGETABLES?
THESE FRESHLY FRIED CROQUETTES ARE DELICIOUS. ♡
FRESHLY BAKED AGUETTES HERE!

Chapter 112: Save the Shopping District!

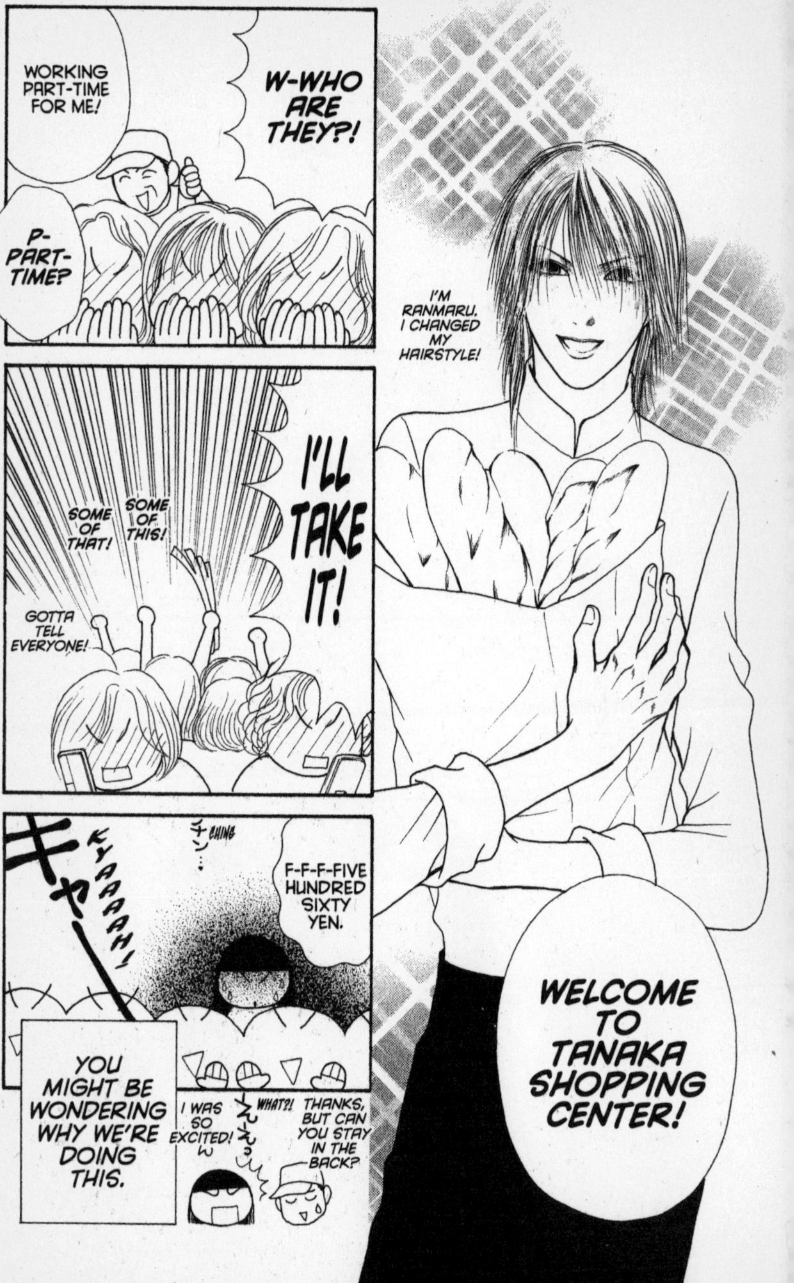
I'M RANMARU. I CHANGED MY HAIRSTYLE!
WELCOME TO TANAKA SHOPPING CENTER!
W-WHO ARE THEY?!
WORKING PART-TIME FOR ME!
P-PART-TIME?
I'LL TAKE IT!
SOME OF THIS!
SOME OF THAT!
GOTTA TELL EVERYONE!
F-F-F-FIVE HUNDRED SIXTY YEN.
チン… CHING
キャー KYAAAAH!
THANKS, BUT CAN YOU STAY IN THE BACK?
WHAT?!
I WAS SO EXCITED!
YOU MIGHT BE WONDERING WHY WE'RE DOING THIS.

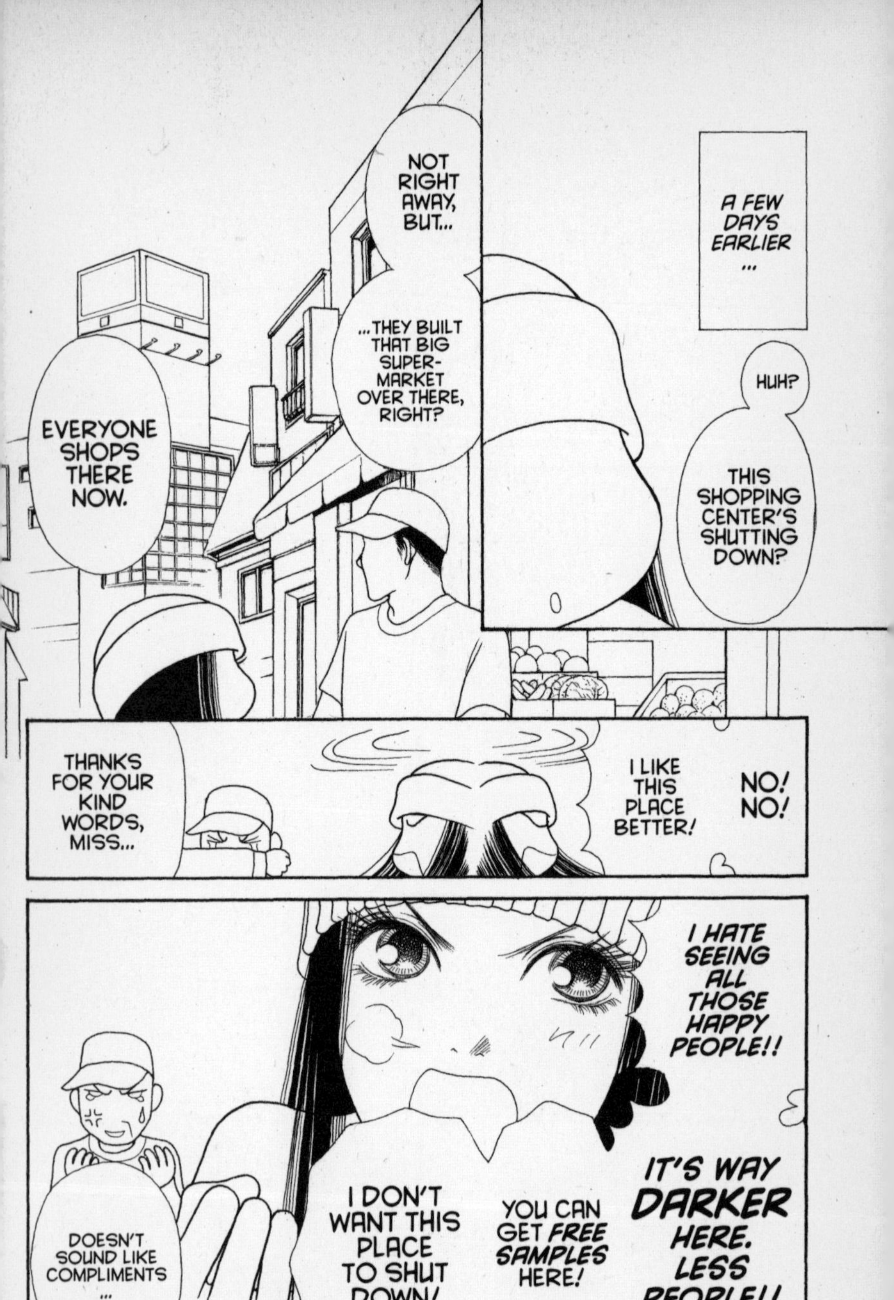
A FEW DAYS EARLIER ...
HUH?
THIS SHOPPING CENTER'S SHUTTING DOWN?
NOT RIGHT AWAY, BUT...
...THEY BUILT THAT BIG SUPER-MARKET OVER THERE, RIGHT?
EVERYONE SHOPS THERE NOW.
NO! NO!
I LIKE THIS PLACE BETTER!
THANKS FOR YOUR KIND WORDS, MISS...
I HATE SEEING ALL THOSE HAPPY PEOPLE!!
IT'S WAY DARKER HERE. LESS PEOPLE!!
YOU CAN GET FREE SAMPLES HERE!
I DON'T WANT THIS PLACE TO SHUT DOWN!
DOESN'T SOUND LIKE COMPLIMENTS ...

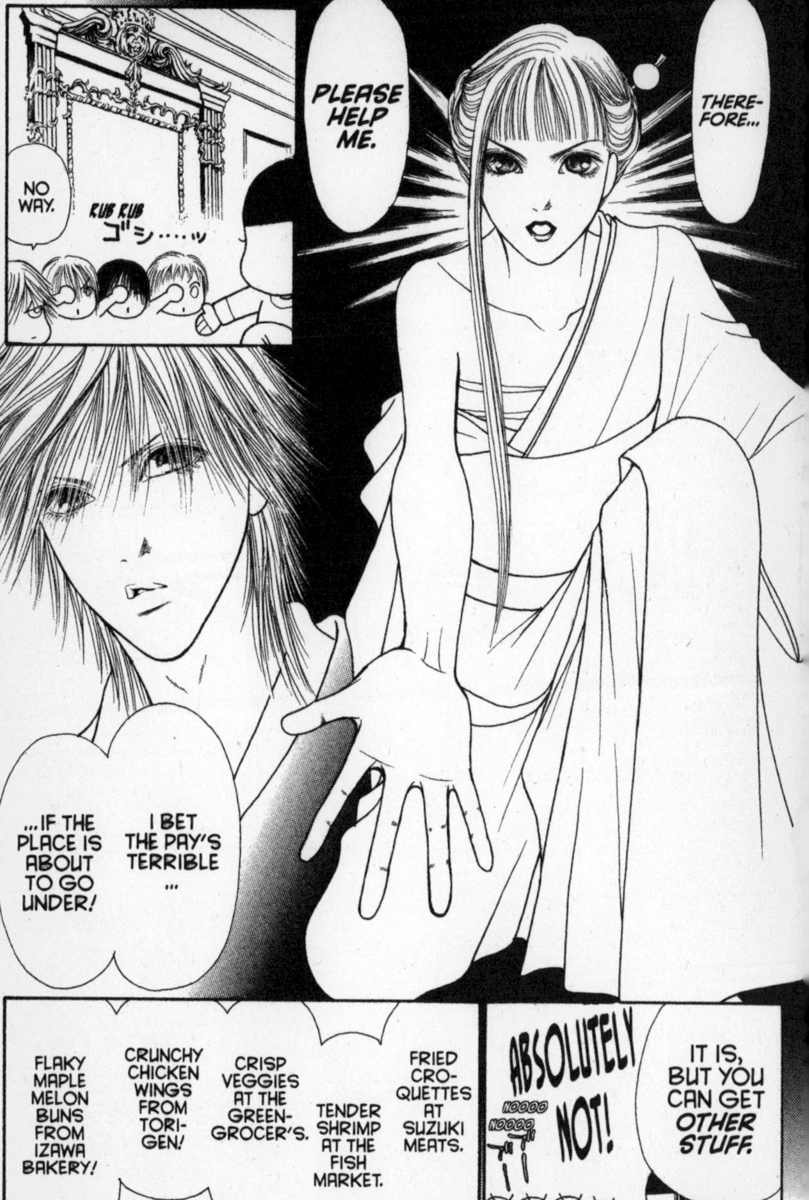
THEREFORE...
PLEASE HELP ME.
NO WAY.
RUB RUB
ゴシ…ッ
I BET THE PAY'S TERRIBLE...
...IF THE PLACE IS ABOUT TO GO UNDER!
IT IS, BUT YOU CAN GET *OTHER STUFF.*
ABSOLUTELY NOT!
NOOOO
NOOOO
FRIED CROQUETTES AT SUZUKI MEATS.
TENDER SHRIMP AT THE FISH MARKET.
CRISP VEGGIES AT THE GREENGROCER'S.
CRUNCHY CHICKEN WINGS FROM TORIGEN!
FLAKY MAPLE MELON BUNS FROM IZAWA BAKERY!

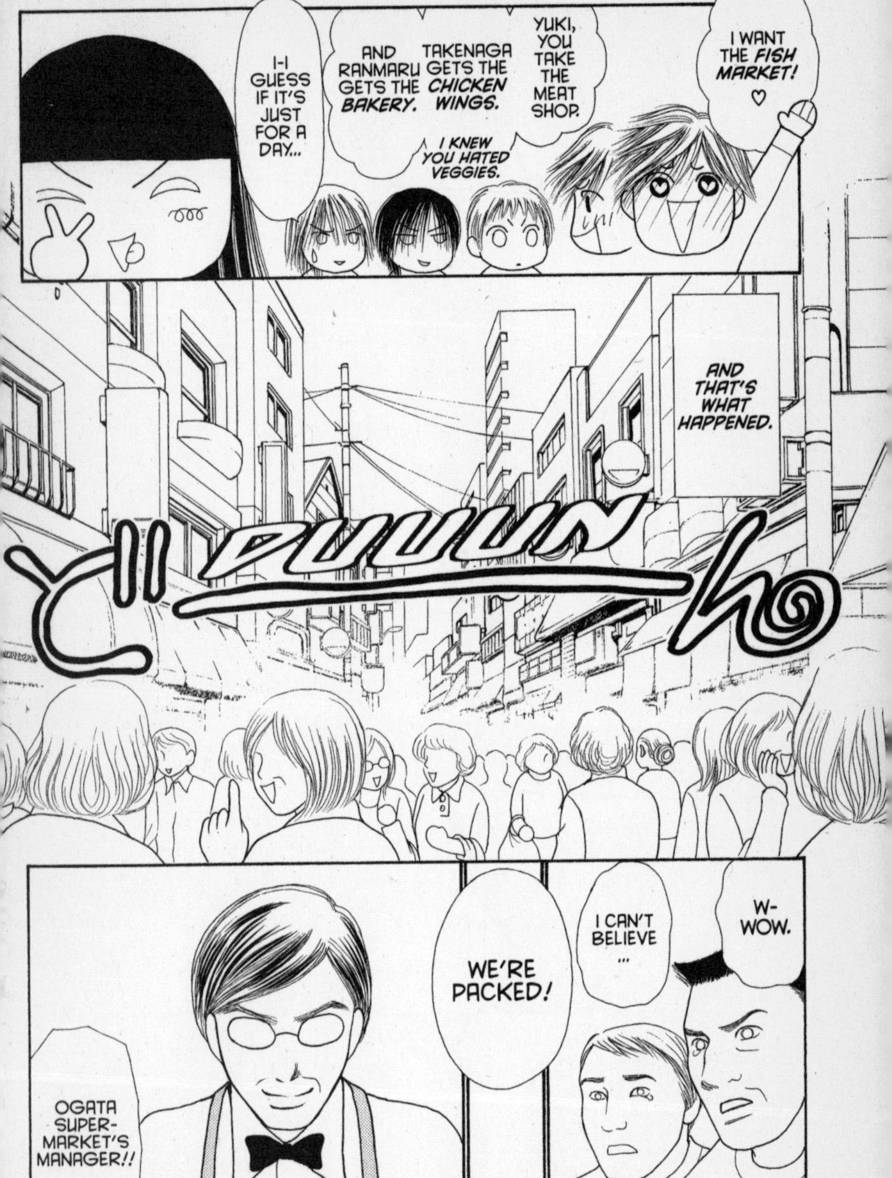
I WANT THE FISH MARKET! ♡
YUKI, YOU TAKE THE MEAT SHOP.
TAKENAGA GETS THE CHICKEN WINGS.
I KNEW YOU HATED VEGGIES.
AND RANMARU GETS THE BAKERY.
I-I GUESS IF IT'S JUST FOR A DAY...
AND THAT'S WHAT HAPPENED.
DUUUN
W-WOW.
I CAN'T BELIEVE ...
WE'RE PACKED!
OGATA SUPER-MARKET'S MANAGER!!

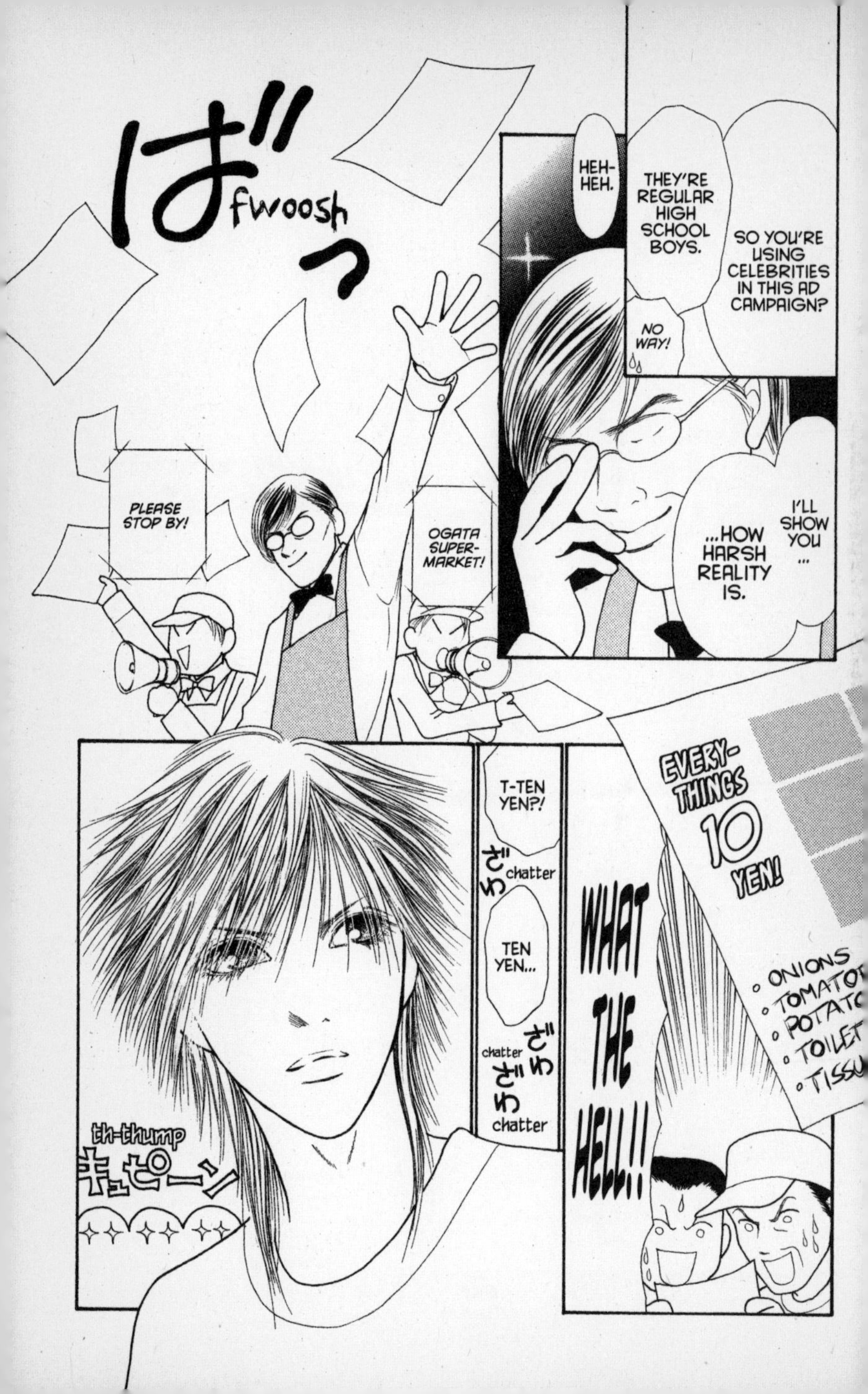
SO YOU'RE USING CELEBRITIES IN THIS AD CAMPAIGN?
THEY'RE REGULAR HIGH SCHOOL BOYS.
NO WAY!
HEH-HEH.
I'LL SHOW YOU ...
...HOW HARSH REALITY IS.
ばっ fwoosh
OGATA SUPER-MARKET!
PLEASE STOP BY!
EVERY-THINGS 10 YEN!
ONIONS
TOILET
WHAT THE HELL!!
T-TEN YEN?!
ざわ chatter
TEN YEN...
ざわ chatter
ざわ chatter
th-thump
キュピーン

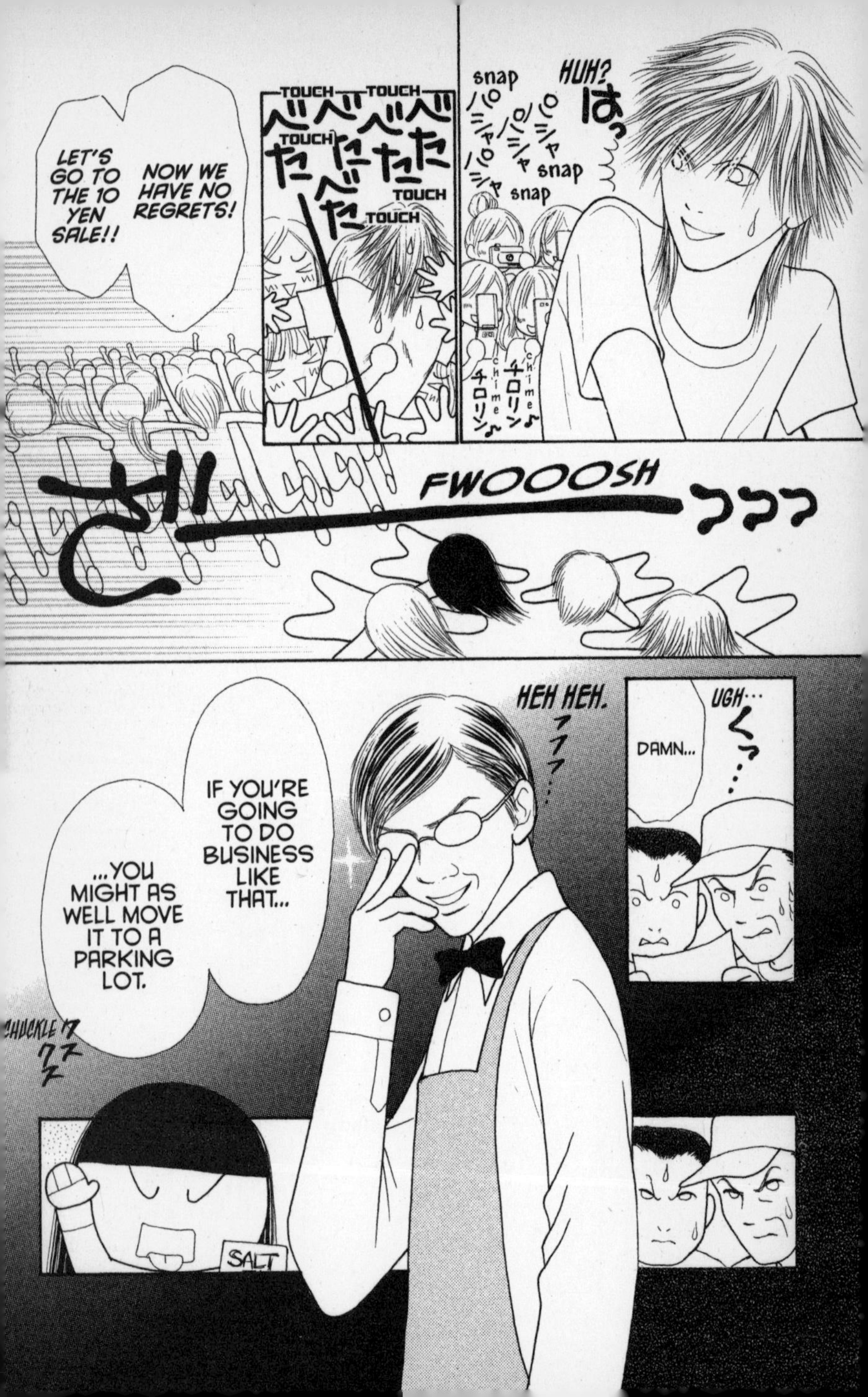
HUH?
はっ
snap snap snap snap
パシャ パシャ パシャ パシャ
TOUCH TOUCH TOUCH TOUCH TOUCH
chime♪ chime♪
チロリン♪ チロリン♪
NOW WE HAVE NO REGRETS!
LET'S GO TO THE 10 YEN SALE!!
FWOOOSH
UGH…
くっ…
DAMN…
HEH HEH.
フフフ…
IF YOU'RE GOING TO DO BUSINESS LIKE THAT…
…YOU MIGHT AS WELL MOVE IT TO A PARKING LOT.
CHUCKLE
SALT

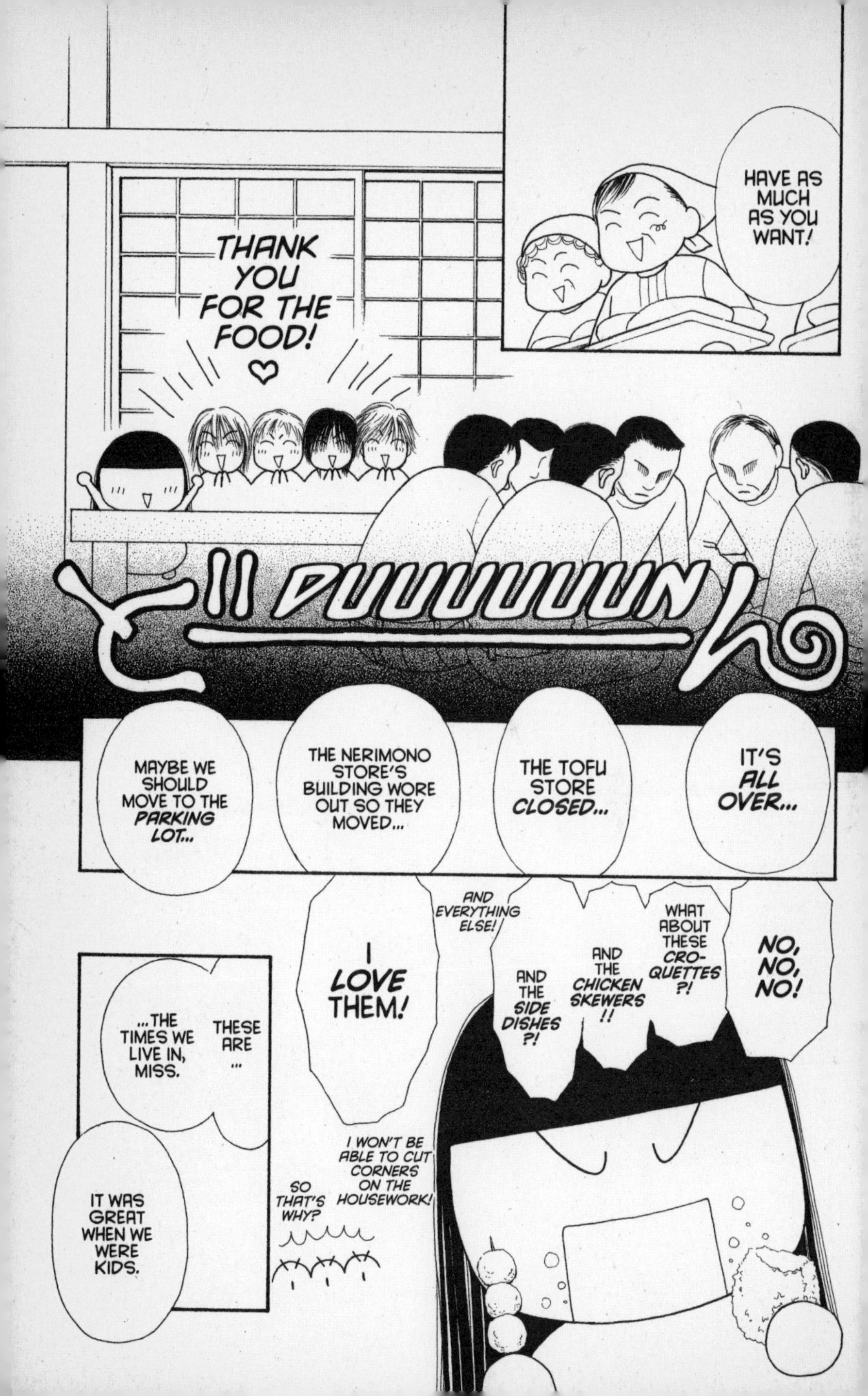
HAVE AS MUCH AS YOU WANT!
THANK YOU FOR THE FOOD! ♡
DUUUUUUN
IT'S ALL OVER...
THE TOFU STORE CLOSED...
THE NERIMONO STORE'S BUILDING WORE OUT SO THEY MOVED...
MAYBE WE SHOULD MOVE TO THE PARKING LOT...
NO, NO, NO!
WHAT ABOUT THESE CROQUETTES?!
AND THE CHICKEN SKEWERS!!
AND THE SIDE DISHES?!
AND EVERYTHING ELSE!
I LOVE THEM!
I WON'T BE ABLE TO CUT CORNERS ON THE HOUSEWORK!
SO THAT'S WHY?
THESE ARE...
...THE TIMES WE LIVE IN, MISS.
IT WAS GREAT WHEN WE WERE KIDS.

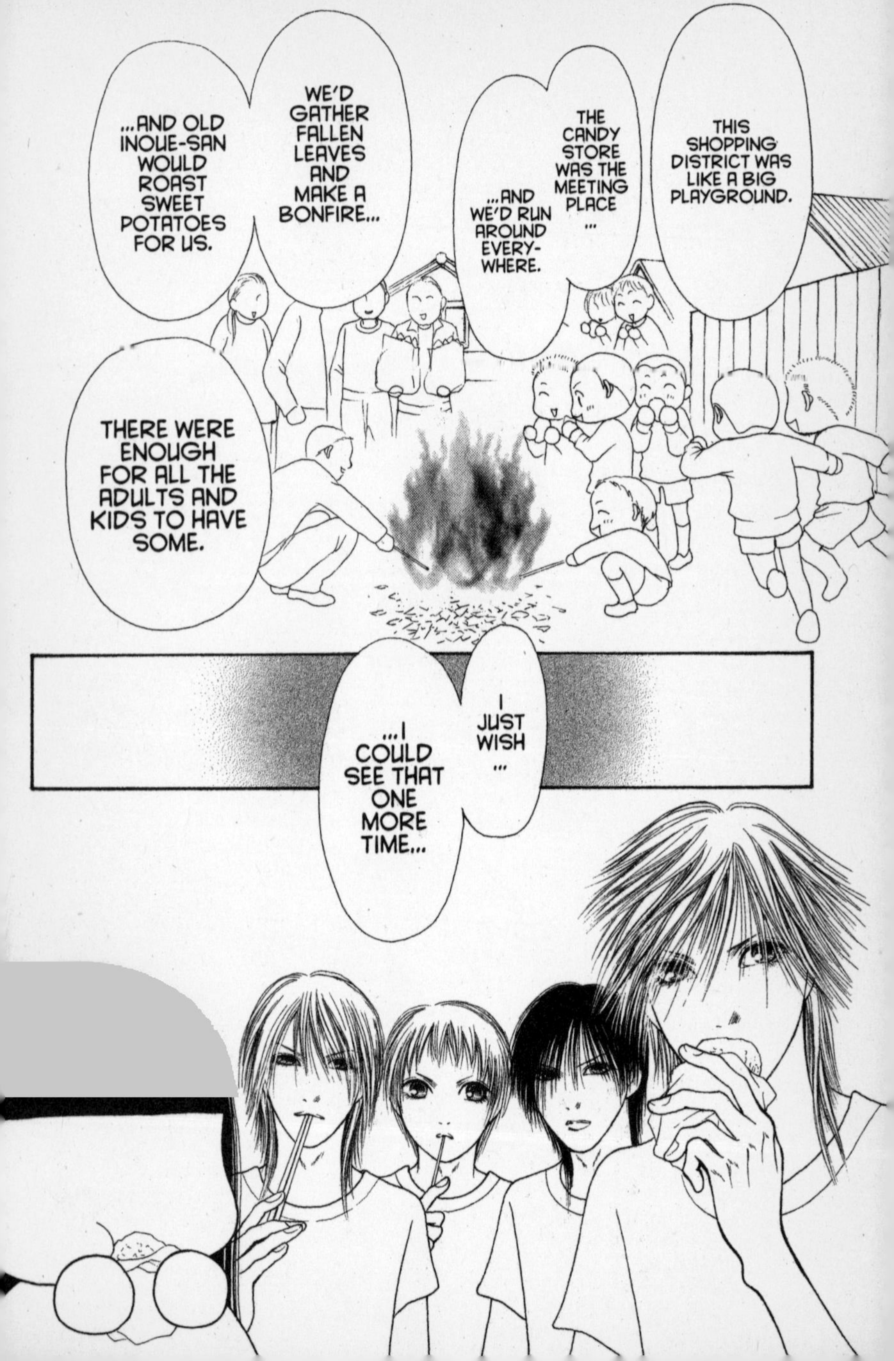
THIS SHOPPING DISTRICT WAS LIKE A BIG PLAYGROUND.
THE CANDY STORE WAS THE MEETING PLACE ...
...AND WE'D RUN AROUND EVERY-WHERE.
WE'D GATHER FALLEN LEAVES AND MAKE A BONFIRE...
...AND OLD INOUE-SAN WOULD ROAST SWEET POTATOES FOR US.
THERE WERE ENOUGH FOR ALL THE ADULTS AND KIDS TO HAVE SOME.
I JUST WISH ...
...I COULD SEE THAT ONE MORE TIME...

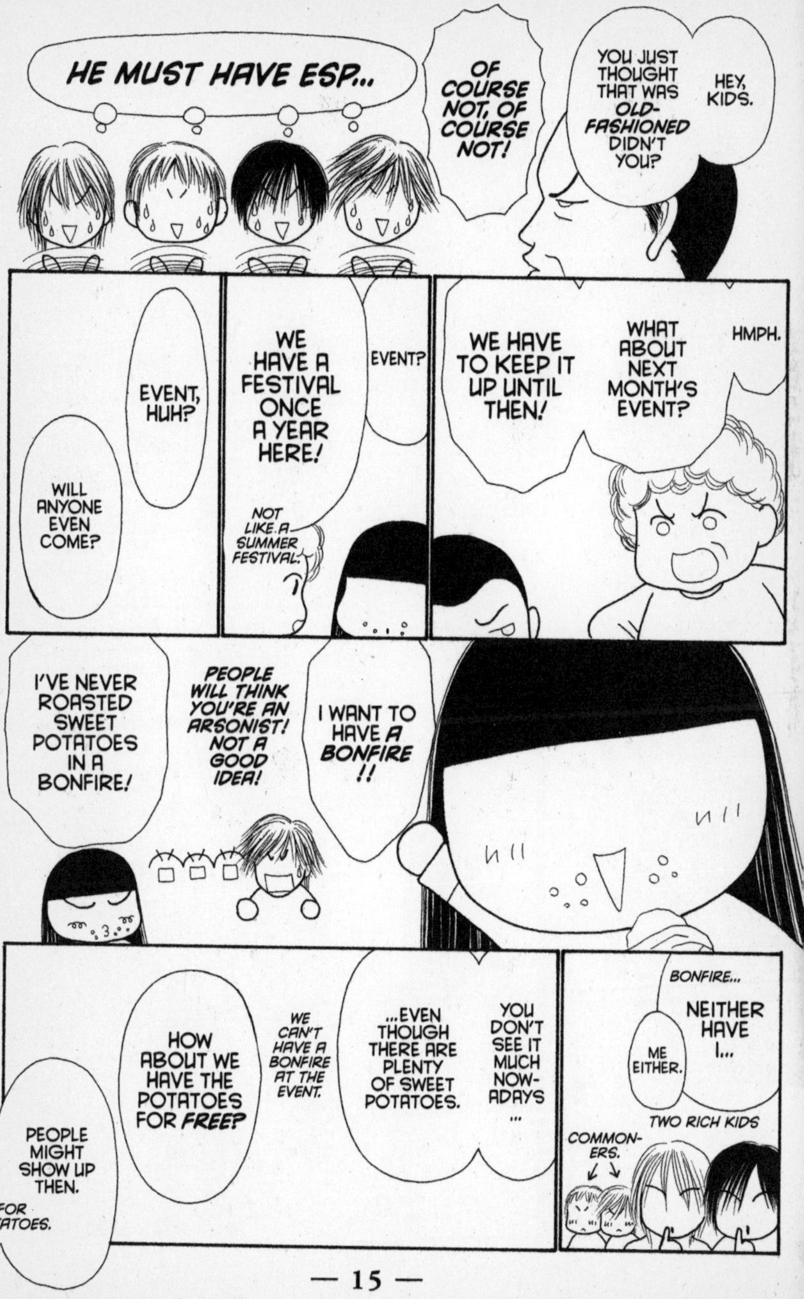
HEY, KIDS.
YOU JUST THOUGHT THAT WAS OLD-FASHIONED DIDN'T YOU?
OF COURSE NOT, OF COURSE NOT!
HE MUST HAVE ESP...
HMPH.
WHAT ABOUT NEXT MONTH'S EVENT?
WE HAVE TO KEEP IT UP UNTIL THEN!
EVENT?
WE HAVE A FESTIVAL ONCE A YEAR HERE!
NOT LIKE A SUMMER FESTIVAL.
EVENT, HUH?
WILL ANYONE EVEN COME?
I WANT TO HAVE A BONFIRE !!
PEOPLE WILL THINK YOU'RE AN ARSONIST! NOT A GOOD IDEA!
I'VE NEVER ROASTED SWEET POTATOES IN A BONFIRE!
BONFIRE...
NEITHER HAVE I...
ME EITHER.
TWO RICH KIDS
COMMONERS.
YOU DON'T SEE IT MUCH NOW-ADAYS...
...EVEN THOUGH THERE ARE PLENTY OF SWEET POTATOES.
WE CAN'T HAVE A BONFIRE AT THE EVENT.
HOW ABOUT WE HAVE THE POTATOES FOR FREE?
PEOPLE MIGHT SHOW UP THEN.
FOR POTATOES.

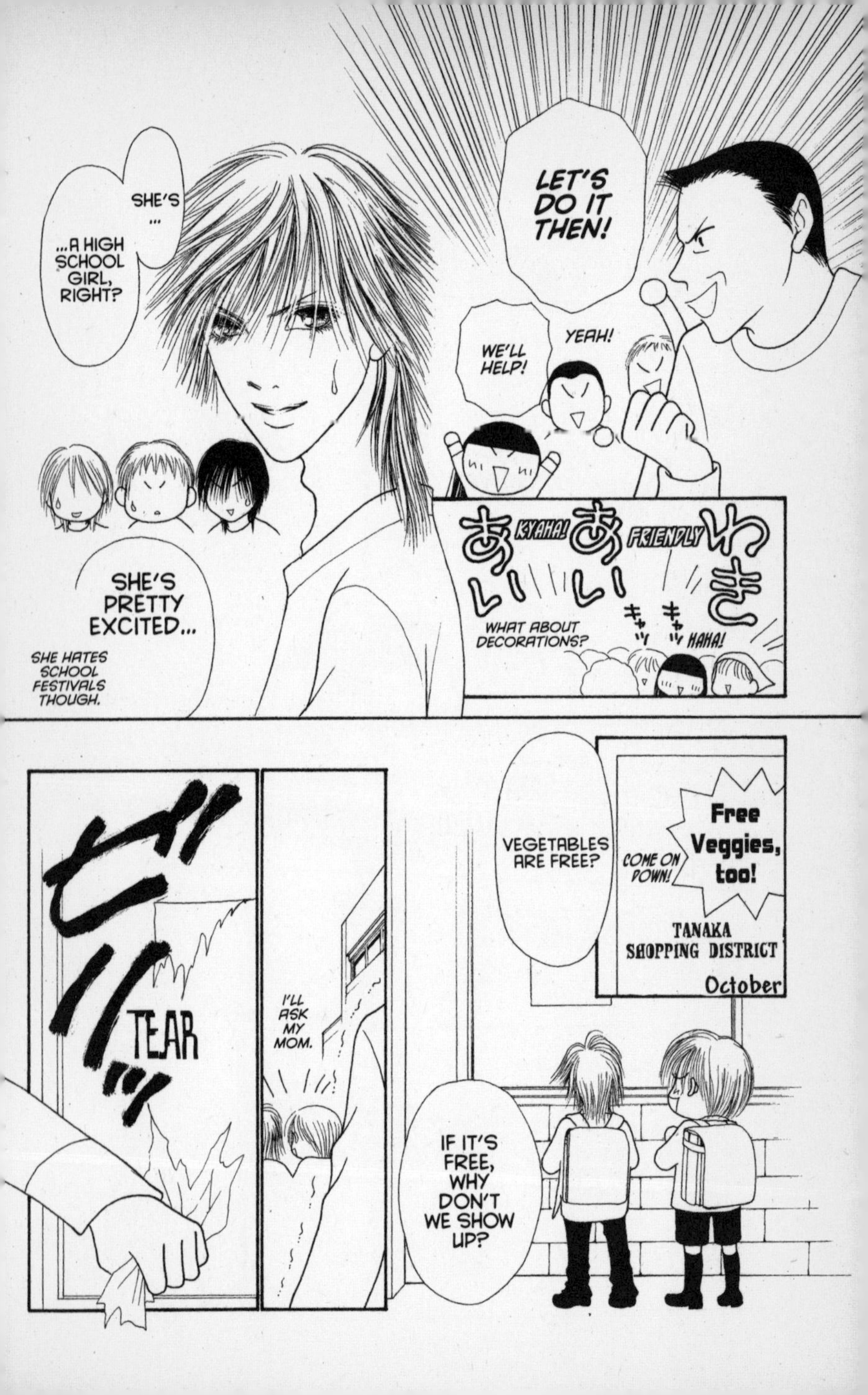
LET'S DO IT THEN!
YEAH!
WE'LL HELP!
SHE'S ...
...A HIGH SCHOOL GIRL, RIGHT?
あいあいわき
KYAHA! FRIENDLY
WHAT ABOUT DECORATIONS?
キャッ キャッ HAHA!
SHE'S PRETTY EXCITED...
SHE HATES SCHOOL FESTIVALS THOUGH.
Free Veggies, too!
COME ON DOWN!
TANAKA SHOPPING DISTRICT
October
VEGETABLES ARE FREE?
IF IT'S FREE, WHY DON'T WE SHOW UP?
I'LL ASK MY MOM.
TEAR

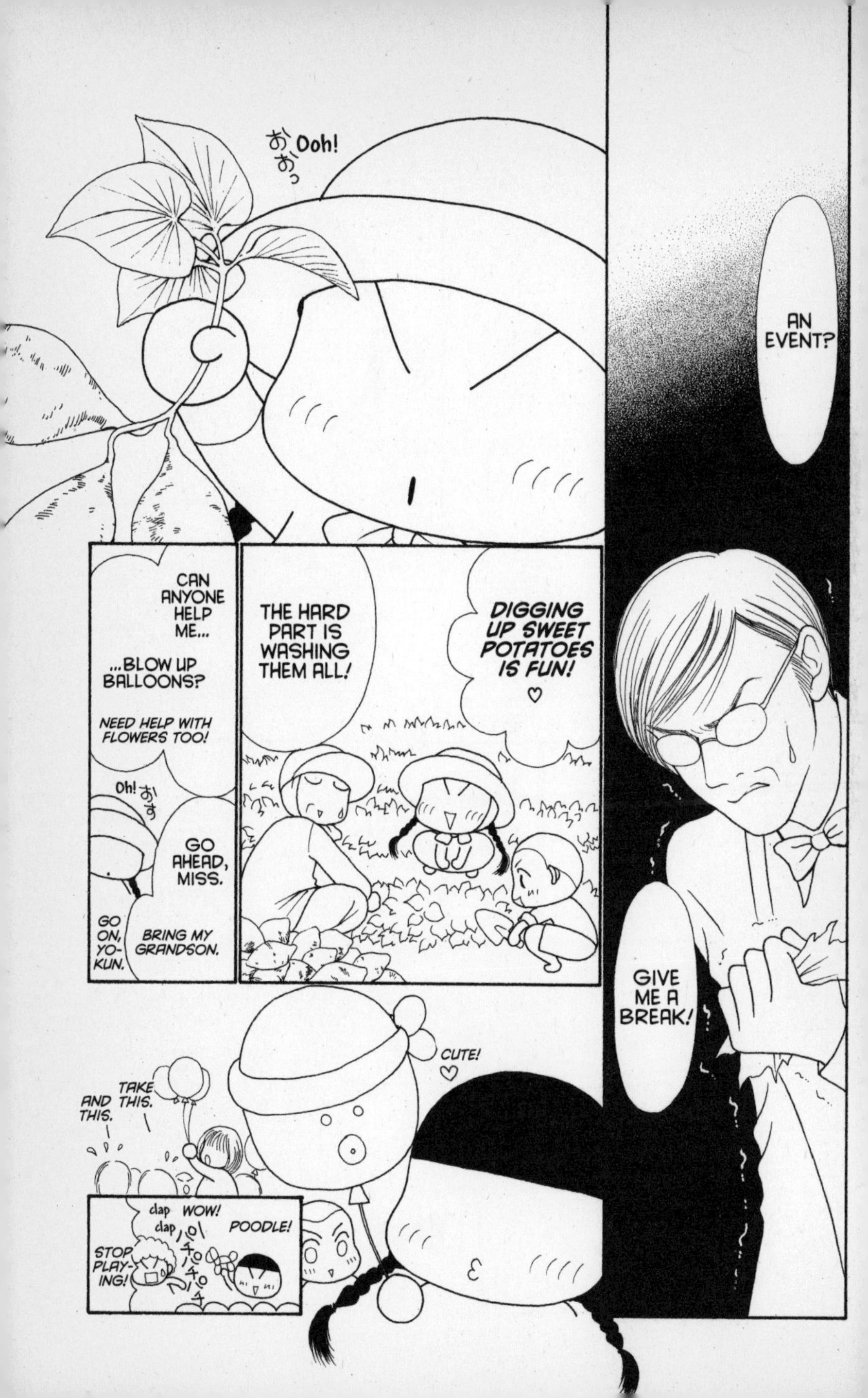
AN EVENT?
GIVE ME A BREAK!
Ooh! おおっ
DIGGING UP SWEET POTATOES IS FUN! ♡
THE HARD PART IS WASHING THEM ALL!
CAN ANYONE HELP ME...
...BLOW UP BALLOONS?
NEED HELP WITH FLOWERS TOO!
Oh! おす
GO AHEAD, MISS.
BRING MY GRANDSON.
GO ON, YO-KUN.
CUTE! ♡
TAKE THIS.
AND THIS.
POODLE!
WOW!
clap clap
STOP PLAY-ING!

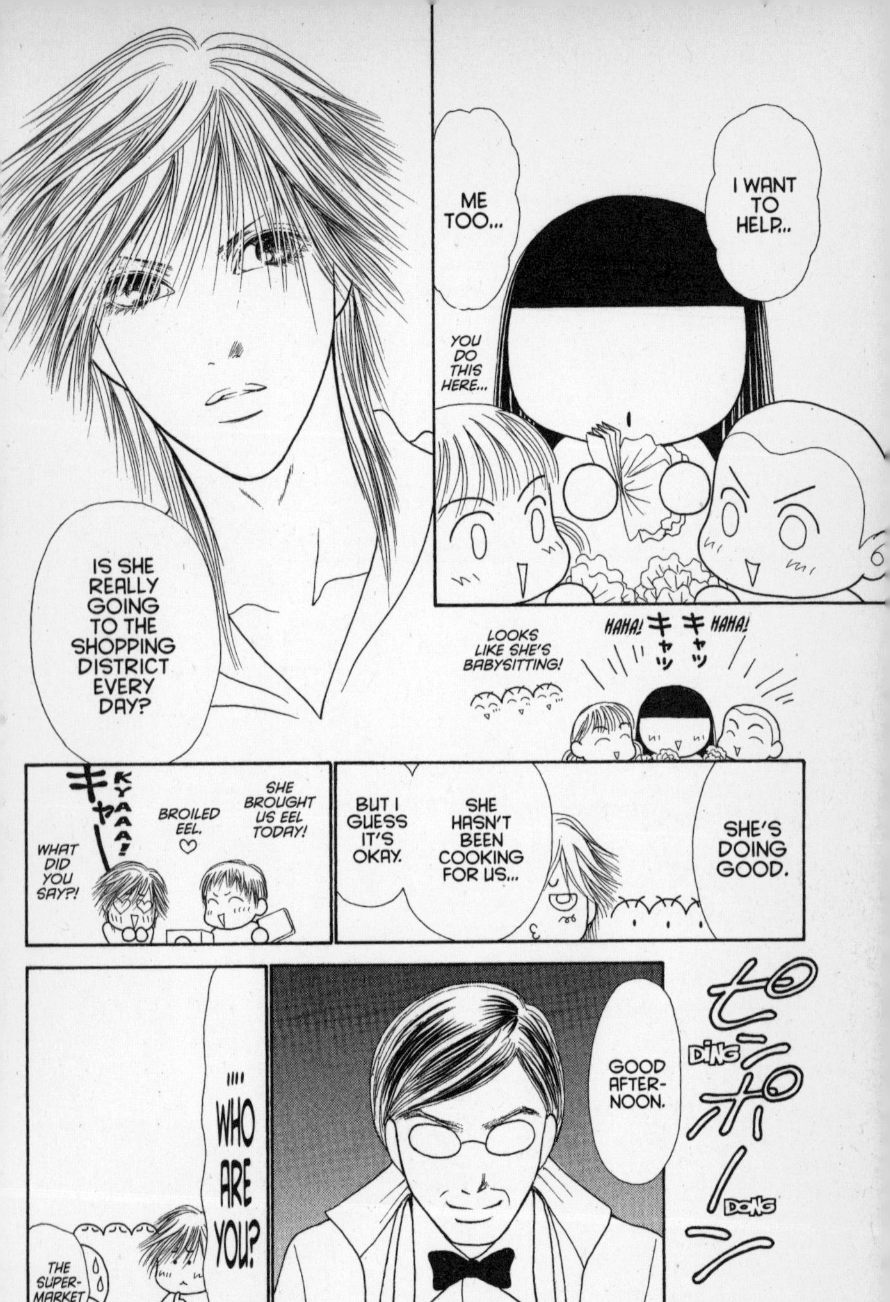
I WANT TO HELP...
ME TOO...
YOU DO THIS HERE...
HAHA!
キャッ
キャッ
HAHA!
LOOKS LIKE SHE'S BABYSITTING!
IS SHE REALLY GOING TO THE SHOPPING DISTRICT EVERY DAY?
SHE'S DOING GOOD.
SHE HASN'T BEEN COOKING FOR US...
BUT I GUESS IT'S OKAY.
SHE BROUGHT US EEL TODAY!
BROILED EEL. ♡
キャー
KYAAAA!
WHAT DID YOU SAY?!
ピンポーン
DING
DONG
GOOD AFTERNOON.
...WHO ARE YOU?
THE SUPERMARKET MANAGER.

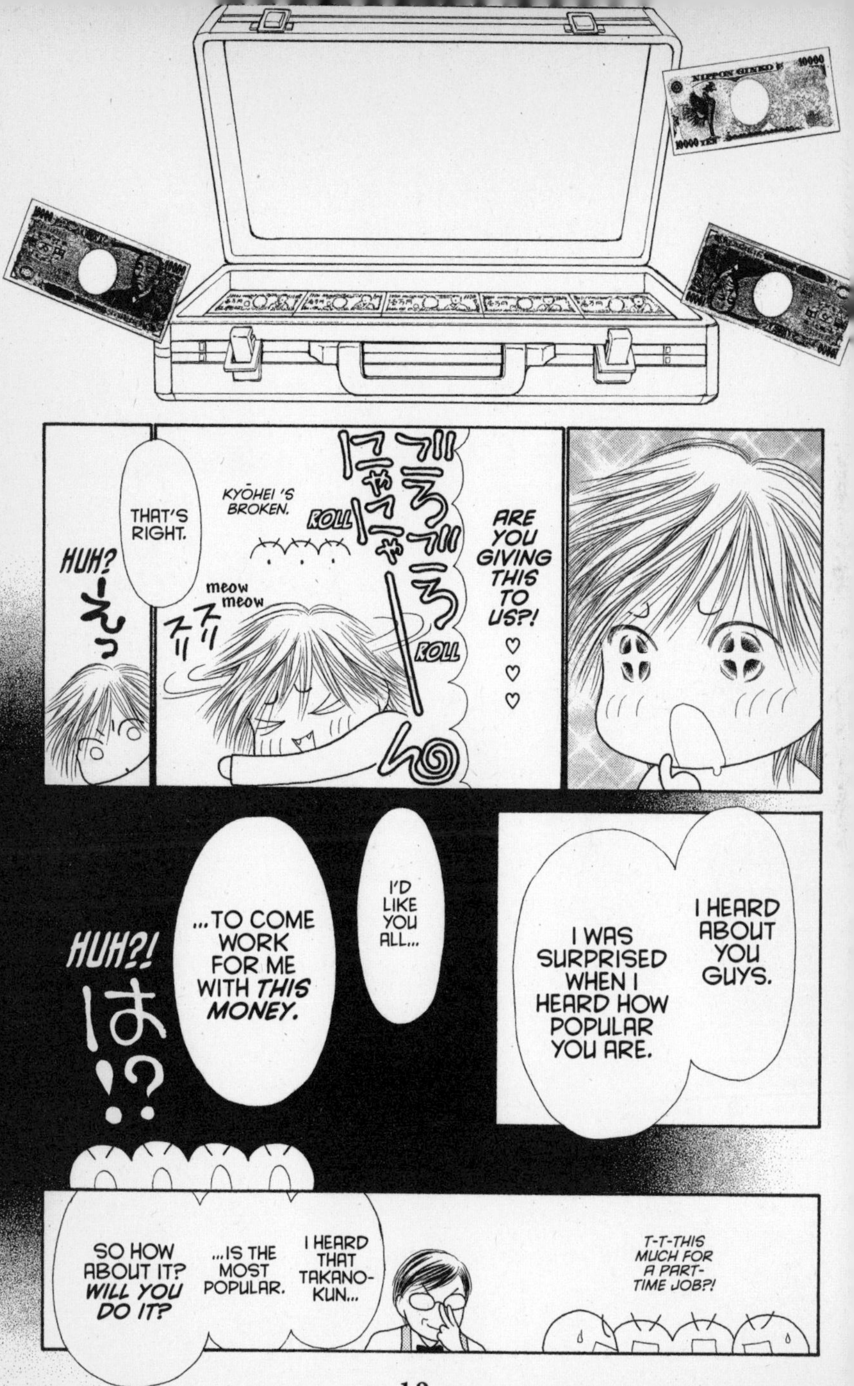
ARE YOU GIVING THIS TO US?! ♡ ♡ ♡
ROLL
ROLL
KYŌHEI'S BROKEN.
meow meow
THAT'S RIGHT.
HUH? えっ
I HEARD ABOUT YOU GUYS.
I WAS SURPRISED WHEN I HEARD HOW POPULAR YOU ARE.
I'D LIKE YOU ALL...
...TO COME WORK FOR ME WITH *THIS MONEY.*
HUH?! は!?
T-T-THIS MUCH FOR A PART-TIME JOB?!
I HEARD THAT TAKANO-KUN...
...IS THE MOST POPULAR.
SO HOW ABOUT IT? *WILL YOU DO IT?*

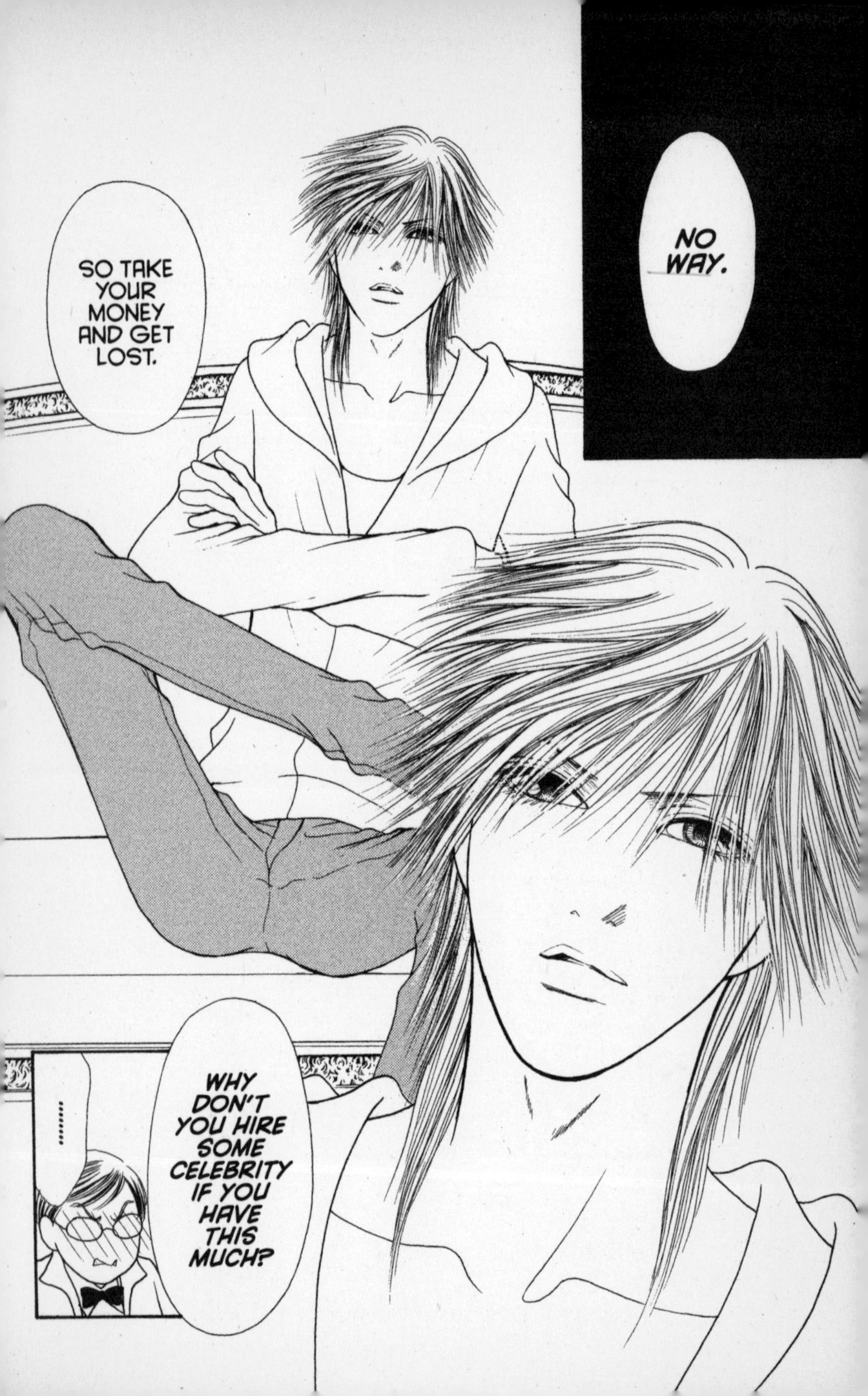
NO WAY.
SO TAKE YOUR MONEY AND GET LOST.
WHY DON'T YOU HIRE SOME CELEBRITY IF YOU HAVE THIS MUCH?
......

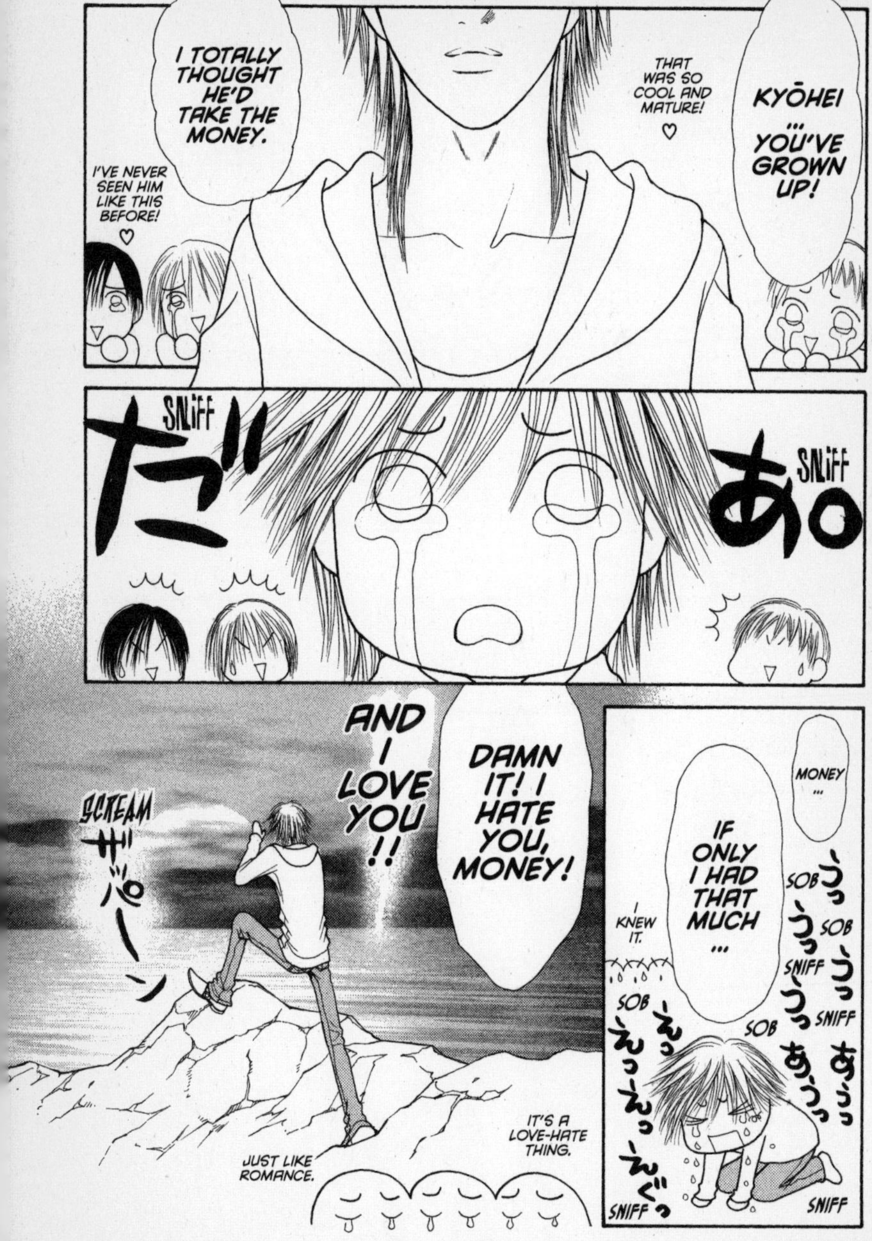
KYŌHEI ... YOU'VE GROWN UP!
THAT WAS SO COOL AND MATURE! ♡
I TOTALLY THOUGHT HE'D TAKE THE MONEY.
I'VE NEVER SEEN HIM LIKE THIS BEFORE! ♡
SNIFF
あ
SNIFF
だ
MONEY ...
IF ONLY I HAD THAT MUCH ...
I KNEW IT.
SOB SOB SNIFF SOB SOB SNIFF SNIFF SNIFF
DAMN IT! I HATE YOU, MONEY!
AND I LOVE YOU!!
SCREAM
ザパーン
IT'S A LOVE-HATE THING.
JUST LIKE ROMANCE.

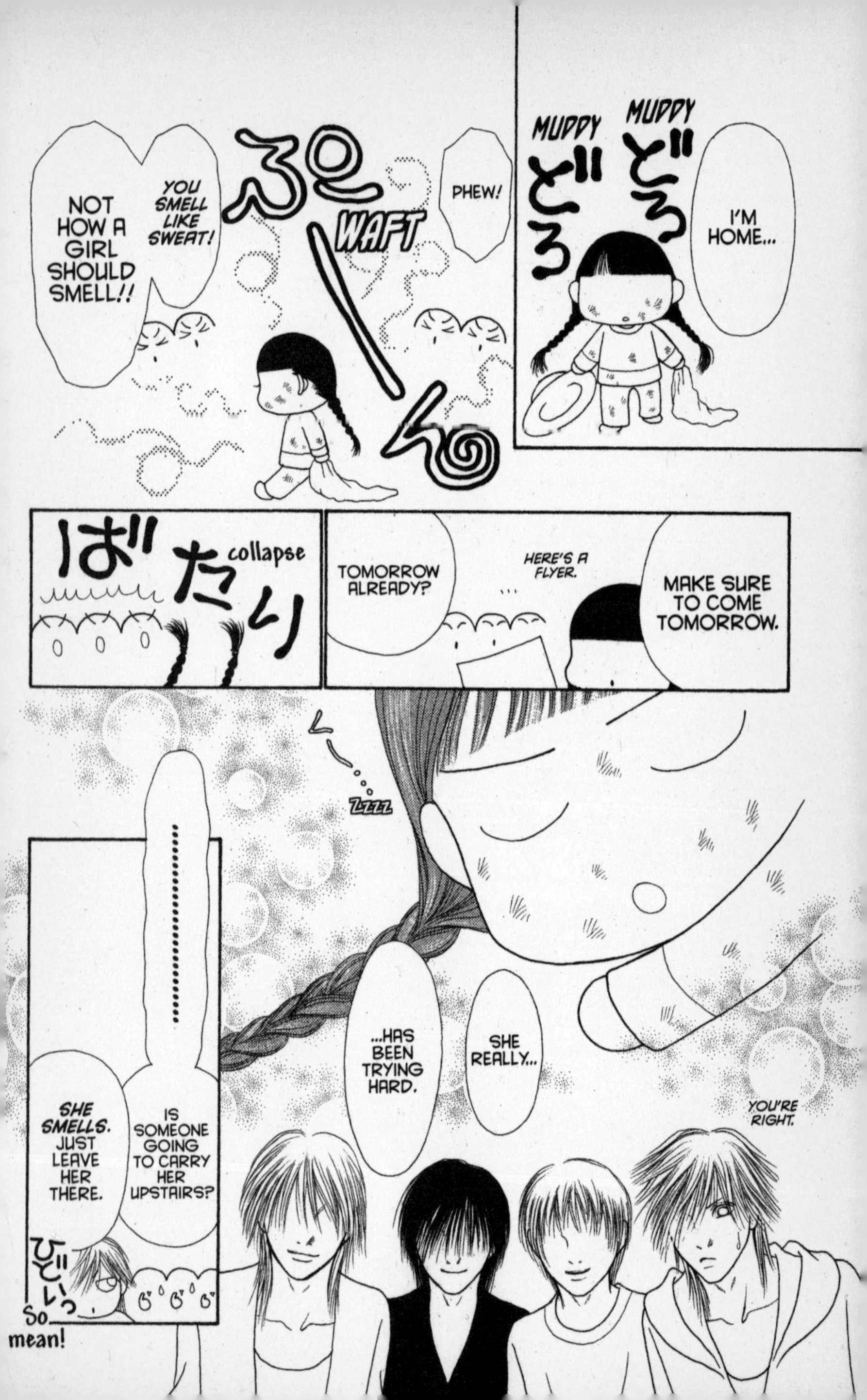
MUDDY
どろ
MUDDY
どろ
I'M HOME...
PHEW!
ぷ～ん
WAFT
YOU SMELL LIKE SWEAT!
NOT HOW A GIRL SHOULD SMELL!!
MAKE SURE TO COME TOMORROW.
HERE'S A FLYER.
...
TOMORROW ALREADY?
ばたり
collapse
Zzzz
YOU'RE RIGHT.
SHE REALLY...
...HAS BEEN TRYING HARD.
......
IS SOMEONE GOING TO CARRY HER UPSTAIRS?
SHE SMELLS. JUST LEAVE HER THERE.
ひどいっ
So mean!

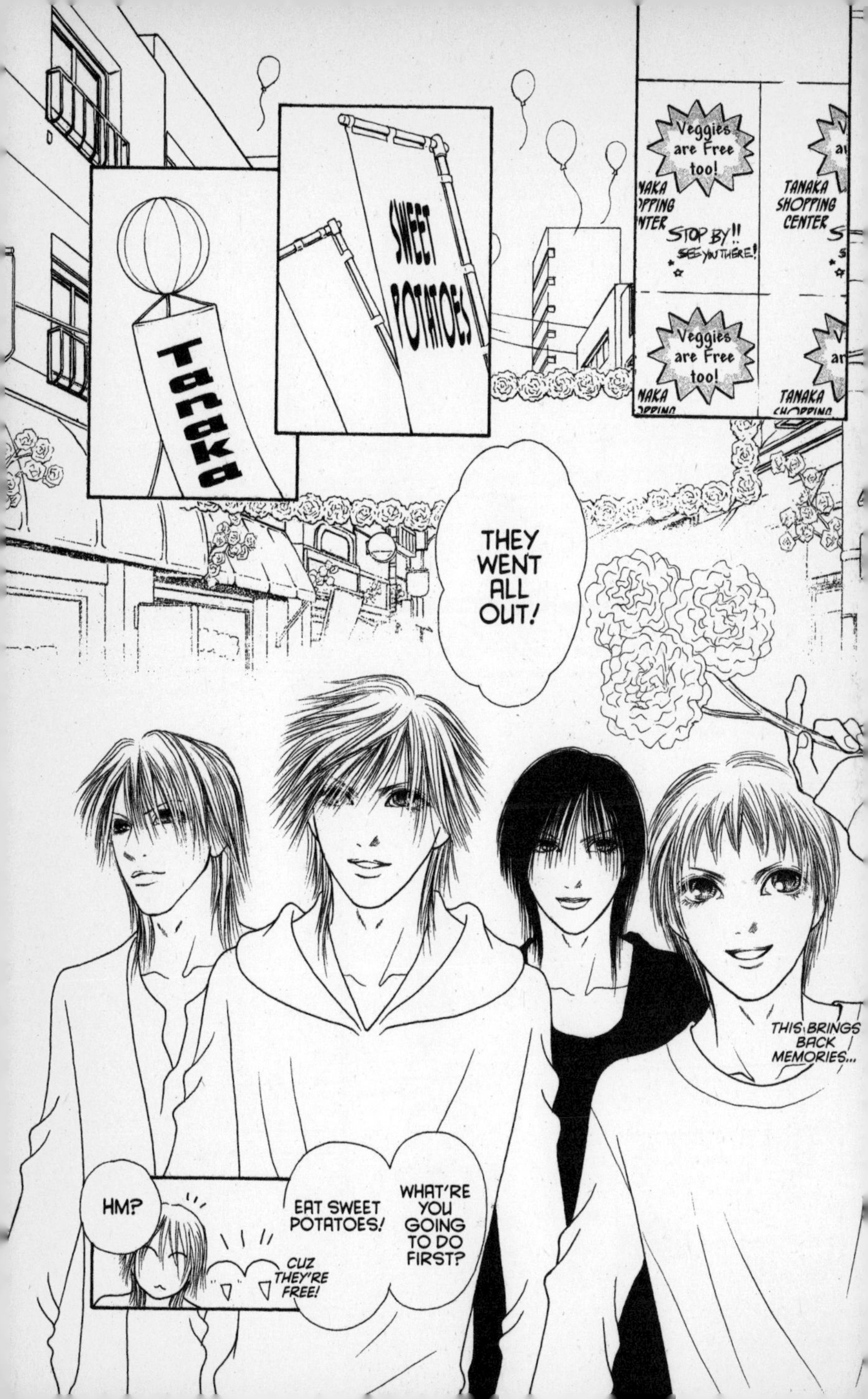
Veggies are Free too!
TANAKA SHOPPING CENTER
STOP BY!!
SEE YOU THERE!
SWEET POTATOES
Tanaka
THEY WENT ALL OUT!
THIS BRINGS BACK MEMORIES...
WHAT'RE YOU GOING TO DO FIRST?
EAT SWEET POTATOES!
CUZ THEY'RE FREE!
HM?

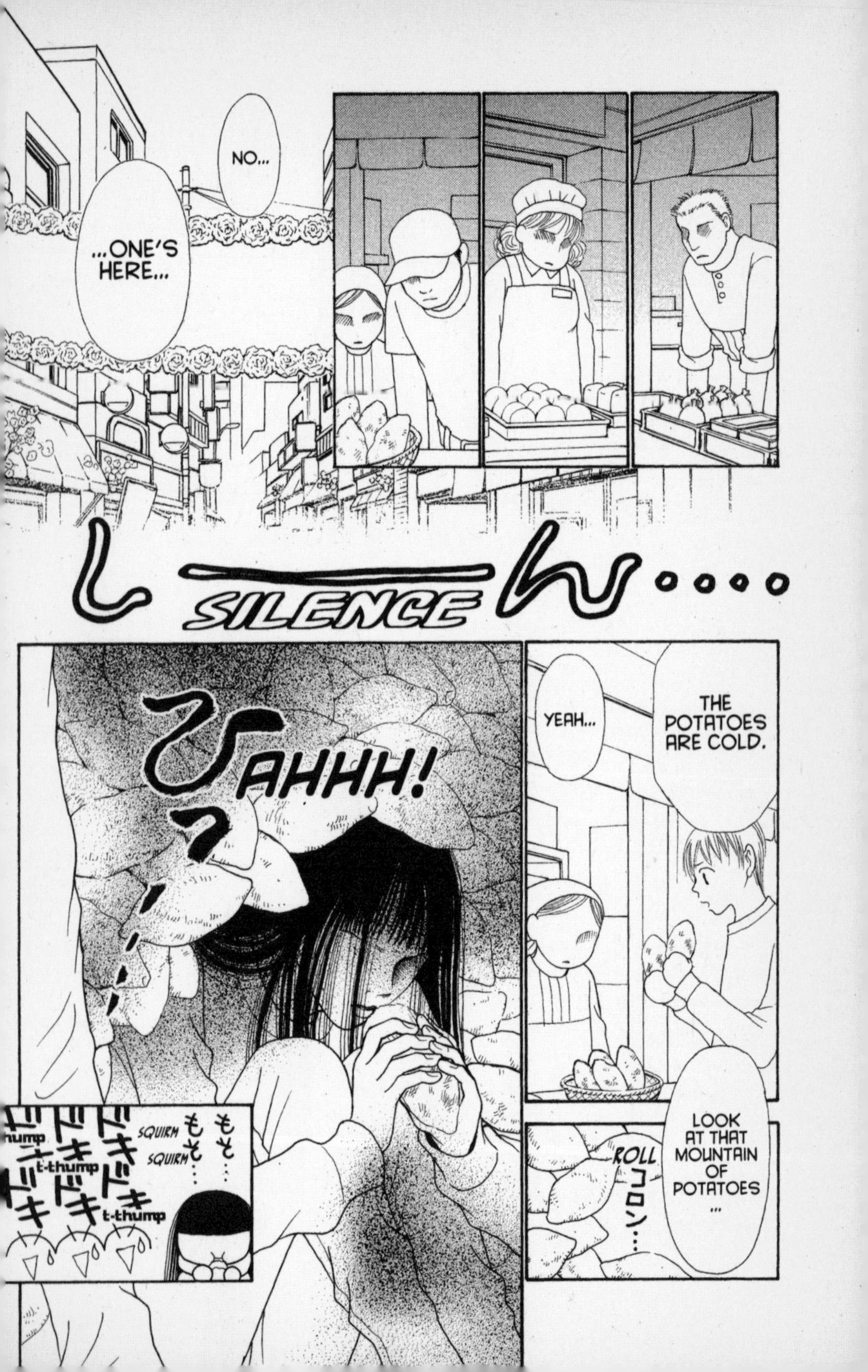
NO...
...ONE'S HERE...
しーーん….
SILENCE
THE POTATOES ARE COLD.
YEAH...
LOOK AT THAT MOUNTAIN OF POTATOES ...
コロン….
ROLL
ひっ
AHHH!
もそ…
SQUIRM
もそ…
SQUIRM
ドキドキ
t-thump
ドキドキ
t-thump

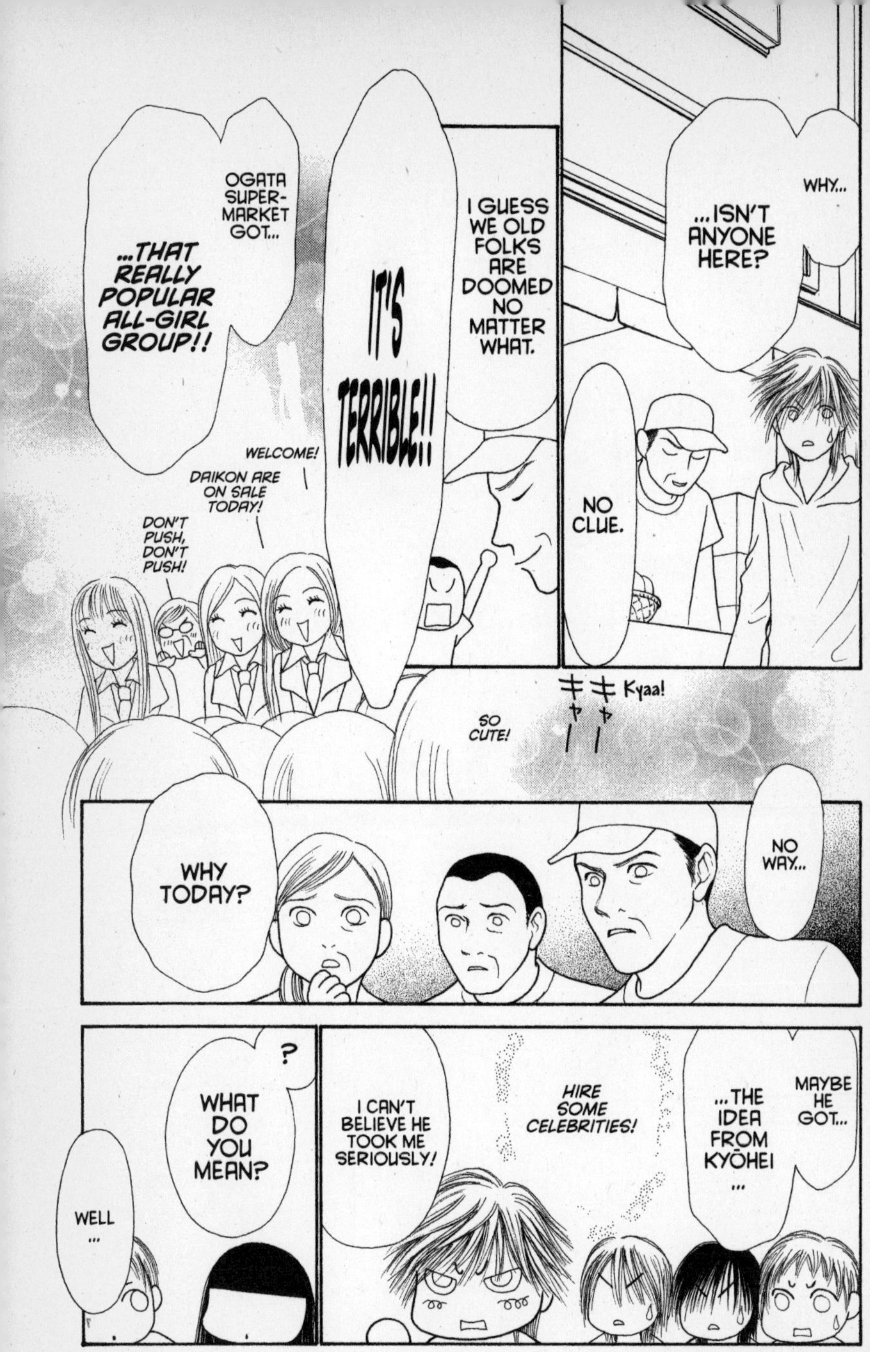
WHY...
...ISN'T ANYONE HERE?
NO CLUE.
I GUESS WE OLD FOLKS ARE DOOMED NO MATTER WHAT.
IT'S TERRIBLE!!
OGATA SUPER-MARKET GOT...
...THAT REALLY POPULAR ALL-GIRL GROUP!!
Kyaa!
SO CUTE!
WELCOME!
DAIKON ARE ON SALE TODAY!
DON'T PUSH, DON'T PUSH!
NO WAY...
WHY TODAY?
MAYBE HE GOT...
...THE IDEA FROM KYŌHEI...
HIRE SOME CELEBRITIES!
I CAN'T BELIEVE HE TOOK ME SERIOUSLY!
?
WHAT DO YOU MEAN?
WELL...

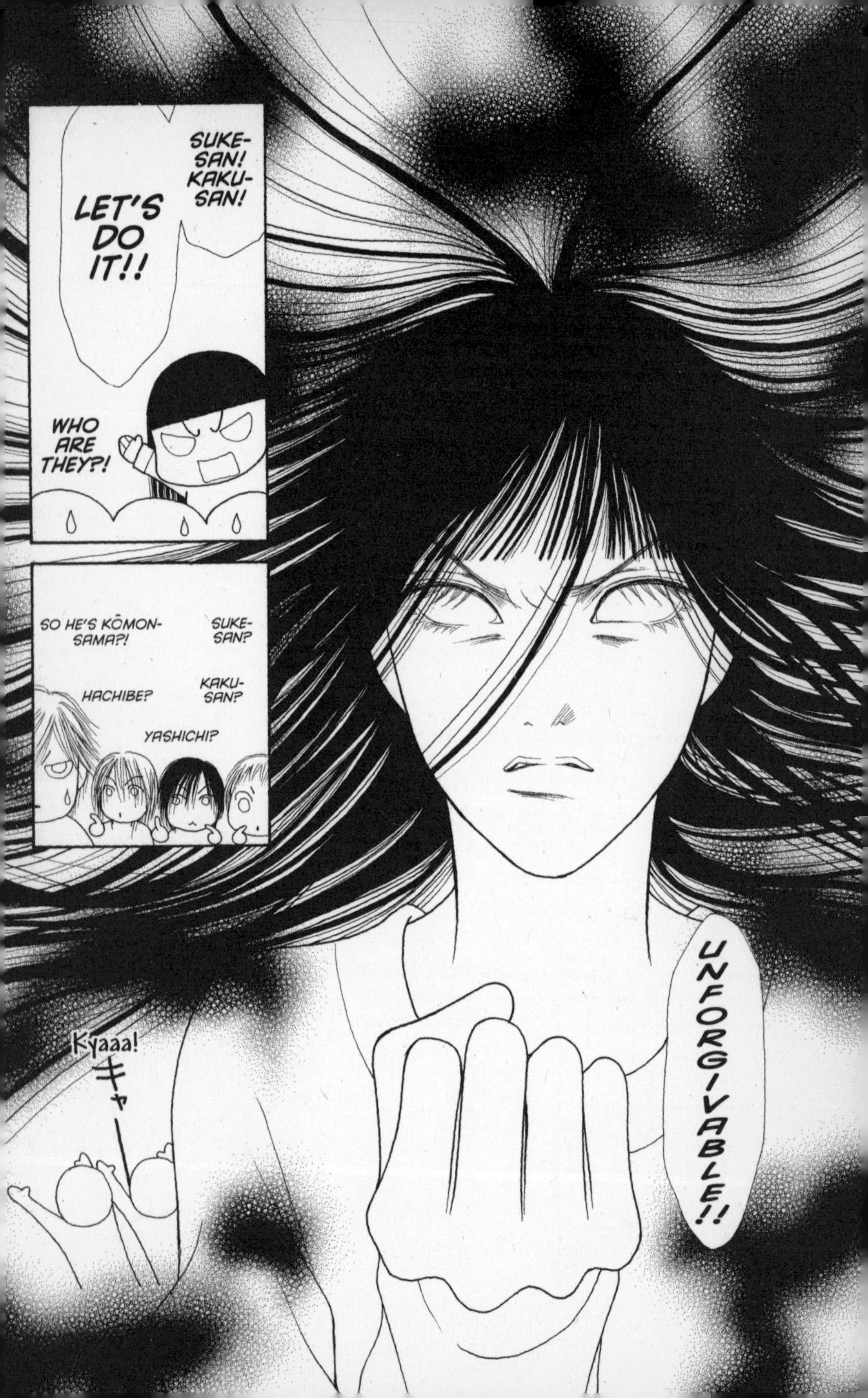
SUKE-SAN! KAKU-SAN!
LET'S DO IT!!
WHO ARE THEY?!
SUKE-SAN?
SO HE'S KŌMON-SAMA?!
KAKU-SAN?
HACHIBE?
YASHICHI?
UNFORGIVABLE!!
Kyaaa!
キャー

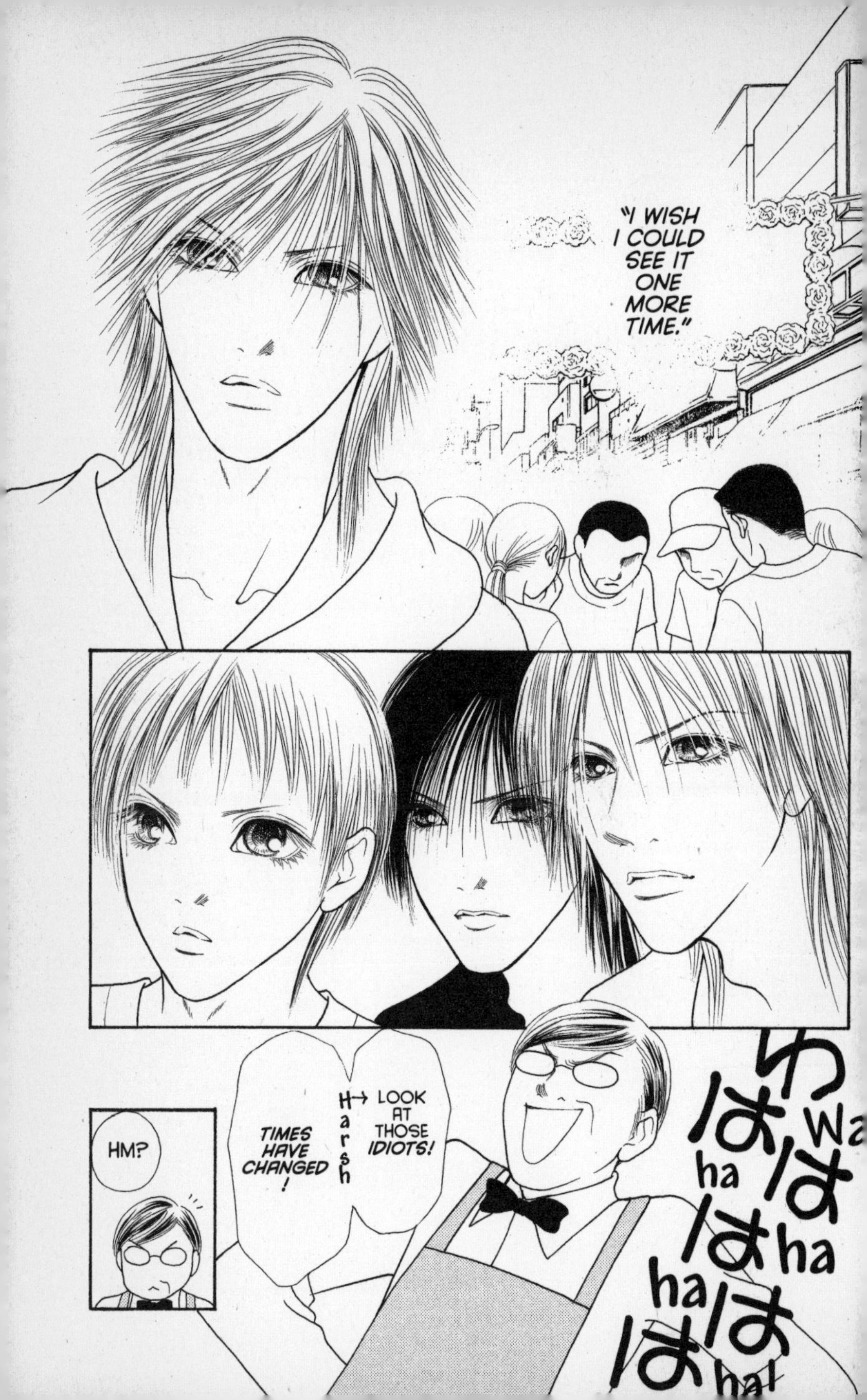
"I WISH I COULD SEE IT ONE MORE TIME."
わははははは
wa ha ha ha ha!
LOOK AT THOSE IDIOTS!
Harsh
TIMES HAVE CHANGED!
HM?

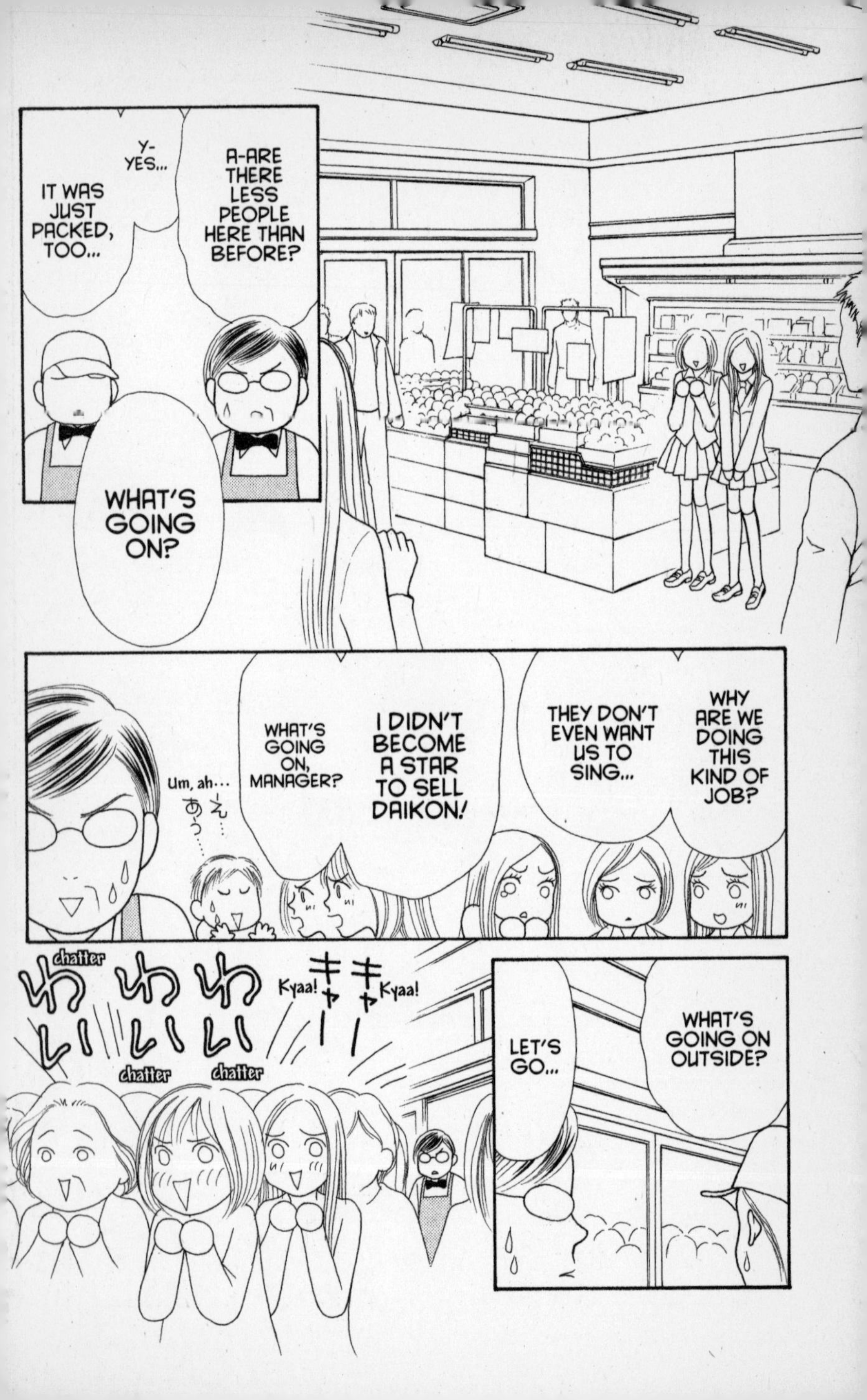
WHAT'S GOING ON?
A-ARE THERE LESS PEOPLE HERE THAN BEFORE?
Y-YES...
IT WAS JUST PACKED, TOO...
WHY ARE WE DOING THIS KIND OF JOB?
THEY DON'T EVEN WANT US TO SING...
I DIDN'T BECOME A STAR TO SELL DAIKON!
WHAT'S GOING ON, MANAGER?
え… あう…
Um, ah…
WHAT'S GOING ON OUTSIDE?
LET'S GO...
キャー Kyaa!
キャー Kyaa!
わいわいわい
chatter
chatter
chatter

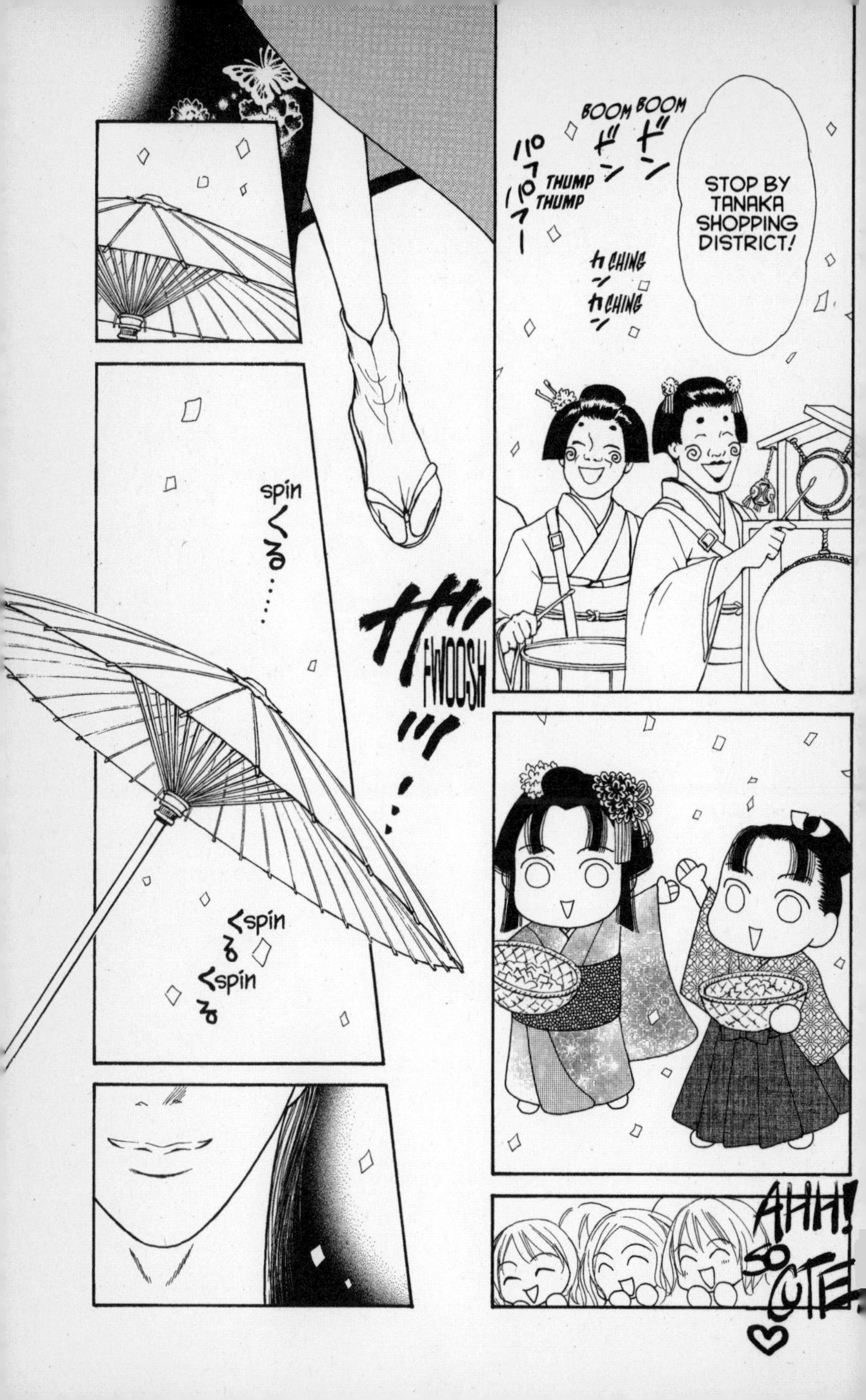
STOP BY TANAKA SHOPPING DISTRICT!
BOOM ドン BOOM ドン
THUMP THUMP
CHING CHING
AHH! SO CUTE
FWOOSH
spin くる…
spin spin

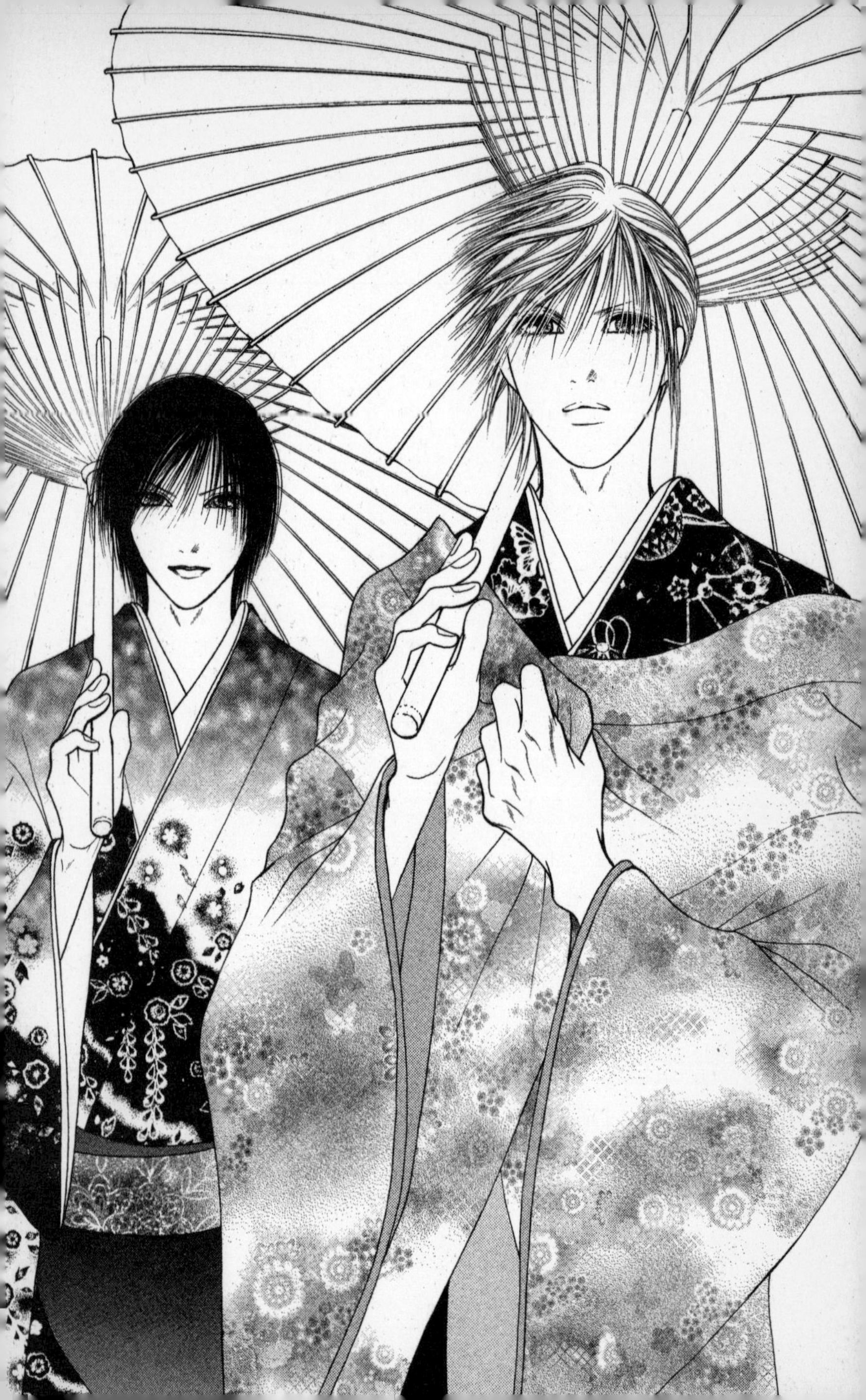

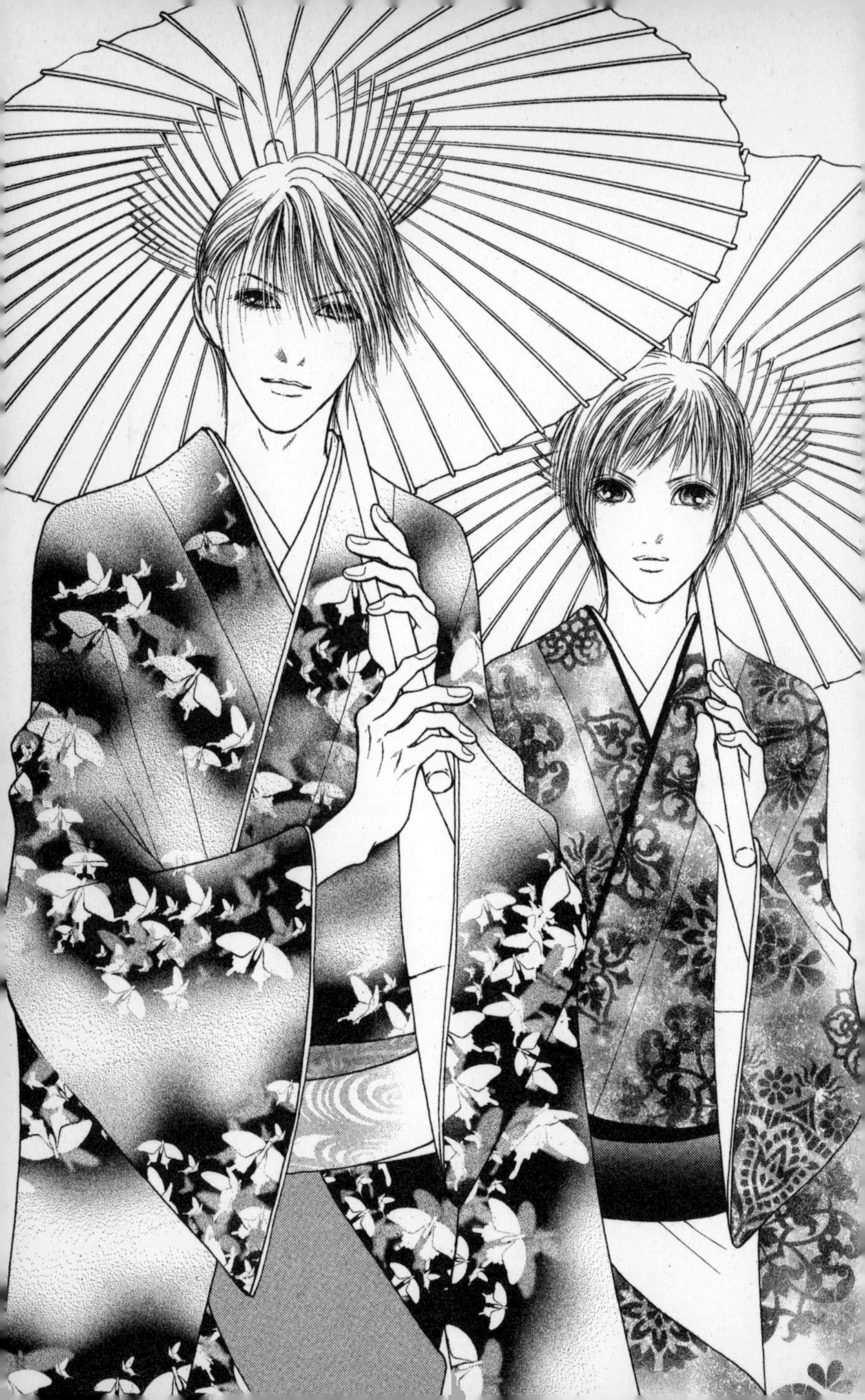

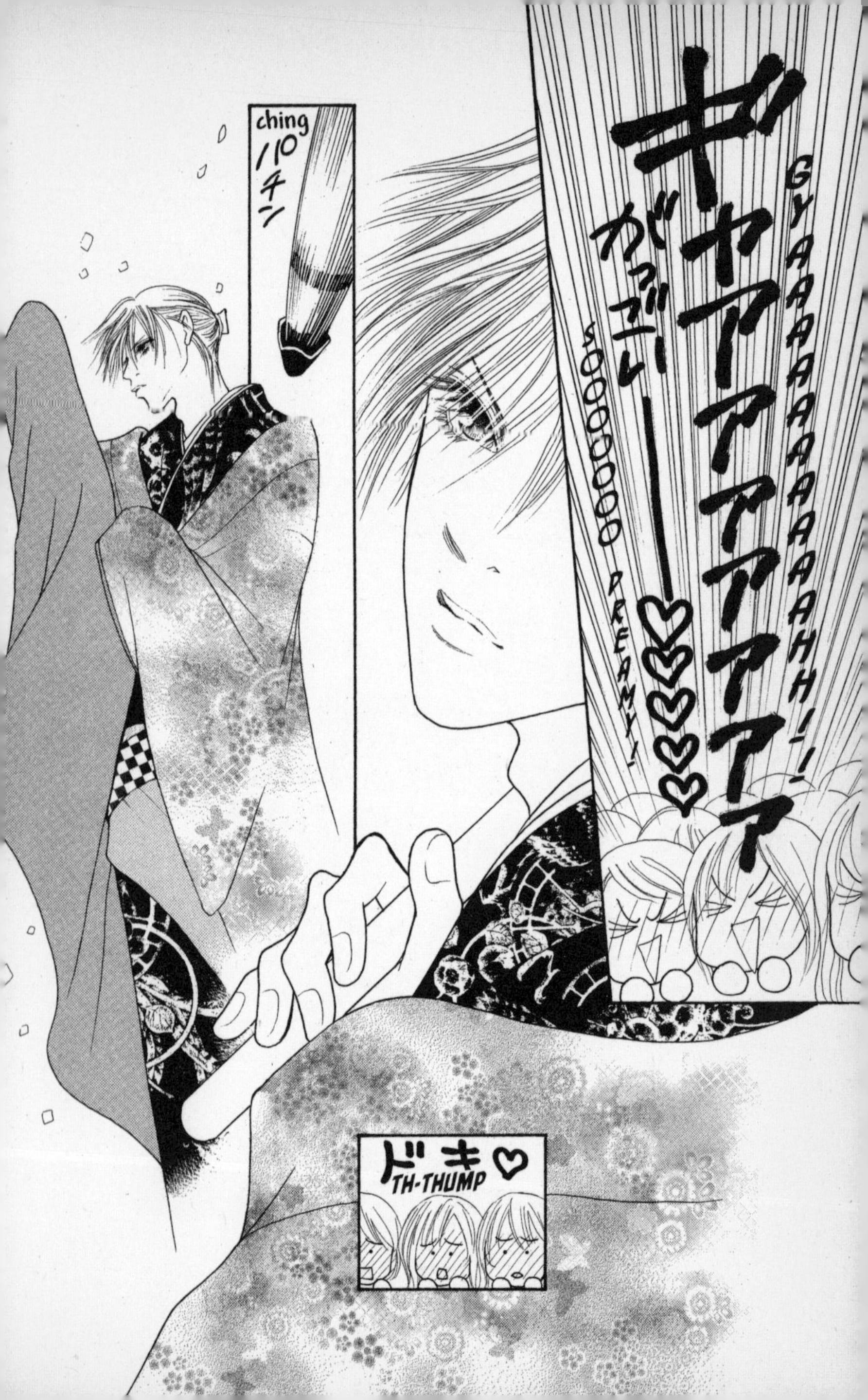
ギャアアアアアア
GYAAAAAAAAAAAH!!
かっこいい―♡♡♡♡♡
SOOOOOOOOO DREAMY!
ching
パチン
ドキ♡
TH-THUMP

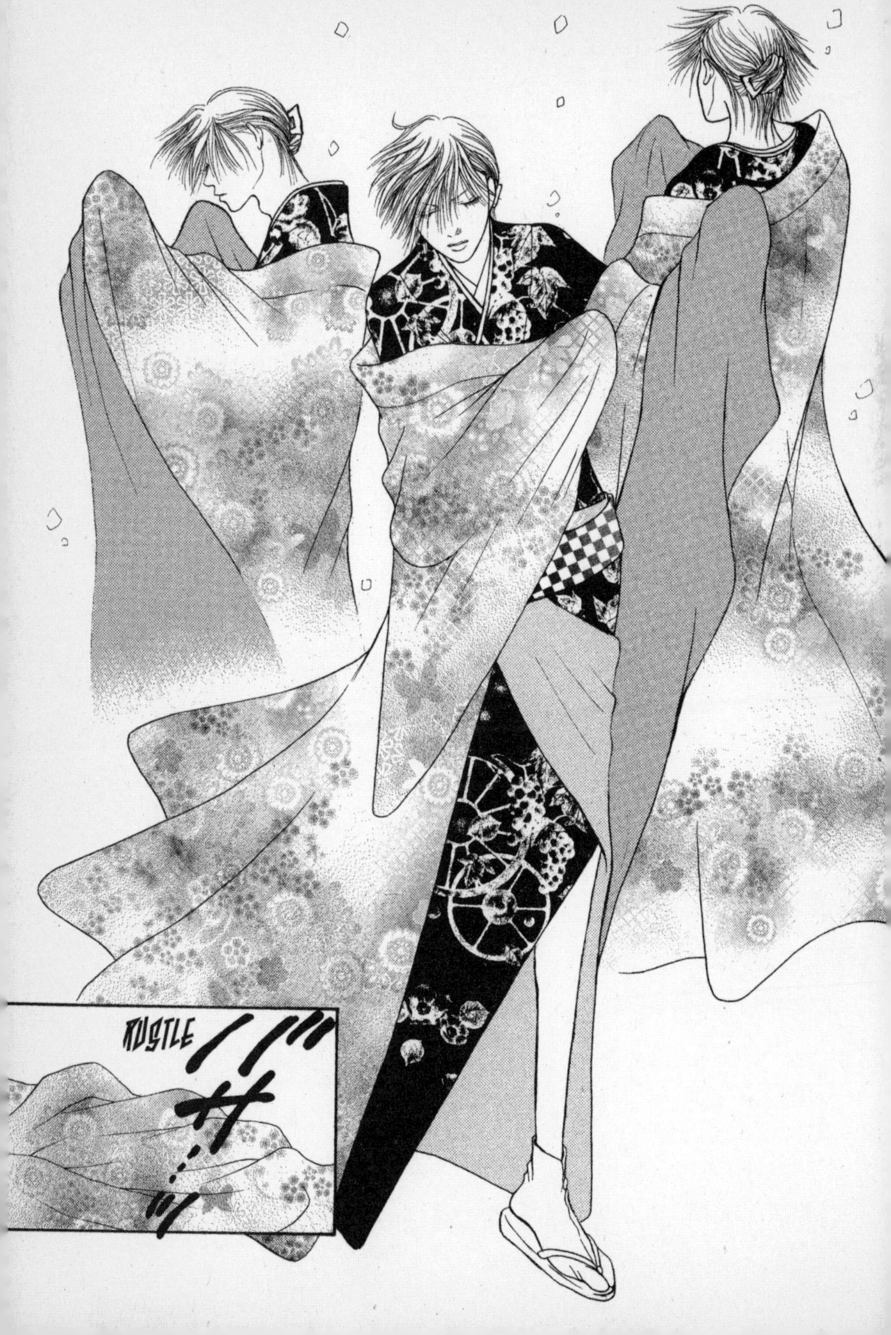
RUSTLE

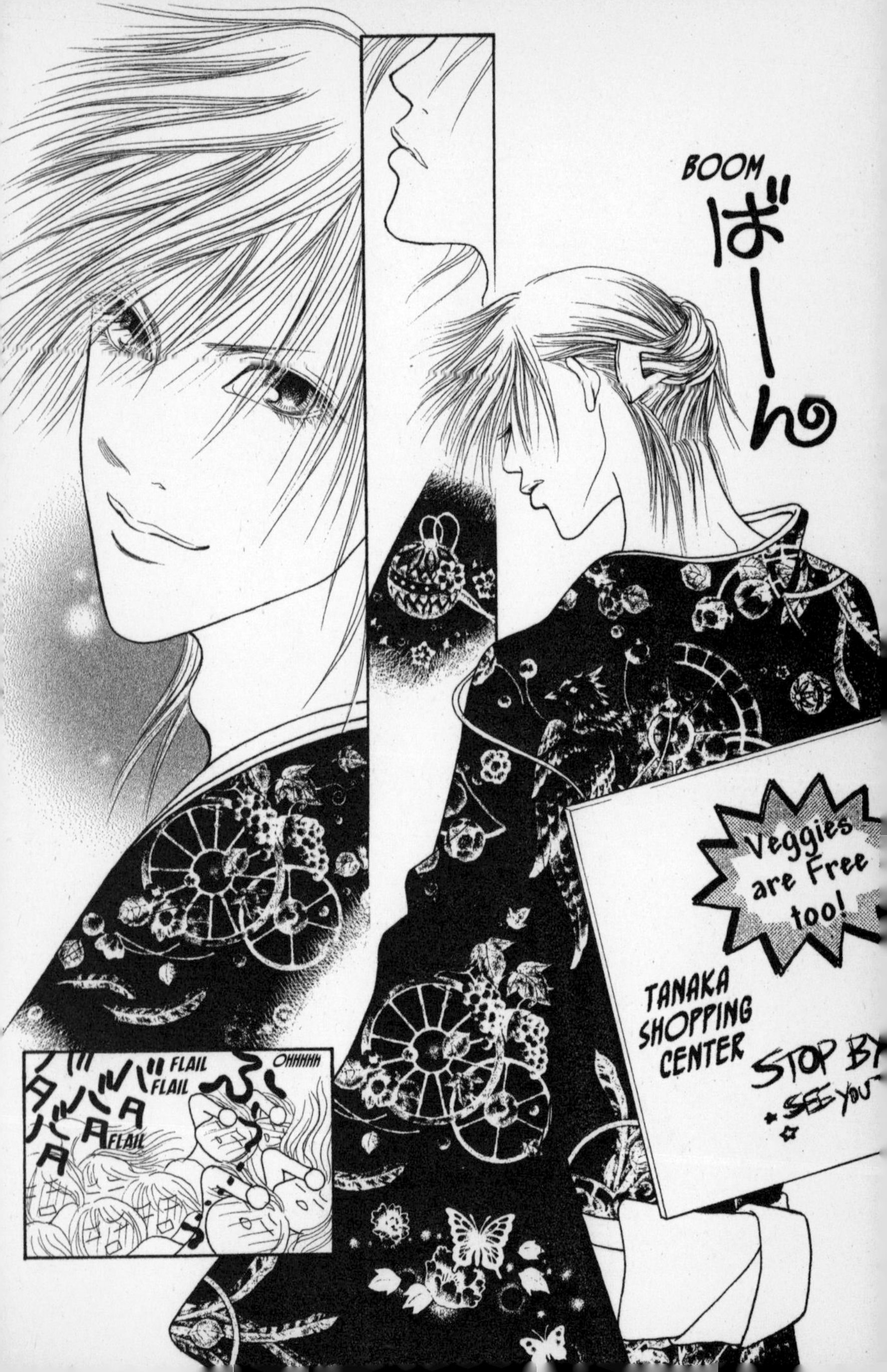
BOOM
ばーん
Veggies are Free too!
TANAKA SHOPPING CENTER
STOP BY
SEE YOU
OHHHHH
FLAIL
FLAIL
FLAIL

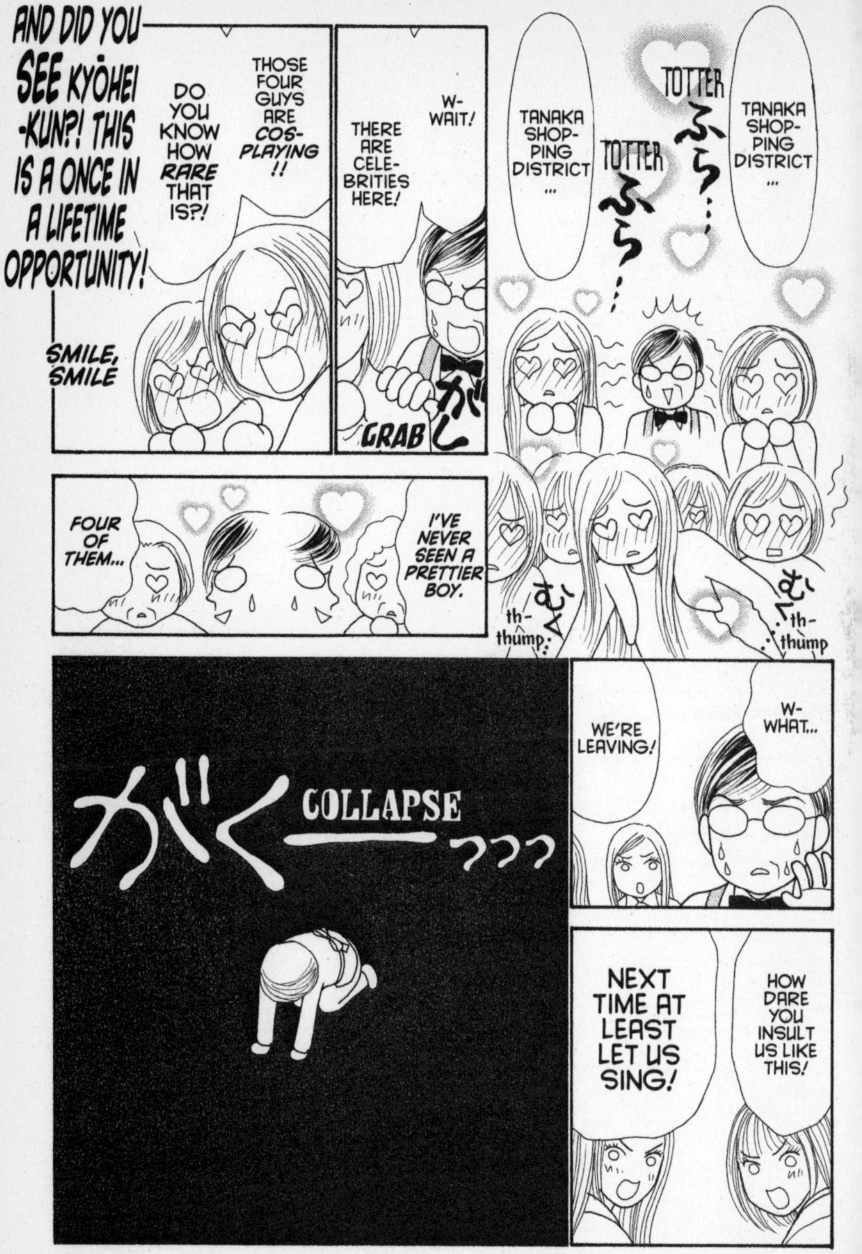

TANAKA SHOPPING DISTRICT...
TOTTER
ふら…
TOTTER
ふら…
TANAKA SHOPPING DISTRICT...
むく
th-thump
むく
th-thump
W-WAIT!
THERE ARE CELEBRITIES HERE!
GRAB
がし
THOSE FOUR GUYS ARE COS-PLAYING!!
DO YOU KNOW HOW RARE THAT IS?!
AND DID YOU SEE KYŌHEI-KUN?! THIS IS A ONCE IN A LIFETIME OPPORTUNITY!
SMILE, SMILE
I'VE NEVER SEEN A PRETTIER BOY.
FOUR OF THEM...
W-WHAT...
WE'RE LEAVING!
HOW DARE YOU INSULT US LIKE THIS!
NEXT TIME AT LEAST LET US SING!
がく
COLLAPSE
つつつ

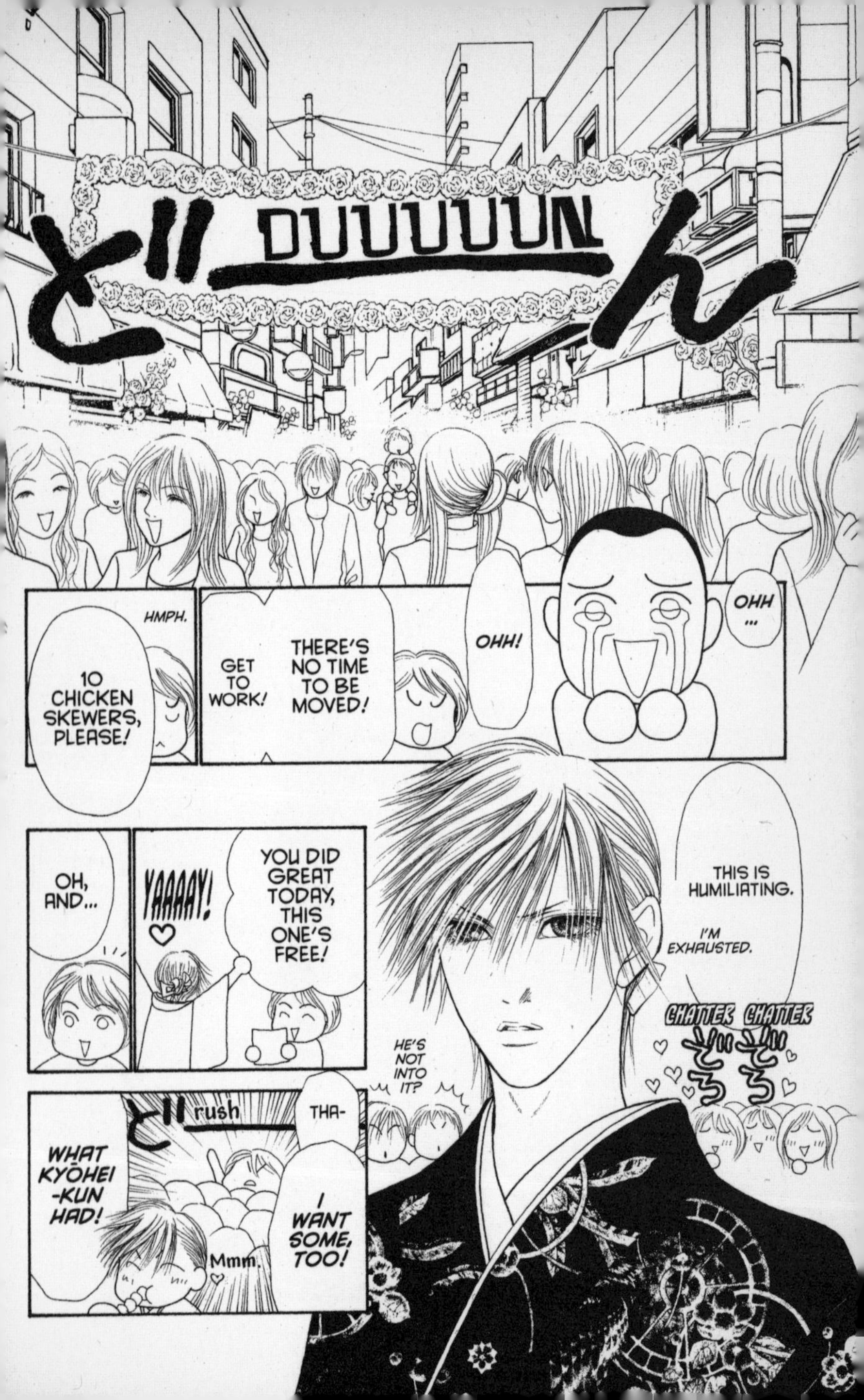

DUUUUUN
OHH ...
OHH!
THERE'S NO TIME TO BE MOVED!
GET TO WORK!
HMPH.
10 CHICKEN SKEWERS, PLEASE!
THIS IS HUMILIATING.
I'M EXHAUSTED.
CHATTER CHATTER
HE'S NOT INTO IT?
YOU DID GREAT TODAY, THIS ONE'S FREE!
YAAAAY! ♡
OH, AND...
THA-
I WANT SOME, TOO!
rush
WHAT KYŌHEI-KUN HAD!
Mmm. ♡

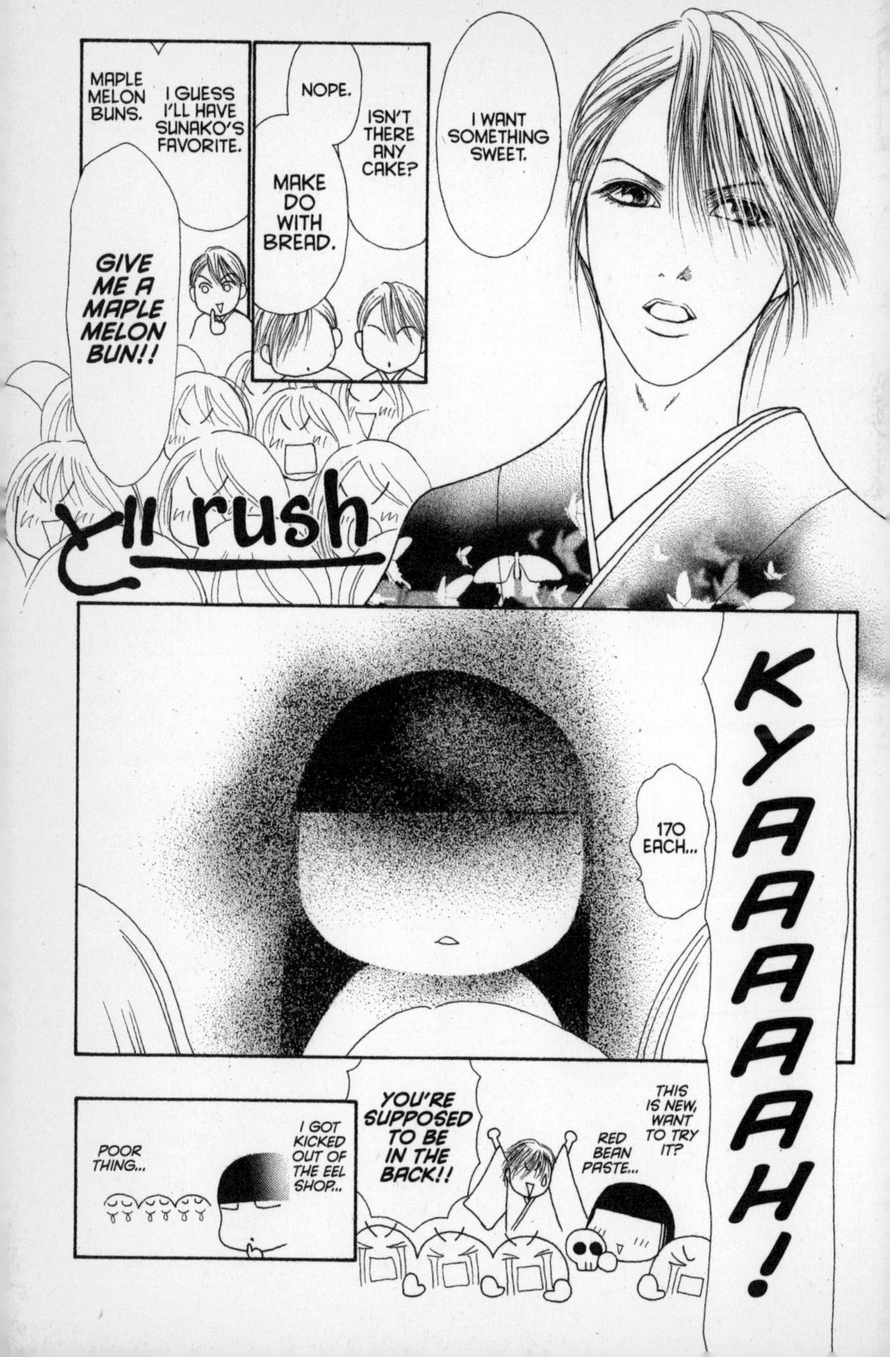
I WANT SOMETHING SWEET.
ISN'T THERE ANY CAKE?
NOPE.
MAKE DO WITH BREAD.
I GUESS I'LL HAVE SUNAKO'S FAVORITE.
MAPLE MELON BUNS.
GIVE ME A MAPLE MELON BUN!!
rush
KYAAAAAAH!
170 EACH...
THIS IS NEW, WANT TO TRY IT?
RED BEAN PASTE...
YOU'RE SUPPOSED TO BE IN THE BACK!!
I GOT KICKED OUT OF THE EEL SHOP...
POOR THING...

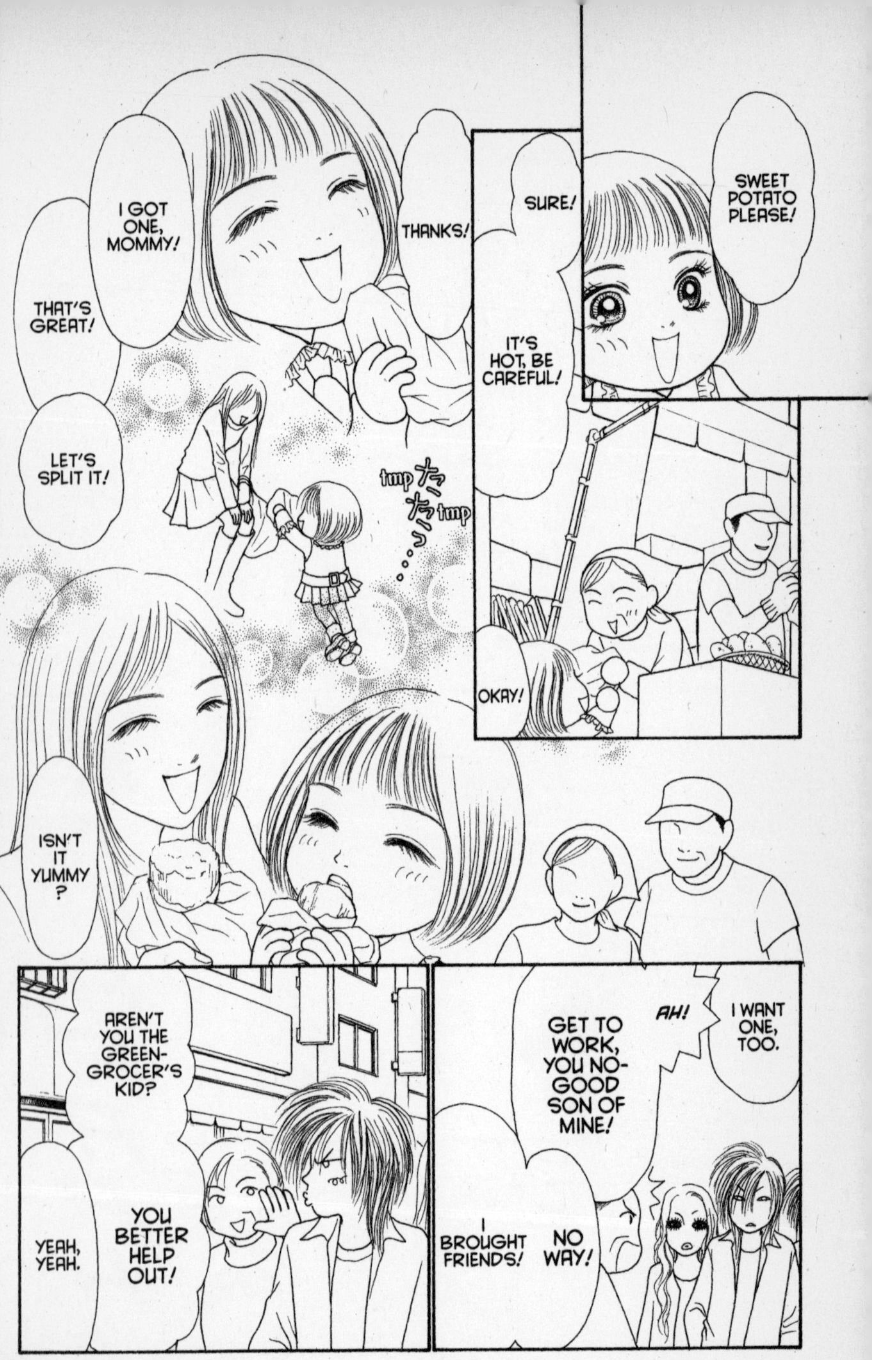
SWEET POTATO PLEASE!
SURE!
IT'S HOT, BE CAREFUL!
OKAY!
THANKS!
I GOT ONE, MOMMY!
THAT'S GREAT!
LET'S SPLIT IT!
tmp tmp
ISN'T IT YUMMY?
I WANT ONE, TOO.
AH!
GET TO WORK, YOU NO-GOOD SON OF MINE!
NO WAY!
I BROUGHT FRIENDS!
AREN'T YOU THE GREEN-GROCER'S KID?
YOU BETTER HELP OUT!
YEAH, YEAH.

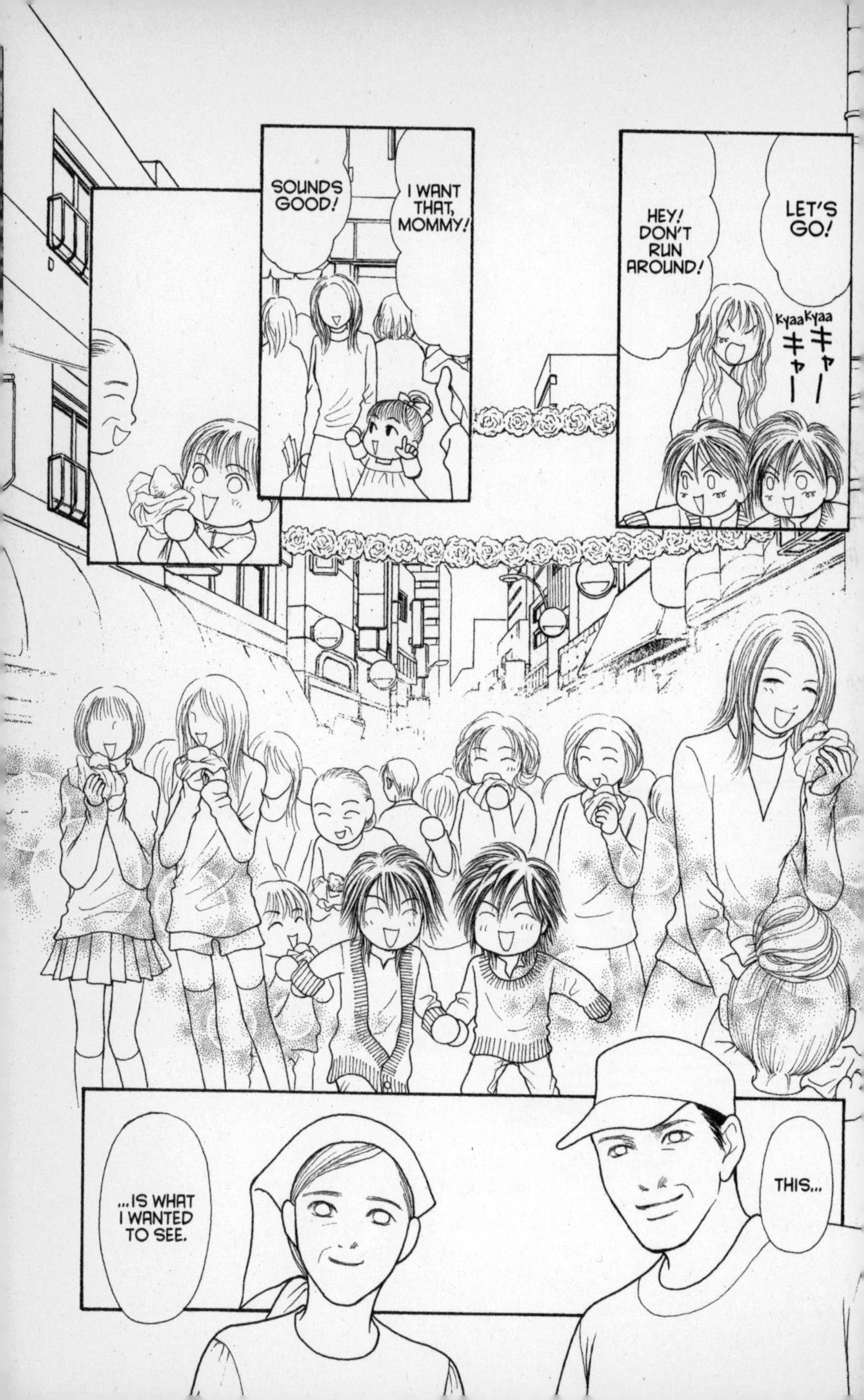
LET'S GO!
HEY! DON'T RUN AROUND!
Kyaa Kyaa
キャーキャー
I WANT THAT, MOMMY!
SOUNDS GOOD!
THIS...
...IS WHAT I WANTED TO SEE.

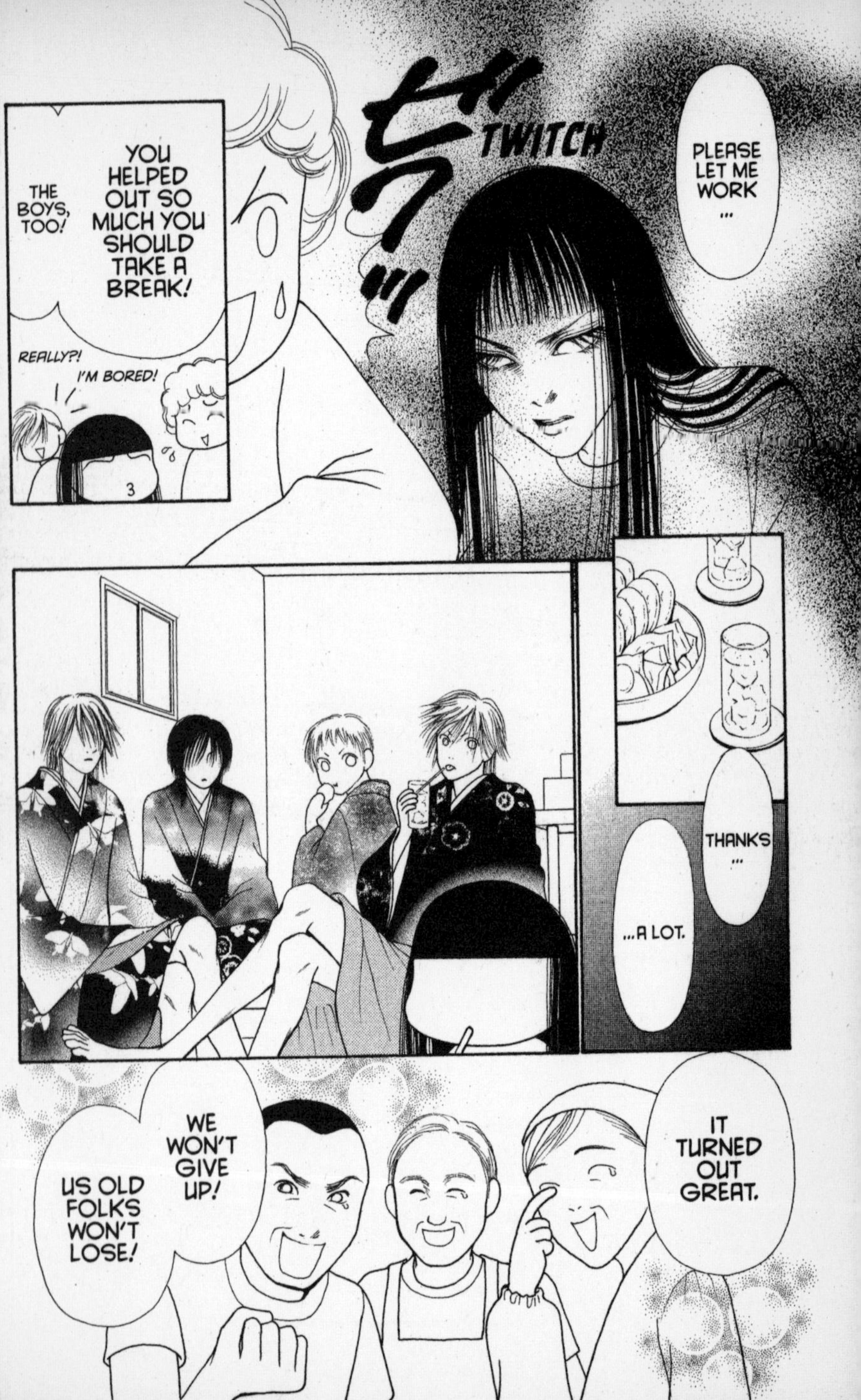
TWITCH
PLEASE LET ME WORK ...
YOU HELPED OUT SO MUCH YOU SHOULD TAKE A BREAK!
THE BOYS, TOO!
REALLY?!
I'M BORED!
THANKS ...
...A LOT.
IT TURNED OUT GREAT.
WE WON'T GIVE UP!
US OLD FOLKS WON'T LOSE!

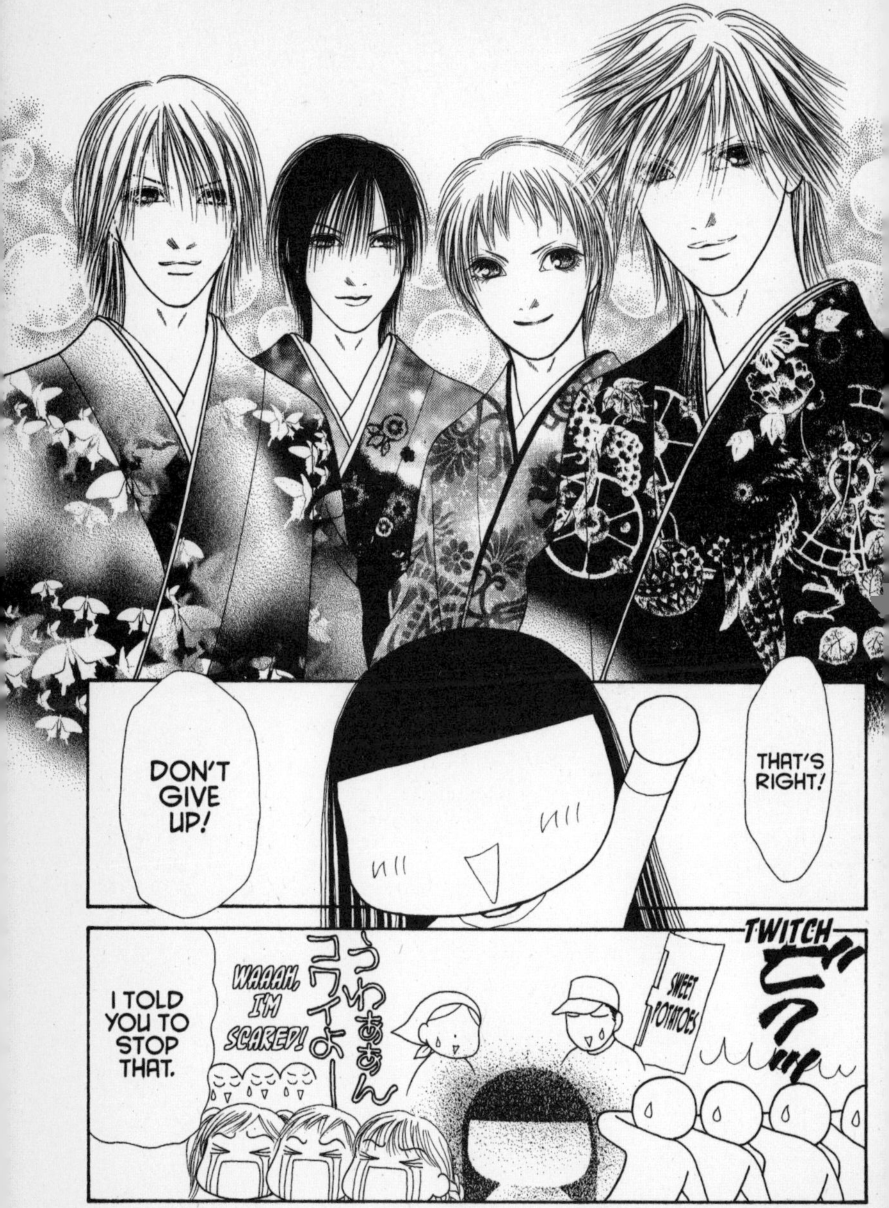
THAT'S RIGHT!
DON'T GIVE UP!
TWITCH
ピク
SWEET POTATOES
うわあぁん コワイよー
WAAAH, I'M SCARED!
I TOLD YOU TO STOP THAT.

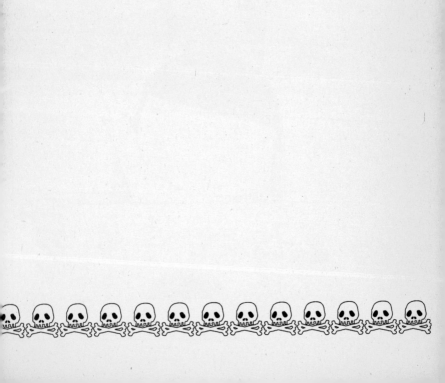

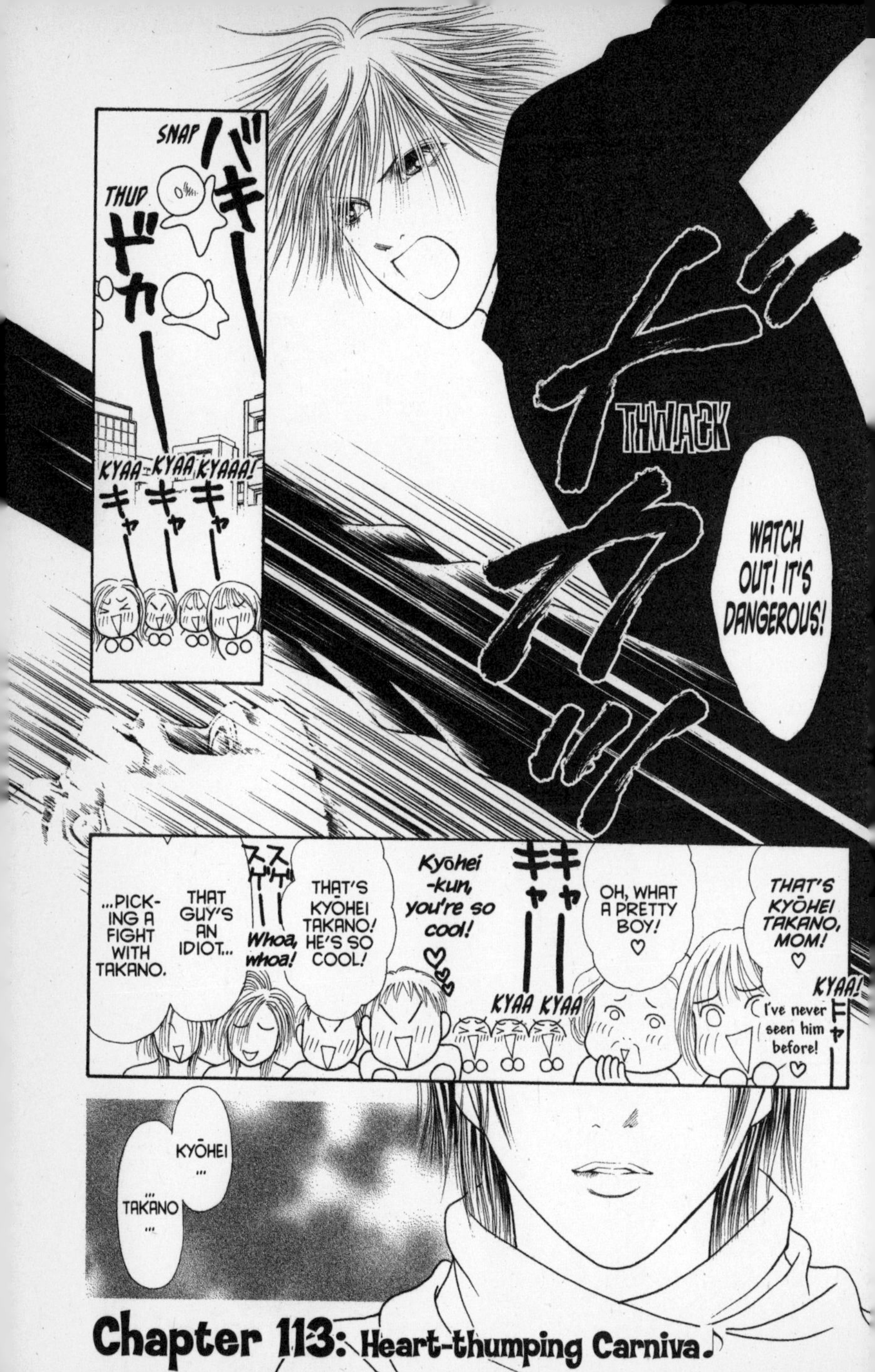
THWACK
WATCH OUT! IT'S DANGEROUS!
SNAP
THUD
KYAAA!
KYAA
KYAA
THAT'S KYŌHEI TAKANO, MOM!
KYAA!
I've never seen him before!
OH, WHAT A PRETTY BOY!
KYAA KYAA
Kyōhei-kun, you're so cool!
THAT'S KYŌHEI TAKANO! HE'S SO COOL!
Whoa, whoa!
THAT GUY'S AN IDIOT...
...PICKING A FIGHT WITH TAKANO.
KYŌHEI ...
... TAKANO ...

Chapter 113: Heart-thumping Carniva♪

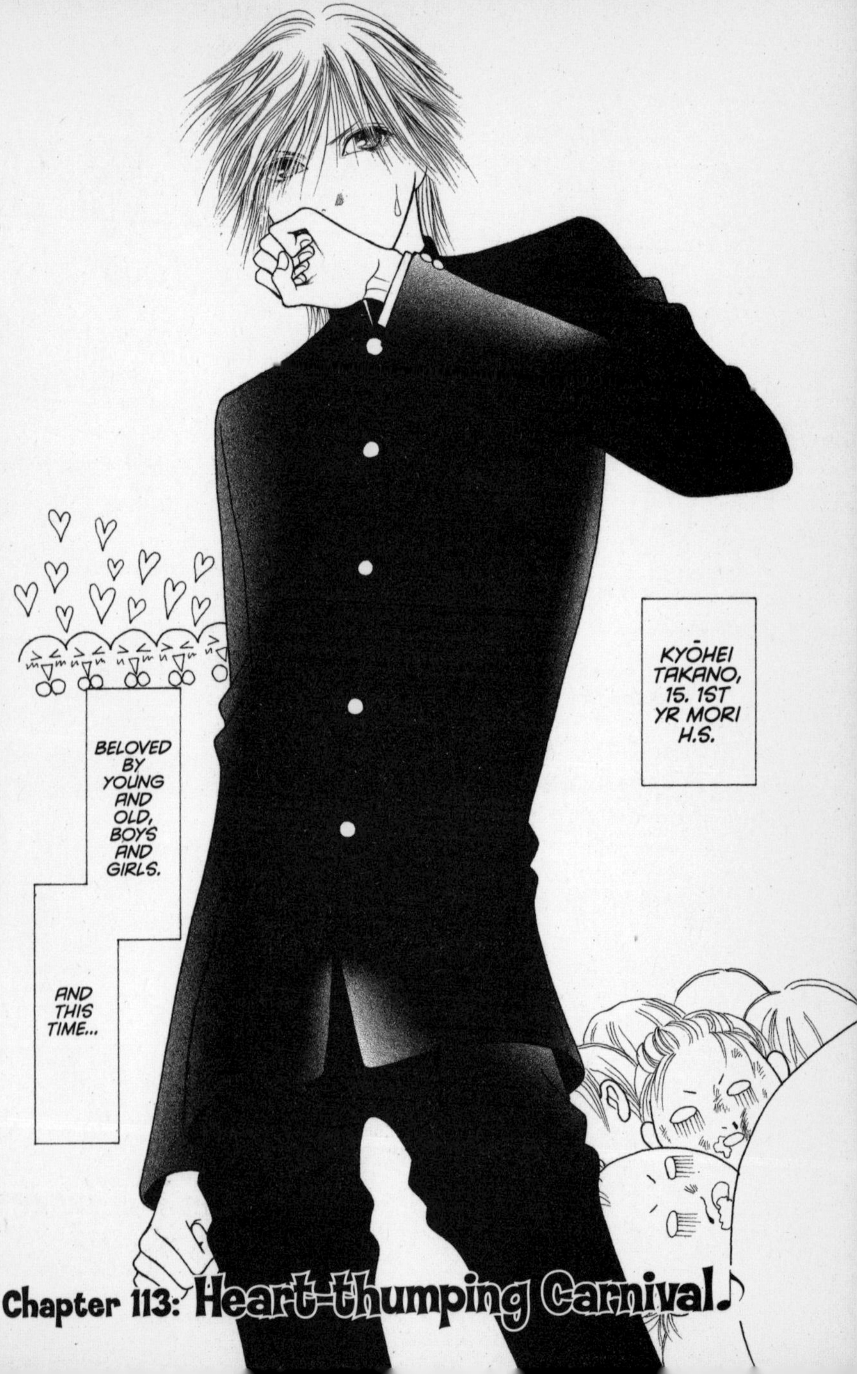
KYŌHEI TAKANO, 15. 1ST YR MORI H.S.
BELOVED BY YOUNG AND OLD, BOYS AND GIRLS.
AND THIS TIME...

Chapter 113: Heart-thumping Carnival♪

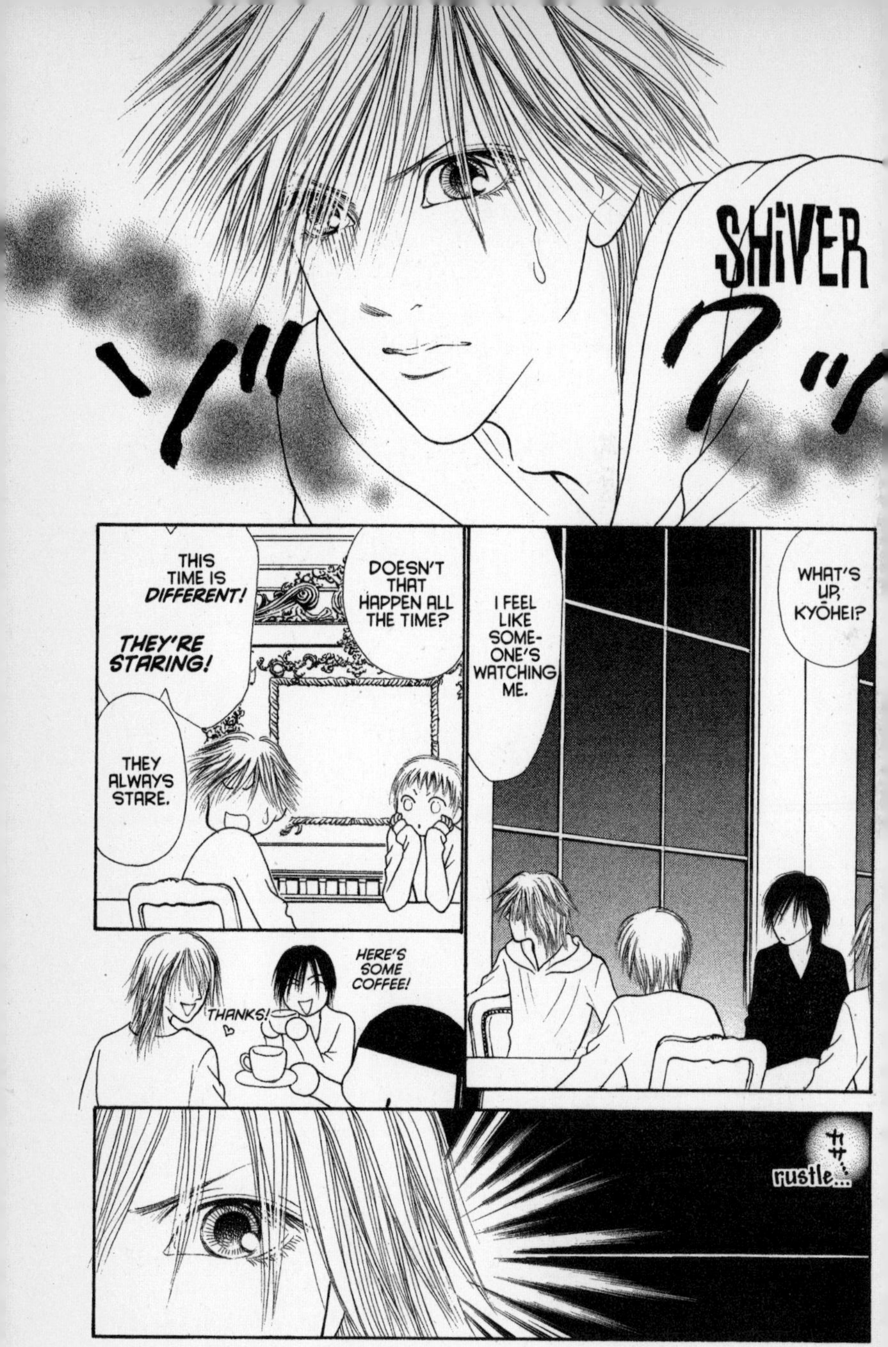

SHIVER
WHAT'S UP, KYŌHEI?
I FEEL LIKE SOME-ONE'S WATCHING ME.
DOESN'T THAT HAPPEN ALL THE TIME?
THIS TIME IS *DIFFERENT!*
THEY'RE STARING!
THEY ALWAYS STARE.
HERE'S SOME COFFEE!
THANKS!
rustle...

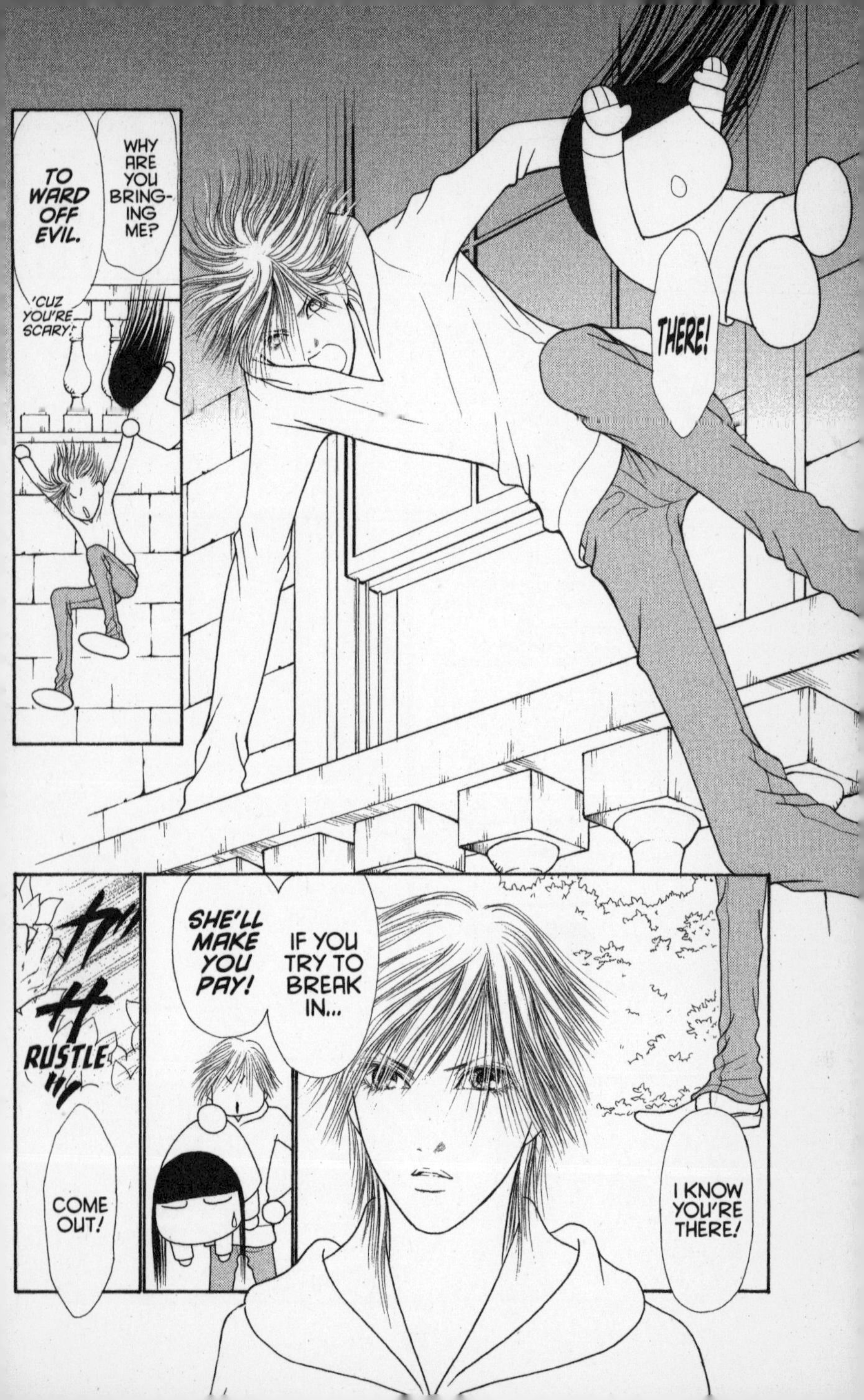
THERE!
WHY ARE YOU BRINGING- ING ME?
TO WARD OFF EVIL.
'CUZ YOU'RE SCARY!
I KNOW YOU'RE THERE!
IF YOU TRY TO BREAK IN...
SHE'LL MAKE YOU PAY!
RUSTLE
COME OUT!

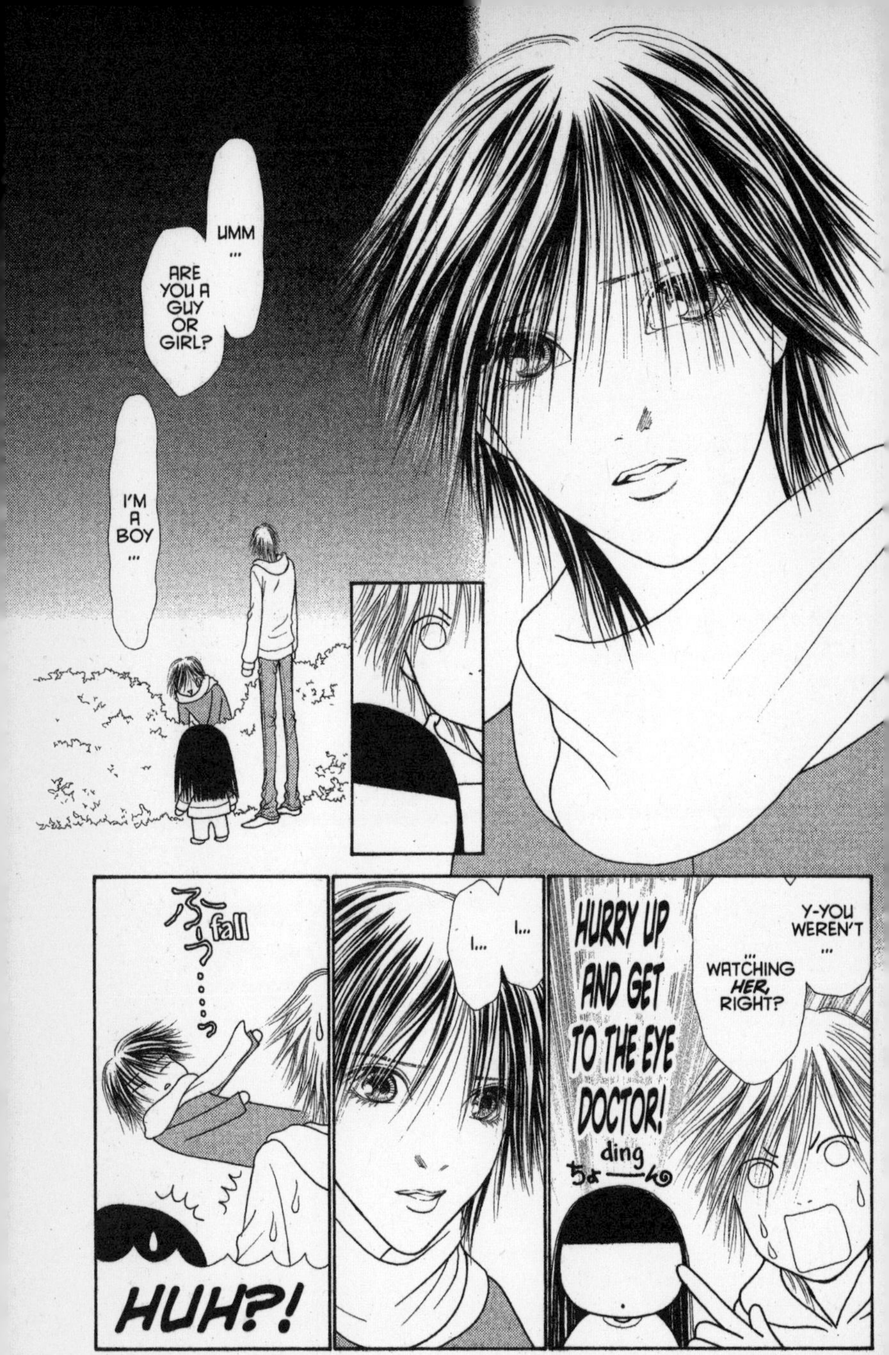
UMM ...
ARE YOU A GUY OR GIRL?
I'M A BOY ...
Y-YOU WEREN'T ...
... WATCHING HER, RIGHT?
HURRY UP AND GET TO THE EYE DOCTOR!
ding ちょーん
I...
I...
ふーっ fall
HUH?!

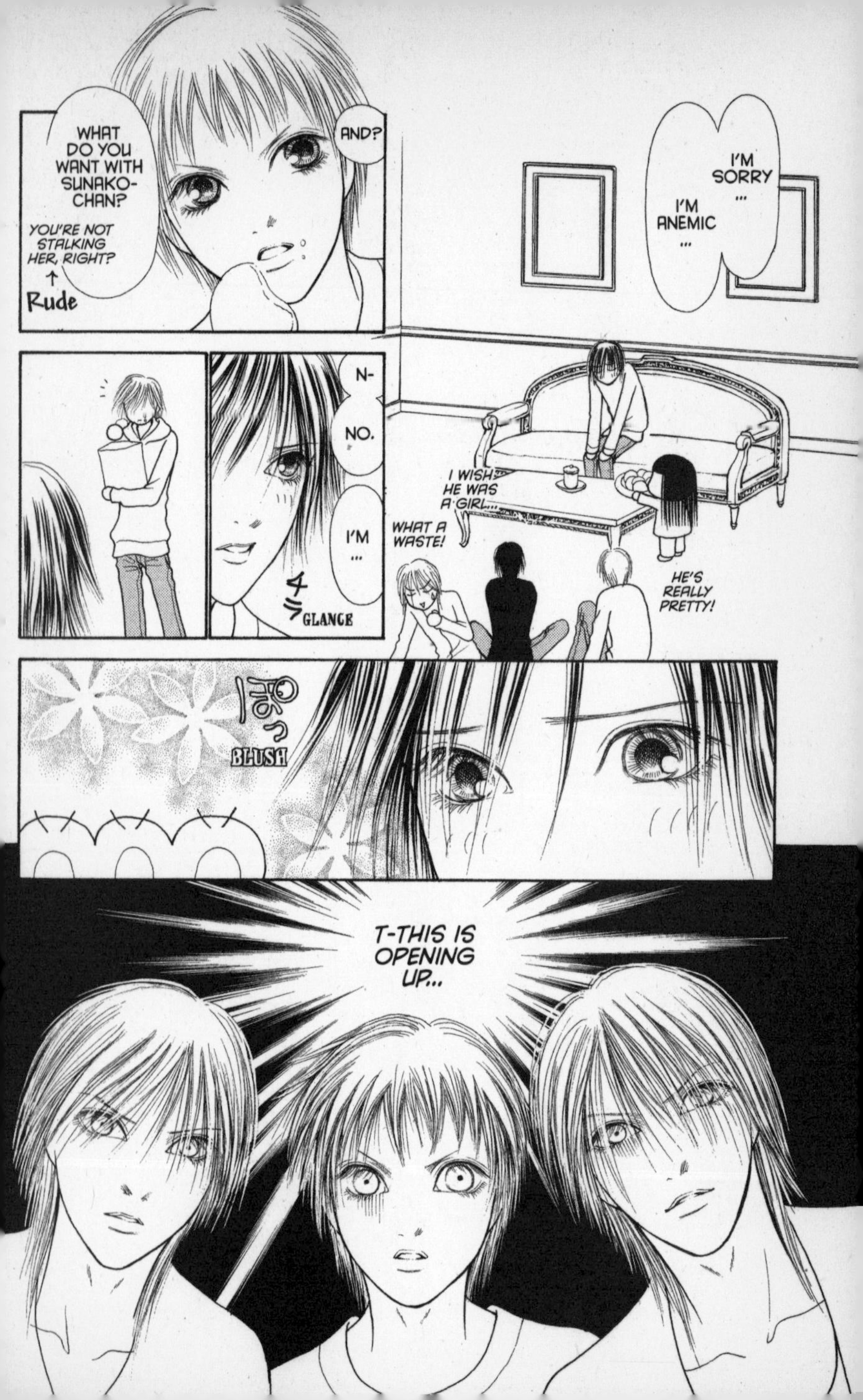

I'M SORRY ...
I'M ANEMIC ...
HE'S REALLY PRETTY!
I WISH HE WAS A GIRL...
WHAT A WASTE!
AND?
WHAT DO YOU WANT WITH SUNAKO-CHAN?
YOU'RE NOT STALKING HER, RIGHT?
↑ Rude
N-
NO.
I'M ...
GLANCE
ぽっ
BLUSH
T-THIS IS OPENING UP...

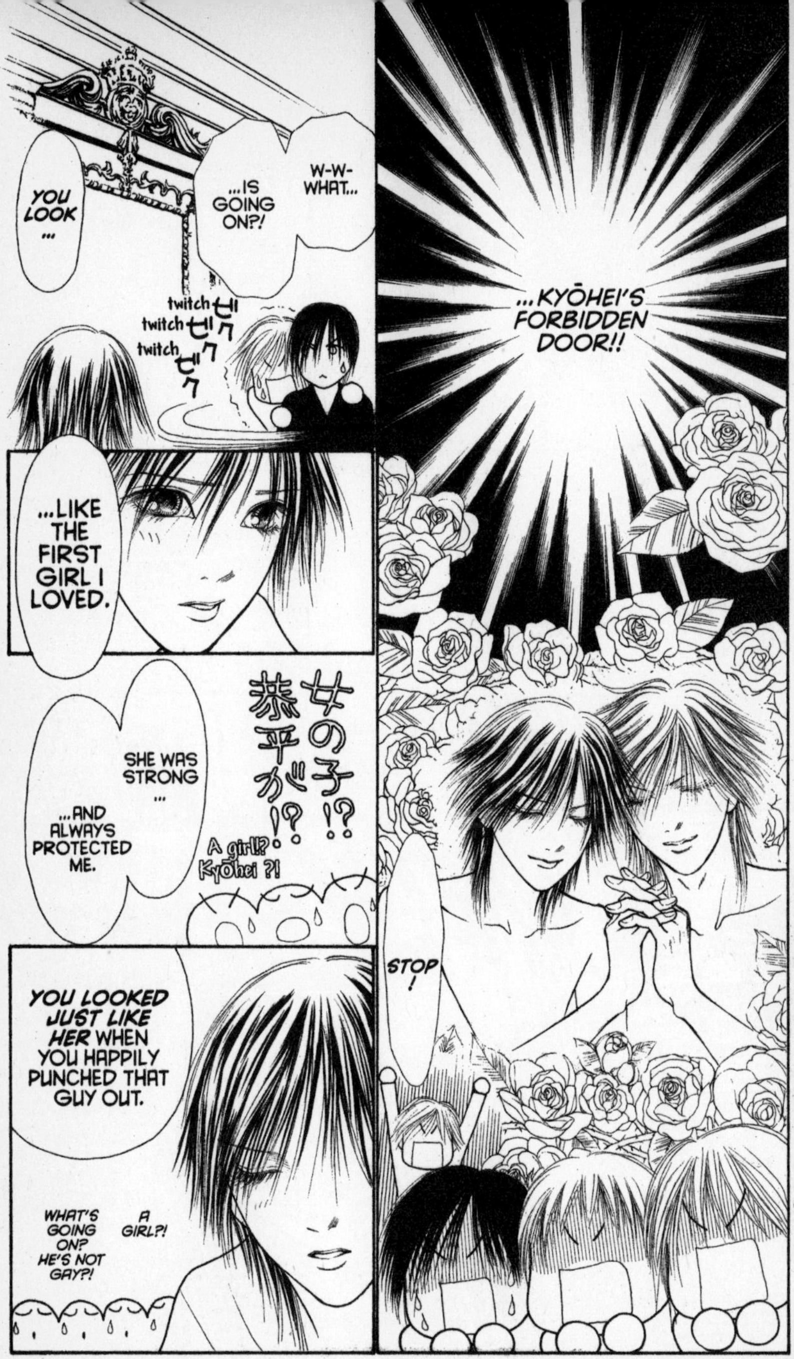

...KYŌHEI'S FORBIDDEN DOOR!!
STOP!
W-W-WHAT...
...IS GOING ON?!
YOU LOOK ...
twitch
twitch
twitch
...LIKE THE FIRST GIRL I LOVED.
女の子!?
恭平が!?
A girl!? Kyōhei ?!
SHE WAS STRONG ...
...AND ALWAYS PROTECTED ME.
YOU LOOKED JUST LIKE HER WHEN YOU HAPPILY PUNCHED THAT GUY OUT.
A GIRL?!
WHAT'S GOING ON? HE'S NOT GAY?!

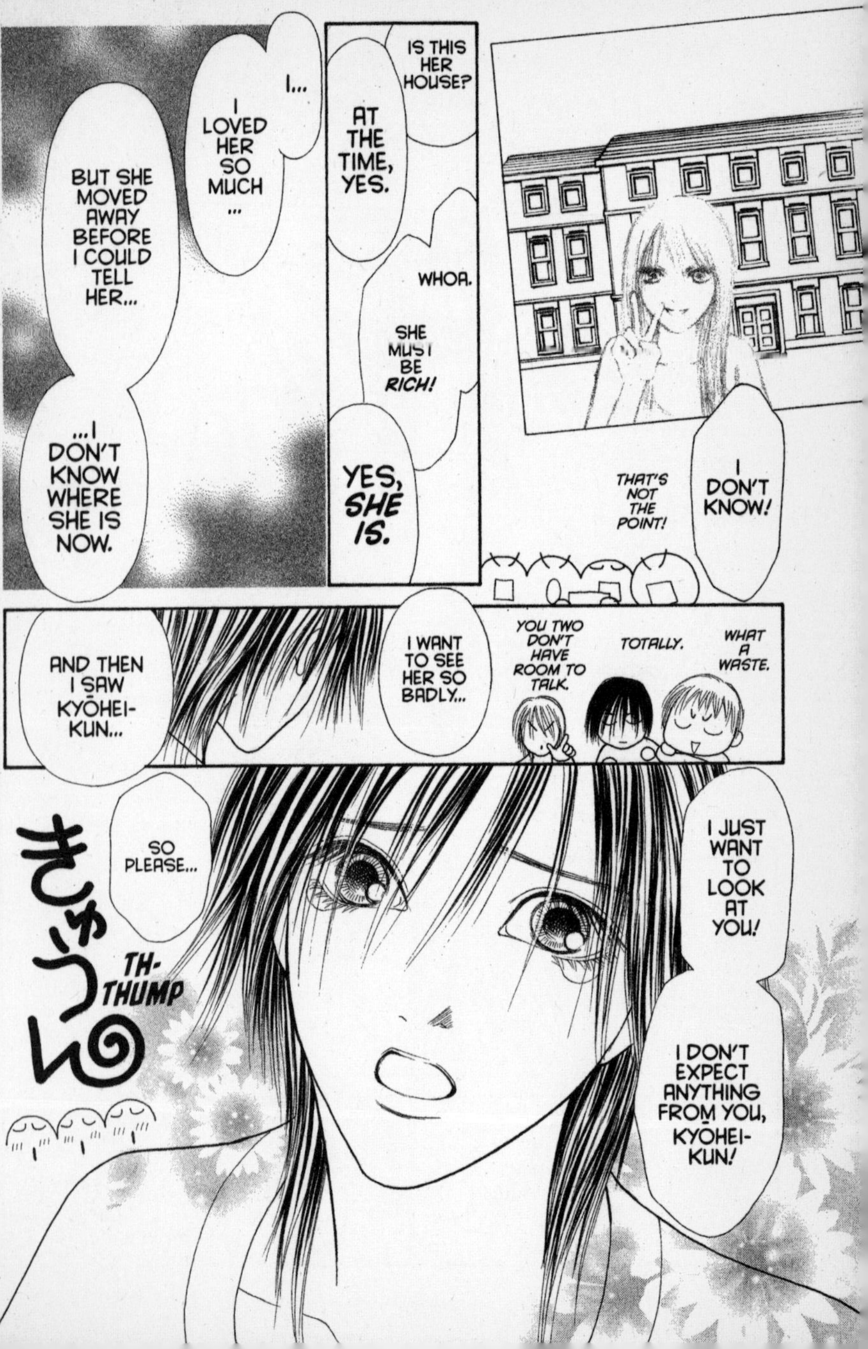

IS THIS HER HOUSE?
AT THE TIME, YES.
WHOA.
SHE MUST BE RICH!
YES, SHE IS.
I DON'T KNOW!
THAT'S NOT THE POINT!
I...
I LOVED HER SO MUCH...
BUT SHE MOVED AWAY BEFORE I COULD TELL HER...
...I DON'T KNOW WHERE SHE IS NOW.
WHAT A WASTE.
TOTALLY.
YOU TWO DON'T HAVE ROOM TO TALK.
I WANT TO SEE HER SO BADLY...
AND THEN I SAW KYŌHEI-KUN...
I JUST WANT TO LOOK AT YOU!
I DON'T EXPECT ANYTHING FROM YOU, KYŌHEI-KUN!
SO PLEASE...
きゅうん
TH-THUMP

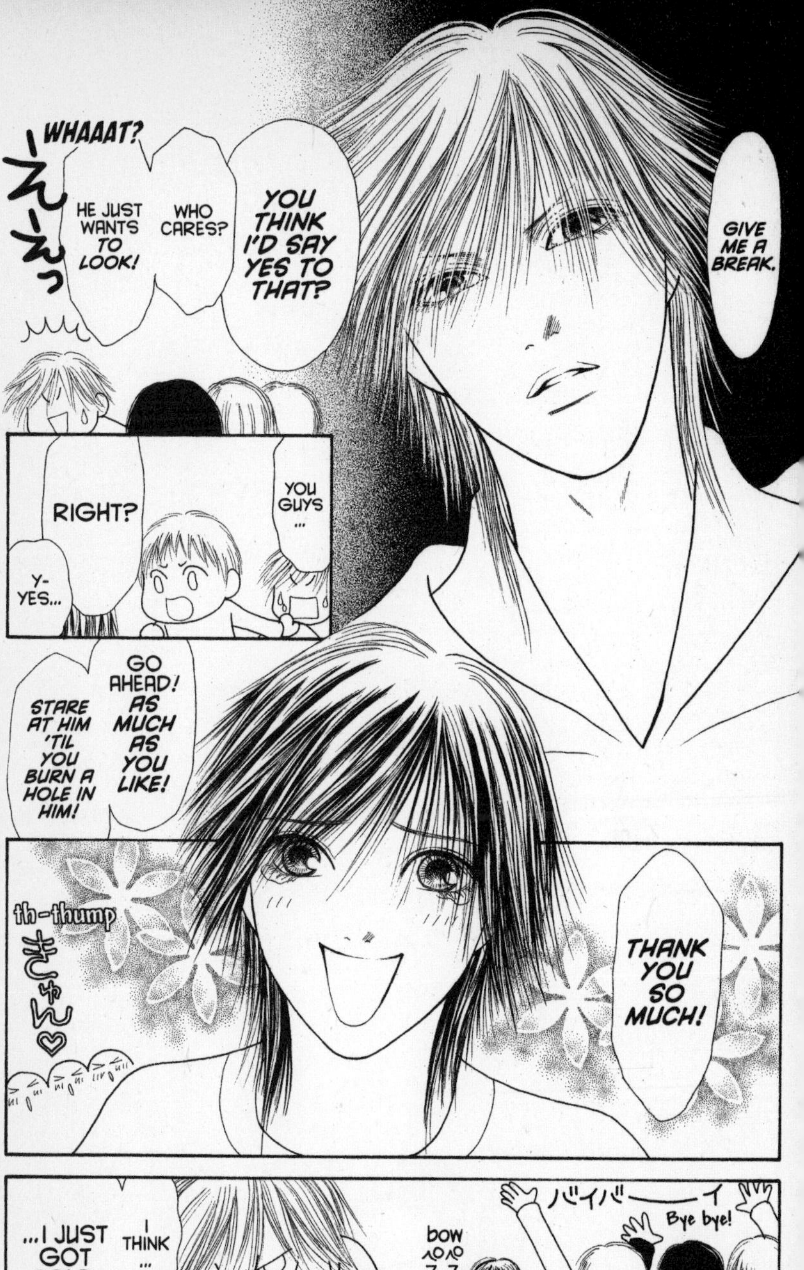
GIVE ME A BREAK.
YOU THINK I'D SAY YES TO THAT?
WHO CARES?
HE JUST WANTS TO LOOK!
WHAAAT?
YOU GUYS ...
RIGHT?
Y- YES...
GO AHEAD! AS MUCH AS YOU LIKE!
STARE AT HIM 'TIL YOU BURN A HOLE IN HIM!
THANK YOU SO MUCH!
th-thump
Bye bye!
bow
I THINK ...
...I JUST GOT SOLD.

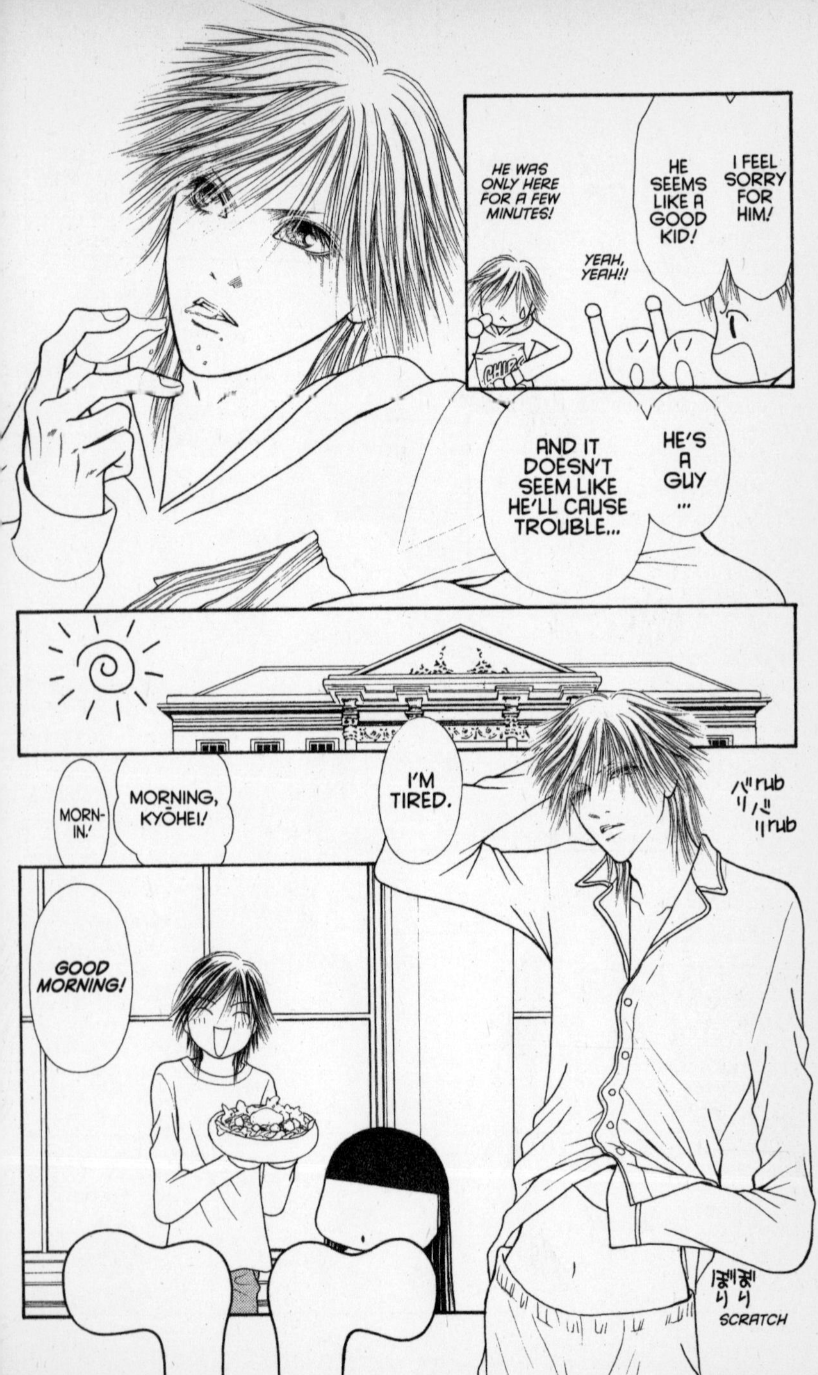
I FEEL SORRY FOR HIM!
HE SEEMS LIKE A GOOD KID!
YEAH, YEAH!!
HE WAS ONLY HERE FOR A FEW MINUTES!
HE'S A GUY ...
AND IT DOESN'T SEEM LIKE HE'LL CAUSE TROUBLE...
I'M TIRED.
バリバリ rub rub
MORNING, KYŌHEI!
MORN-IN.'
GOOD MORNING!
ぽりぽり SCRATCH

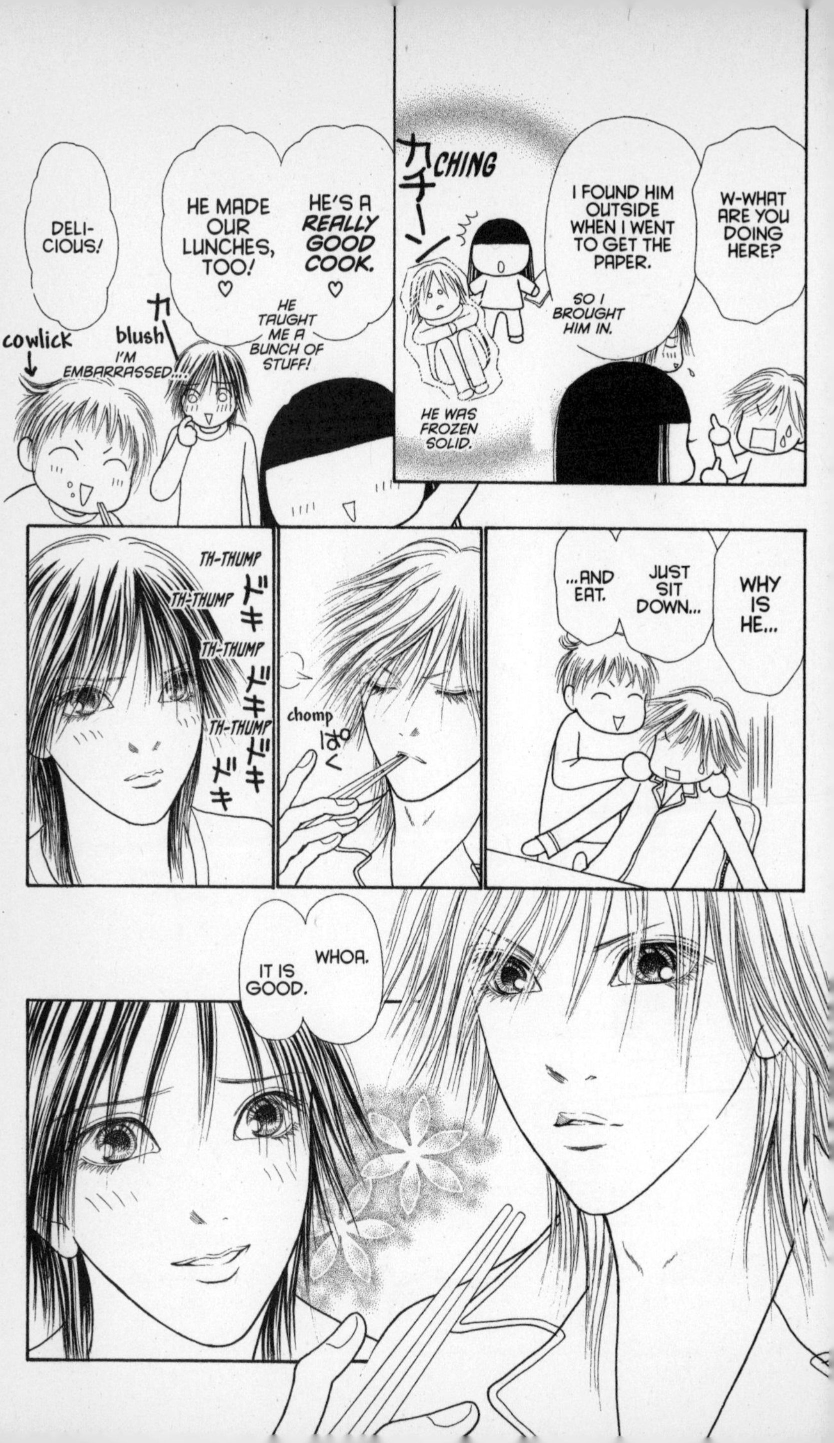
W-WHAT ARE YOU DOING HERE?
I FOUND HIM OUTSIDE WHEN I WENT TO GET THE PAPER.
SO I BROUGHT HIM IN.
カチーン
CHING
HE WAS FROZEN SOLID.
HE'S A REALLY GOOD COOK. ♡
HE MADE OUR LUNCHES, TOO! ♡
HE TAUGHT ME A BUNCH OF STUFF!
カー
blush
I'M EMBARRASSED...
DELI-CIOUS!
cowlick
WHY IS HE...
JUST SIT DOWN...
...AND EAT.
ぱく
chomp
ドキ
TH-THUMP
ドキ
TH-THUMP
ドキ
TH-THUMP
ドキ
TH-THUMP
WHOA.
IT IS GOOD.

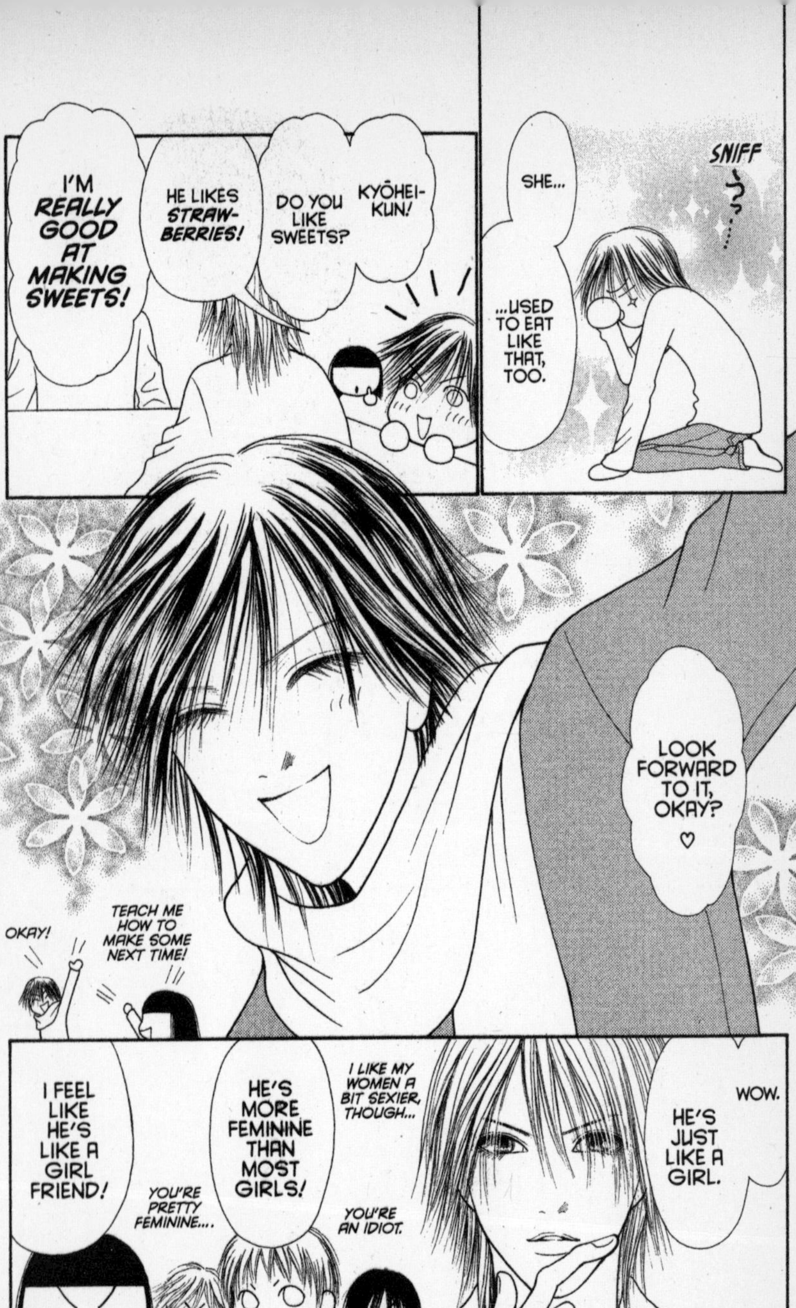
SNIFF
SHE...
...USED TO EAT LIKE THAT, TOO.
KYŌHEI-KUN!
DO YOU LIKE SWEETS?
HE LIKES STRAWBERRIES!
I'M REALLY GOOD AT MAKING SWEETS!
LOOK FORWARD TO IT, OKAY? ♡
TEACH ME HOW TO MAKE SOME NEXT TIME!
OKAY!
WOW.
HE'S JUST LIKE A GIRL.
I LIKE MY WOMEN A BIT SEXIER, THOUGH...
YOU'RE AN IDIOT.
HE'S MORE FEMININE THAN MOST GIRLS!
YOU'RE PRETTY FEMININE....
I FEEL LIKE HE'S LIKE A GIRL FRIEND!

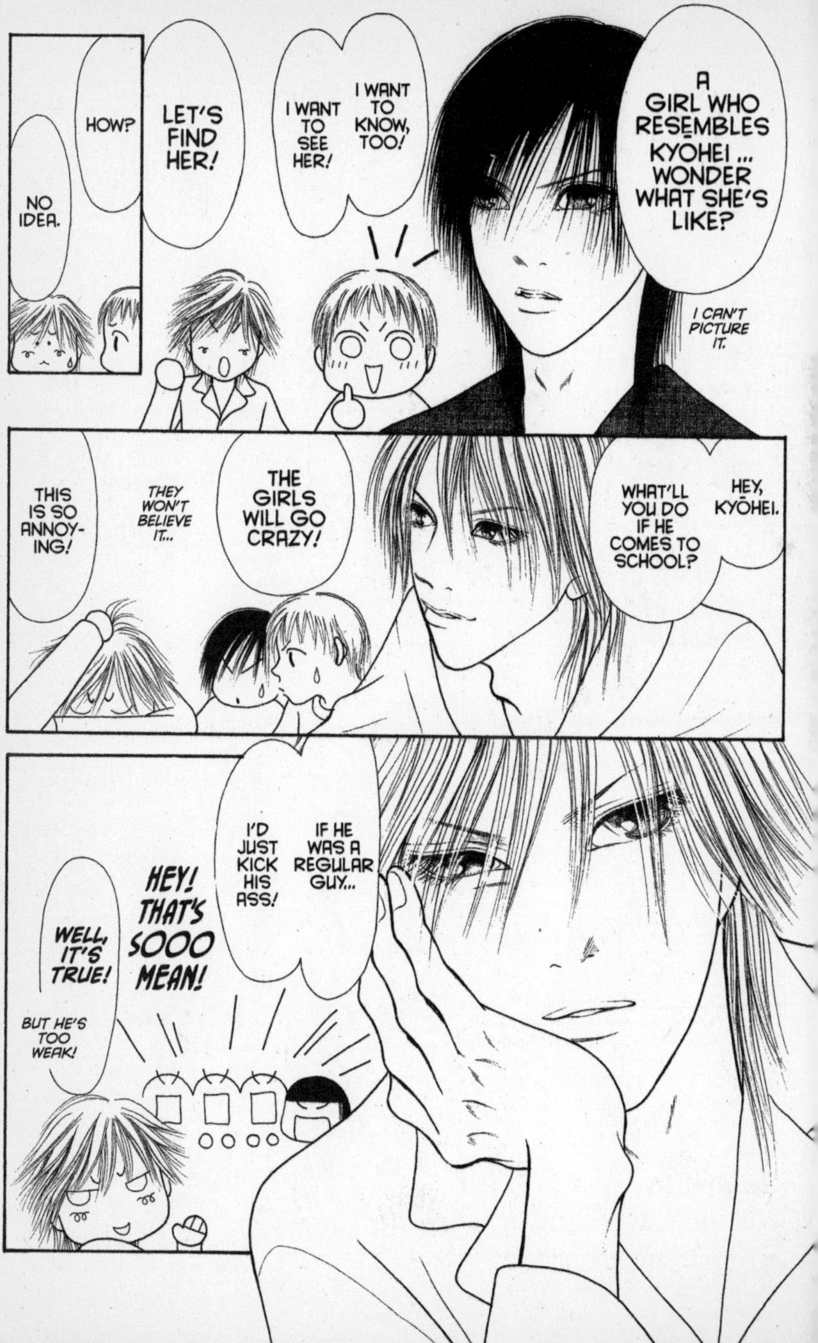
A GIRL WHO RESEMBLES KYOHEI ... WONDER WHAT SHE'S LIKE?
I CAN'T PICTURE IT.
I WANT TO KNOW, TOO!
I WANT TO SEE HER!
LET'S FIND HER!
HOW?
NO IDEA.
HEY, KYŌHEI.
WHAT'LL YOU DO IF HE COMES TO SCHOOL?
THE GIRLS WILL GO CRAZY!
THEY WON'T BELIEVE IT...
THIS IS SO ANNOYING!
IF HE WAS A REGULAR GUY...
I'D JUST KICK HIS ASS!
HEY! THAT'S SOOO MEAN!
WELL, IT'S TRUE!
BUT HE'S TOO WEAK!

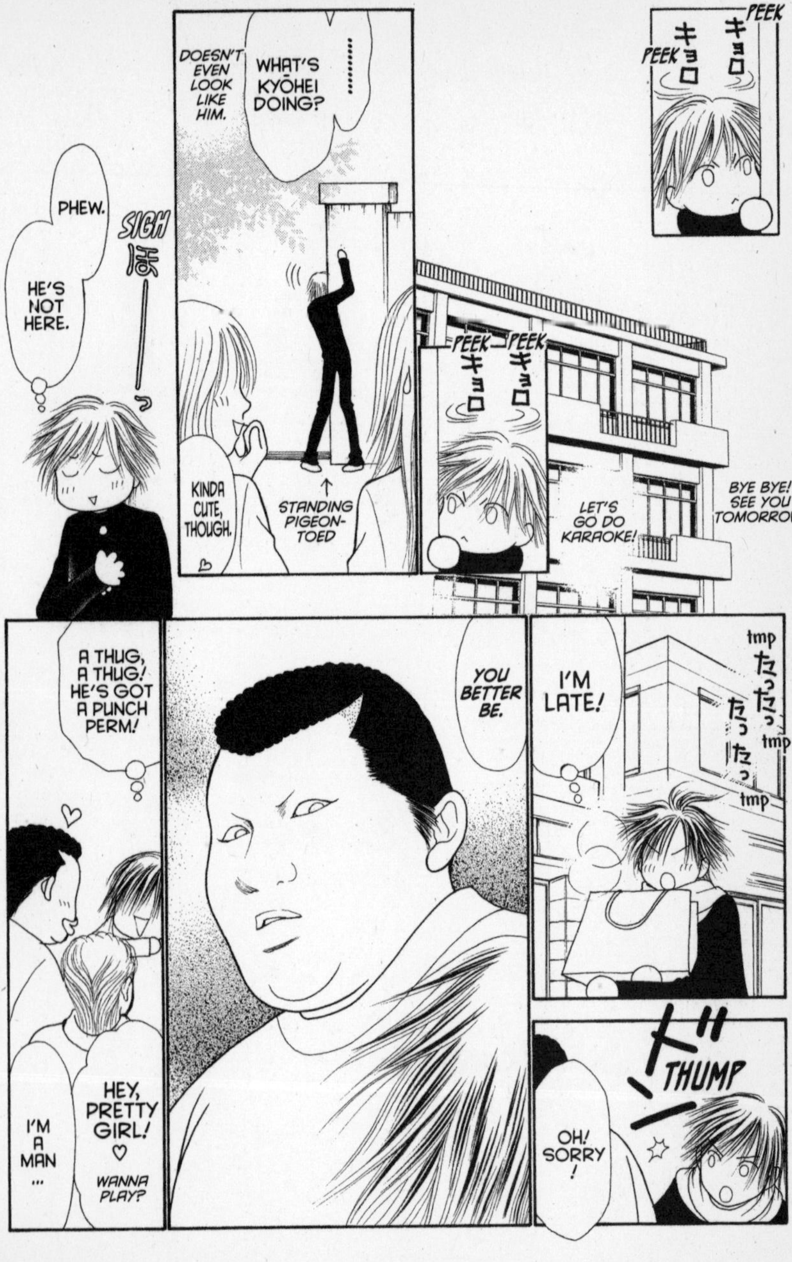
PEEK
キョロ
PEEK
キョロ
BYE BYE! SEE YOU TOMORROW!
LET'S GO DO KARAOKE!
PEEK
キョロ
PEEK
キョロ
......
WHAT'S KYŌHEI DOING?
DOESN'T EVEN LOOK LIKE HIM.
STANDING PIGEON-TOED
KINDA CUTE, THOUGH.
SIGH
ほーっ
PHEW.
HE'S NOT HERE.
tmp
たったっ
tmp
たったっ
tmp
I'M LATE!
ドッ
THUMP
OH! SORRY!
YOU BETTER BE.
A THUG, A THUG! HE'S GOT A PUNCH PERM!
HEY, PRETTY GIRL! ♡
WANNA PLAY?
I'M A MAN ...

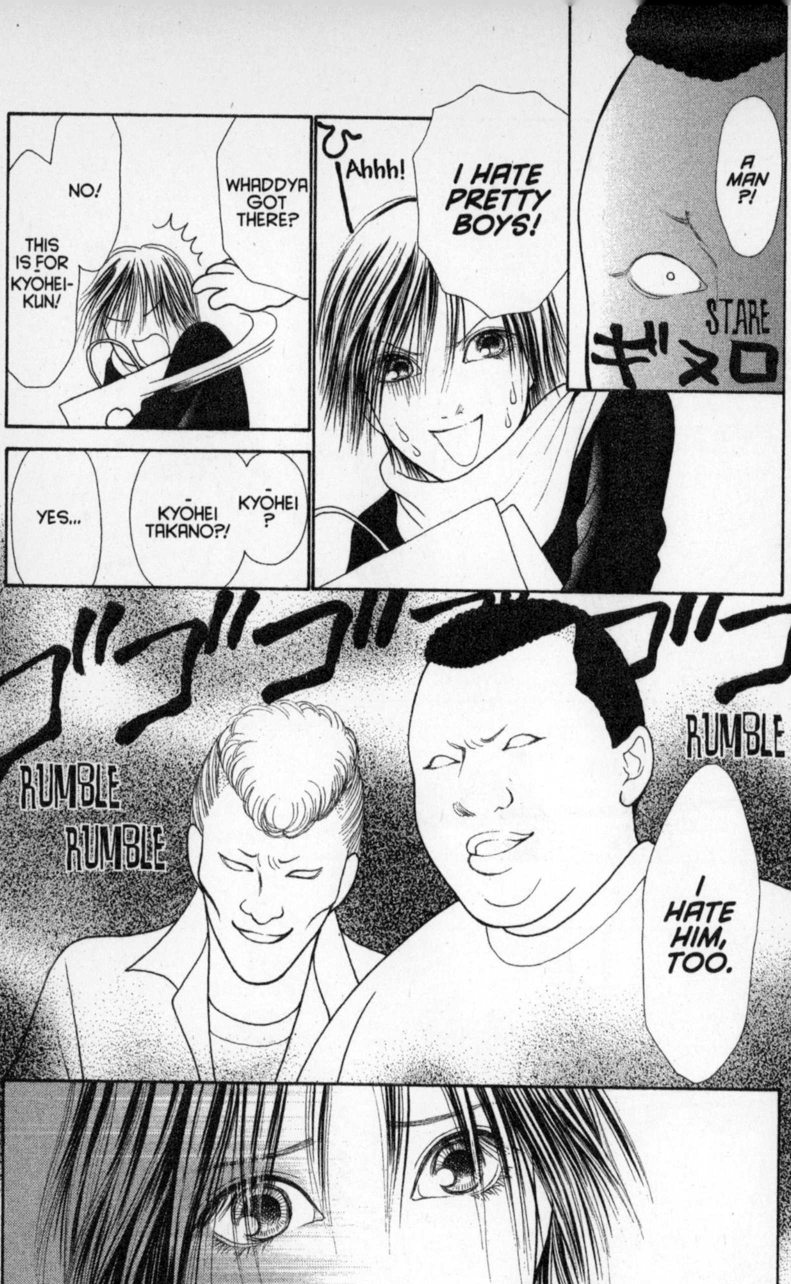
A MAN?!
STARE
ギヌロ
ひ
Ahhh!
I HATE PRETTY BOYS!
WHADDYA GOT THERE?
NO!
THIS IS FOR KYŌHEI-KUN!
KYŌHEI?
KYŌHEI TAKANO?!
YES...
ゴゴゴゴゴ
RUMBLE
RUMBLE
RUMBLE
I HATE HIM, TOO.

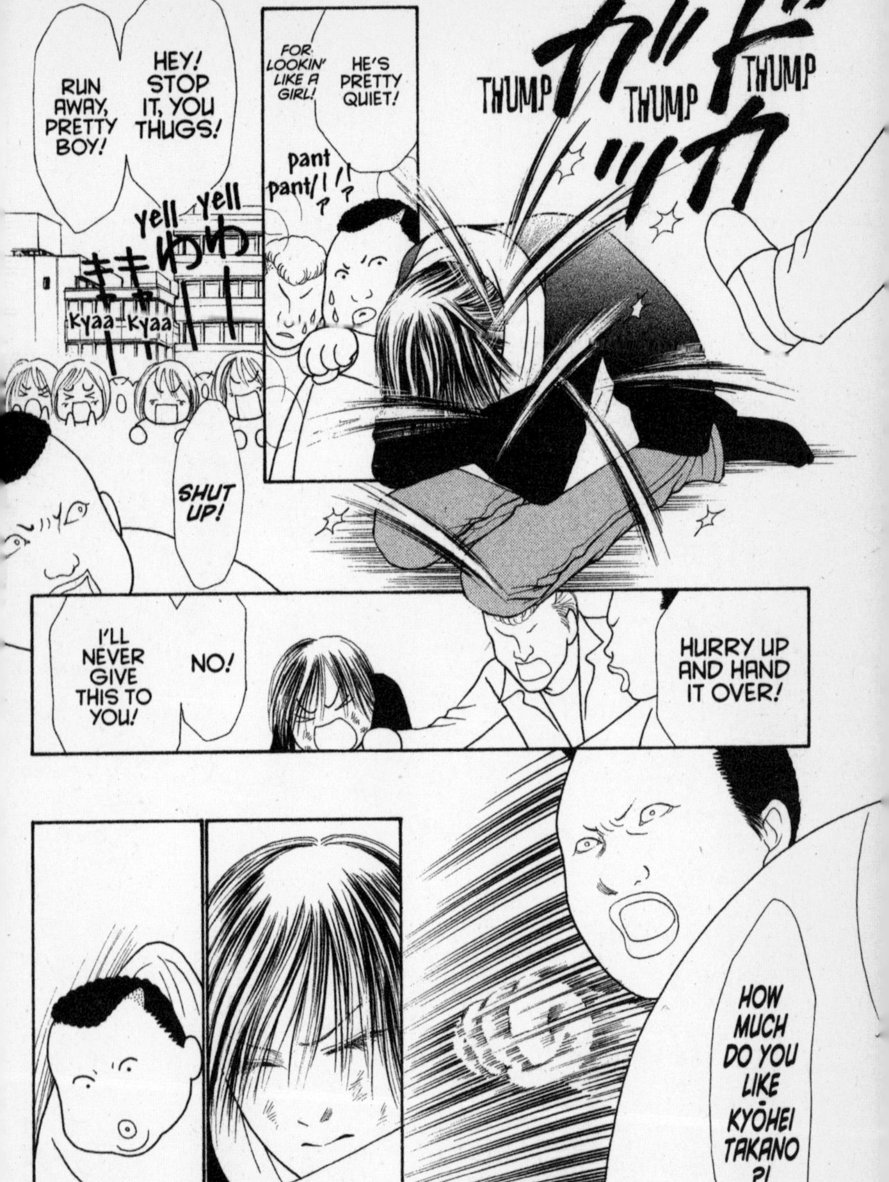
THUMP THUMP THUMP
HE'S PRETTY QUIET!
FOR LOOKIN' LIKE A GIRL!
pant pant
HEY! STOP IT, YOU THUGS!
RUN AWAY, PRETTY BOY!
yell yell
Kyaa Kyaa
SHUT UP!
HURRY UP AND HAND IT OVER!
NO!
I'LL NEVER GIVE THIS TO YOU!
HOW MUCH DO YOU LIKE KYŌHEI TAKANO?!

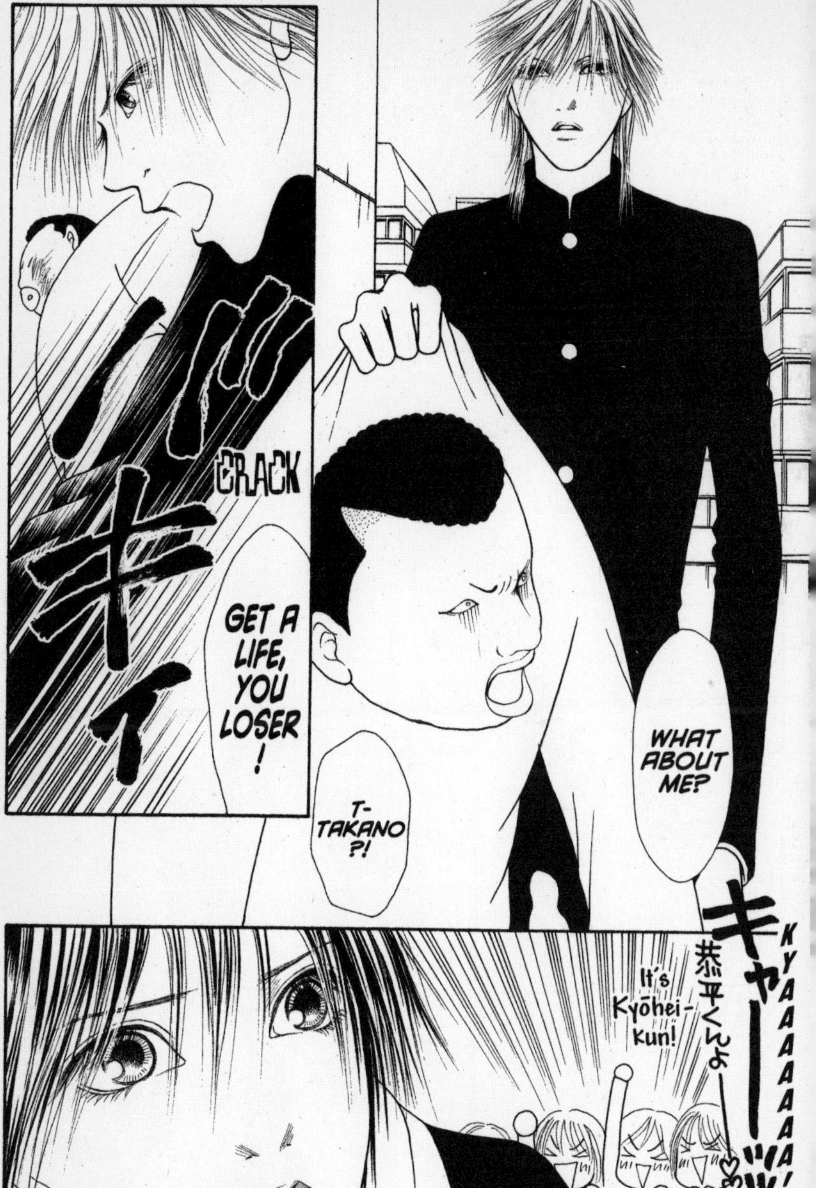
WHAT ABOUT ME?
T-TAKANO?!
GET A LIFE, YOU LOSER!
CRACK
KYAAAAAAAAA!
恭平くんよ
It's Kyōhei-kun!

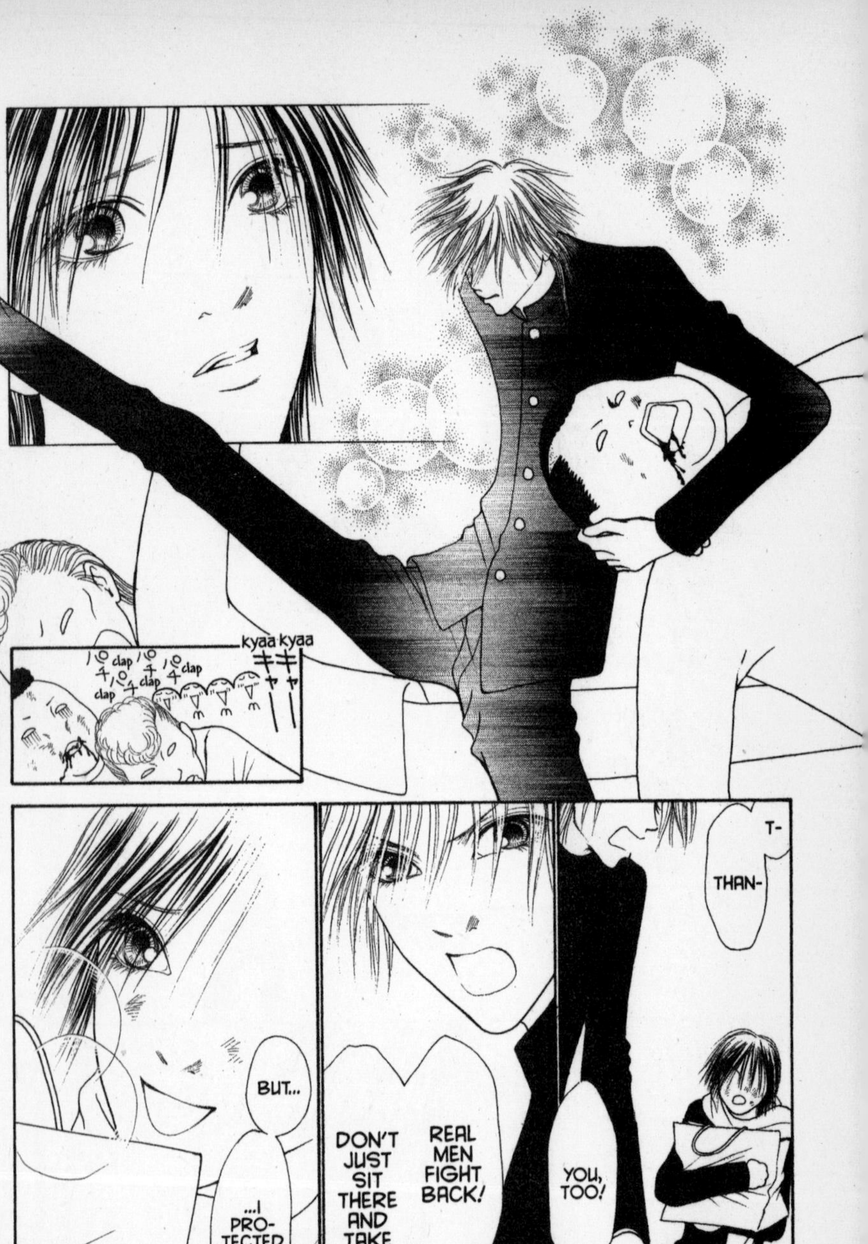
kyaa kyaa
キャー キャー
パチ clap パチ clap パチ clap
T-
THAN-
YOU, TOO!
REAL MEN FIGHT BACK!
DON'T JUST SIT THERE AND TAKE IT!
BUT...
...I PROTECTED THIS.

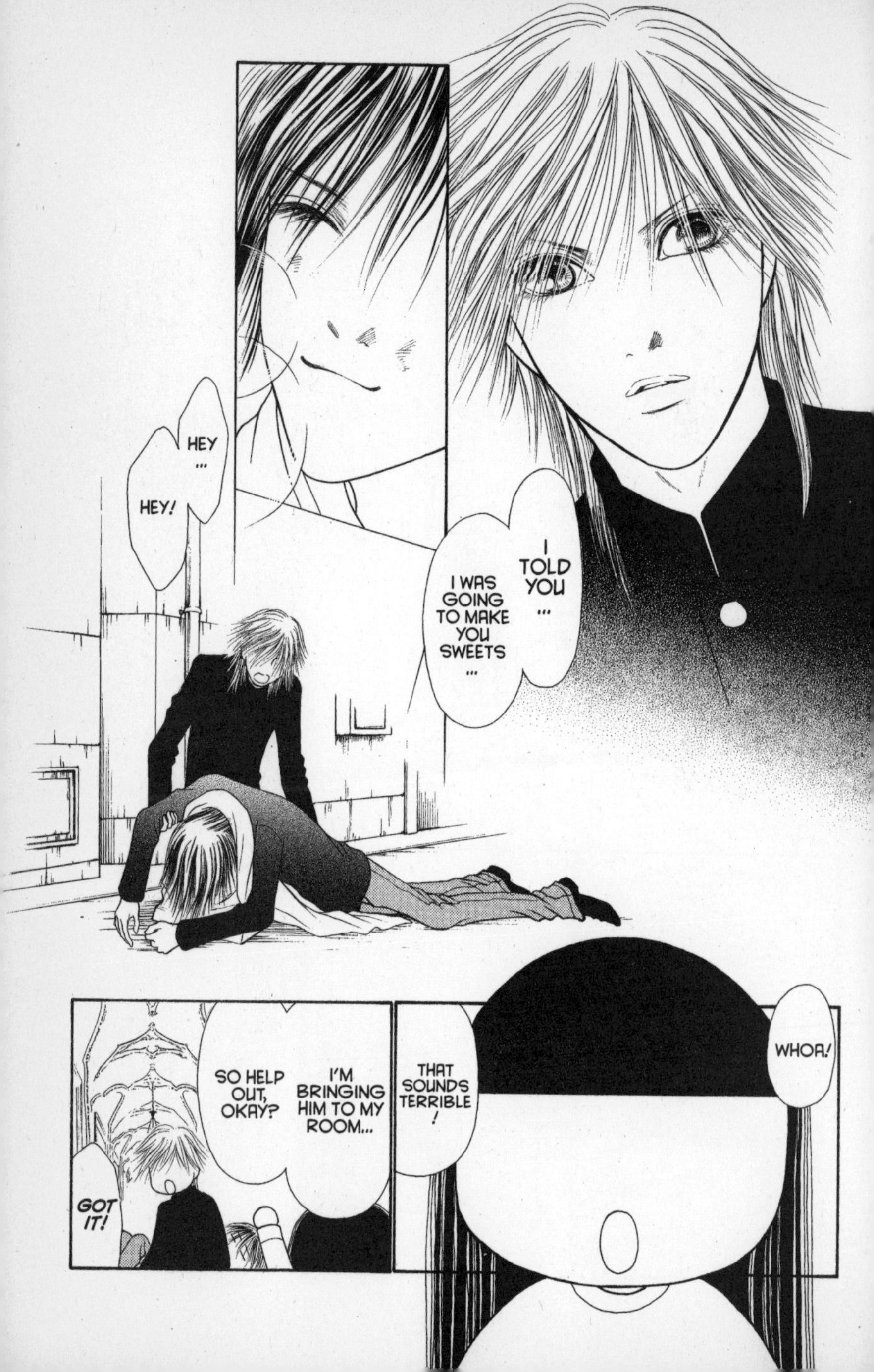
I TOLD YOU ...
I WAS GOING TO MAKE YOU SWEETS ...
HEY ...
HEY!
WHOA!
THAT SOUNDS TERRIBLE!
I'M BRINGING HIM TO MY ROOM...
SO HELP OUT, OKAY?
GOT IT!

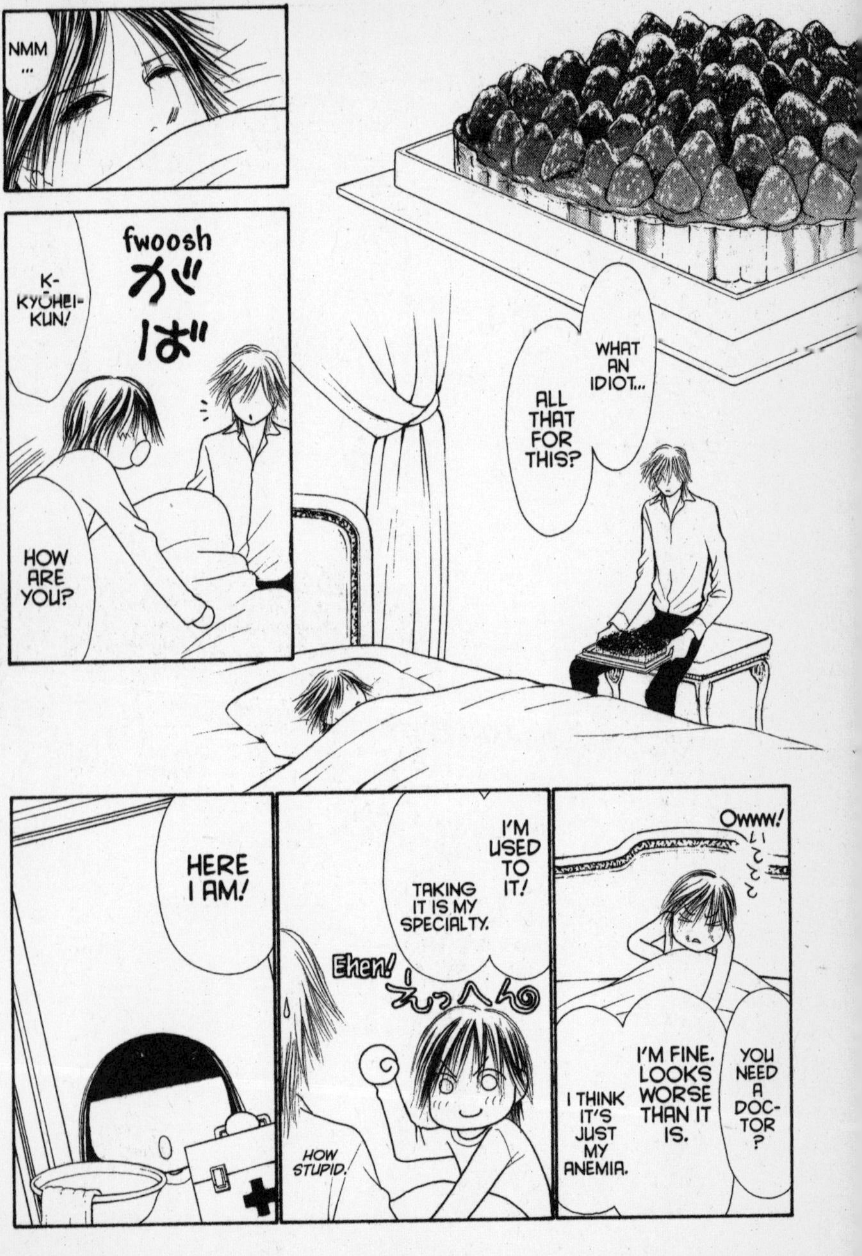
WHAT AN IDIOT...
ALL THAT FOR THIS?
NMM ...
K-KYŌHEI-KUN!
fwoosh
がば
HOW ARE YOU?
Owww!
いててて
YOU NEED A DOC-TOR?
I'M FINE. LOOKS WORSE THAN IT IS.
I THINK IT'S JUST MY ANEMIA.
I'M USED TO IT!
TAKING IT IS MY SPECIALTY.
Ehen!
えっへん
HOW STUPID.
HERE I AM!

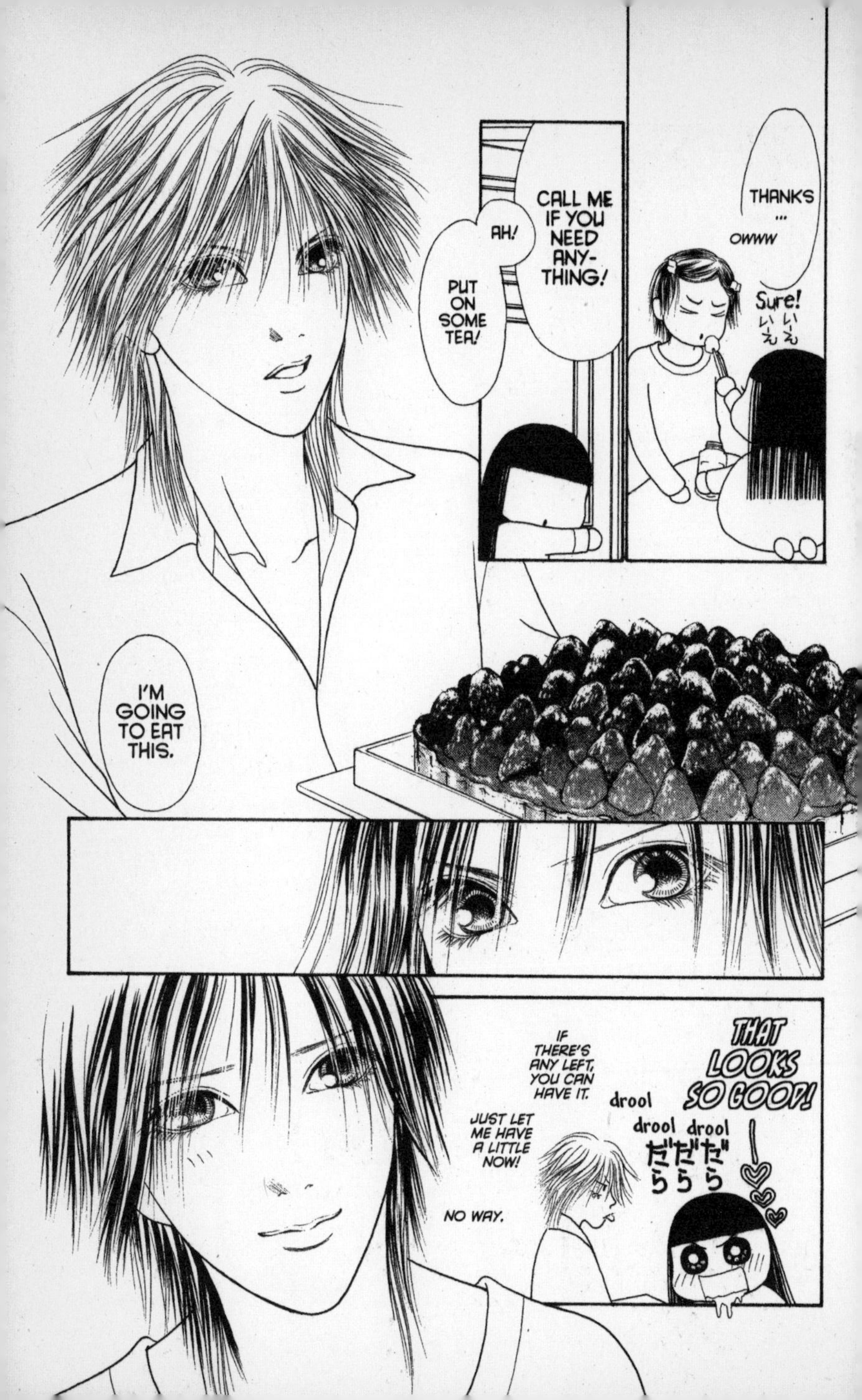
THANKS ... OWWW
Sure!
いいえ いいえ
CALL ME IF YOU NEED ANYTHING!
AH! PUT ON SOME TEA!
I'M GOING TO EAT THIS.
THAT LOOKS SO GOOD!
drool drool drool
だらだらだら
IF THERE'S ANY LEFT, YOU CAN HAVE IT.
JUST LET ME HAVE A LITTLE NOW!
NO WAY.

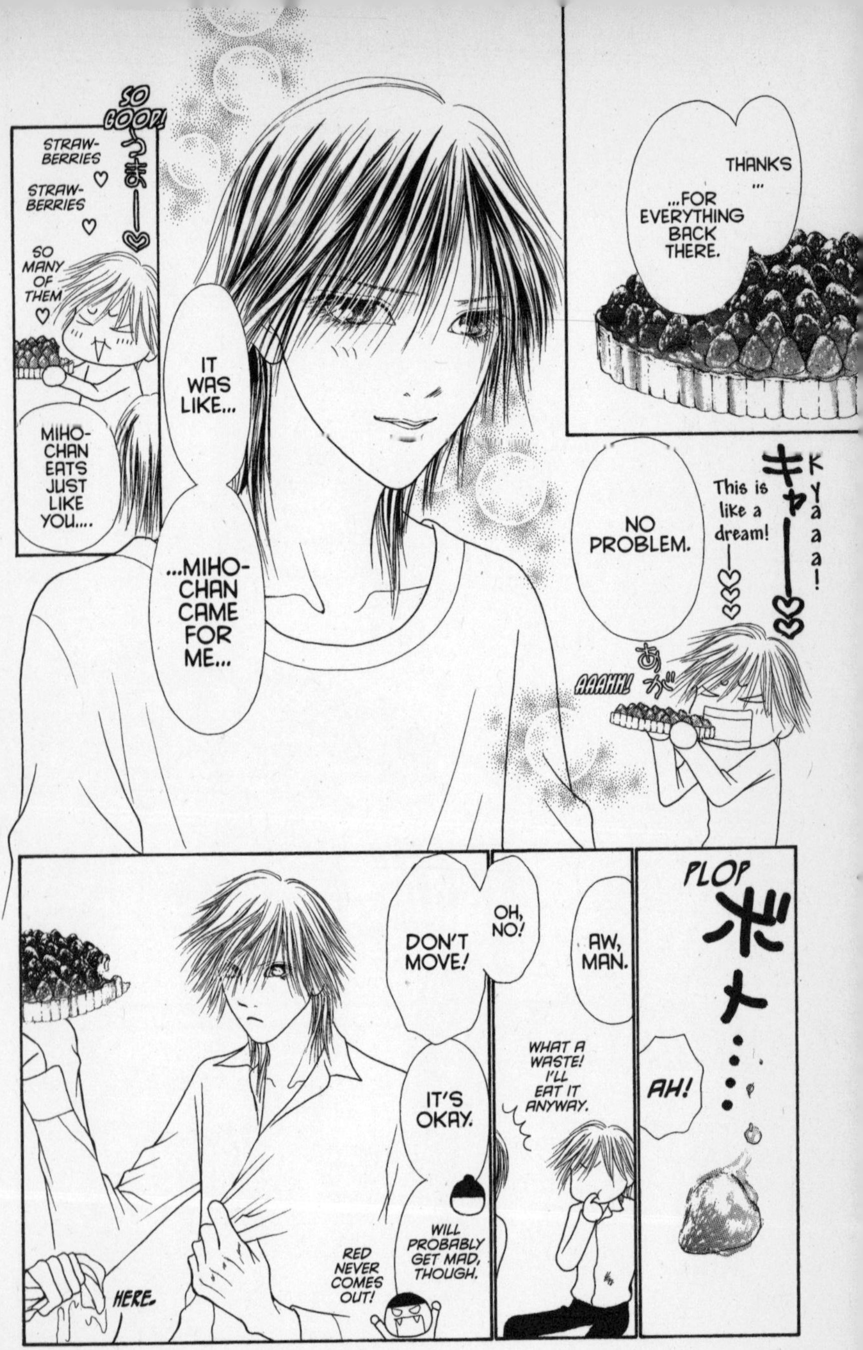
THANKS ...
...FOR EVERYTHING BACK THERE.
NO PROBLEM.
This is like a dream!
KYaaa!
AAAHH!
IT WAS LIKE...
...MIHO-CHAN CAME FOR ME...
SO GOOD!
STRAWBERRIES ♡
STRAWBERRIES ♡
SO MANY OF THEM ♡
MIHO-CHAN EATS JUST LIKE YOU....
PLOP
AH!
AW, MAN.
OH, NO!
WHAT A WASTE! I'LL EAT IT ANYWAY.
DON'T MOVE!
IT'S OKAY.
HERE.
WILL PROBABLY GET MAD, THOUGH.
RED NEVER COMES OUT!

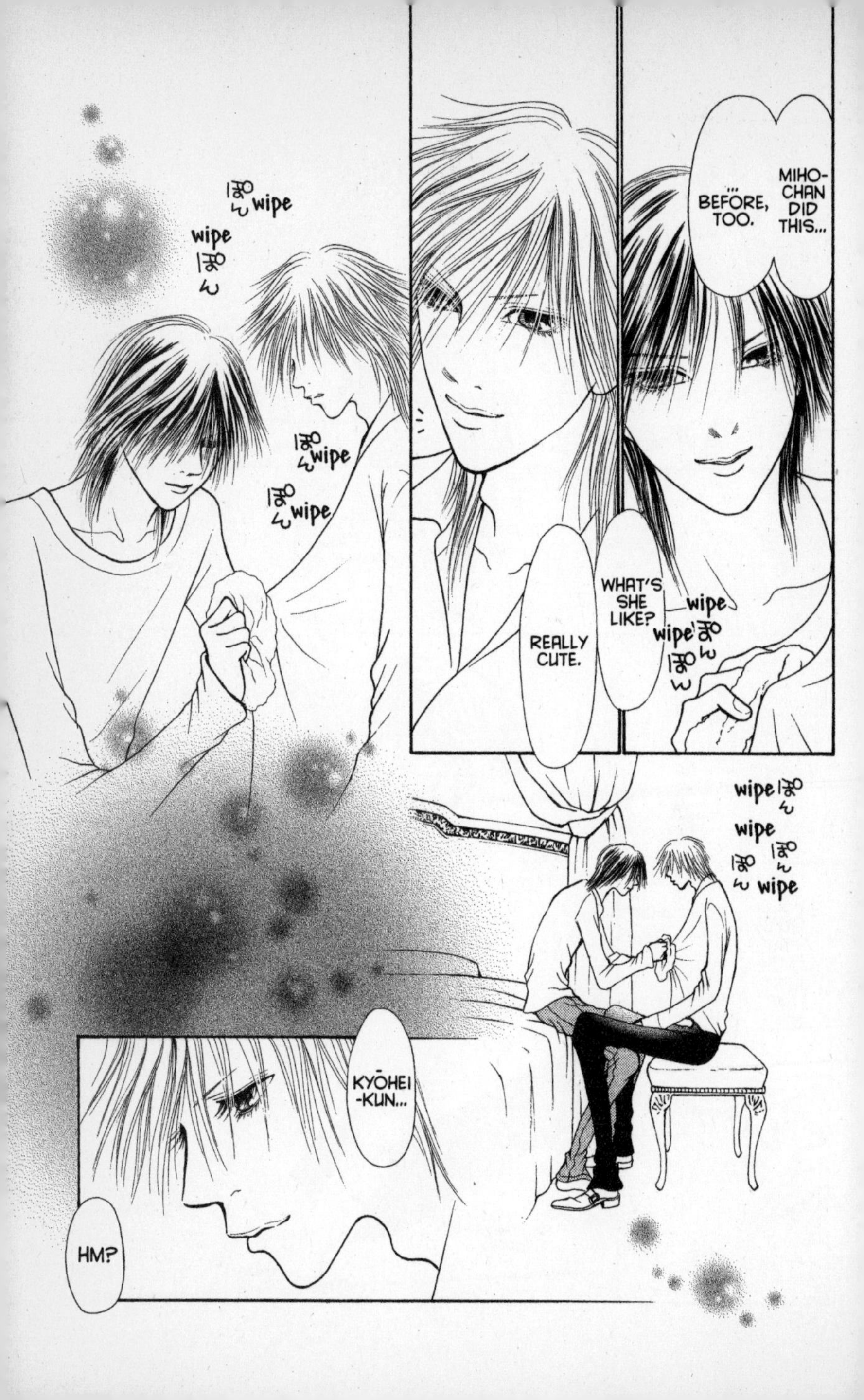
MIHO-CHAN DID THIS...
...BEFORE, TOO.
WHAT'S SHE LIKE?
wipe ぽん
wipe ぽん
REALLY CUTE.
ぽん wipe
wipe ぽん
ぽん wipe
ぽん wipe
wipe ぽん
wipe ぽん
ぽん wipe
KYŌHEI-KUN...
HM?

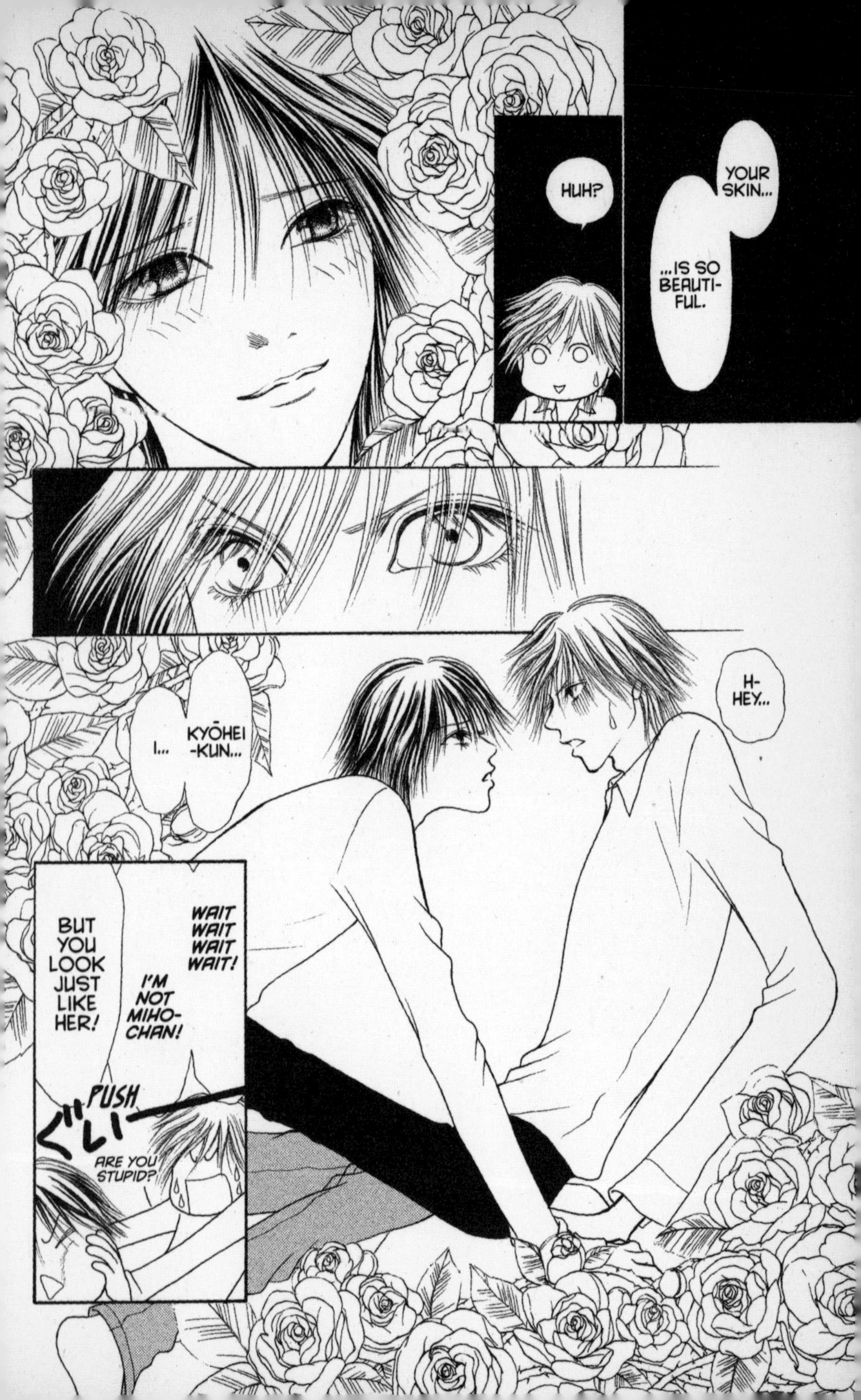
YOUR SKIN...
...IS SO BEAUTIFUL.
HUH?
H-HEY...
KYŌHEI-KUN...
I...
WAIT WAIT WAIT WAIT!
I'M NOT MIHO-CHAN!
BUT YOU LOOK JUST LIKE HER!
PUSH
ぐい
ARE YOU STUPID?

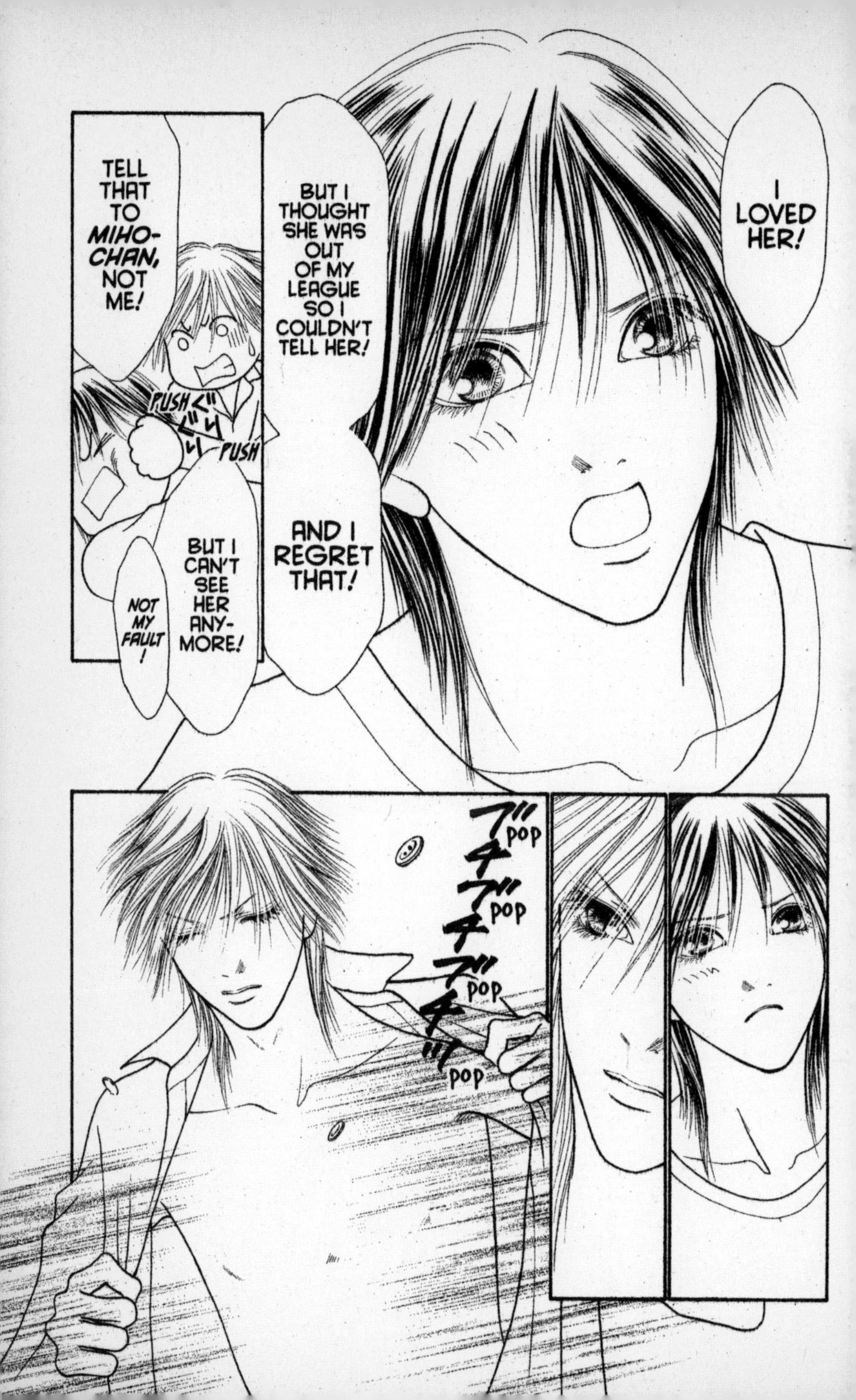
I LOVED HER!
BUT I THOUGHT SHE WAS OUT OF MY LEAGUE SO I COULDN'T TELL HER!
AND I REGRET THAT!
TELL THAT TO *MIHO-CHAN,* NOT ME!
PUSH
PUSH
BUT I CAN'T SEE HER ANYMORE!
NOT MY FAULT!
POP
POP
POP
POP

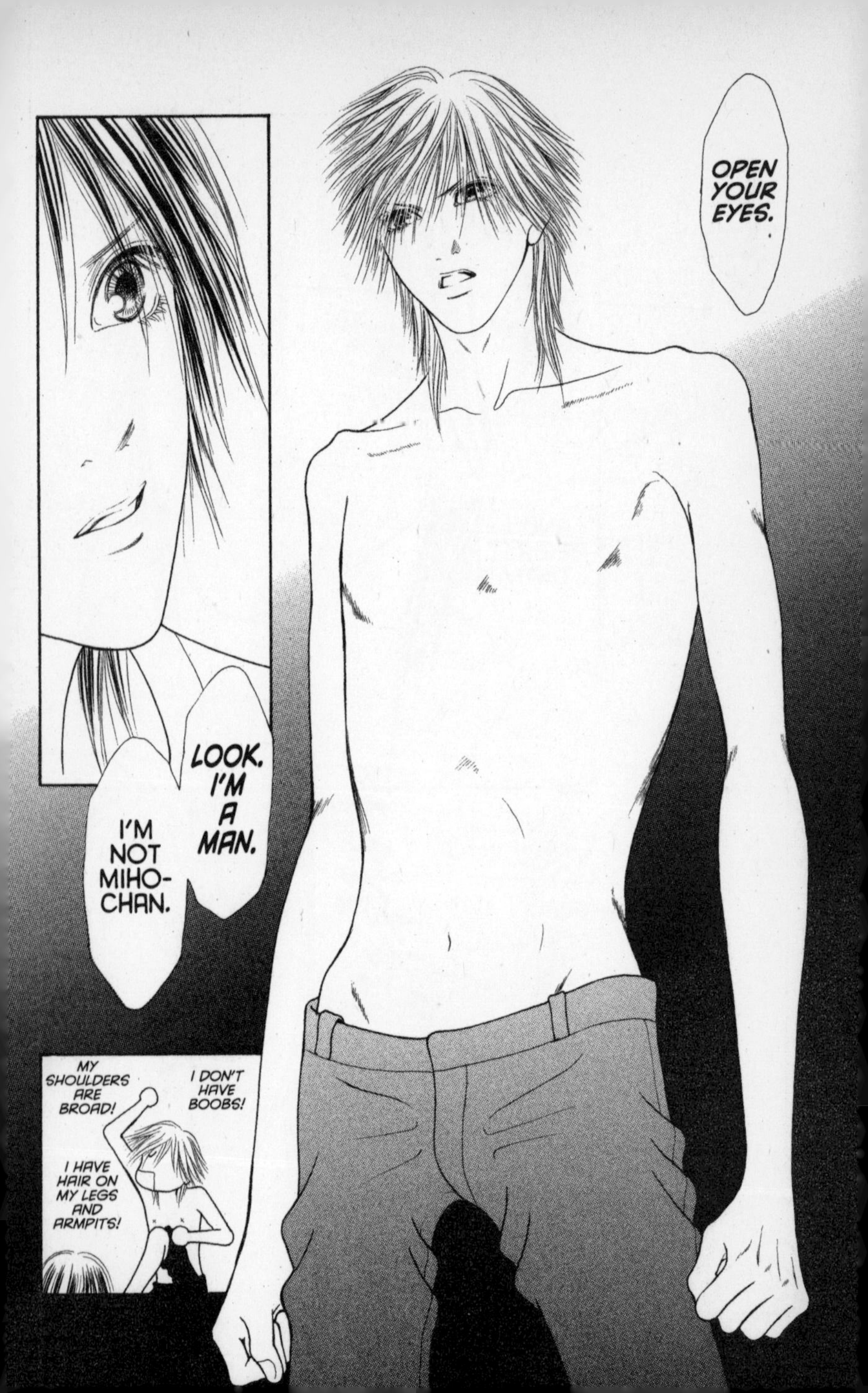
OPEN YOUR EYES.
LOOK. I'M A MAN.
I'M NOT MIHO-CHAN.
I DON'T HAVE BOOBS!
MY SHOULDERS ARE BROAD!
I HAVE HAIR ON MY LEGS AND ARMPITS!

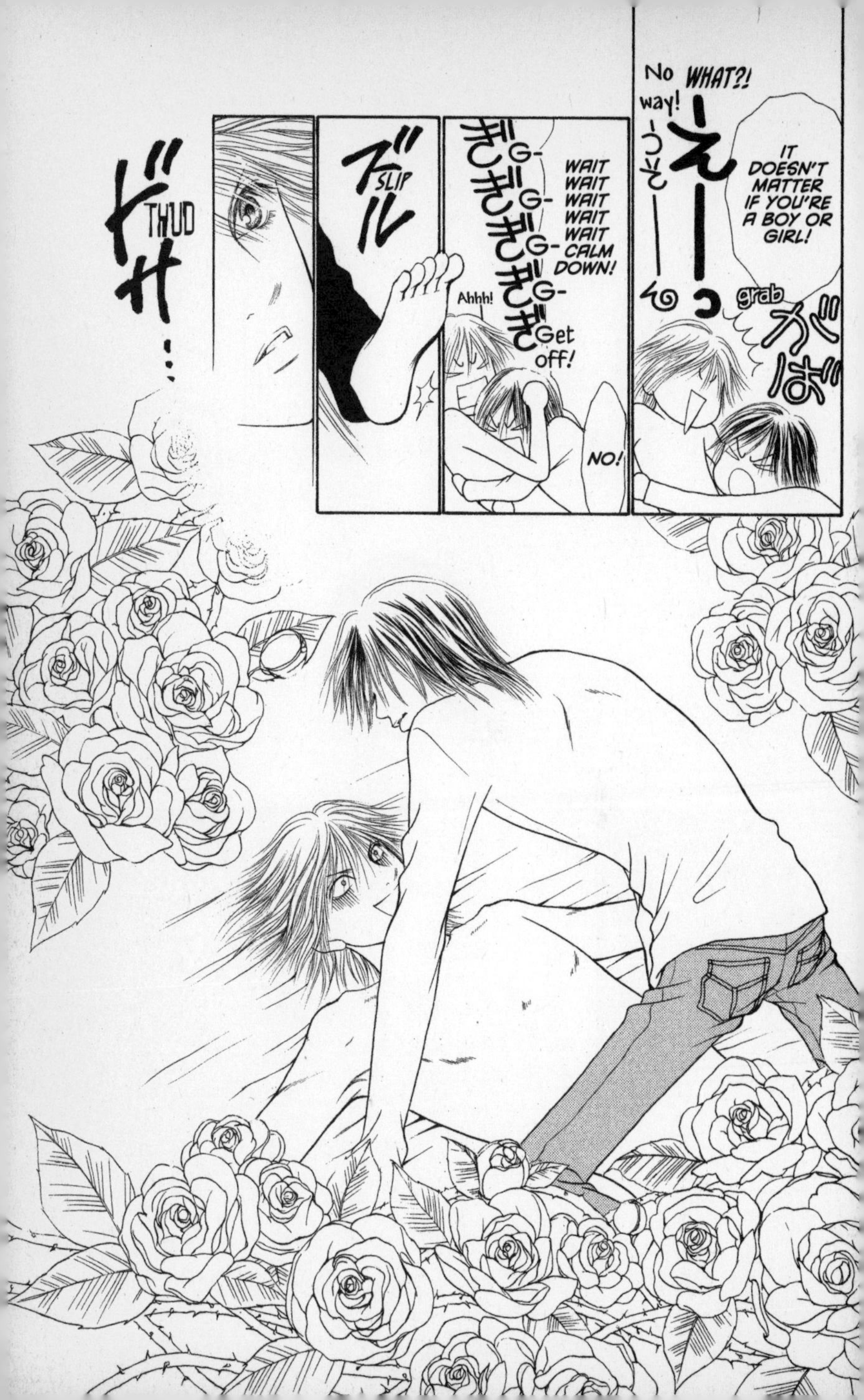
IT DOESN'T MATTER IF YOU'RE A BOY OR GIRL!
がば
grab
えーっ
WHAT?!
うそーん
No way!
WAIT WAIT WAIT WAIT WAIT CALM DOWN!
ぎぎぎぎ
G- G- G- G-
Get off!
Ahhh!
NO!
ズル
SLIP
ドサ…
THUD

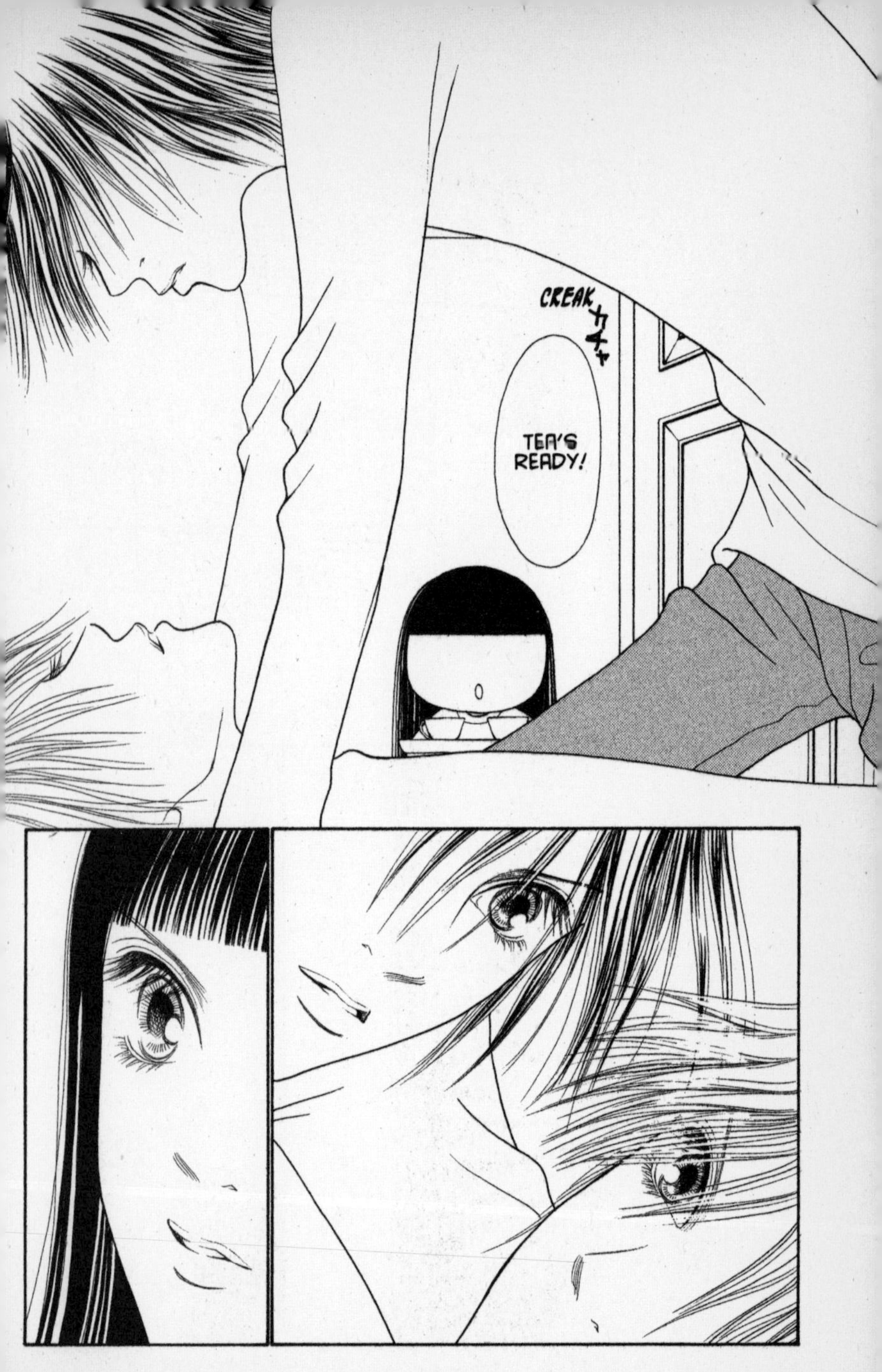
CREAK
TEA'S READY!

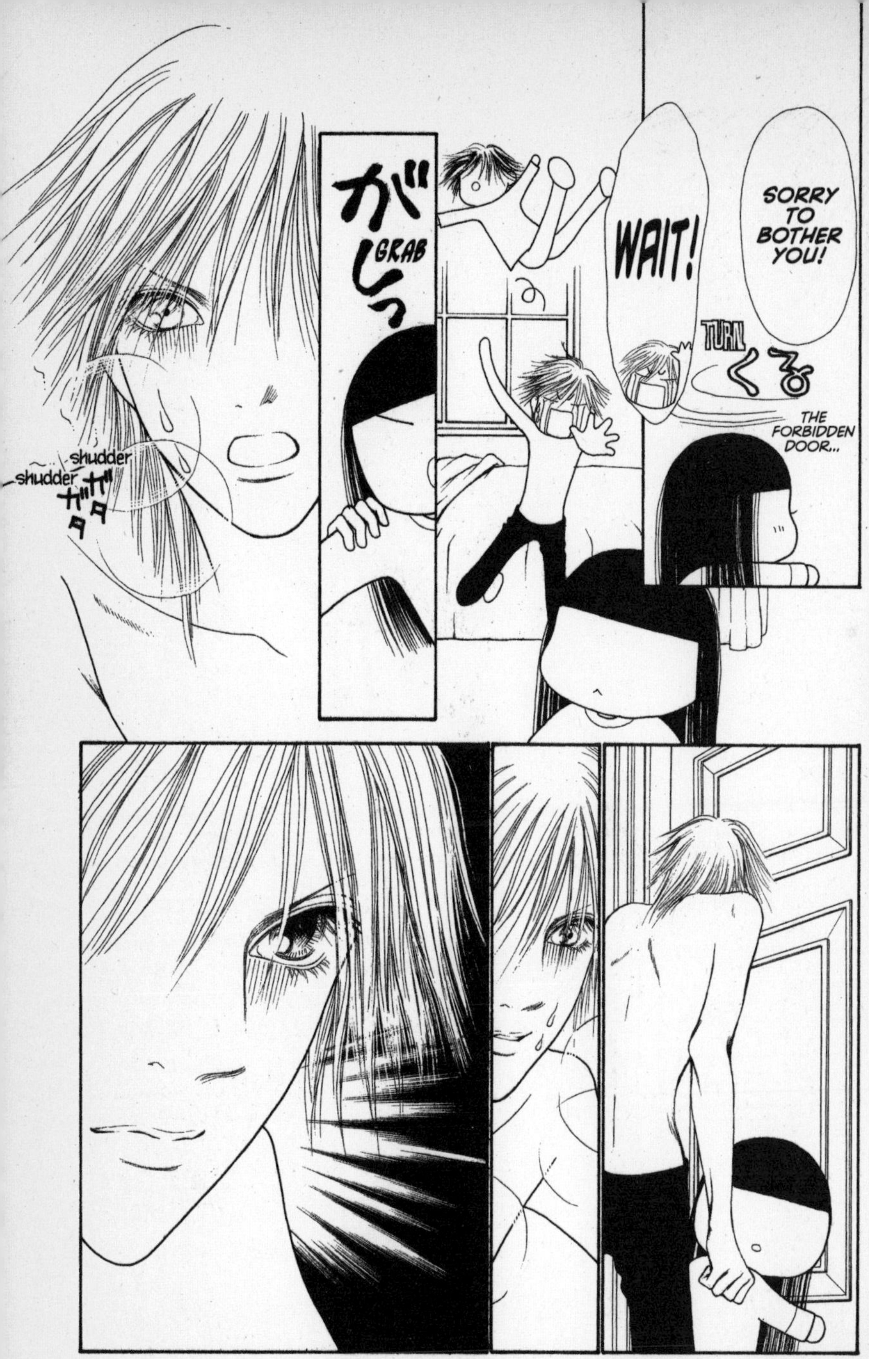
SORRY TO BOTHER YOU!
TURN
くる
THE FORBIDDEN DOOR...
WAIT!
がしっ
GRAB
shudder
shudder
ガタガタ

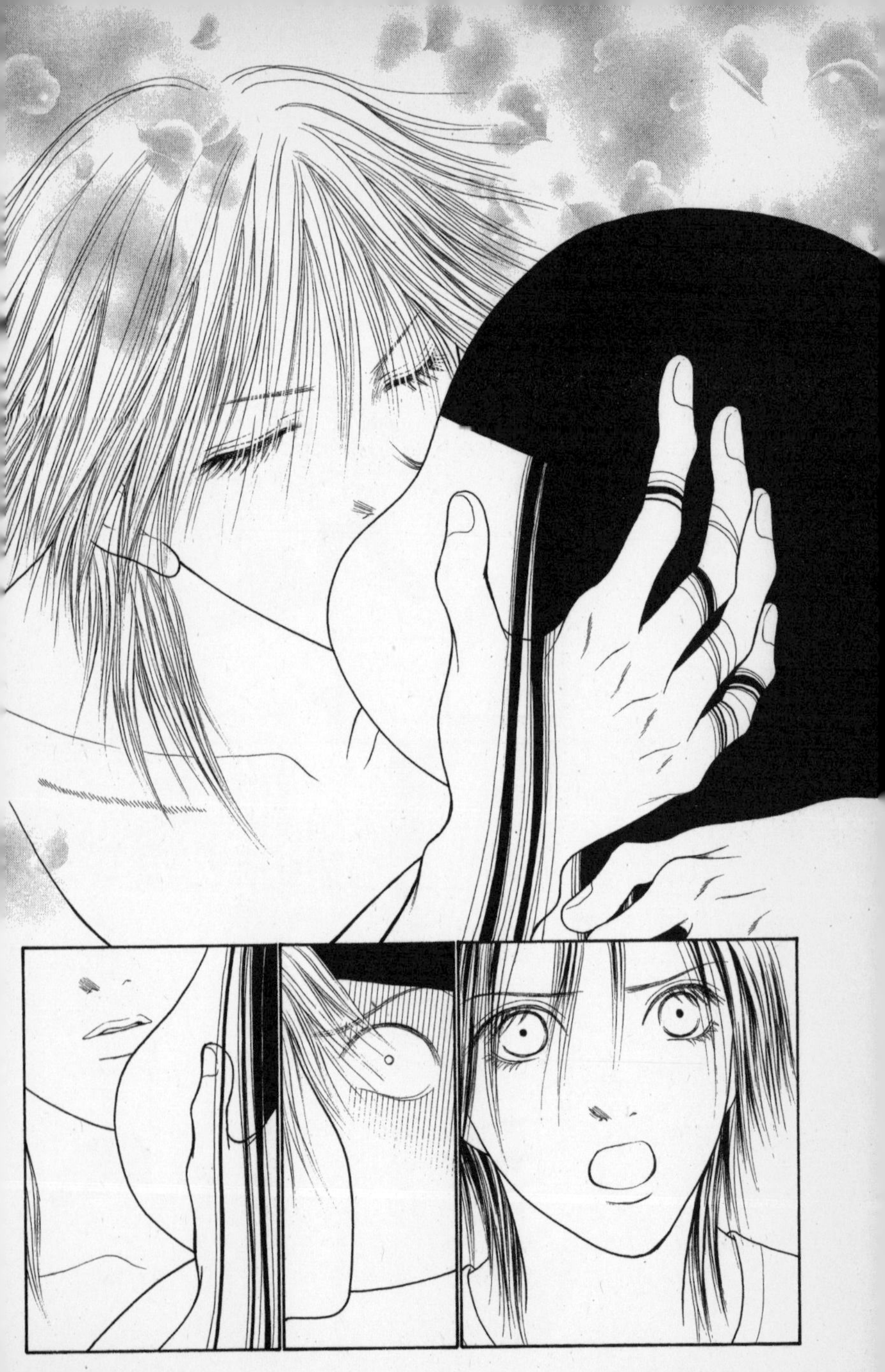

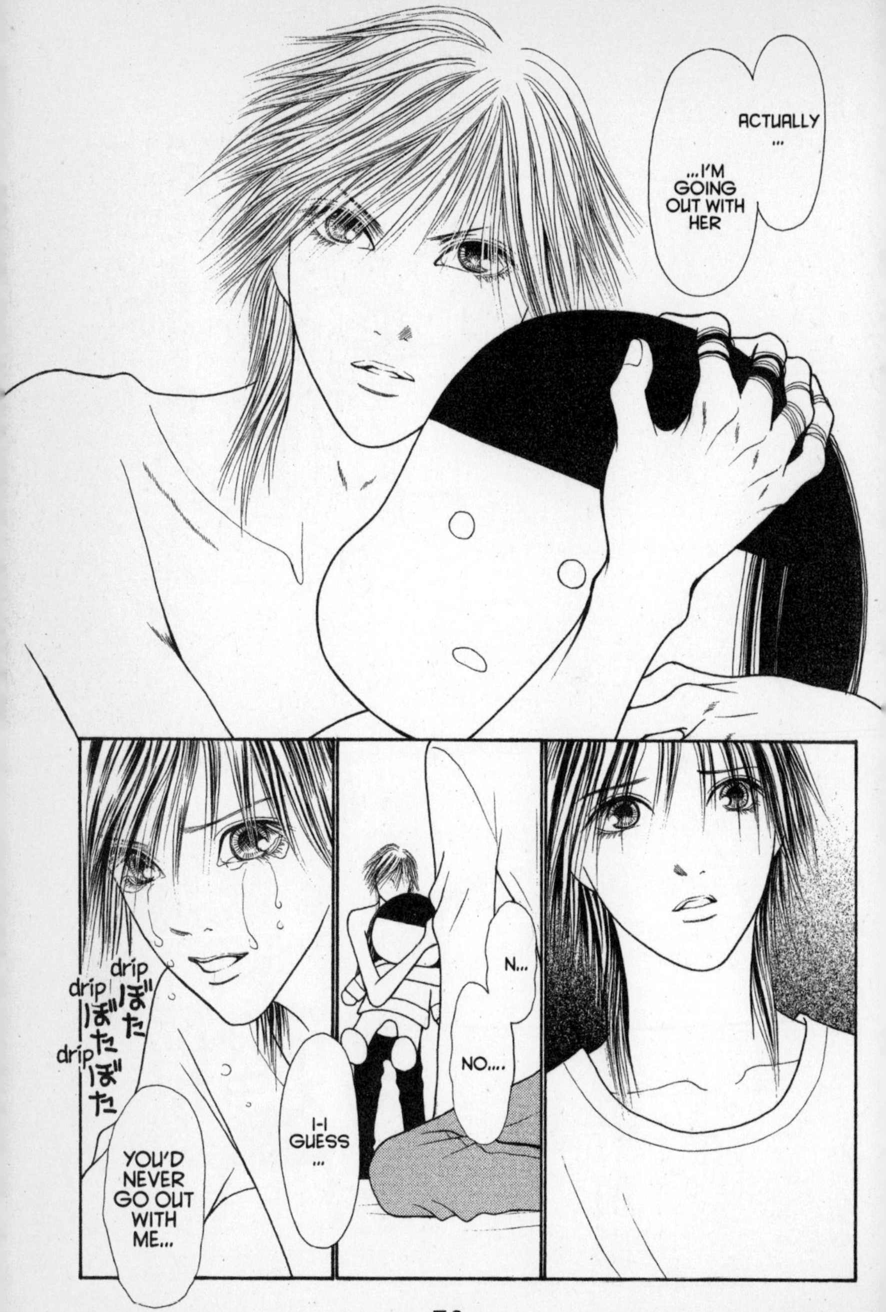
ACTUALLY ...
...I'M GOING OUT WITH HER
N...
NO....
I-I GUESS ...
drip ぼた
drip ぼた
drip ぼた
YOU'D NEVER GO OUT WITH ME...

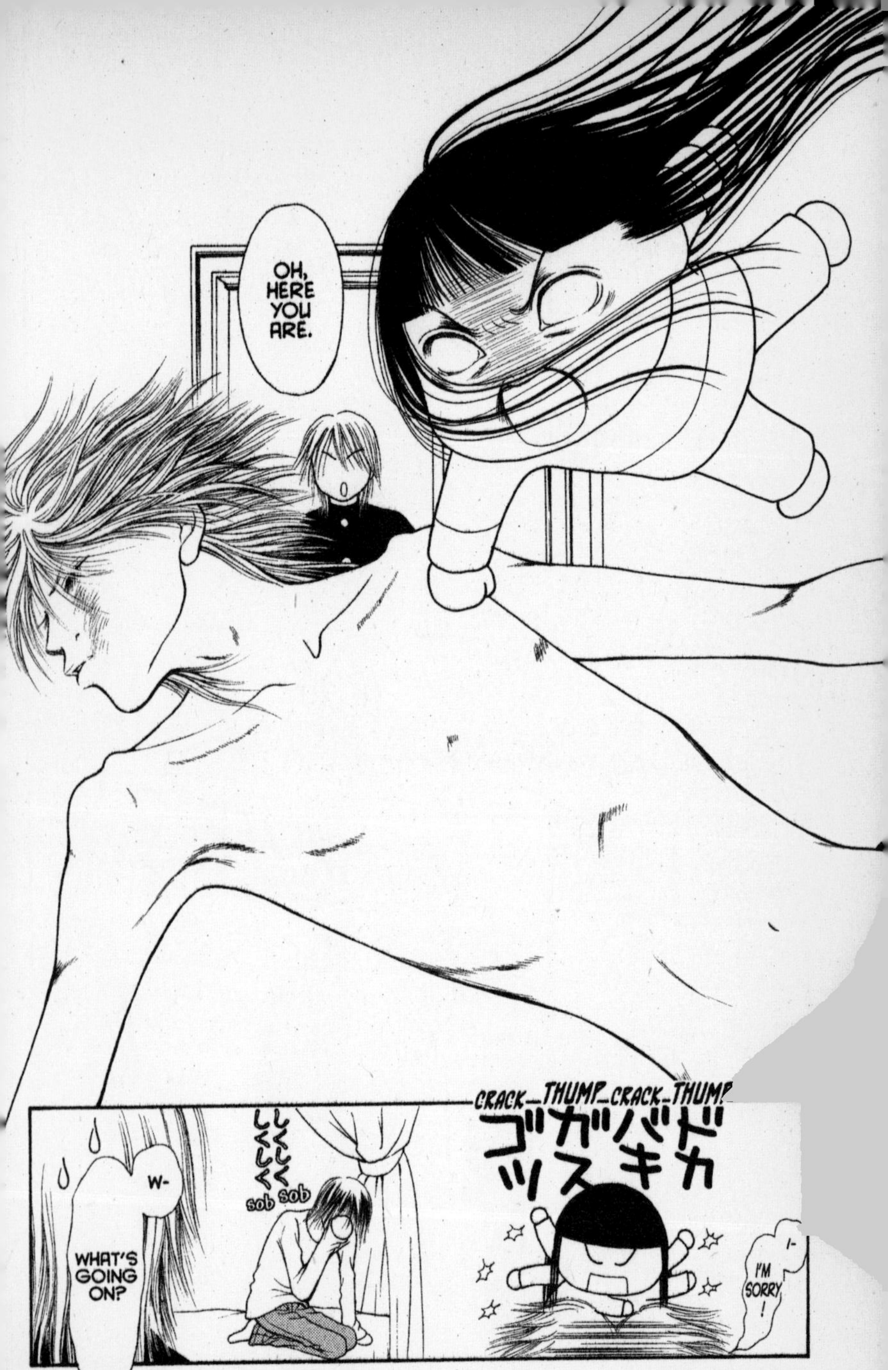
OH, HERE YOU ARE.
CRACK-THUMP-CRACK-THUMP
ドカバキガスゴッ
I- I'M SORRY!
しくしく しくしく
sob sob
W-
WHAT'S GOING ON?

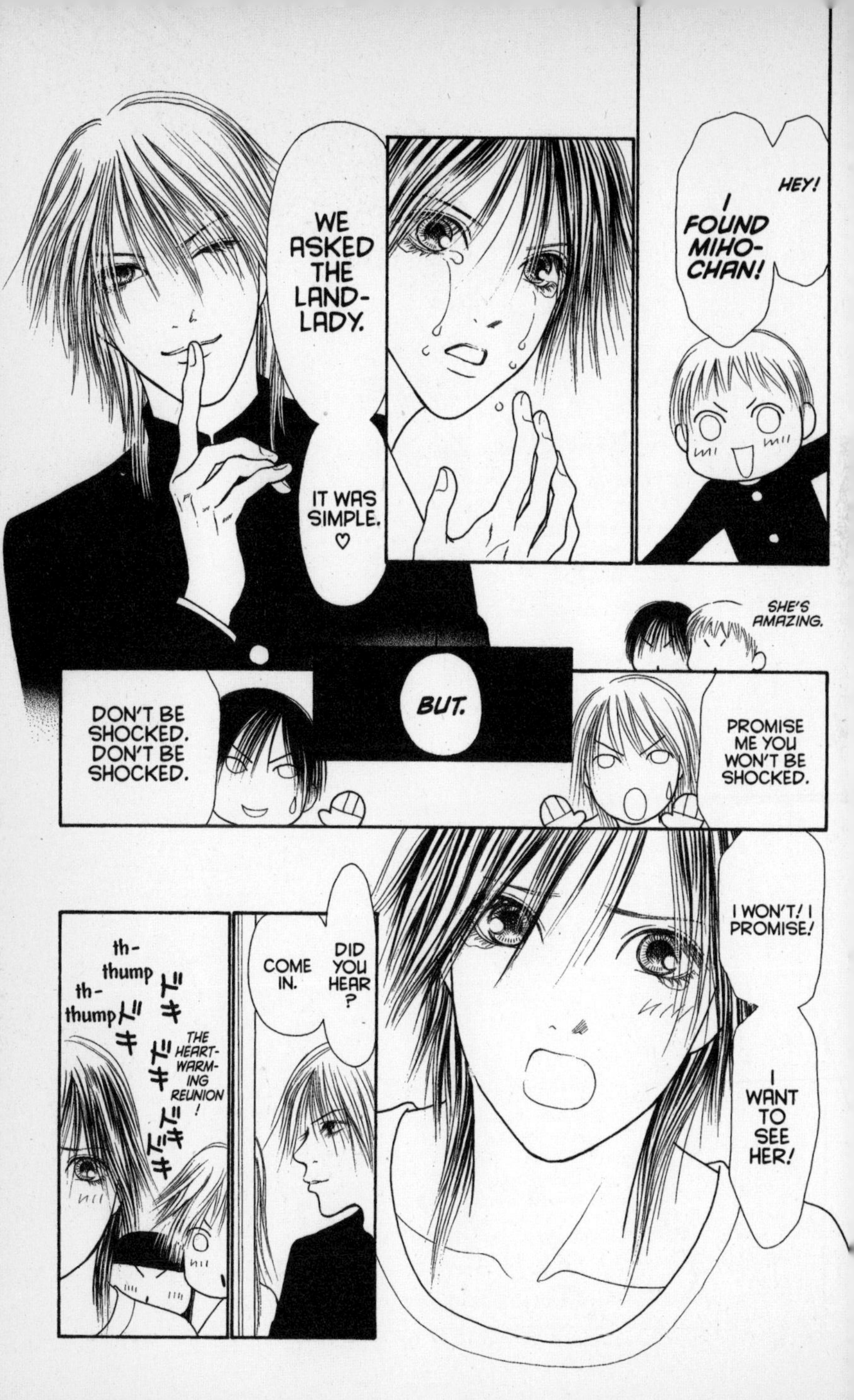
HEY!
I FOUND MIHO-CHAN!
WE ASKED THE LAND-LADY.
IT WAS SIMPLE. ♡
SHE'S AMAZING.
PROMISE ME YOU WON'T BE SHOCKED.
BUT.
DON'T BE SHOCKED. DON'T BE SHOCKED.
I WON'T! I PROMISE!
I WANT TO SEE HER!
DID YOU HEAR?
COME IN.
th-thump th-thump
ドキドキ ドキドキ ドキドキ
THE HEART-WARMING REUNION!

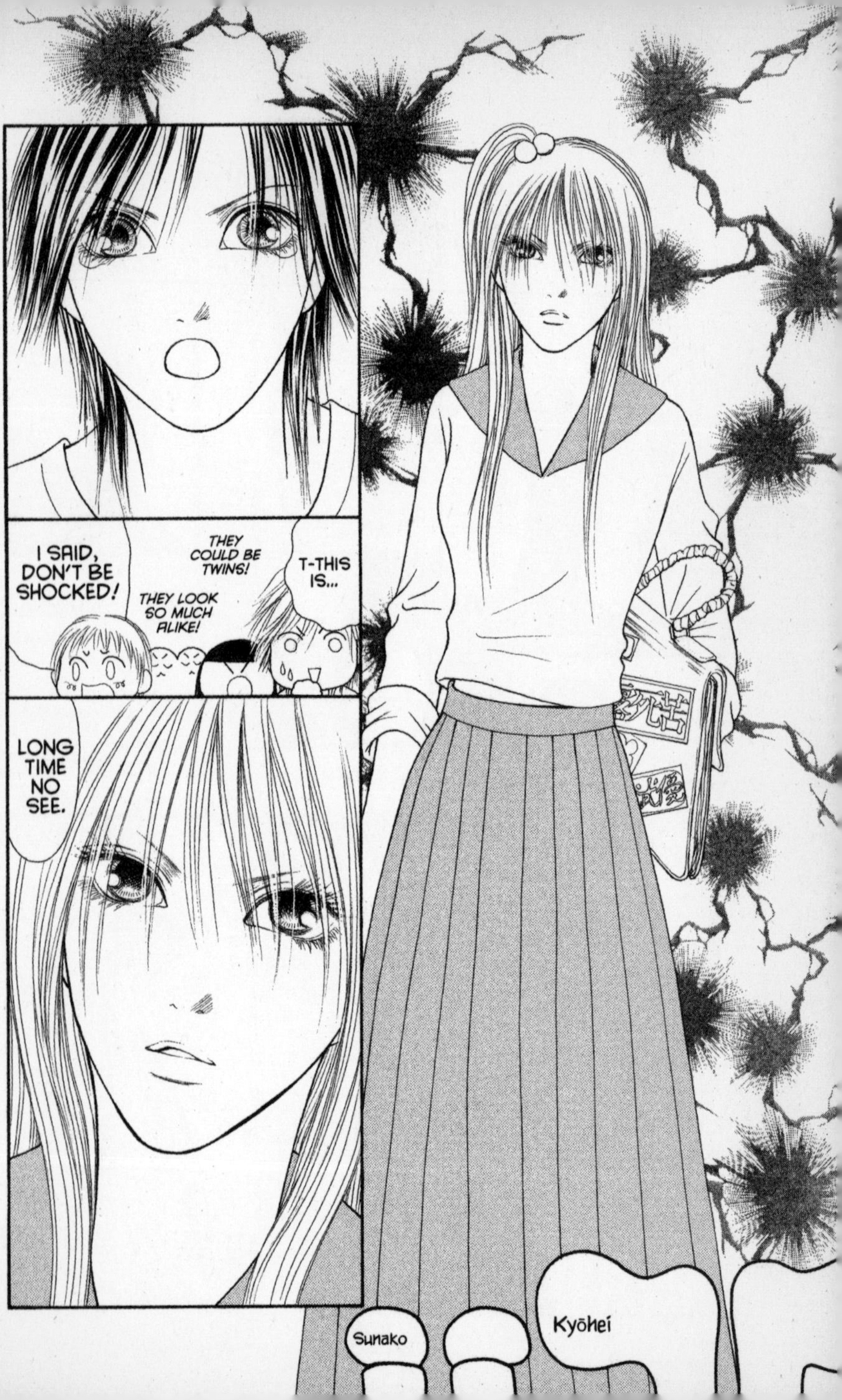
Kyōhei
Sunako
T-THIS IS...
THEY COULD BE TWINS!
THEY LOOK SO MUCH ALIKE!
I SAID, DON'T BE SHOCKED!
LONG TIME NO SEE.

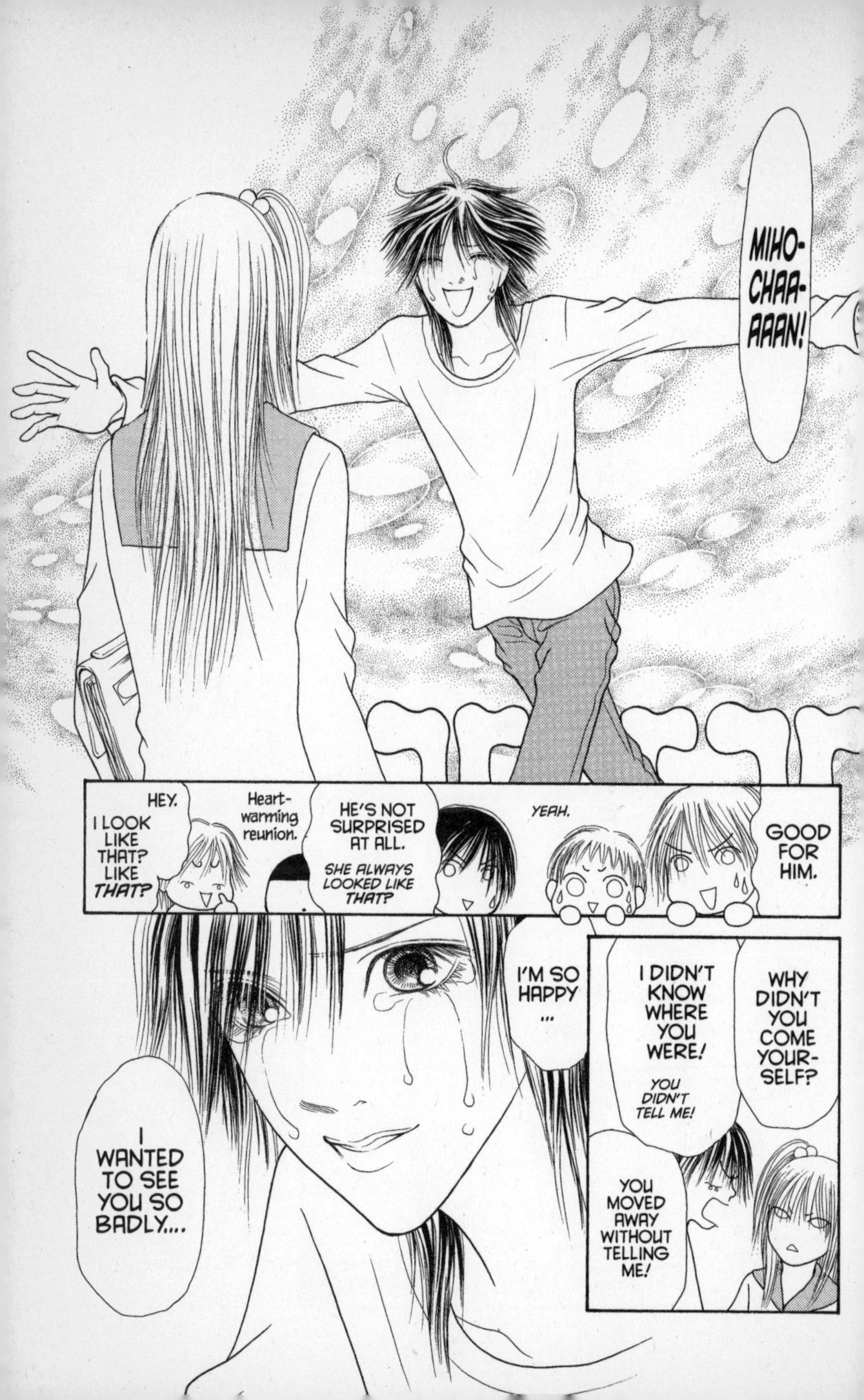
MIHO-CHAA-AAAN!
GOOD FOR HIM.
YEAH.
HE'S NOT SURPRISED AT ALL.
SHE ALWAYS LOOKED LIKE *THAT*?
Heart-warming reunion.
HEY. I LOOK LIKE THAT? LIKE *THAT*?
WHY DIDN'T YOU COME YOURSELF?
I DIDN'T KNOW WHERE YOU WERE!
YOU DIDN'T TELL ME!
YOU MOVED AWAY WITHOUT TELLING ME!
I'M SO HAPPY ...
I WANTED TO SEE YOU SO BADLY....

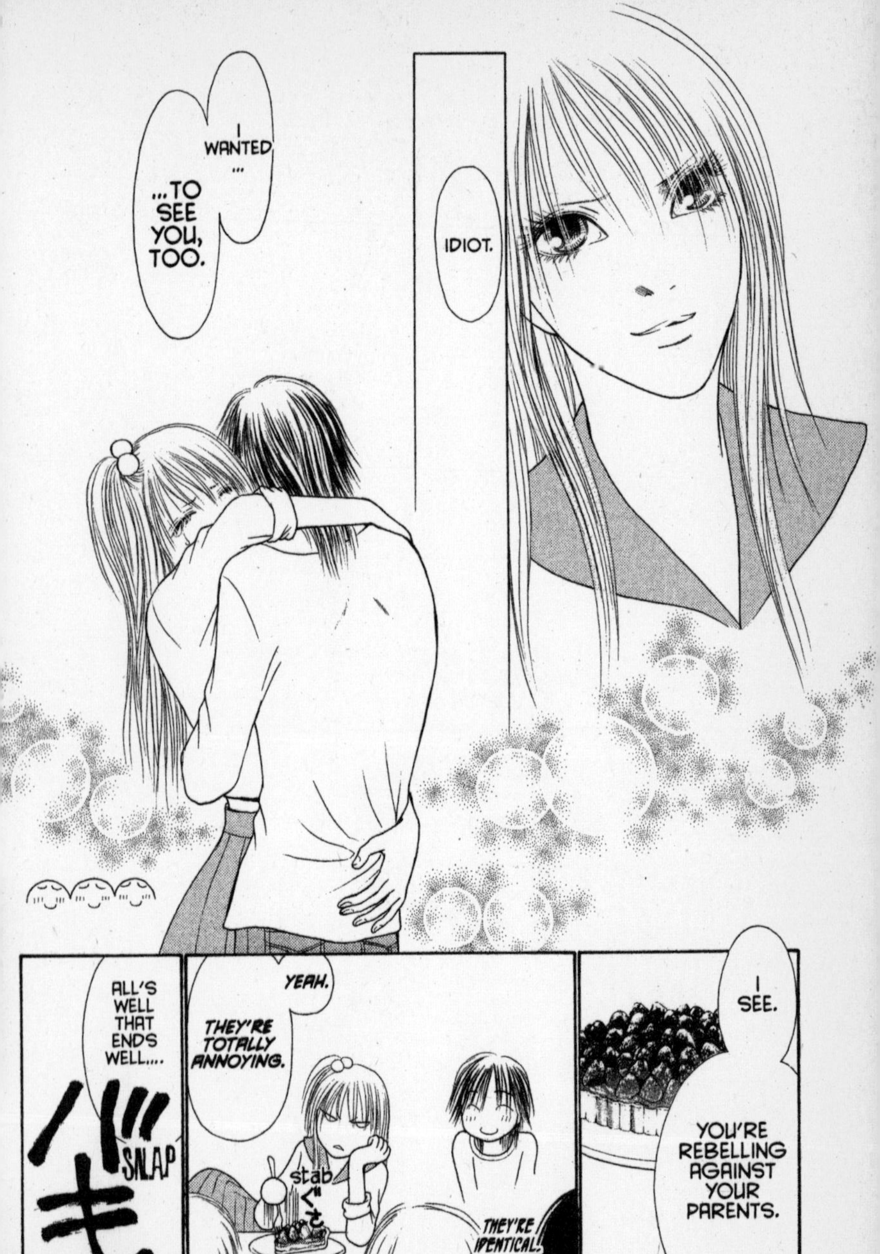
IDIOT.
I WANTED ...
...TO SEE YOU, TOO.
I SEE.
YOU'RE REBELLING AGAINST YOUR PARENTS.
YEAH.
THEY'RE TOTALLY ANNOYING.
stab
ぐさ
THEY'RE IDENTICAL!
ALL'S WELL THAT ENDS WELL....
バキィ
SNAP

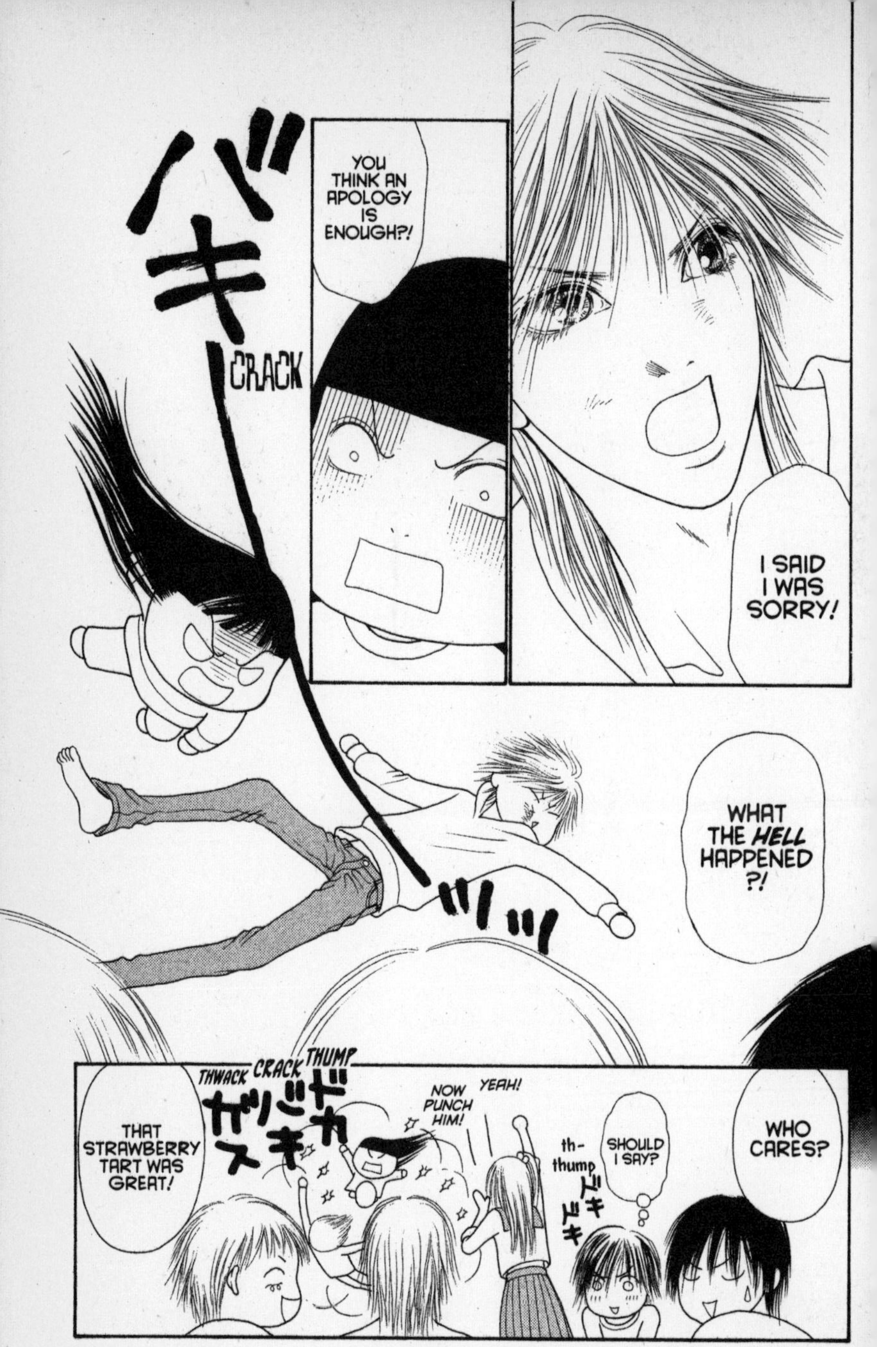
I SAID I WAS SORRY!
YOU THINK AN APOLOGY IS ENOUGH?!
バキ
CRACK
WHAT THE HELL HAPPENED ?!
ツッ
WHO CARES?
th-thump
ドキドキ
SHOULD I SAY?
YEAH!
NOW PUNCH HIM!
THUMP
ドカ
CRACK
バキ
THWACK
ガス
THAT STRAWBERRY TART WAS GREAT!

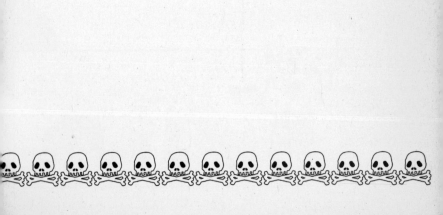

Chapter 114
Case of the Crooked Pharmacist (Part 1)

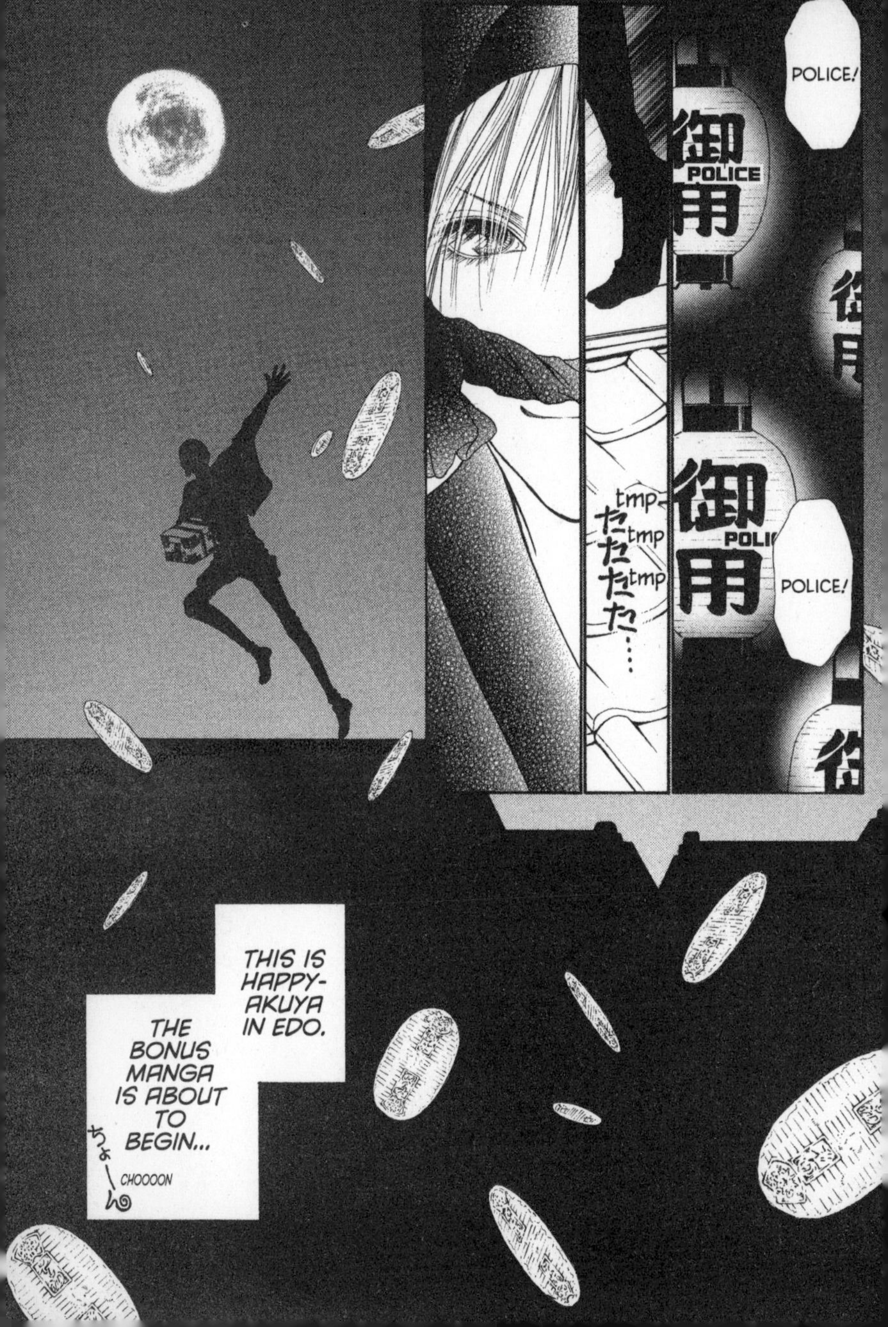
POLICE!
御用
POLICE
御用
POLICE!
POLI
tmp tmp tmp
たたたた…
THIS IS HAPPY-AKUYA IN EDO.
THE BONUS MANGA IS ABOUT TO BEGIN...
ちょーん
CHOOOON

Chapter 114 Case of the Crooked Pharmacist (Part 1)

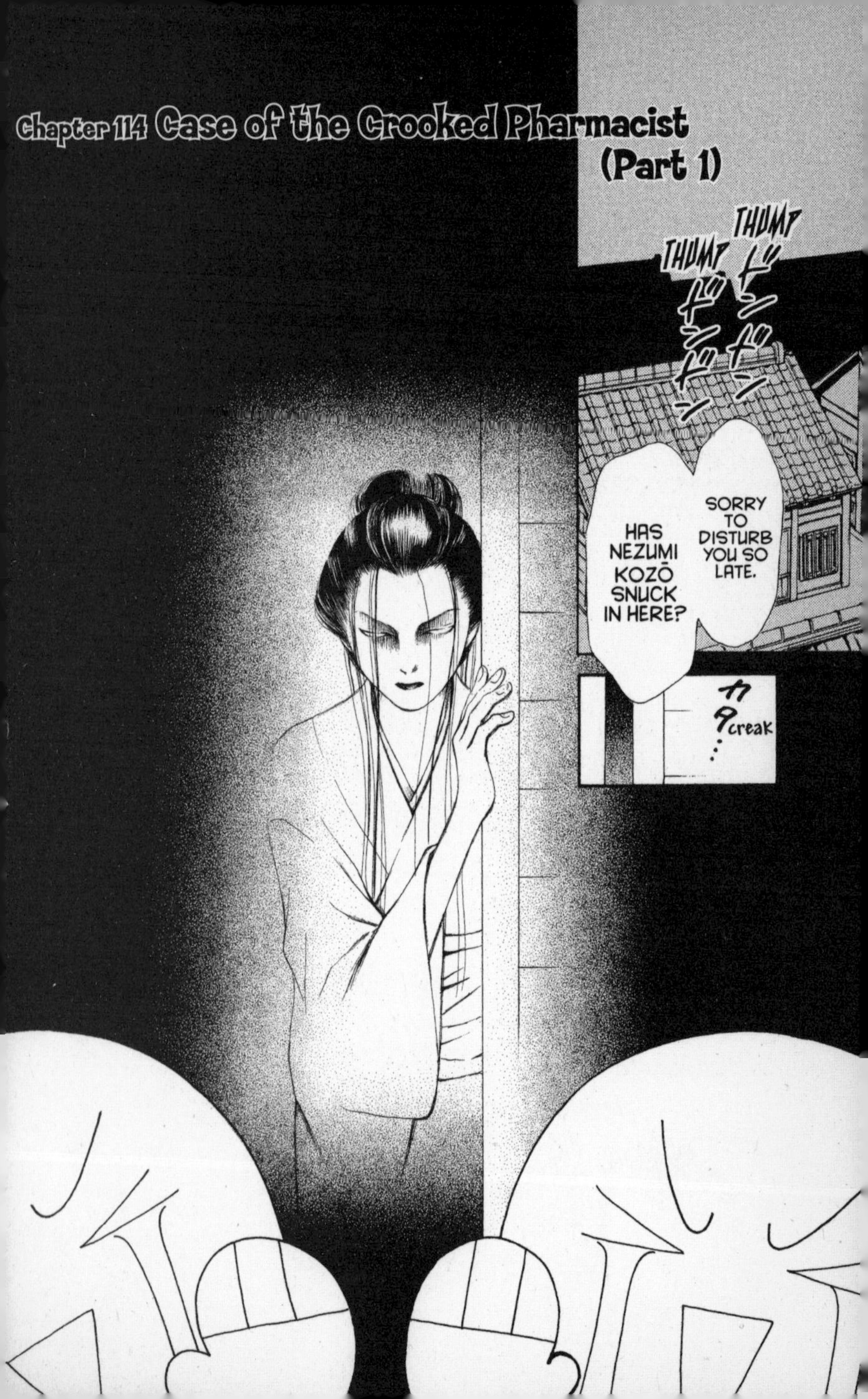
THUMP
THUMP
SORRY TO DISTURB YOU SO LATE.
HAS NEZUMI KOZŌ SNUCK IN HERE?
creak

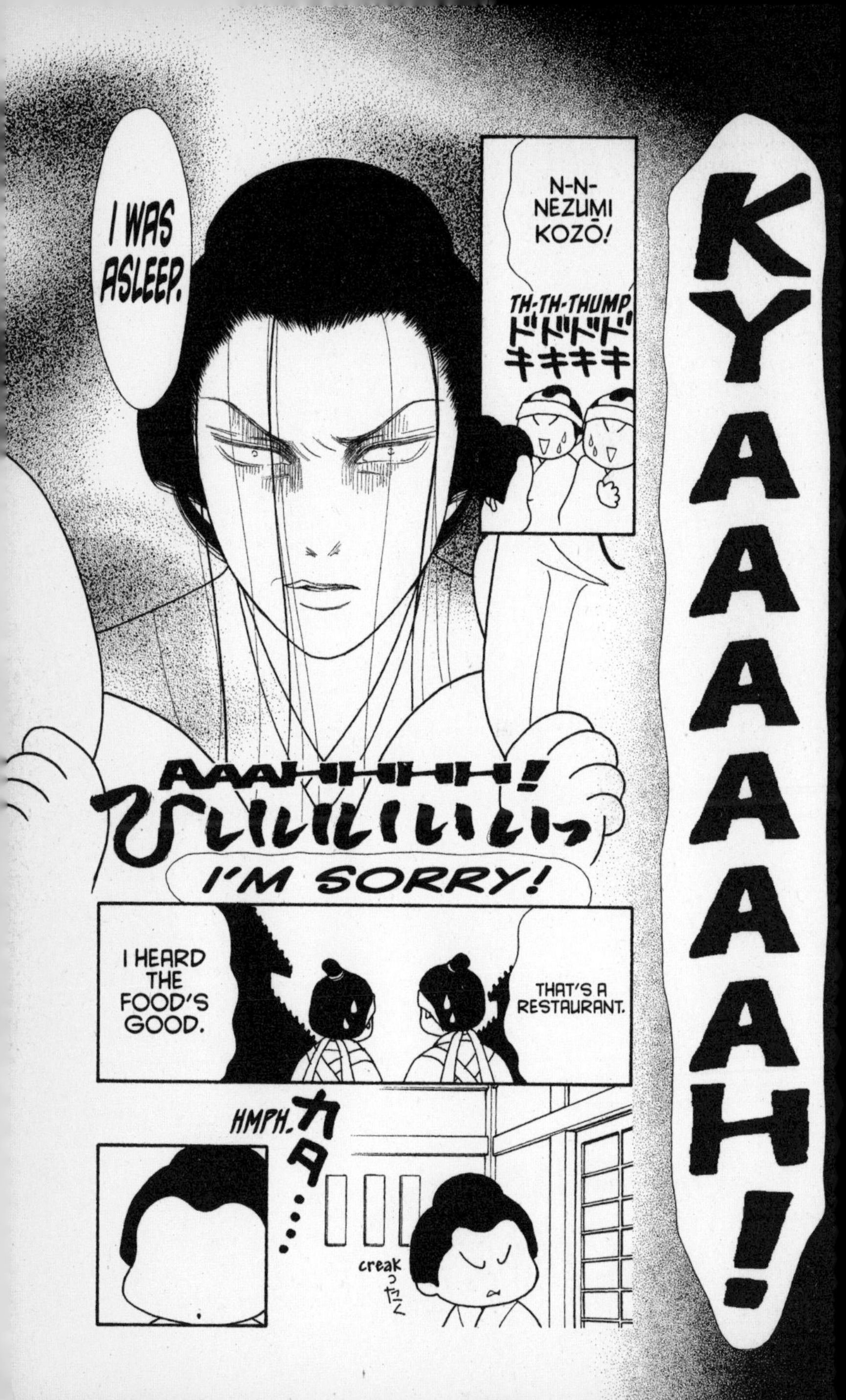

KYAAAAAH!
N-N-NEZUMI KOZŌ!
TH-TH-THUMP
ドドドド
キキキキ
I WAS ASLEEP.
AAAHHHHH!
ひぃぃぃぃっ
I'M SORRY!
THAT'S A RESTAURANT.
I HEARD THE FOOD'S GOOD.
creak
っ
たく
カタ...
HMPH.

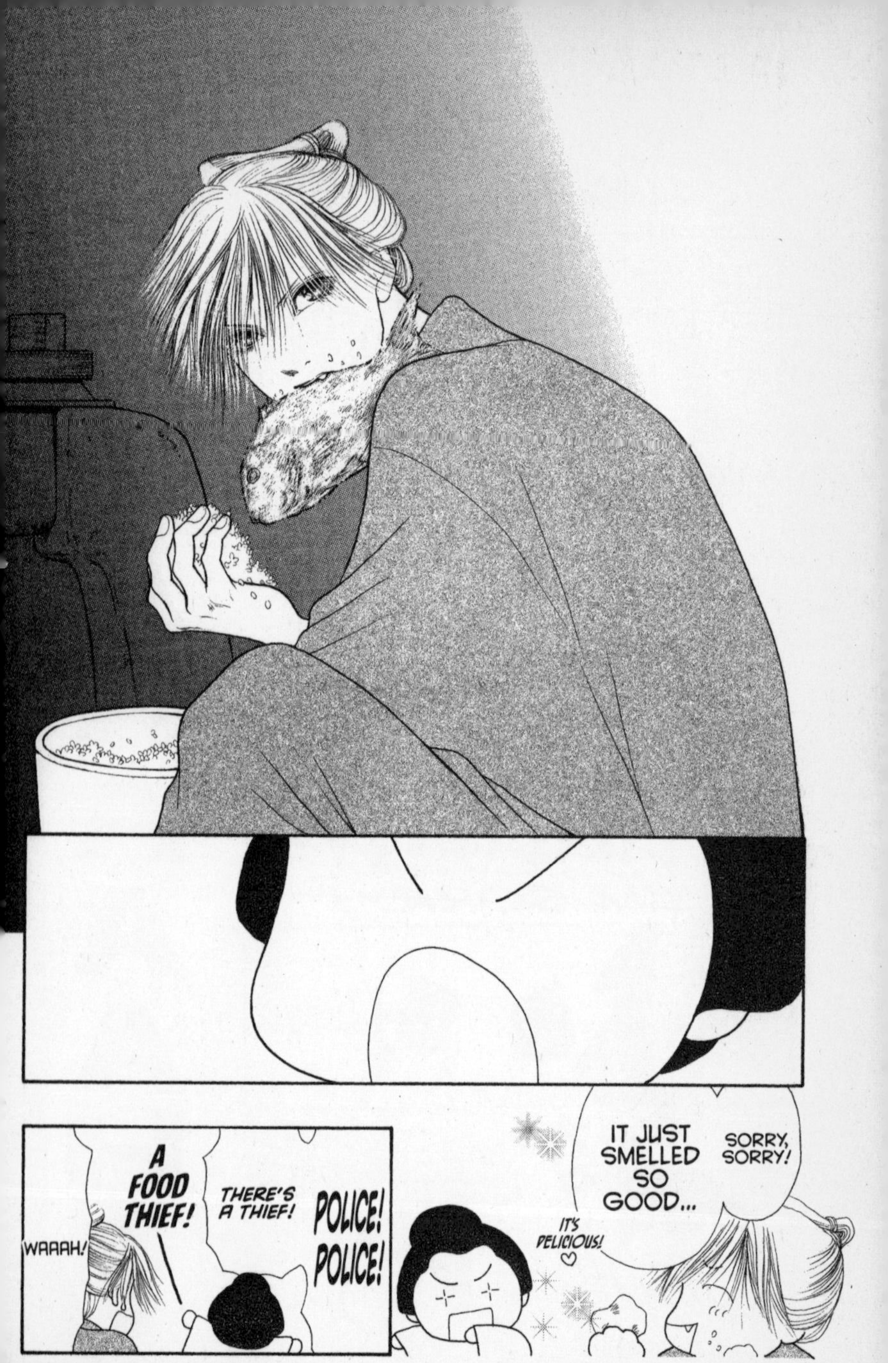
SORRY, SORRY!
IT JUST SMELLED SO GOOD...
IT'S DELICIOUS!
POLICE! POLICE!
THERE'S A THIEF!
A FOOD THIEF!
WAAAH!

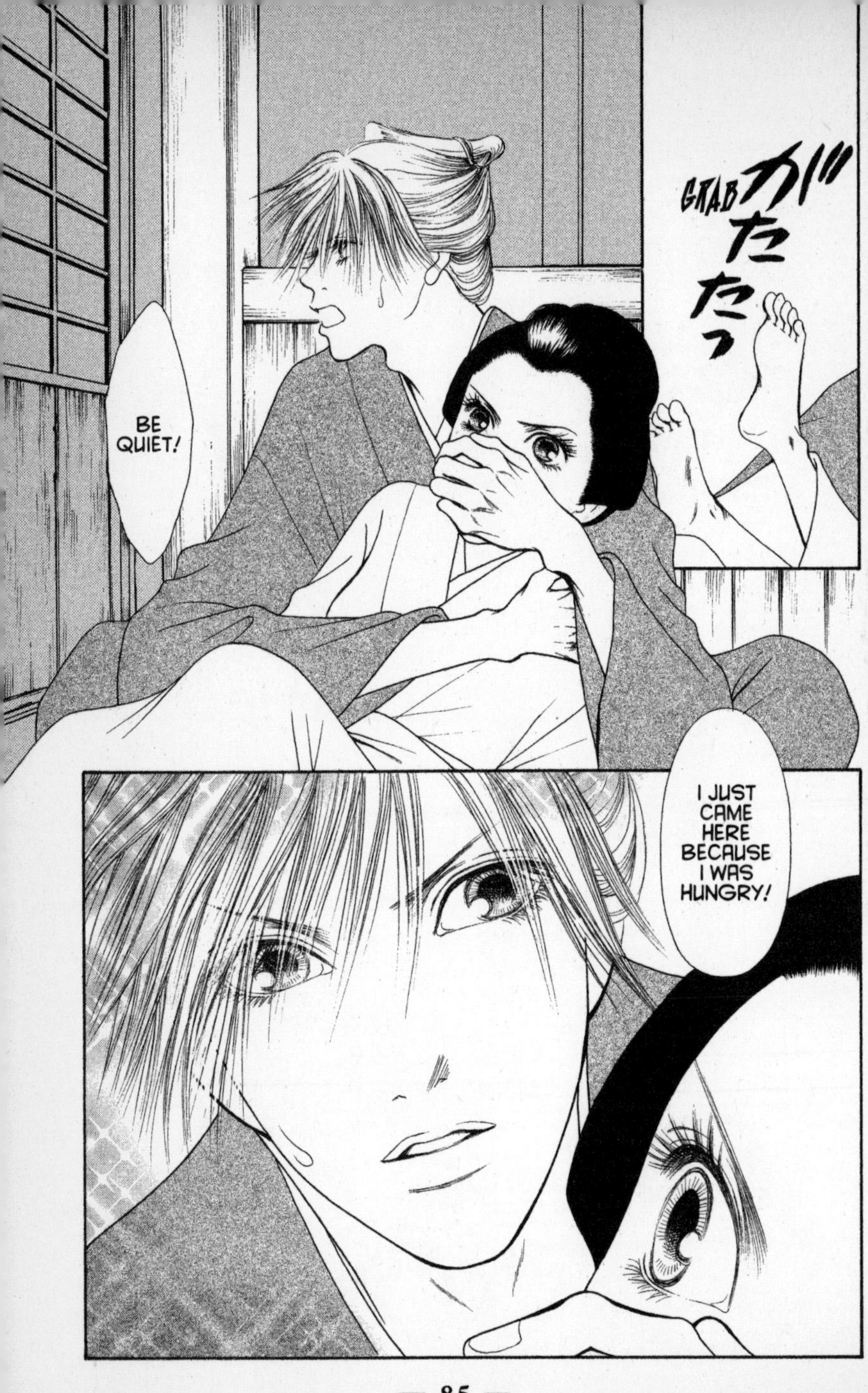
GRAB
がたたっ
BE QUIET!
I JUST CAME HERE BECAUSE I WAS HUNGRY!

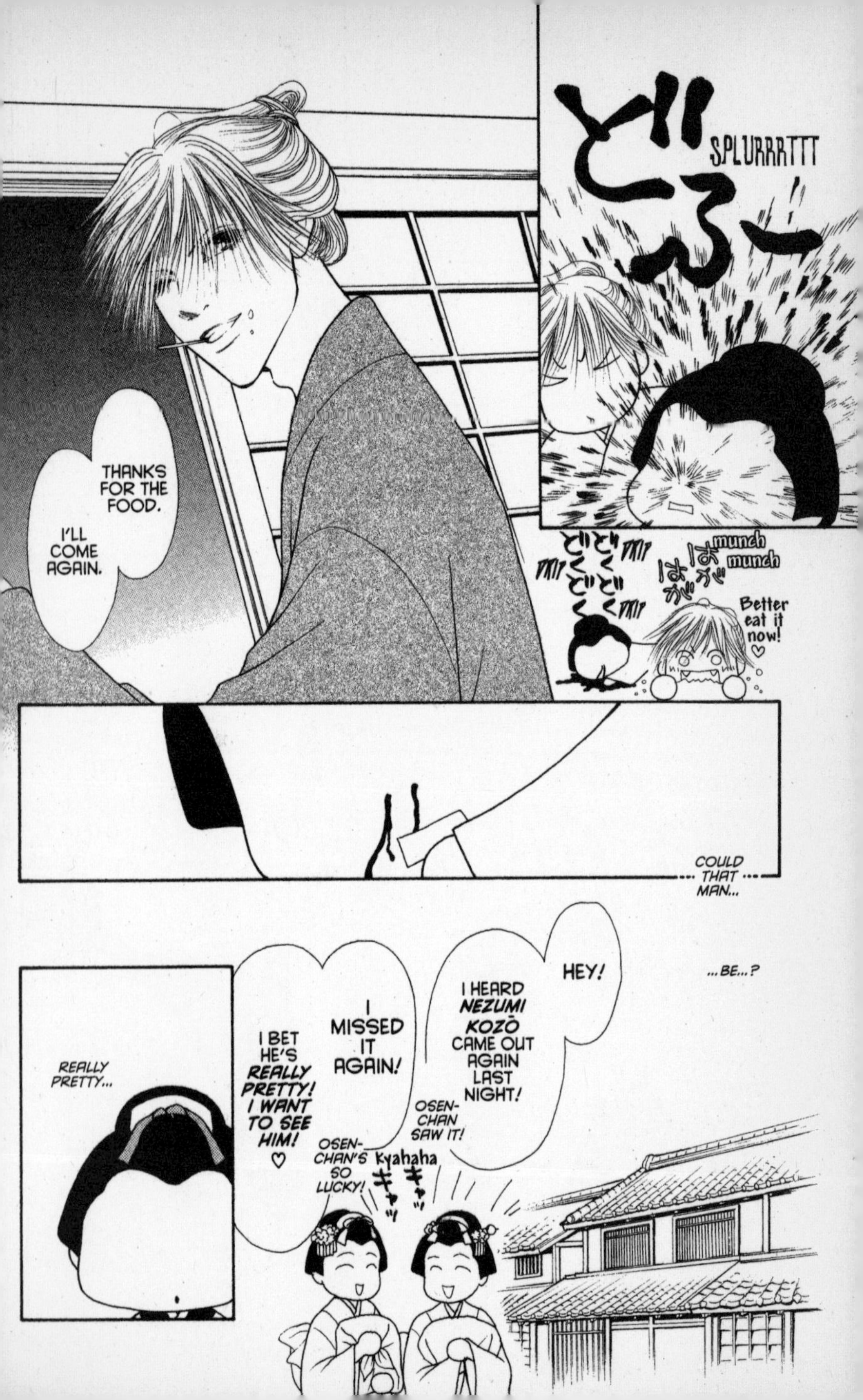

SPLURRRTTT
munch munch
Better eat it now! ♡
THANKS FOR THE FOOD.
I'LL COME AGAIN.
...COULD THAT MAN...
...BE...?
HEY!
I HEARD NEZUMI KOZŌ CAME OUT AGAIN LAST NIGHT!
OSEN-CHAN SAW IT!
I MISSED IT AGAIN!
I BET HE'S REALLY PRETTY! I WANT TO SEE HIM! ♡
Kyahaha
キャッ キャッ
OSEN-CHAN'S SO LUCKY!
REALLY PRETTY...

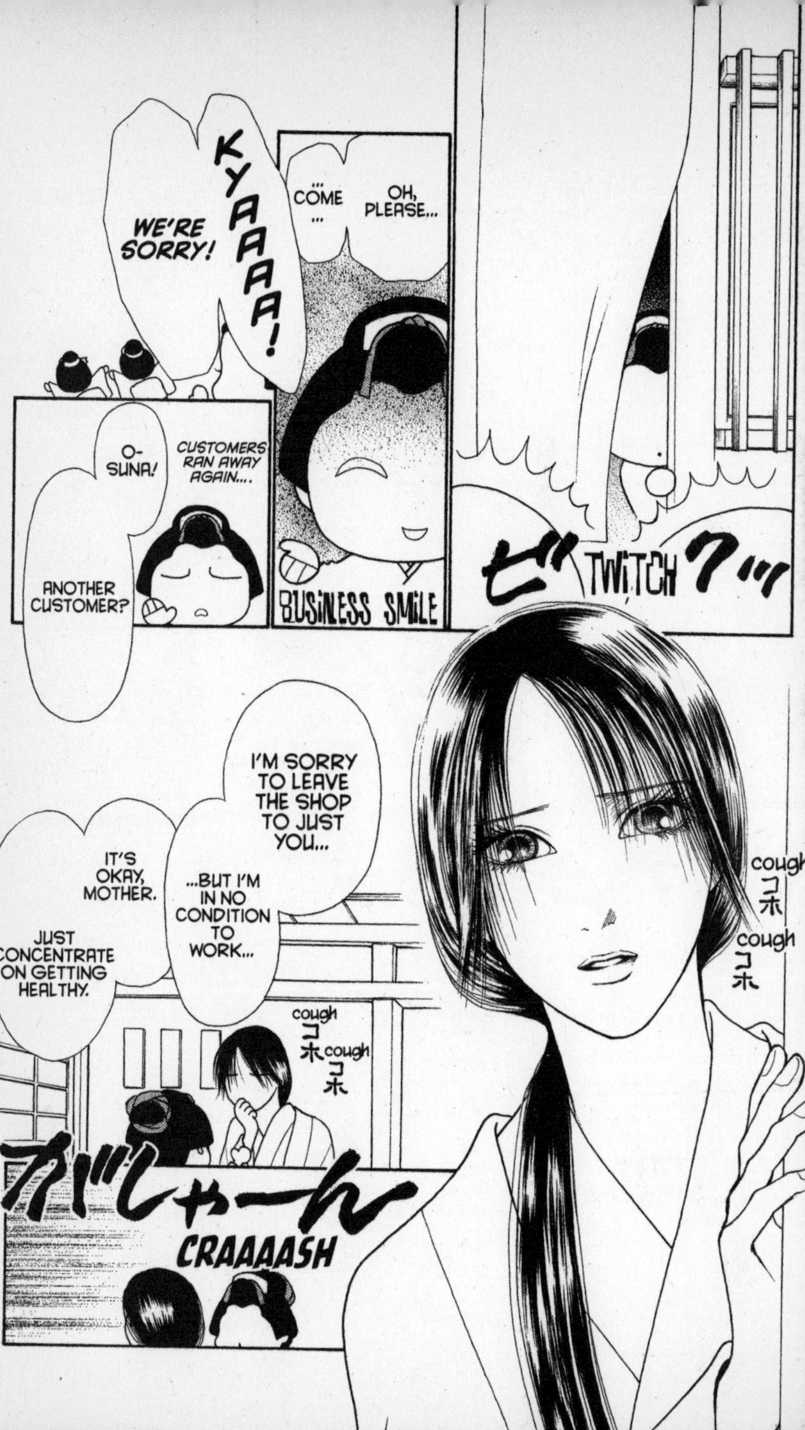
ビクッ
TWITCH
OH, PLEASE...
...COME...
BUSINESS SMILE
KYAAAA!
WE'RE SORRY!
CUSTOMERS RAN AWAY AGAIN....
O-SUNA!
ANOTHER CUSTOMER?
cough
コホ
cough
コホ
I'M SORRY TO LEAVE THE SHOP TO JUST YOU...
...BUT I'M IN NO CONDITION TO WORK...
IT'S OKAY, MOTHER.
JUST CONCENTRATE ON GETTING HEALTHY.
cough
コホ
cough
コホ
ガシャーン
CRAAAASH

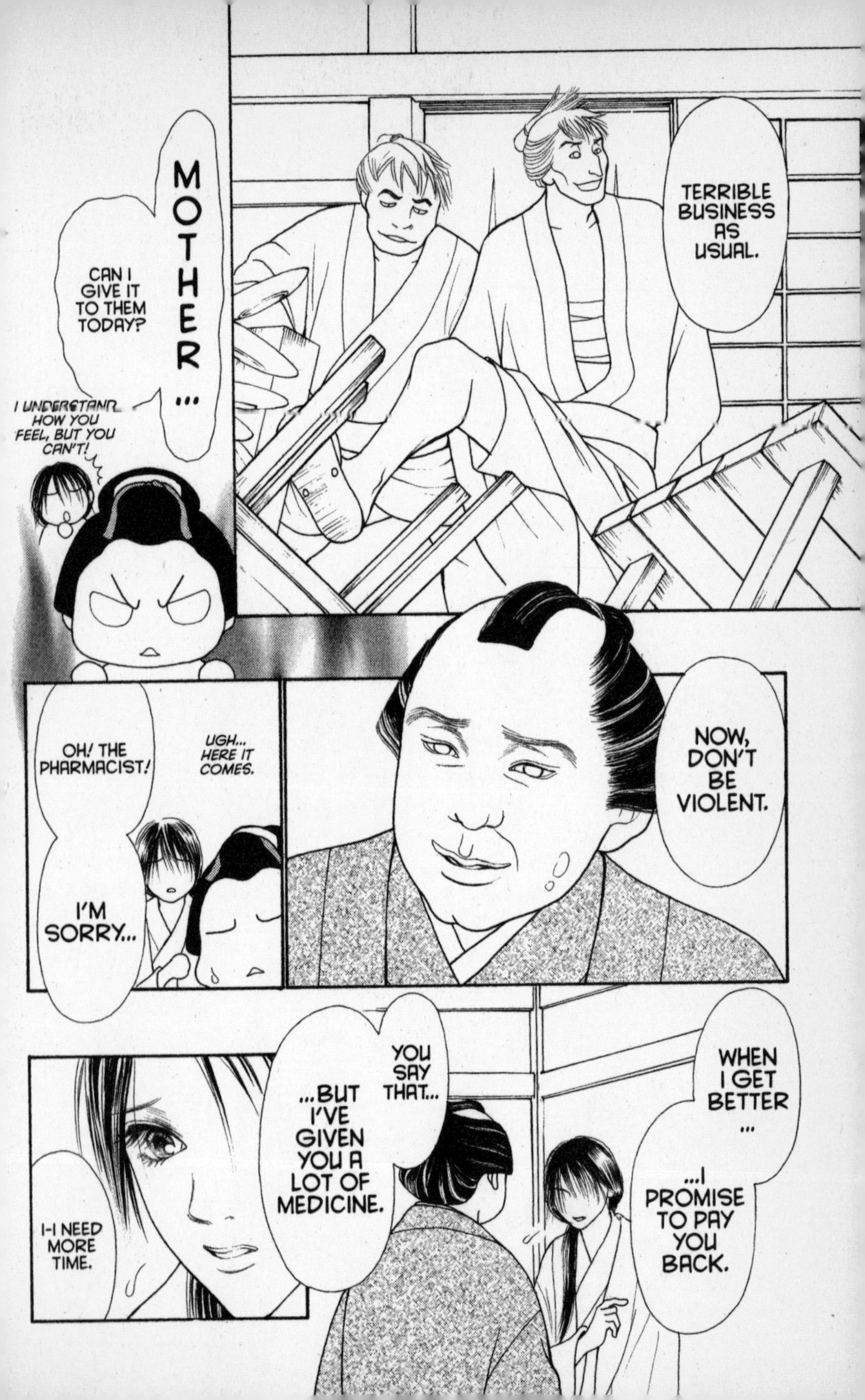
TERRIBLE BUSINESS AS USUAL.
MOTHER ...
CAN I GIVE IT TO THEM TODAY?
I UNDERSTAND HOW YOU FEEL, BUT YOU CAN'T!
NOW, DON'T BE VIOLENT.
UGH... HERE IT COMES.
OH! THE PHARMACIST!
I'M SORRY...
WHEN I GET BETTER ...
...I PROMISE TO PAY YOU BACK.
YOU SAY THAT...
...BUT I'VE GIVEN YOU A LOT OF MEDICINE.
I-I NEED MORE TIME.

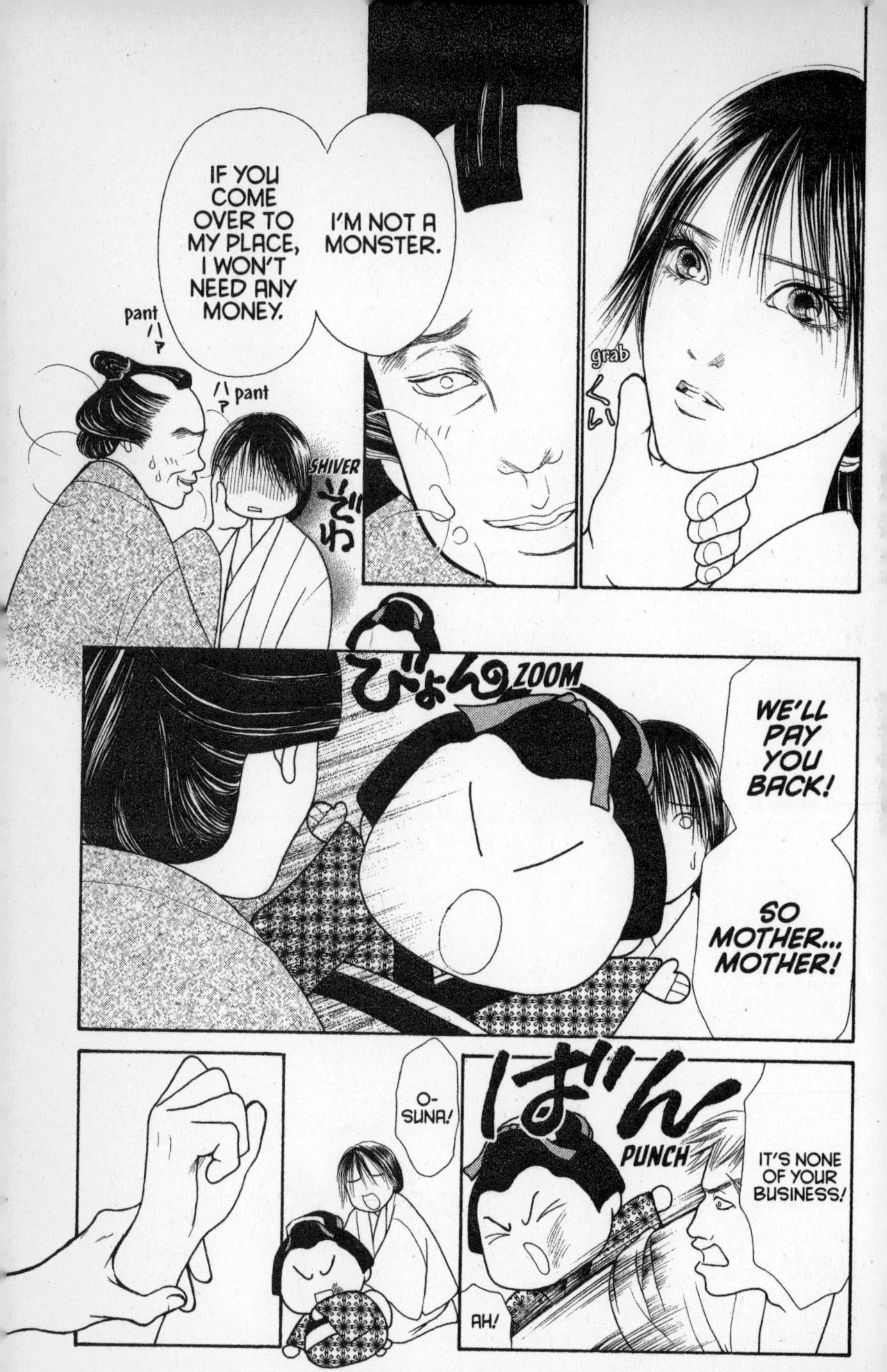
grab
I'M NOT A MONSTER.
IF YOU COME OVER TO MY PLACE, I WON'T NEED ANY MONEY.
pant
pant
SHIVER
びょん ZOOM
WE'LL PAY YOU BACK!
SO MOTHER... MOTHER!
ばん PUNCH
IT'S NONE OF YOUR BUSINESS!
AH!
O-SUNA!

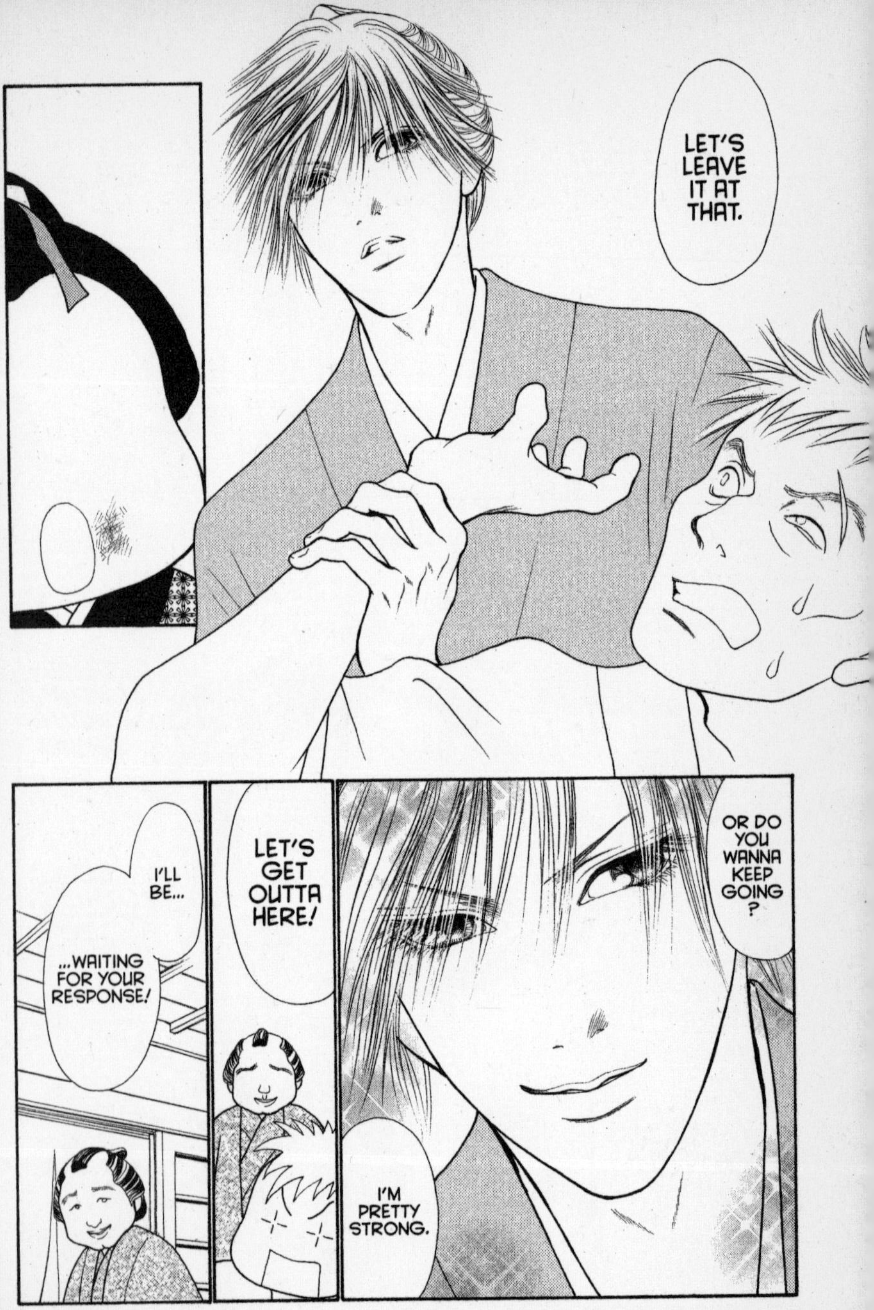
LET'S LEAVE IT AT THAT.
OR DO YOU WANNA KEEP GOING?
I'M PRETTY STRONG.
LET'S GET OUTTA HERE!
I'LL BE...
...WAITING FOR YOUR RESPONSE!

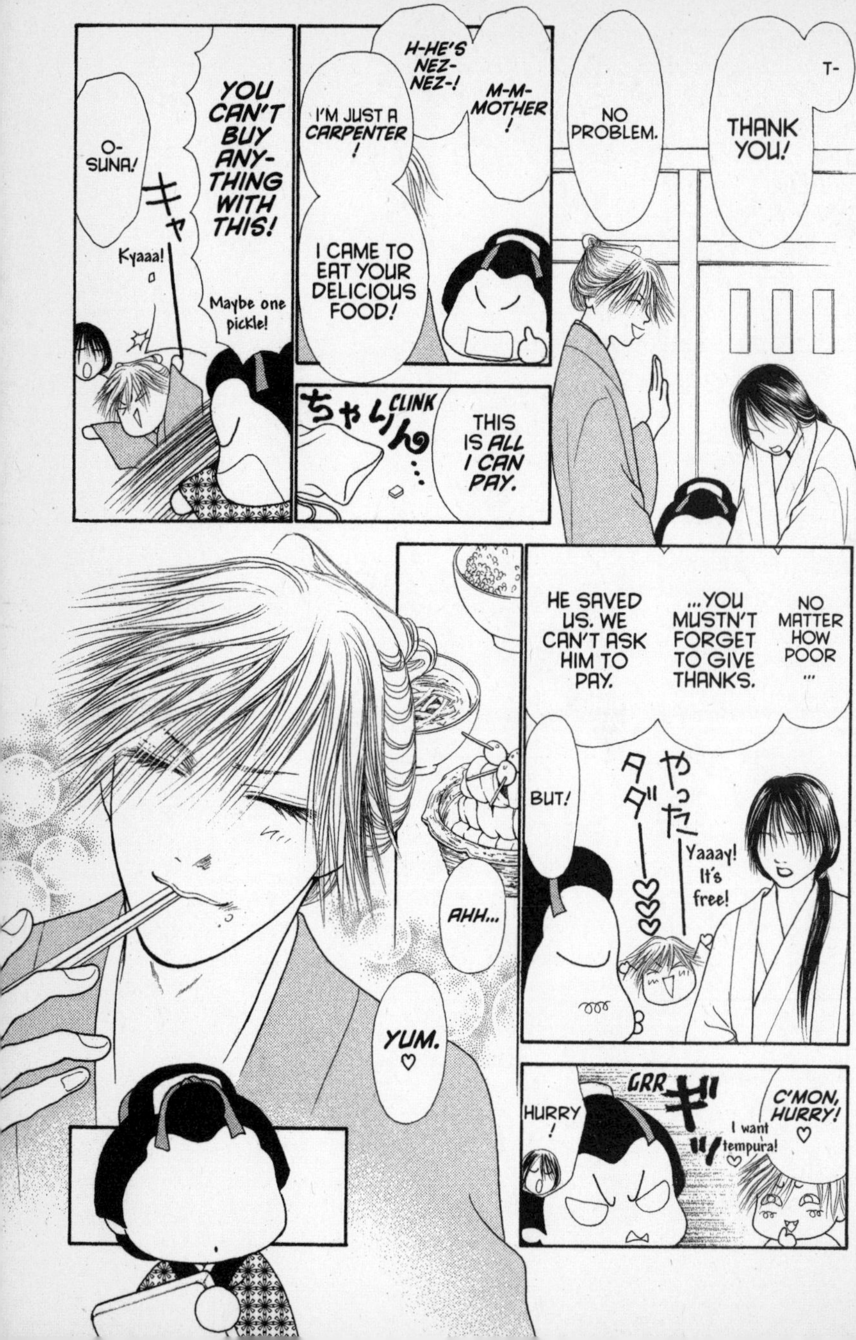
T-
THANK YOU!
NO PROBLEM.
M-M-MOTHER!
H-HE'S NEZ-NEZ-!
I'M JUST A CARPENTER!
I CAME TO EAT YOUR DELICIOUS FOOD!
THIS IS ALL I CAN PAY.
ちゃりん
CLINK
YOU CAN'T BUY ANYTHING WITH THIS!
O-SUNA!
キャ
Kyaaa!
Maybe one pickle!
NO MATTER HOW POOR...
...YOU MUSTN'T FORGET TO GIVE THANKS.
HE SAVED US. WE CAN'T ASK HIM TO PAY.
BUT!
やったー
Yaaay!
タダー
It's free!
C'MON, HURRY! ♡
I want tempura! ♡
ギッ
GRR
HURRY!
AHH...
YUM. ♡

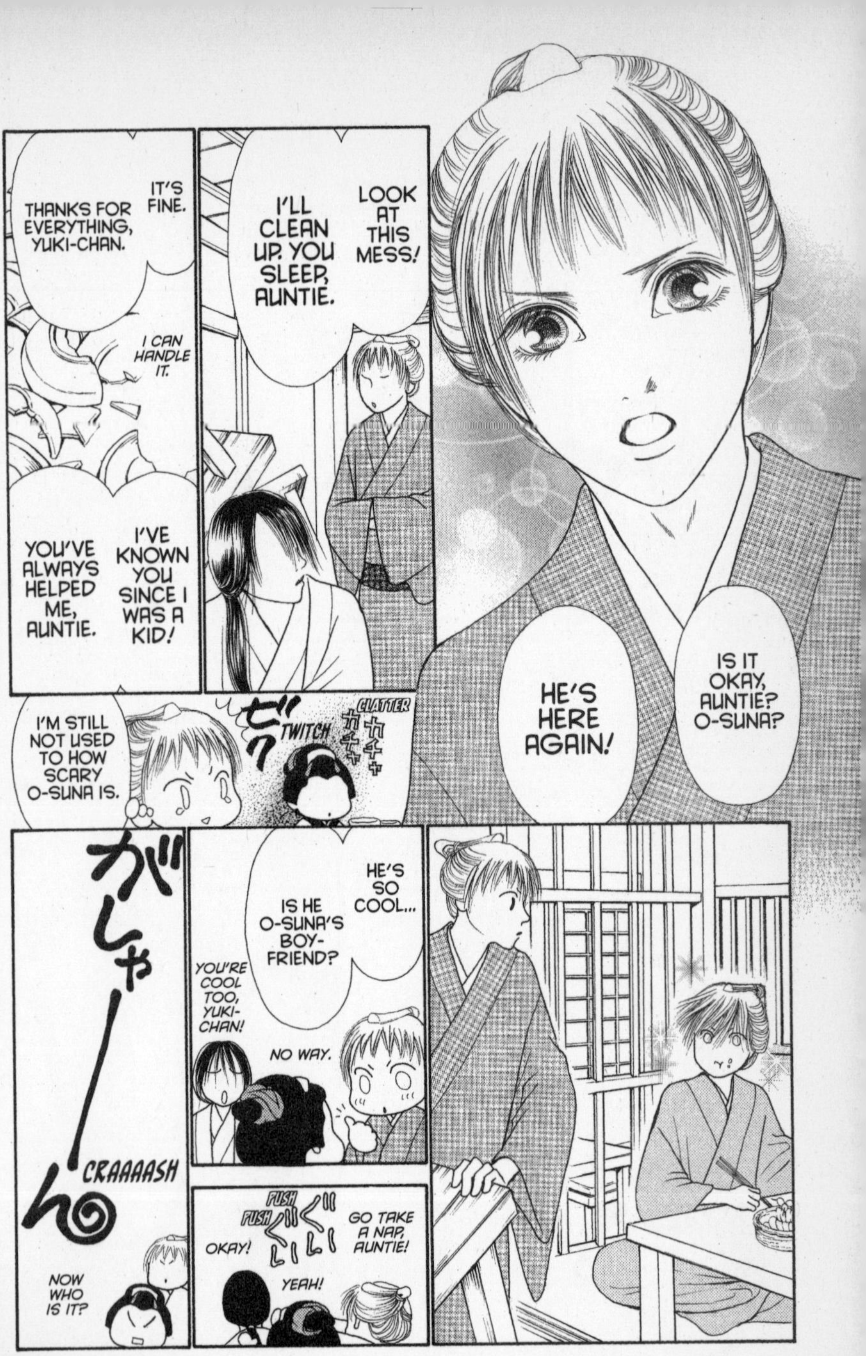
IS IT OKAY, AUNTIE? O-SUNA?
HE'S HERE AGAIN!
LOOK AT THIS MESS!
I'LL CLEAN UP. YOU SLEEP, AUNTIE.
IT'S FINE.
THANKS FOR EVERYTHING, YUKI-CHAN.
I CAN HANDLE IT.
I'VE KNOWN YOU SINCE I WAS A KID!
YOU'VE ALWAYS HELPED ME, AUNTIE.
CLATTER
カチャカチャ
ビク
TWITCH
I'M STILL NOT USED TO HOW SCARY O-SUNA IS.
HE'S SO COOL...
IS HE O-SUNA'S BOY-FRIEND?
YOU'RE COOL TOO, YUKI-CHAN!
NO WAY.
GO TAKE A NAP, AUNTIE!
PUSH
PUSH
ぐいぐい
OKAY!
YEAH!
がしゃーーん
CRAAAASH
NOW WHO IS IT?

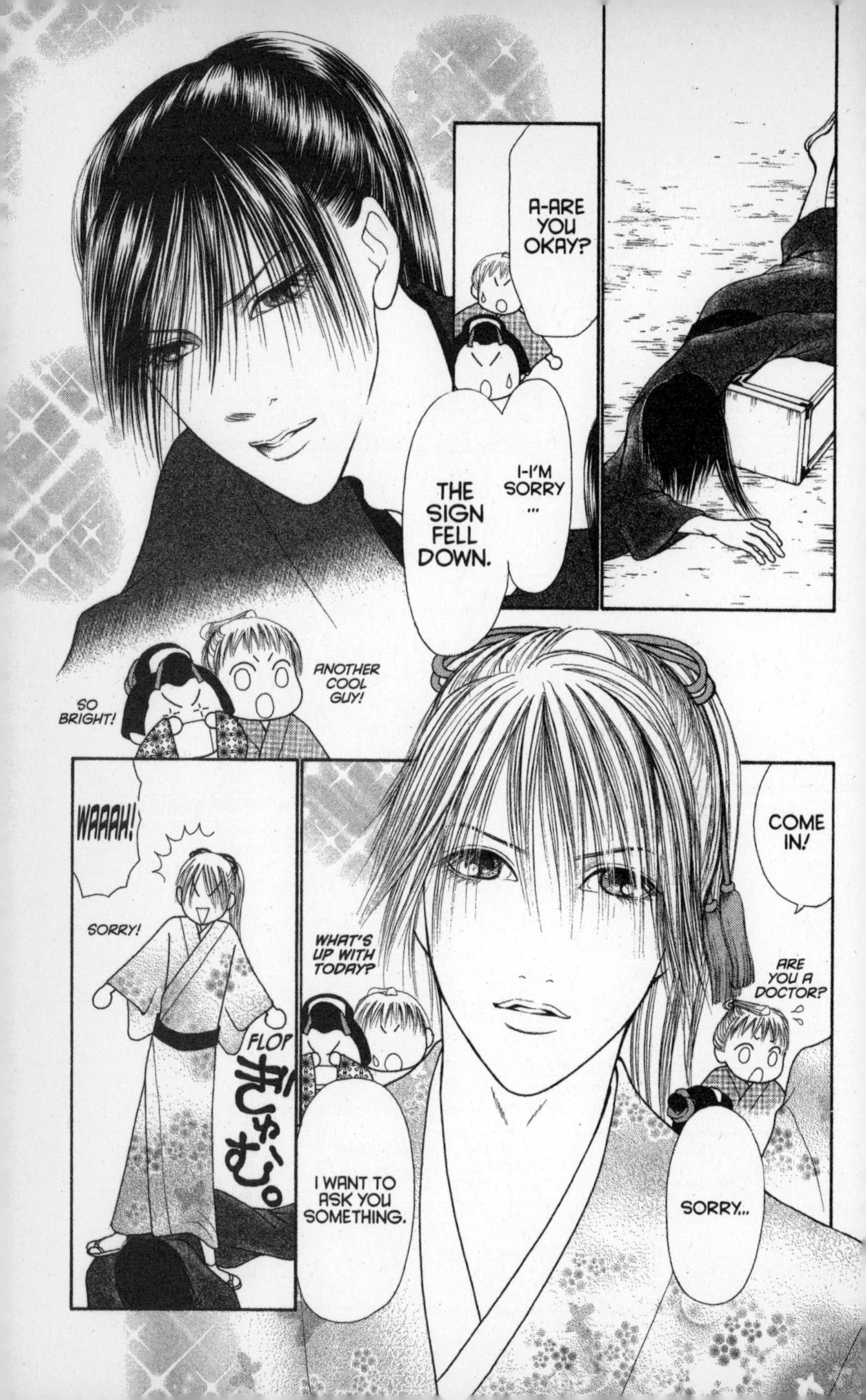
A-ARE YOU OKAY?
I-I'M SORRY ...
THE SIGN FELL DOWN.
ANOTHER COOL GUY!
SO BRIGHT!
COME IN!
ARE YOU A DOCTOR?
SORRY...
WHAT'S UP WITH TODAY?
I WANT TO ASK YOU SOMETHING.
WAAAH!
SORRY!
FLOP

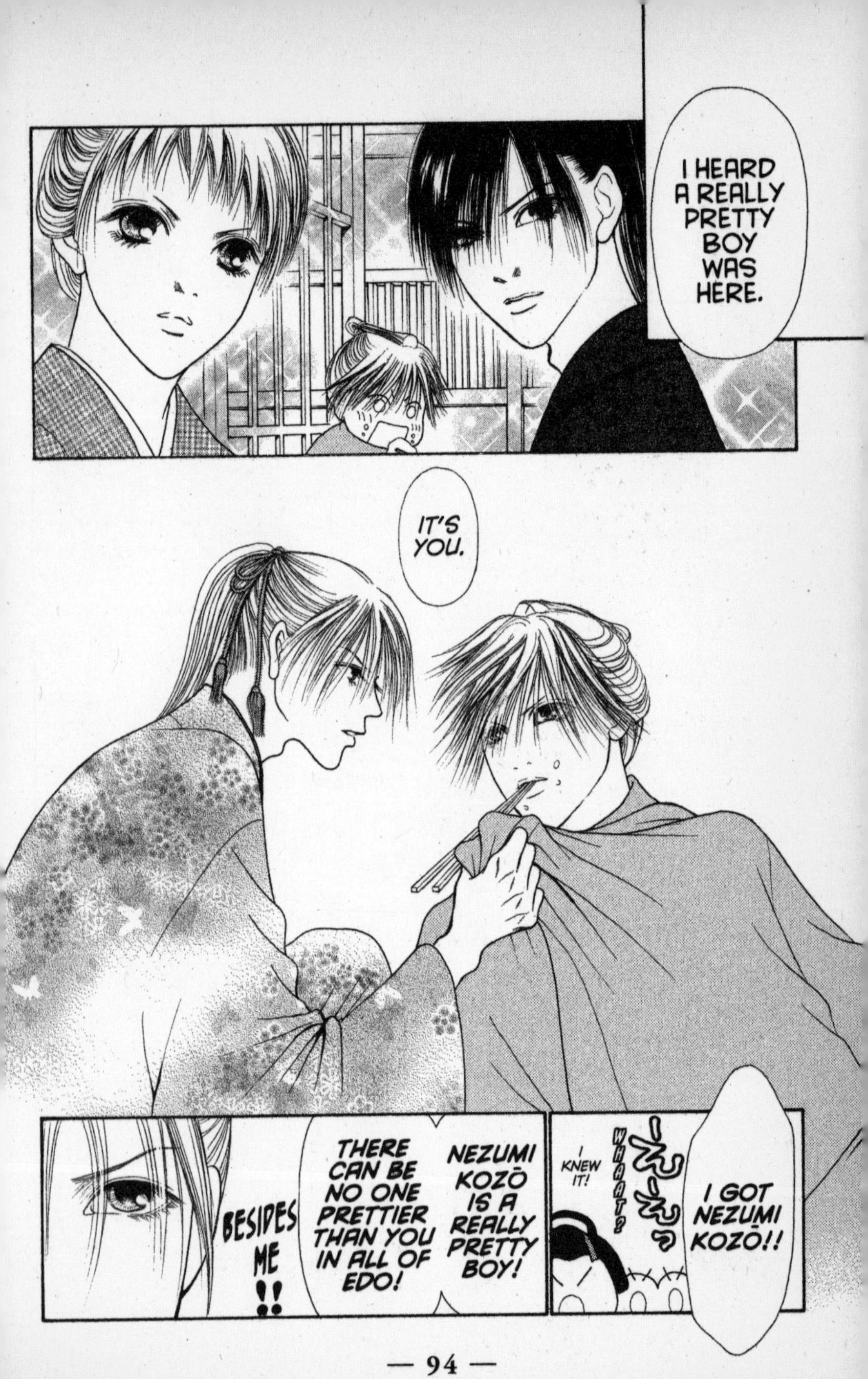
I HEARD A REALLY PRETTY BOY WAS HERE.
IT'S YOU.
I GOT NEZUMI KOZŌ!!
WHAAAT?
I KNEW IT!
NEZUMI KOZŌ IS A REALLY PRETTY BOY!
THERE CAN BE NO ONE PRETTIER THAN YOU IN ALL OF EDO!
BESIDES ME!!

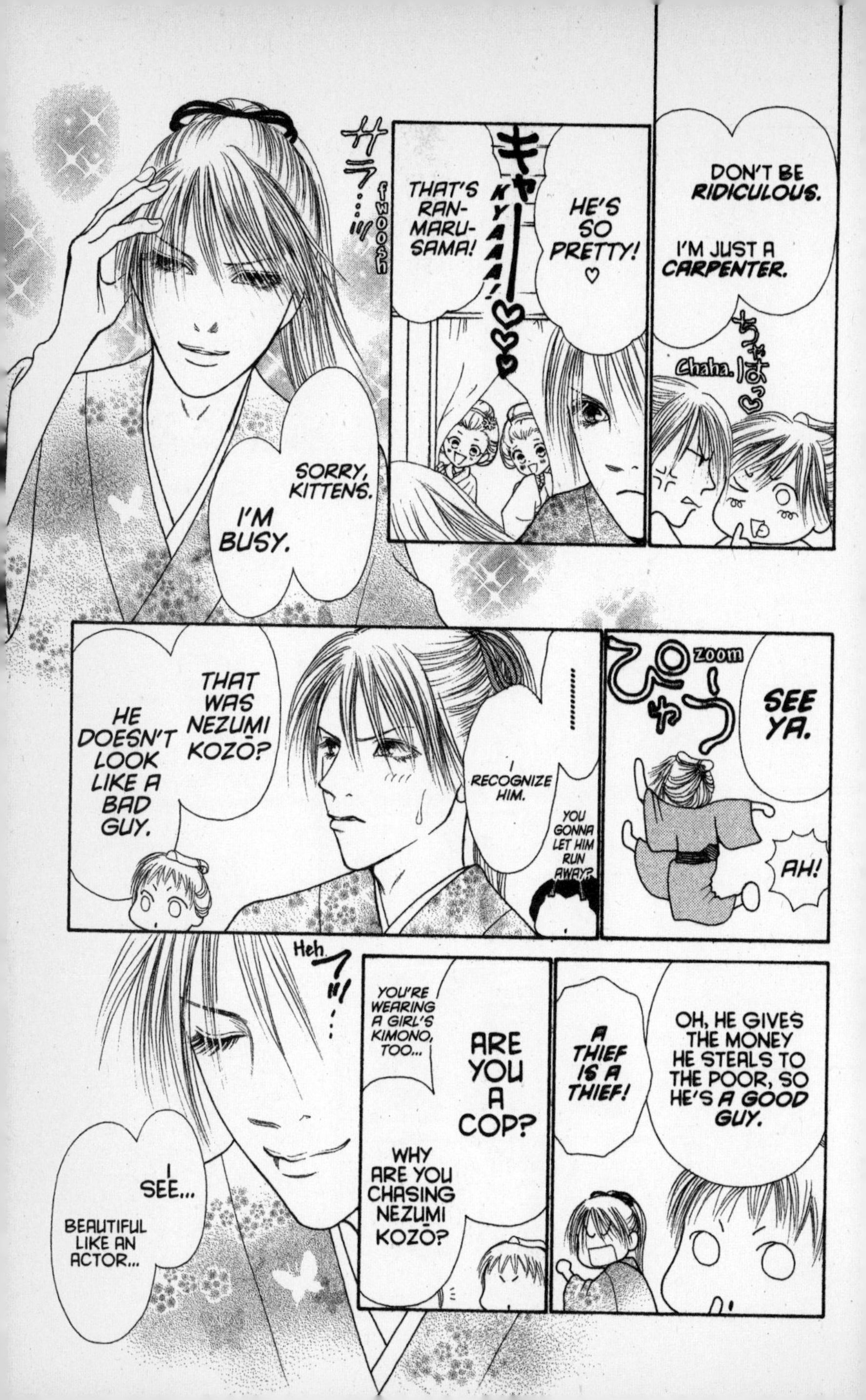
DON'T BE RIDICULOUS.
I'M JUST A CARPENTER.
Chaha.
HE'S SO PRETTY! ♡
キャー
KYAAAA!
THAT'S RAN-MARU-SAMA!
サラ…
fwoosh
SORRY, KITTENS.
I'M BUSY.
SEE YA.
ぴゅう
zoom
AH!
......
I RECOGNIZE HIM.
YOU GONNA LET HIM RUN AWAY?
THAT WAS NEZUMI KOZŌ?
HE DOESN'T LOOK LIKE A BAD GUY.
OH, HE GIVES THE MONEY HE STEALS TO THE POOR, SO HE'S A GOOD GUY.
A THIEF IS A THIEF!
ARE YOU A COP?
YOU'RE WEARING A GIRL'S KIMONO, TOO...
WHY ARE YOU CHASING NEZUMI KOZŌ?
Heh.
I SEE...
BEAUTIFUL LIKE AN ACTOR...

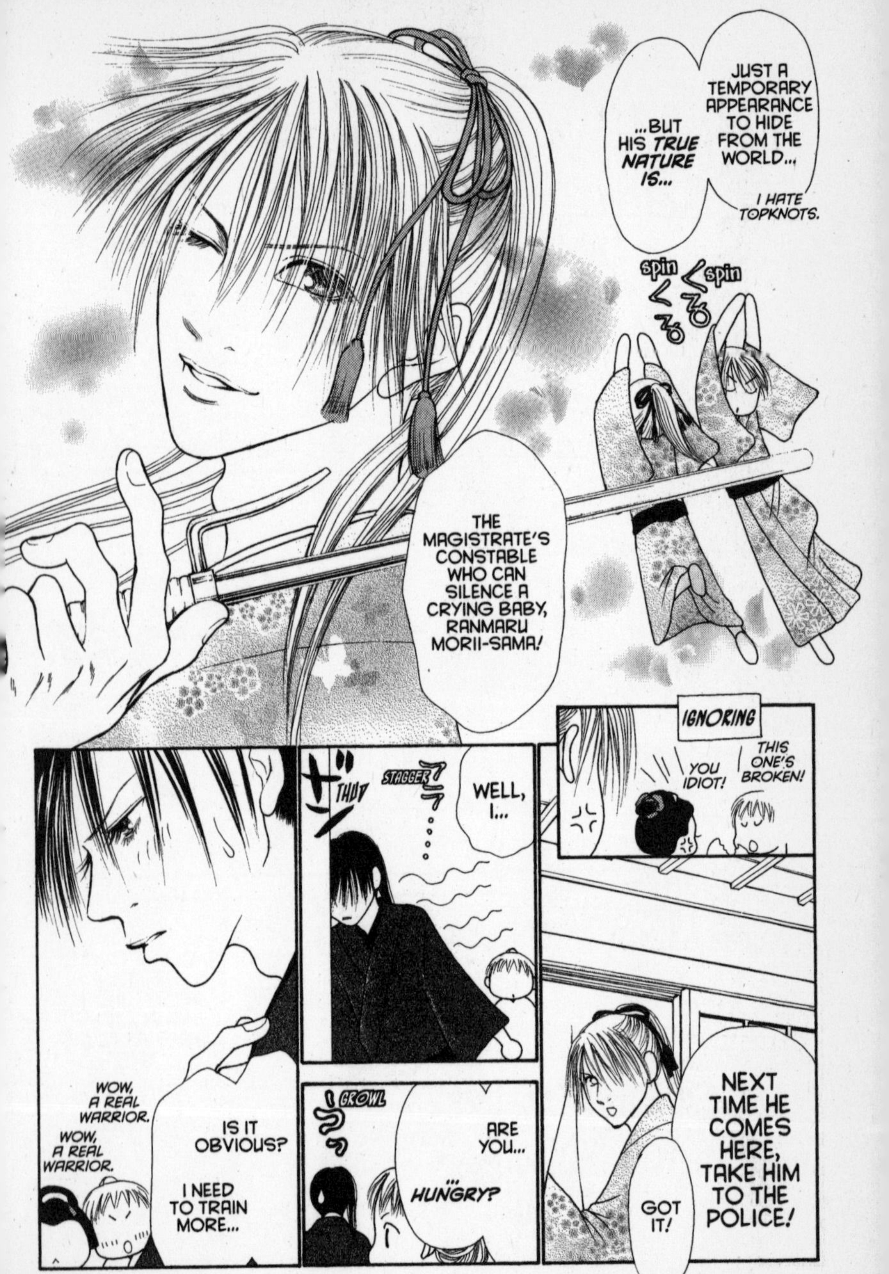
JUST A TEMPORARY APPEARANCE TO HIDE FROM THE WORLD...
...BUT HIS TRUE NATURE IS...
I HATE TOPKNOTS.
spin
spin
THE MAGISTRATE'S CONSTABLE WHO CAN SILENCE A CRYING BABY, RANMARU MORII-SAMA!
IGNORING
THIS ONE'S BROKEN!
YOU IDIOT!
NEXT TIME HE COMES HERE, TAKE HIM TO THE POLICE!
GOT IT!
STAGGER
THUD
WELL, I...
GROWL
ARE YOU...
...HUNGRY?
IS IT OBVIOUS?
I NEED TO TRAIN MORE...
WOW, A REAL WARRIOR.
WOW, A REAL WARRIOR.

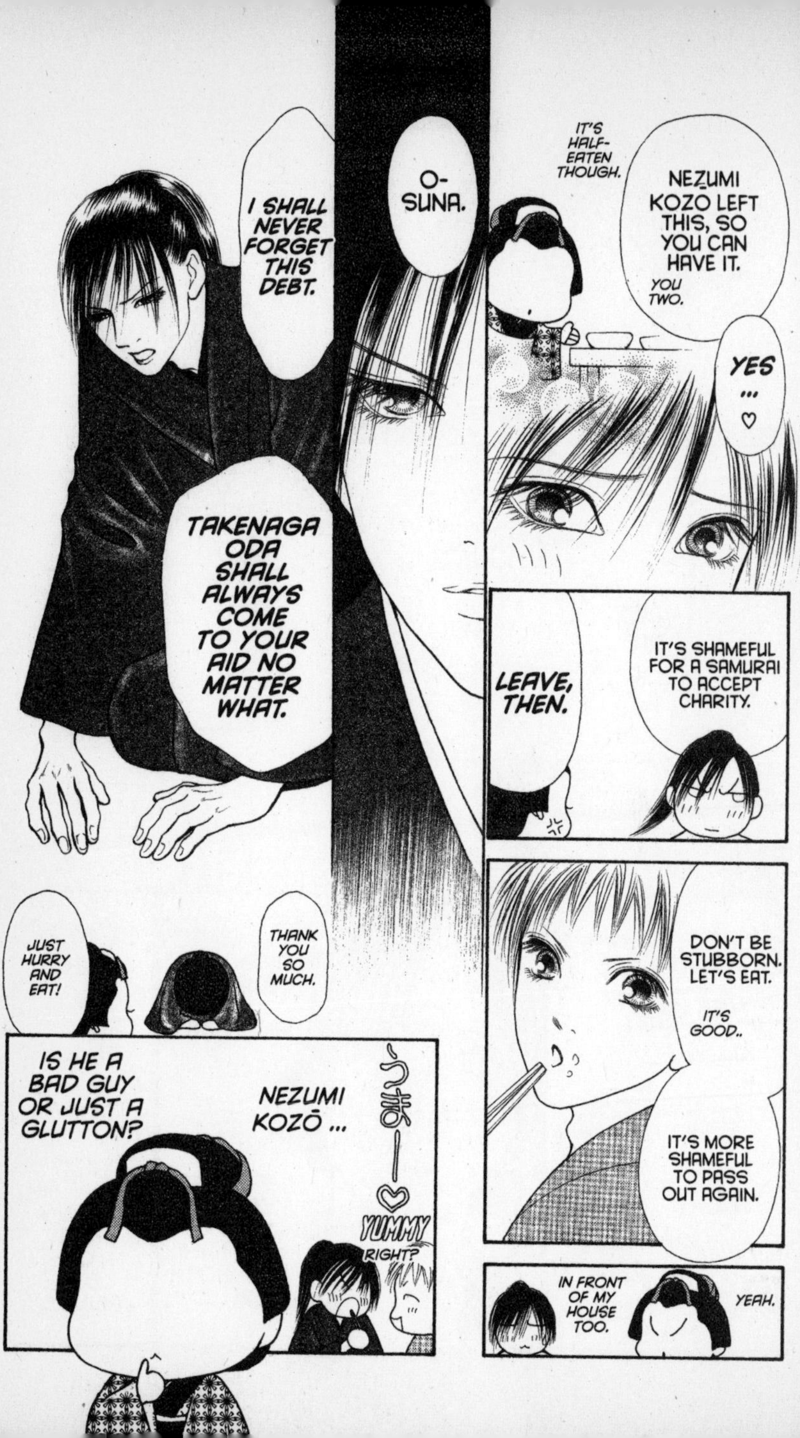
IT'S HALF-EATEN THOUGH.
NEZUMI KOZO LEFT THIS, SO YOU CAN HAVE IT.
YOU TWO.
YES ... ♡
IT'S SHAMEFUL FOR A SAMURAI TO ACCEPT CHARITY.
LEAVE, THEN.
DON'T BE STUBBORN. LET'S EAT.
IT'S GOOD..
IT'S MORE SHAMEFUL TO PASS OUT AGAIN.
IN FRONT OF MY HOUSE TOO.
YEAH.
O-SUNA.
I SHALL NEVER FORGET THIS DEBT.
TAKENAGA ODA SHALL ALWAYS COME TO YOUR AID NO MATTER WHAT.
THANK YOU SO MUCH.
JUST HURRY AND EAT!
うまーー♡
YUMMY
RIGHT?
NEZUMI KOZŌ ...
IS HE A BAD GUY OR JUST A GLUTTON?

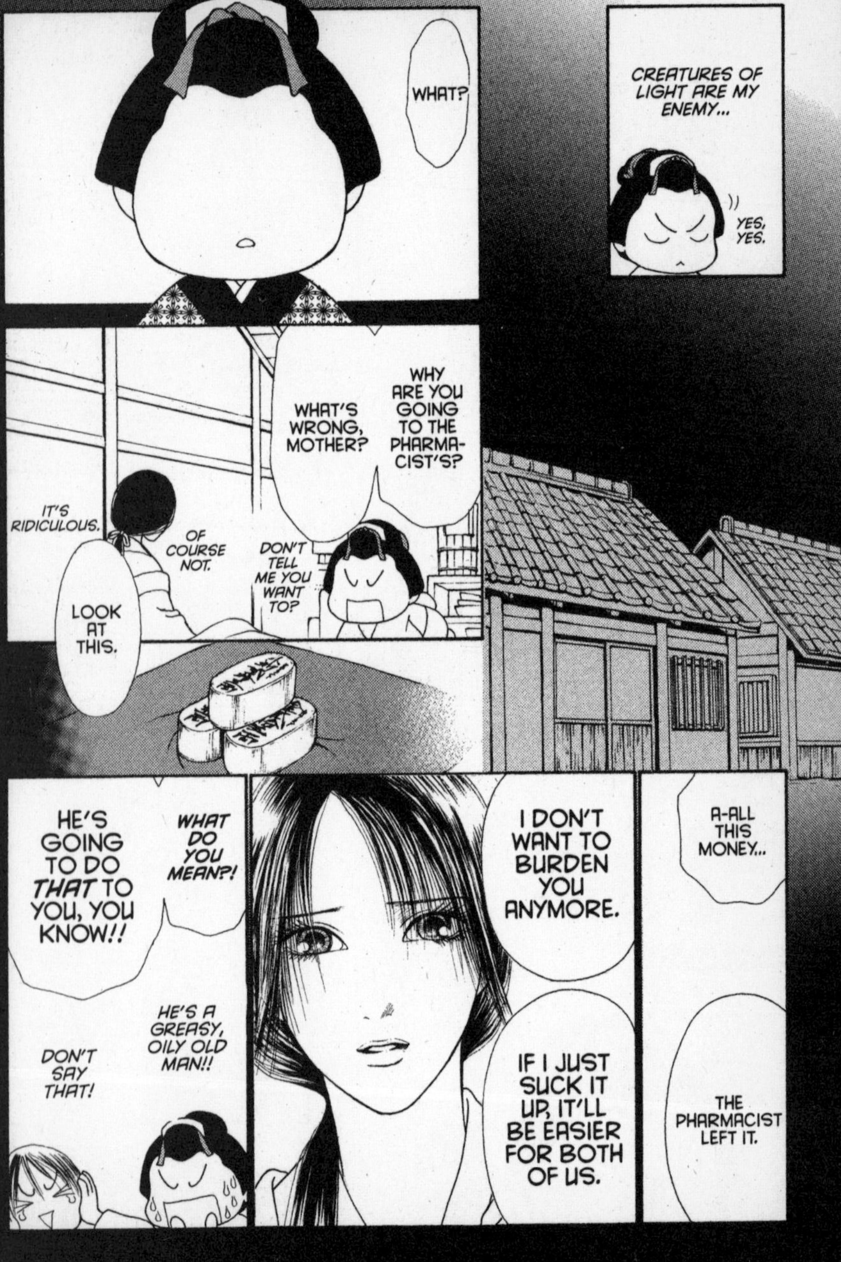
CREATURES OF LIGHT ARE MY ENEMY...
YES, YES.
WHAT?
WHY ARE YOU GOING TO THE PHARMACIST'S?
WHAT'S WRONG, MOTHER?
DON'T TELL ME YOU WANT TO?
OF COURSE NOT.
IT'S RIDICULOUS.
LOOK AT THIS.
A-ALL THIS MONEY...
THE PHARMACIST LEFT IT.
I DON'T WANT TO BURDEN YOU ANYMORE.
IF I JUST SUCK IT UP, IT'LL BE EASIER FOR BOTH OF US.
WHAT DO YOU MEAN?!
HE'S GOING TO DO *THAT* TO YOU, YOU KNOW!!
HE'S A GREASY, OILY OLD MAN!!
DON'T SAY THAT!

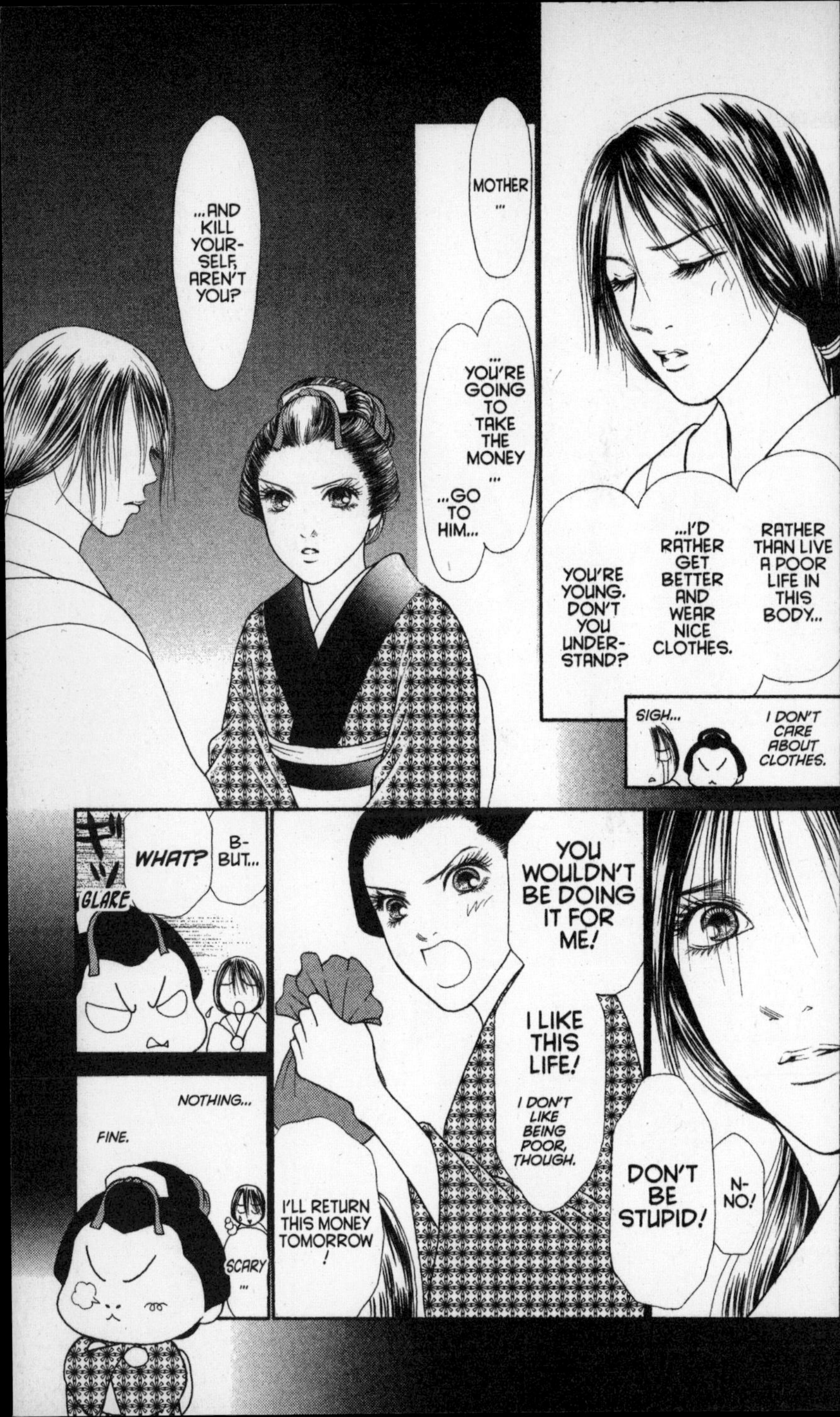

RATHER THAN LIVE A POOR LIFE IN THIS BODY...
...I'D RATHER GET BETTER AND WEAR NICE CLOTHES.
YOU'RE YOUNG. DON'T YOU UNDERSTAND?
I DON'T CARE ABOUT CLOTHES.
SIGH...
MOTHER...
...YOU'RE GOING TO TAKE THE MONEY...
...GO TO HIM...
...AND KILL YOURSELF, AREN'T YOU?
N-NO!
DON'T BE STUPID!
YOU WOULDN'T BE DOING IT FOR ME!
I LIKE THIS LIFE!
I DON'T LIKE BEING POOR, THOUGH.
I'LL RETURN THIS MONEY TOMORROW!
B-BUT...
WHAT?
GLARE
NOTHING...
FINE.
SCARY...

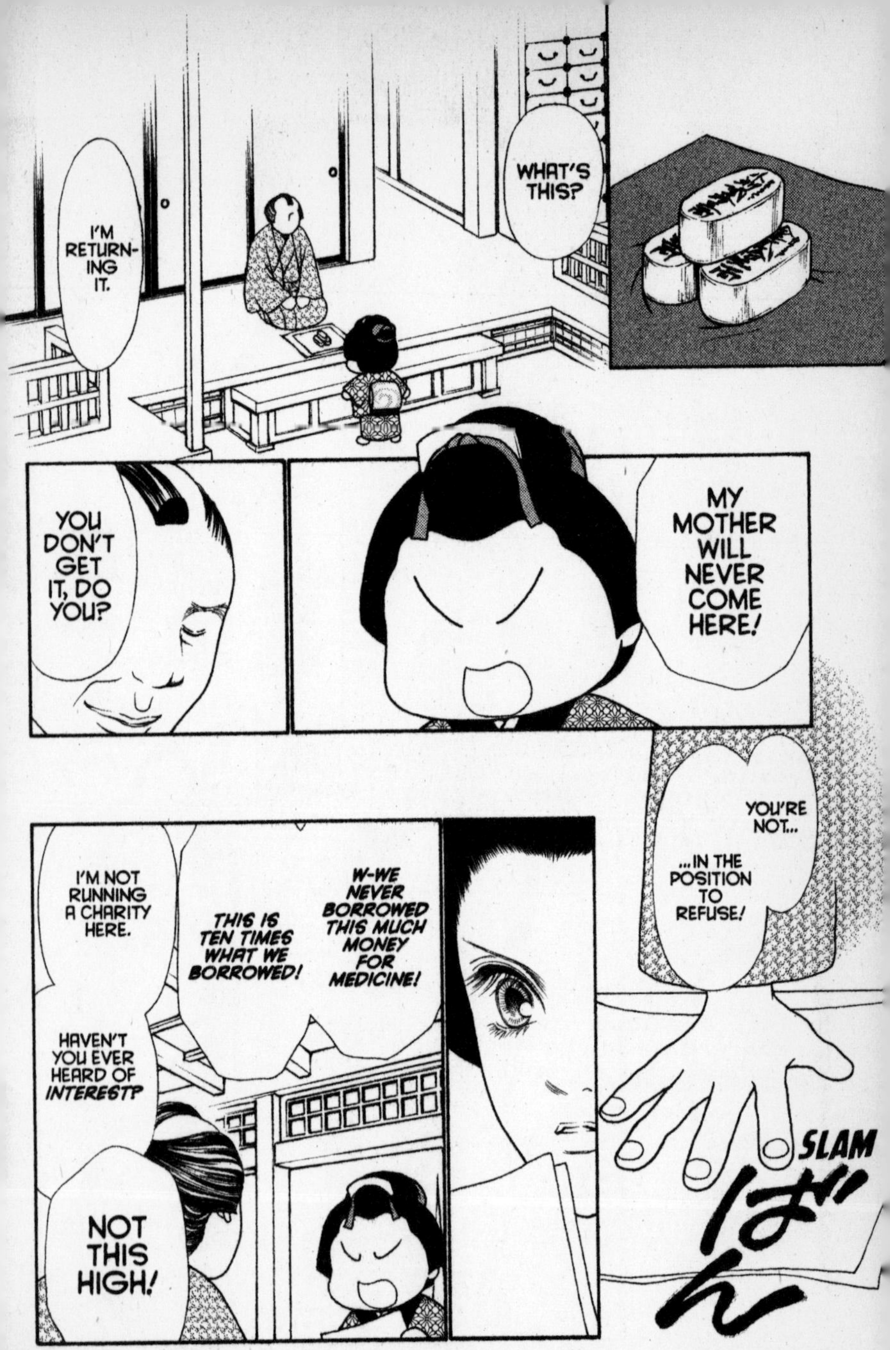
WHAT'S THIS?
I'M RETURNING IT.
MY MOTHER WILL NEVER COME HERE!
YOU DON'T GET IT, DO YOU?
YOU'RE NOT...
...IN THE POSITION TO REFUSE!
SLAM
ばん
W-WE NEVER BORROWED THIS MUCH MONEY FOR MEDICINE!
THIS IS TEN TIMES WHAT WE BORROWED!
I'M NOT RUNNING A CHARITY HERE.
HAVEN'T YOU EVER HEARD OF *INTEREST*?
NOT THIS HIGH!

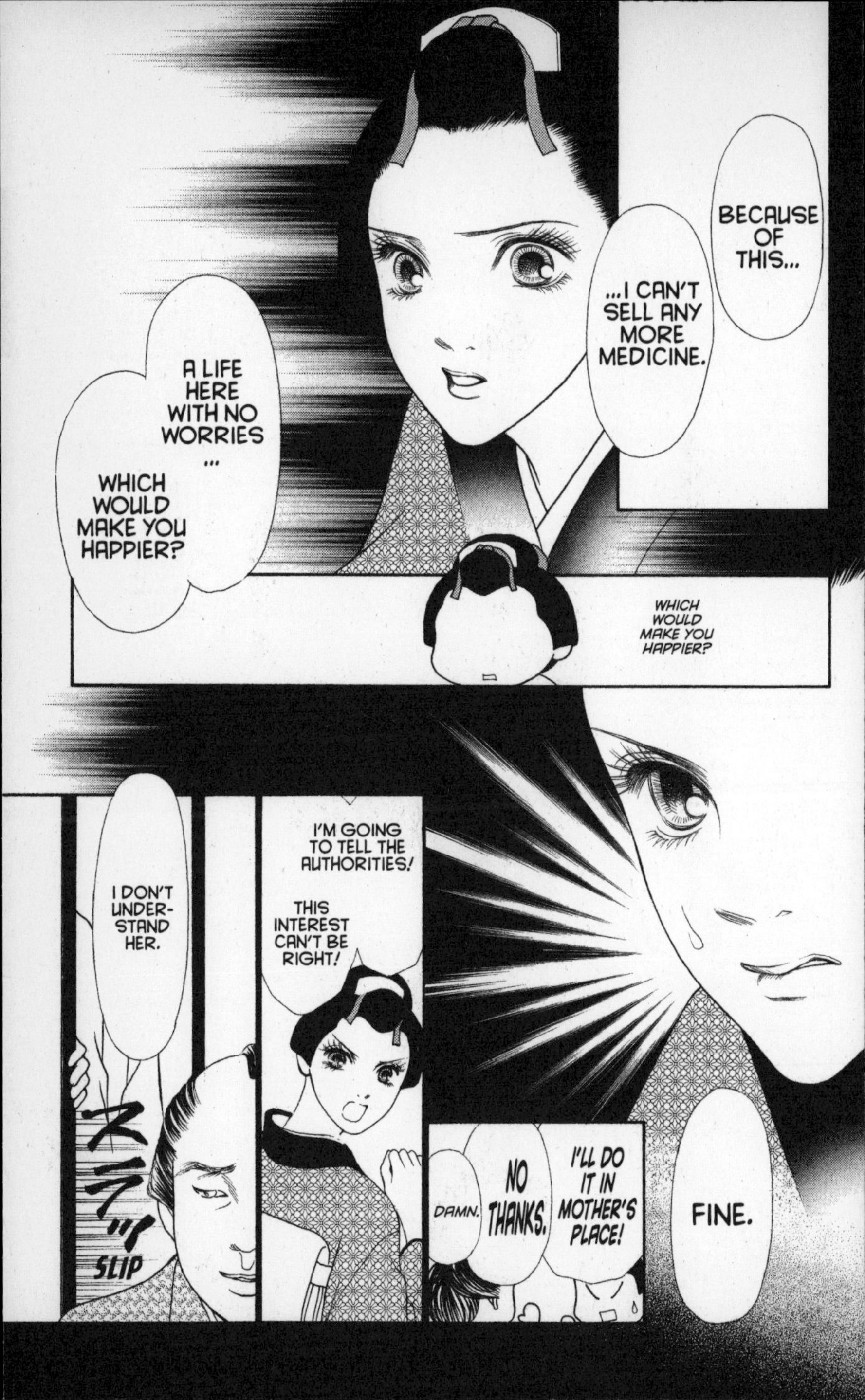
BECAUSE OF THIS...
...I CAN'T SELL ANY MORE MEDICINE.
A LIFE HERE WITH NO WORRIES ... WHICH WOULD MAKE YOU HAPPIER?
WHICH WOULD MAKE YOU HAPPIER?
FINE.
I'LL DO IT IN MOTHER'S PLACE!
NO THANKS.
DAMN.
I'M GOING TO TELL THE AUTHORITIES!
THIS INTEREST CAN'T BE RIGHT!
I DON'T UNDER-STAND HER.
SLIP

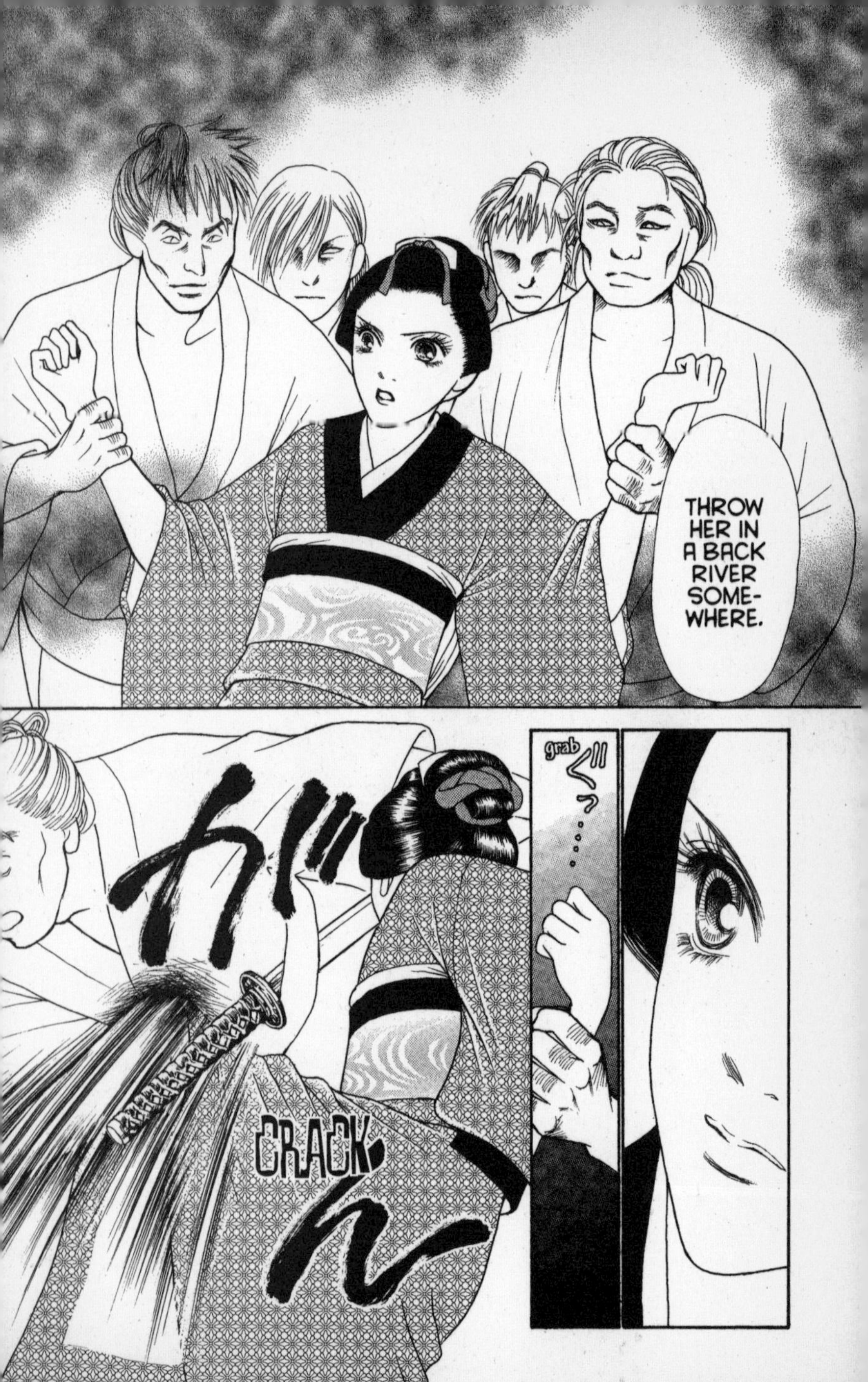
THROW HER IN A BACK RIVER SOME-WHERE.
grab
CRACK

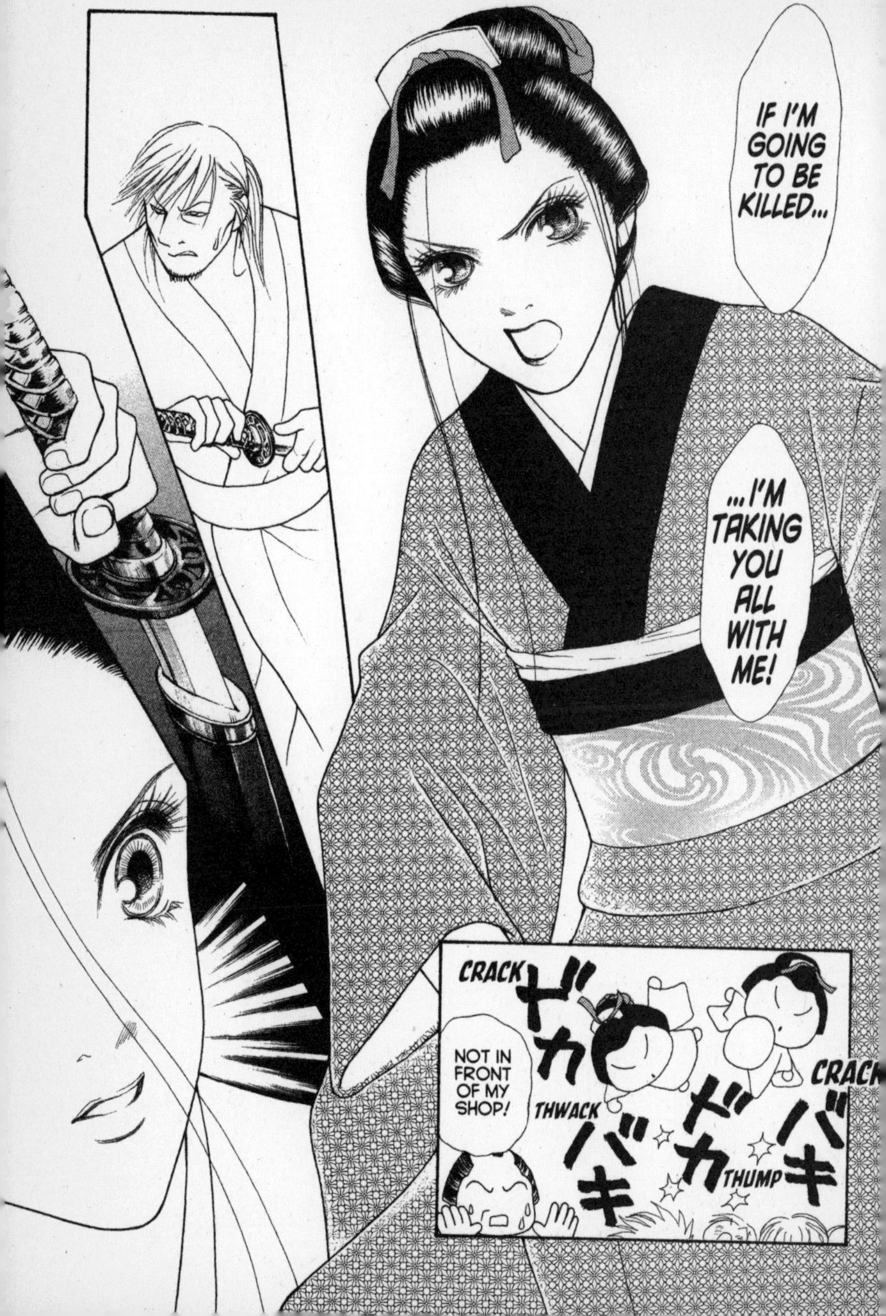
IF I'M GOING TO BE KILLED...
...I'M TAKING YOU ALL WITH ME!
CRACK
バキ
THUMP
ドカ
バキ
THWACK
CRACK
ドカ
NOT IN FRONT OF MY SHOP!

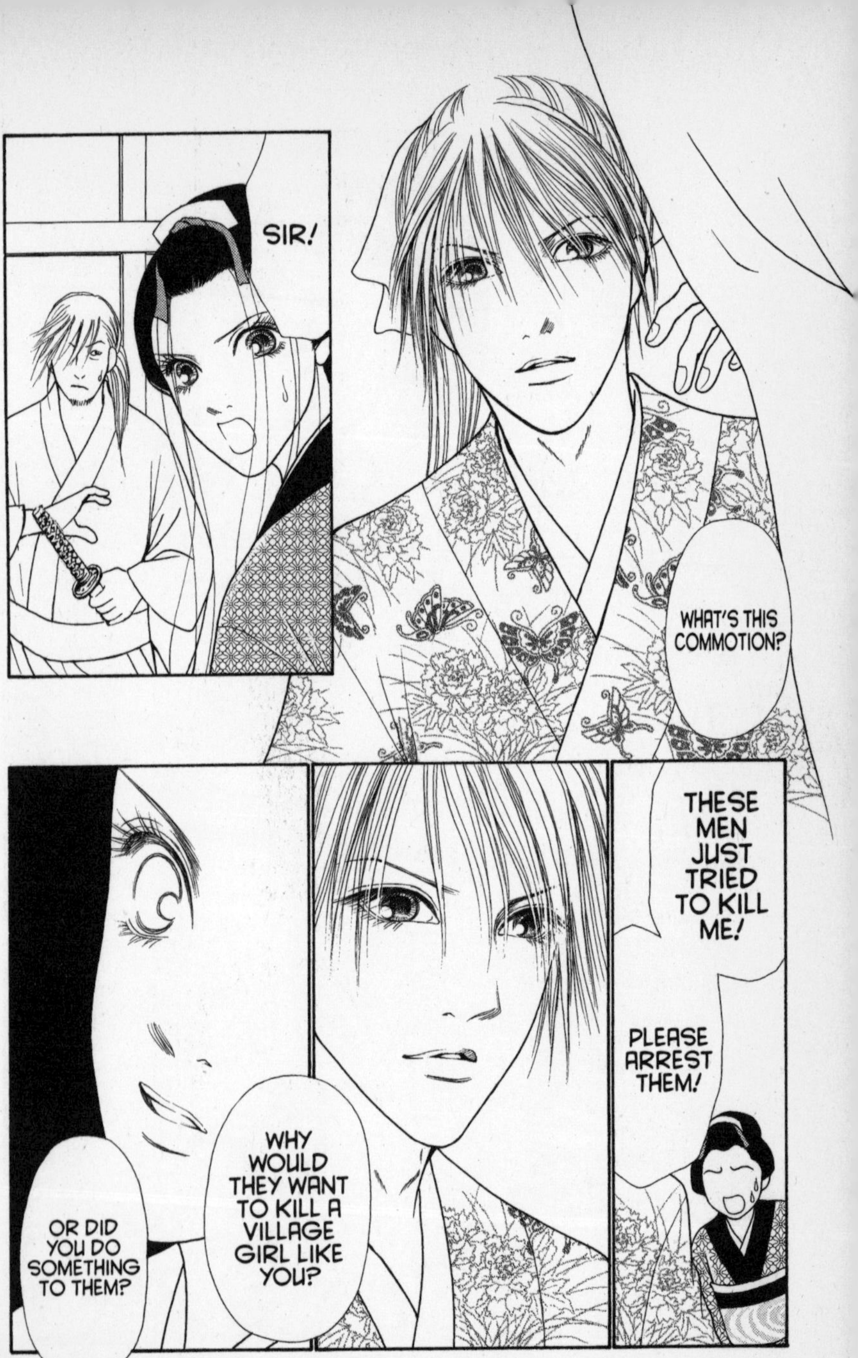
WHAT'S THIS COMMOTION?
SIR!
THESE MEN JUST TRIED TO KILL ME!
PLEASE ARREST THEM!
WHY WOULD THEY WANT TO KILL A VILLAGE GIRL LIKE YOU?
OR DID YOU DO SOMETHING TO THEM?

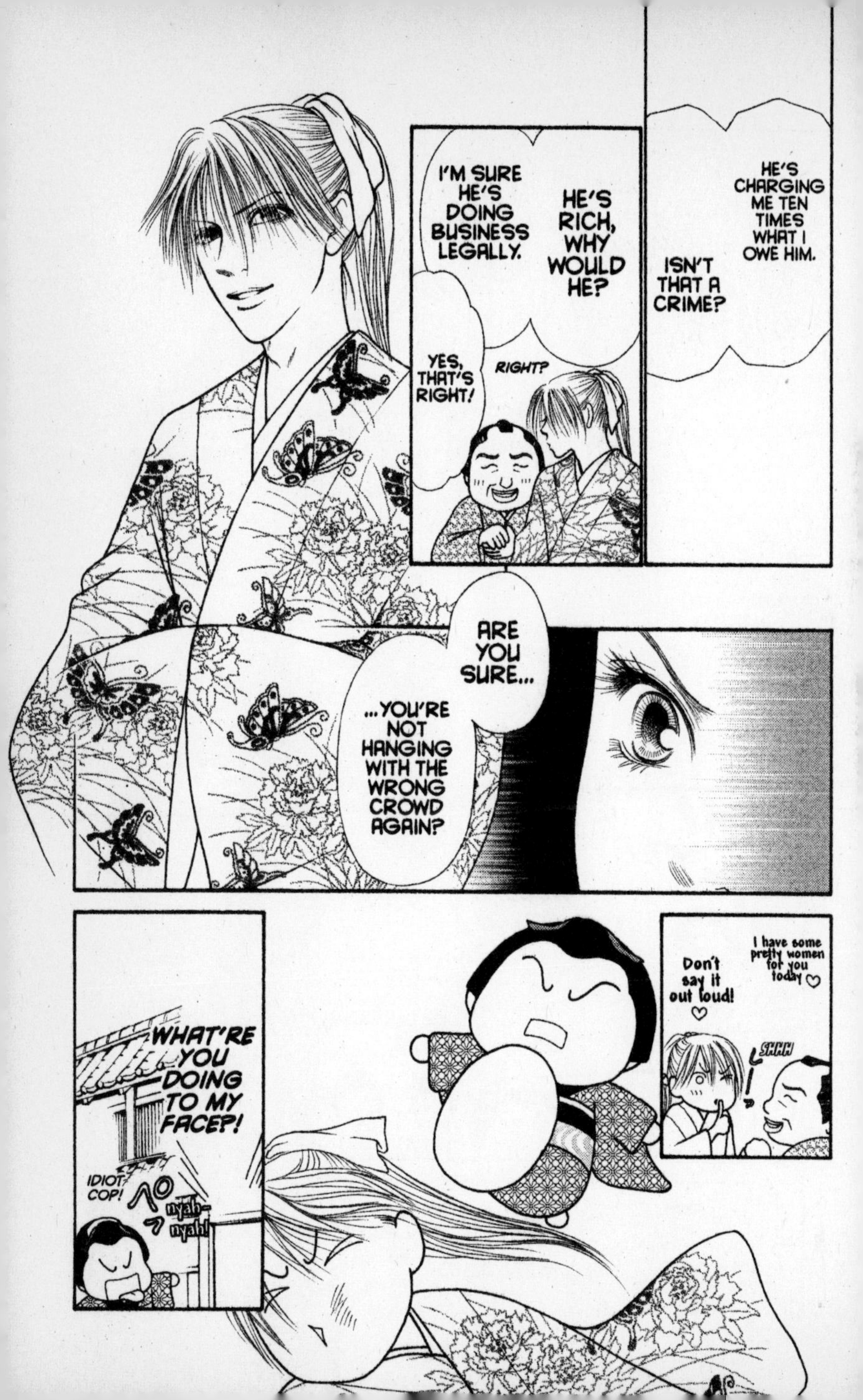
HE'S CHARGING ME TEN TIMES WHAT I OWE HIM.
ISN'T THAT A CRIME?
HE'S RICH, WHY WOULD HE?
I'M SURE HE'S DOING BUSINESS LEGALLY.
RIGHT?
YES, THAT'S RIGHT!
ARE YOU SURE...
...YOU'RE NOT HANGING WITH THE WRONG CROWD AGAIN?
I have some pretty women for you today ♡
Don't say it out loud! ♡
SHHH
WHAT'RE YOU DOING TO MY FACE?!
IDIOT COP!
nyah-nyah!

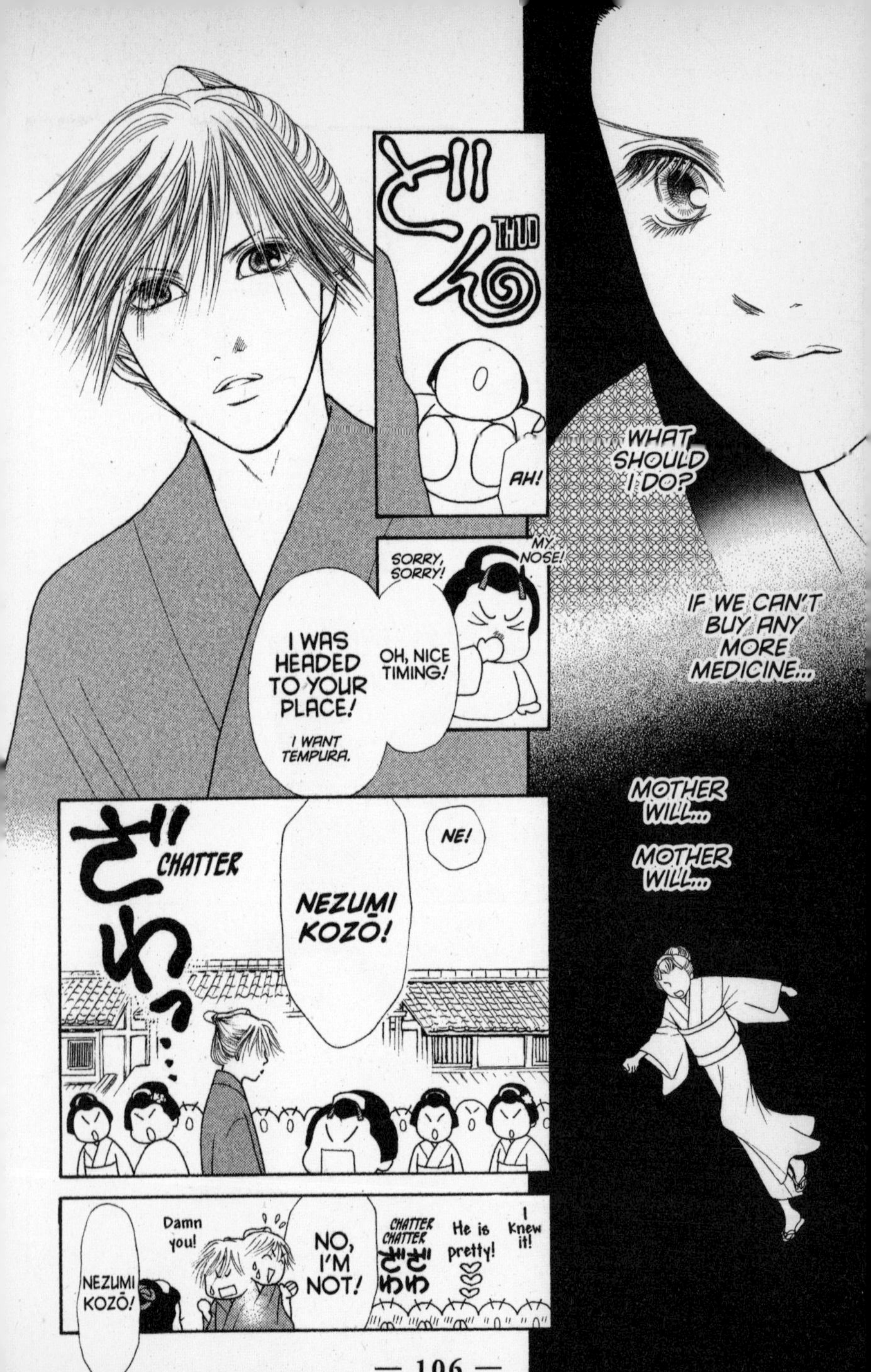
WHAT SHOULD I DO?
IF WE CAN'T BUY ANY MORE MEDICINE...
MOTHER WILL...
MOTHER WILL...
どん THUD
AH!
MY NOSE!
SORRY, SORRY!
OH, NICE TIMING!
I WAS HEADED TO YOUR PLACE!
I WANT TEMPURA.
NE!
NEZUMI KOZŌ!
ざわっ CHATTER
I knew it!
He is pretty!
ざざわわ CHATTER CHATTER
NO, I'M NOT!
Damn you!
NEZUMI KOZŌ!

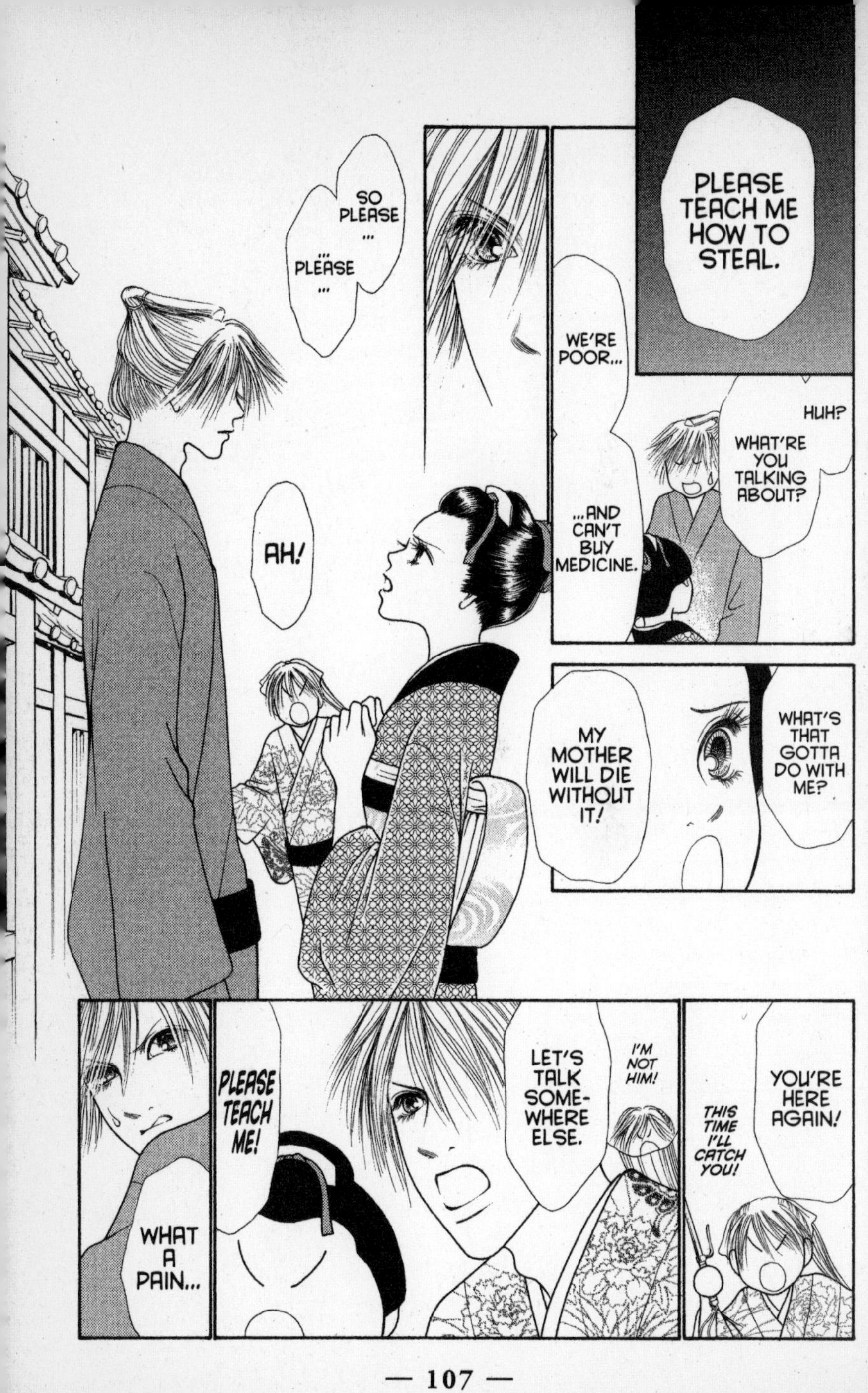
PLEASE TEACH ME HOW TO STEAL.
HUH?
WHAT'RE YOU TALKING ABOUT?
WE'RE POOR...
...AND CAN'T BUY MEDICINE.
WHAT'S THAT GOTTA DO WITH ME?
MY MOTHER WILL DIE WITHOUT IT!
SO PLEASE ...
... PLEASE ...
AH!
YOU'RE HERE AGAIN!
THIS TIME I'LL CATCH YOU!
I'M NOT HIM!
LET'S TALK SOMEWHERE ELSE.
PLEASE TEACH ME!
WHAT A PAIN...

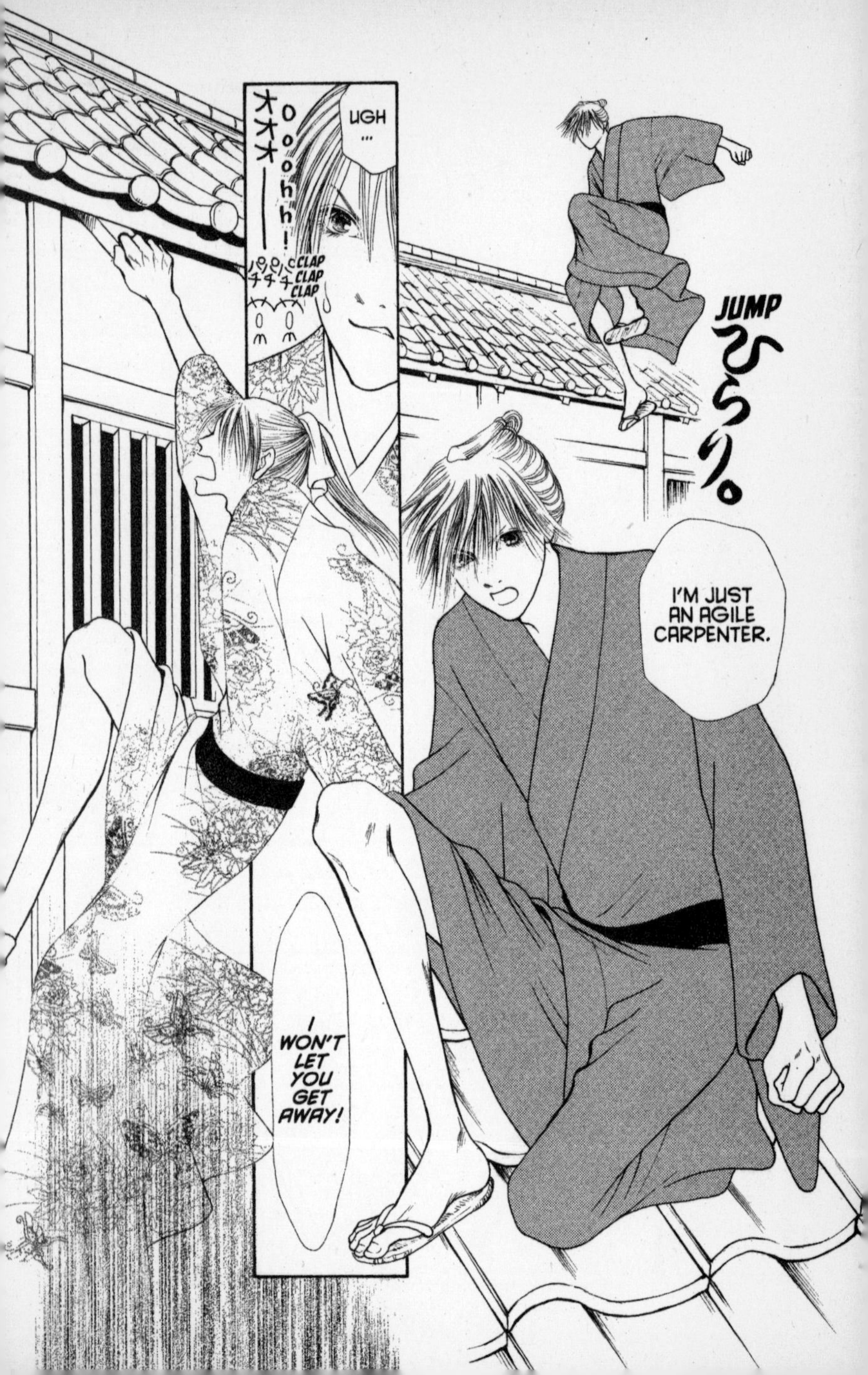
JUMP
ひらり。
I'M JUST AN AGILE CARPENTER.
UGH ...
Ooohh!
オオオーー
CLAP CLAP CLAP
パチパチ
I WON'T LET YOU GET AWAY!

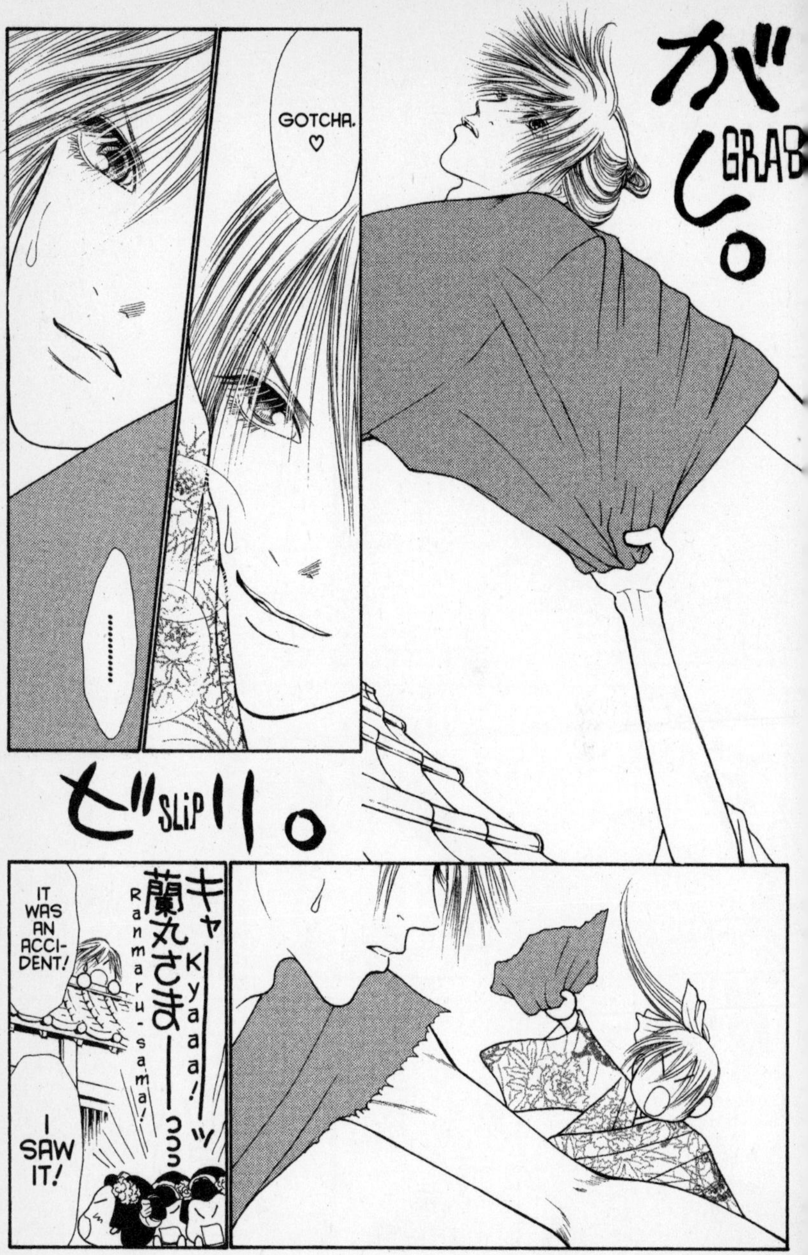
GRAB
GOTCHA. ♡
......
SLIP
キャーッ 蘭丸さまーっっっ
Kyaaa!! Ranmaru-sama!
IT WAS AN ACCIDENT!
I SAW IT!

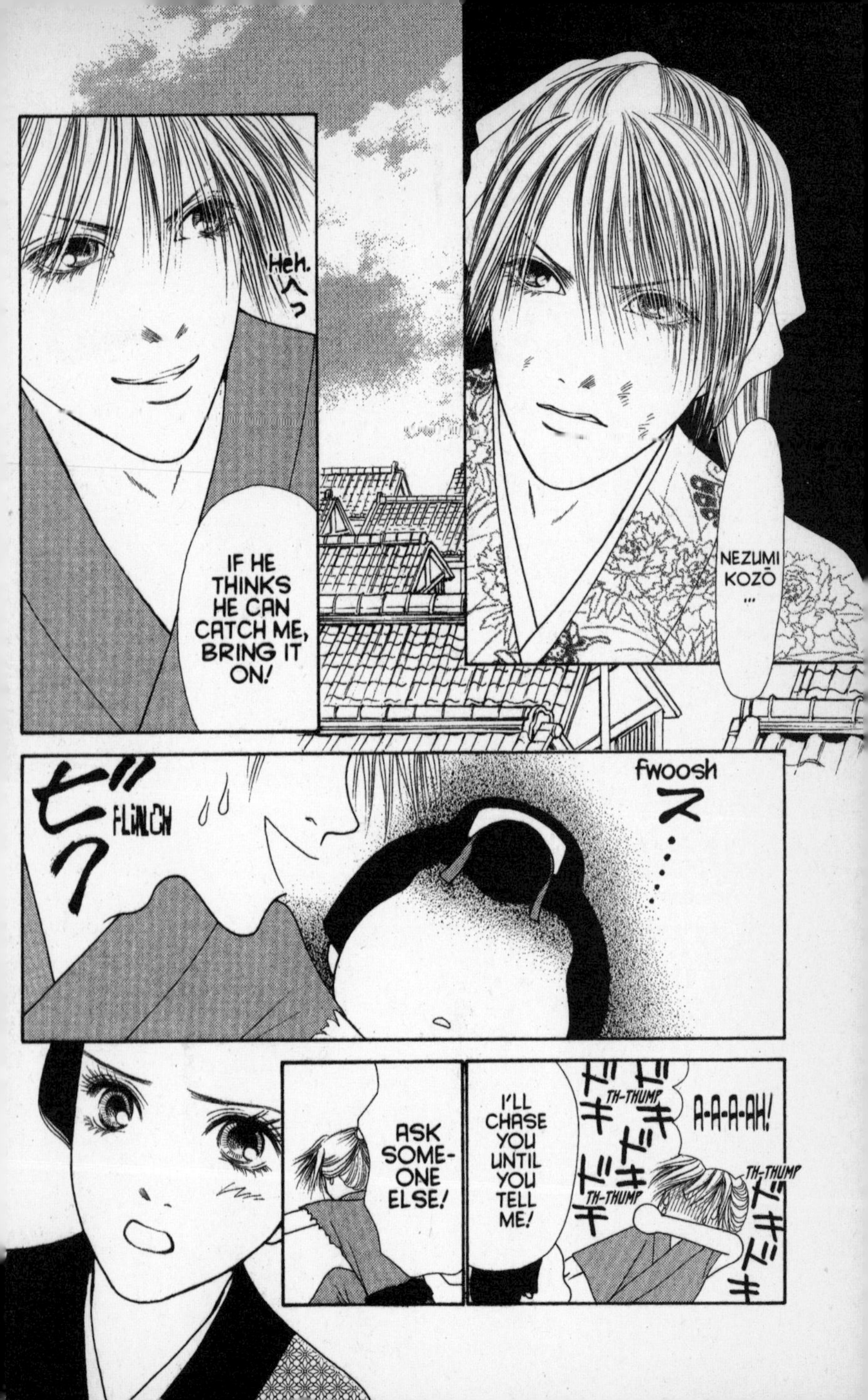
NEZUMI KOZŌ ...
Heh. へっ
IF HE THINKS HE CAN CATCH ME, BRING IT ON!
fwoosh ス…
ビクッ FLINCH
A-A-A-AH!
I'LL CHASE YOU UNTIL YOU TELL ME!
TH-THUMP ドキドキ
TH-THUMP ドキドキ
TH-THUMP ドキドキ
ASK SOME-ONE ELSE!

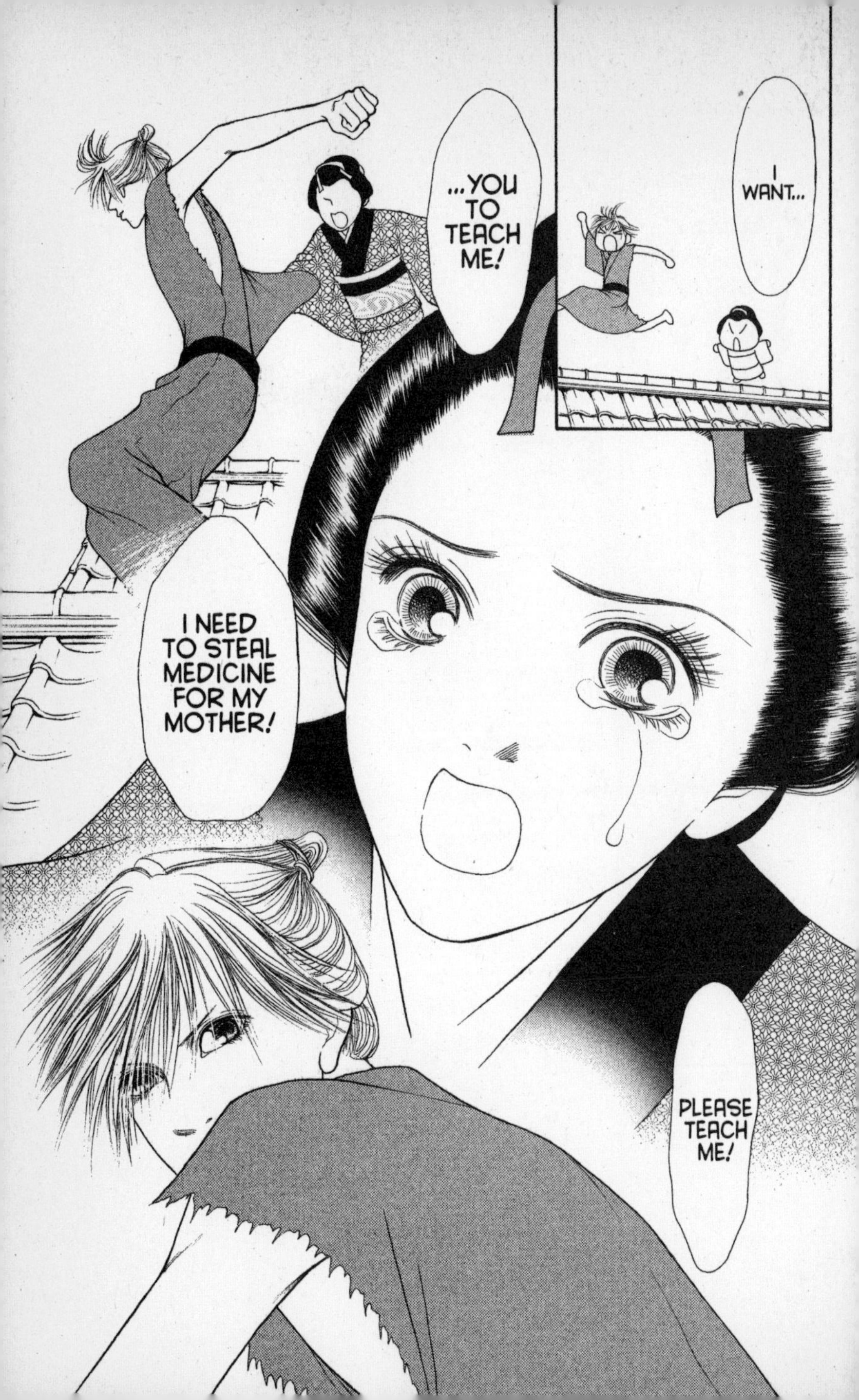
I WANT...
...YOU TO TEACH ME!
I NEED TO STEAL MEDICINE FOR MY MOTHER!
PLEASE TEACH ME!

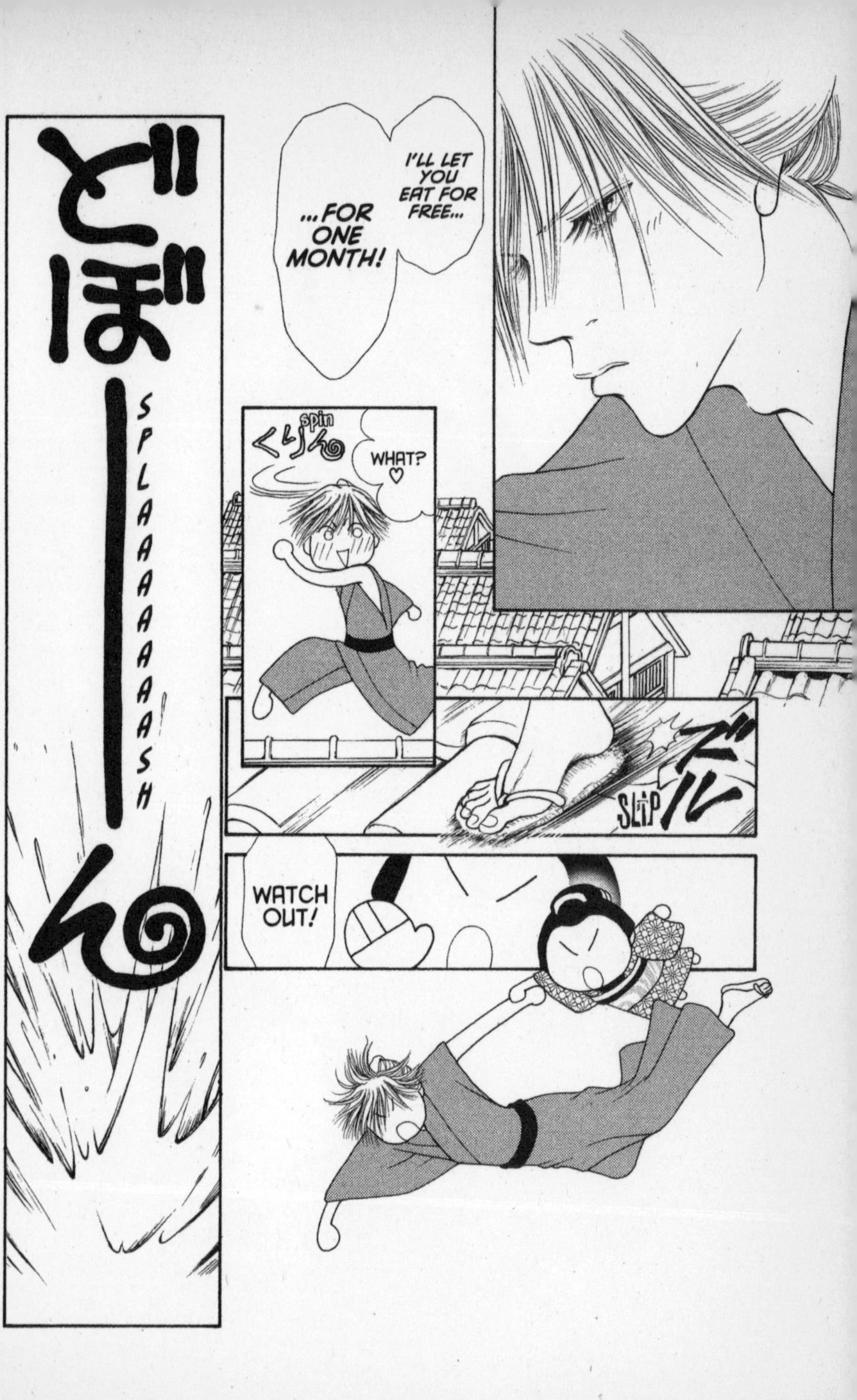
I'LL LET YOU EAT FOR FREE...
...FOR ONE MONTH!
spin
くるりん
WHAT? ♡
ズル
SLIP
WATCH OUT!
どぼーん
SPLAAAAAAAAASH

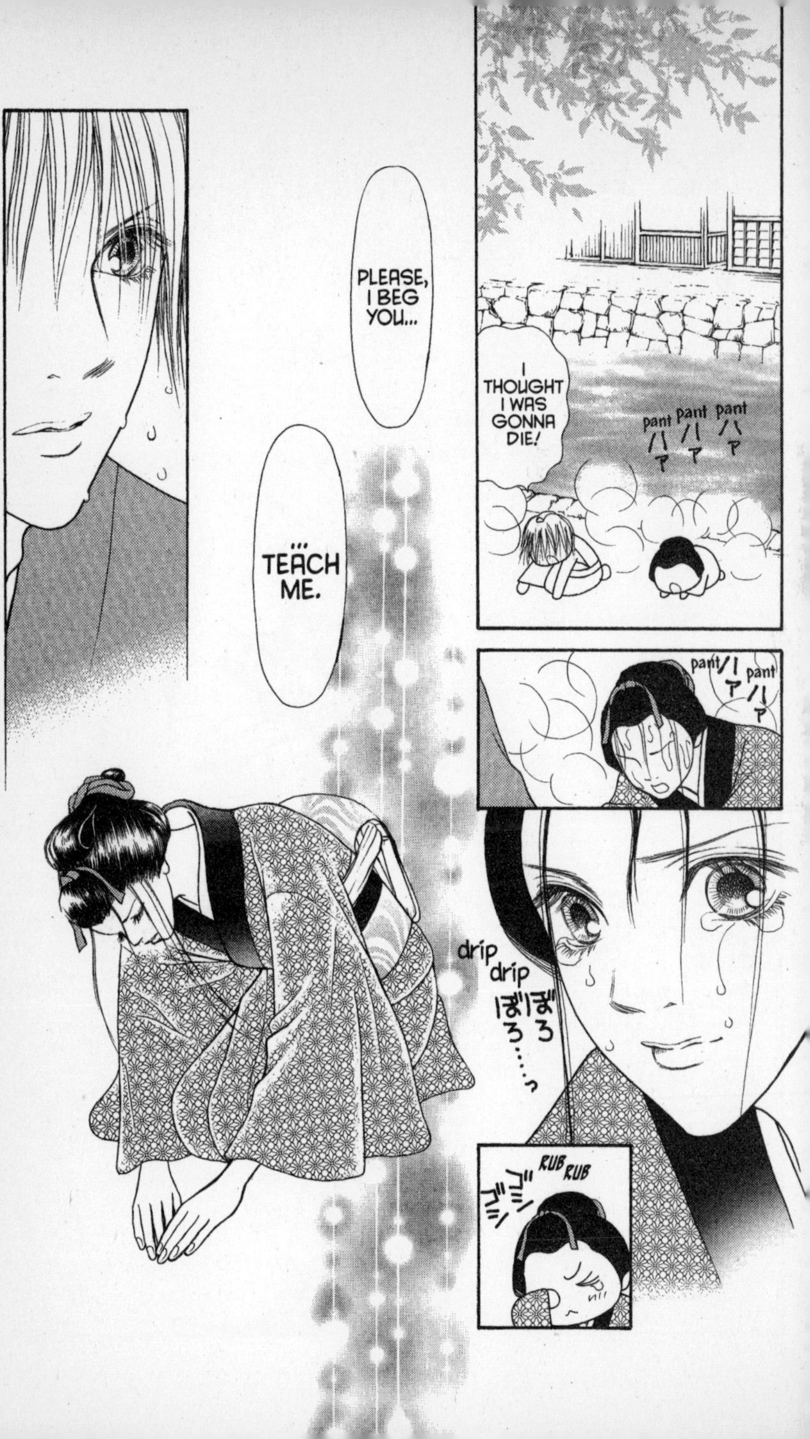
I THOUGHT I WAS GONNA DIE!
pant ハア pant ハア pant ハア
pant ハア pant ハア
drip drip ぼろぼろ…っ
RUB RUB ゴシゴシ
PLEASE, I BEG YOU...
...TEACH ME.

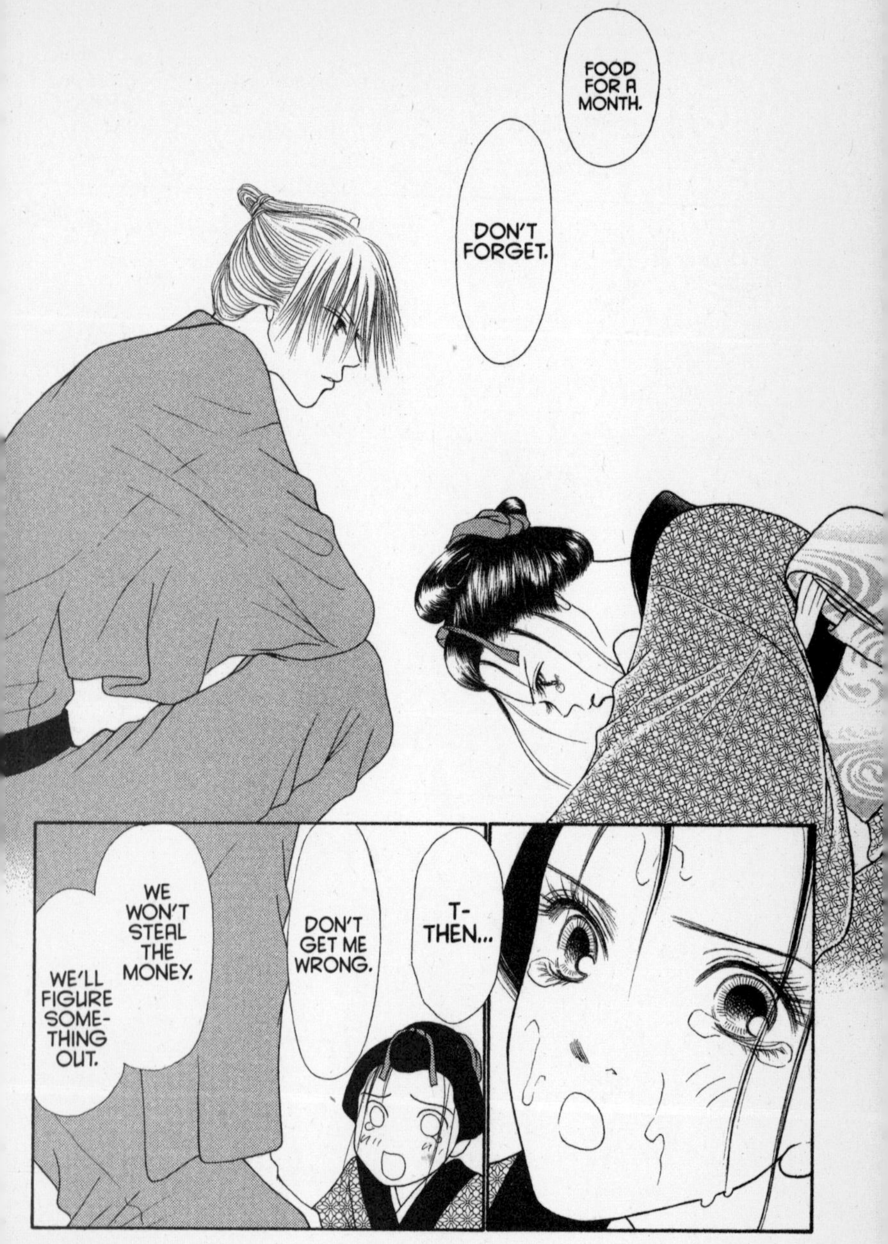
FOOD FOR A MONTH.
DON'T FORGET.
T-THEN...
DON'T GET ME WRONG.
WE WON'T STEAL THE MONEY.
WE'LL FIGURE SOME-THING OUT.

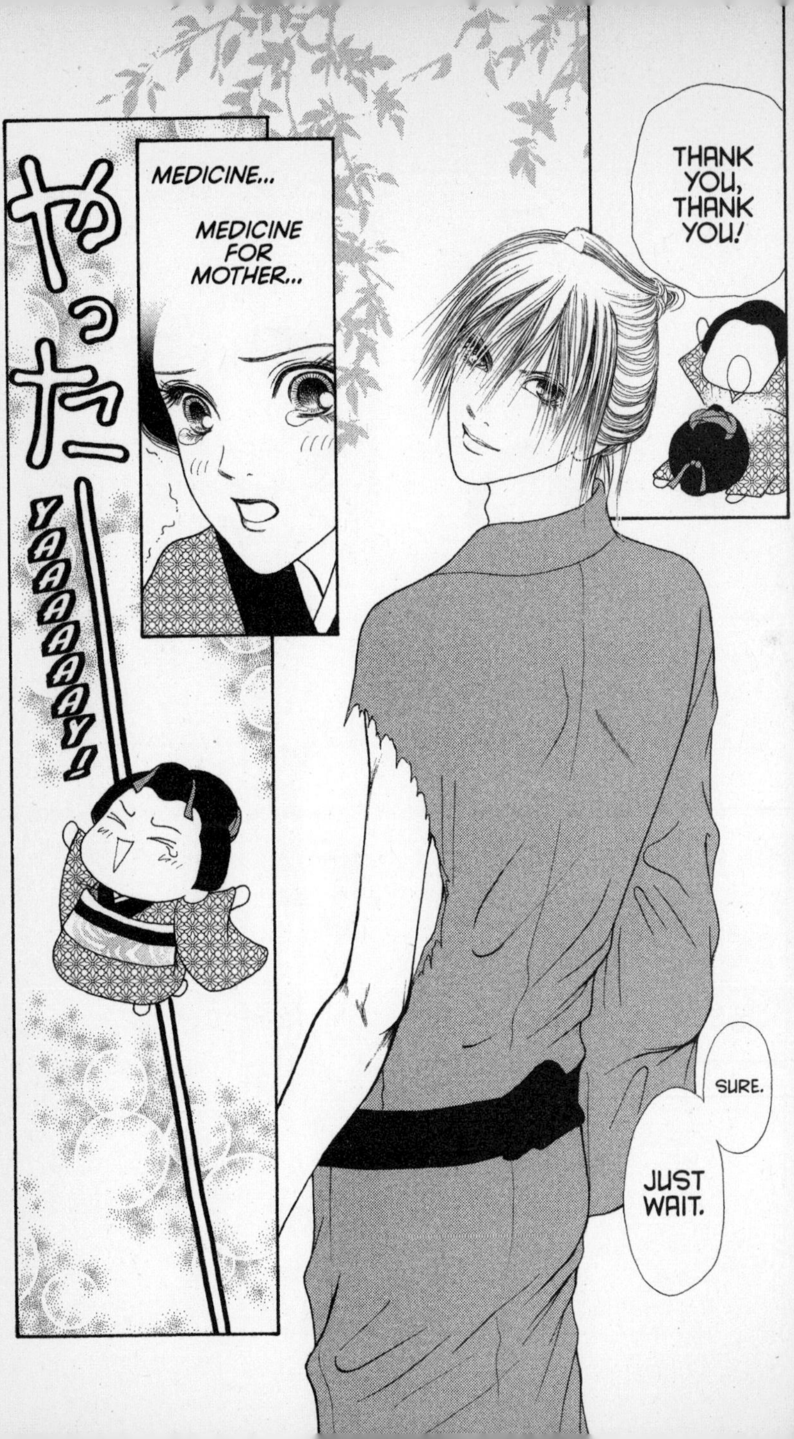
THANK YOU, THANK YOU!
SURE.
JUST WAIT.
MEDICINE...
MEDICINE FOR MOTHER...
やったー
YAAAAAAY!

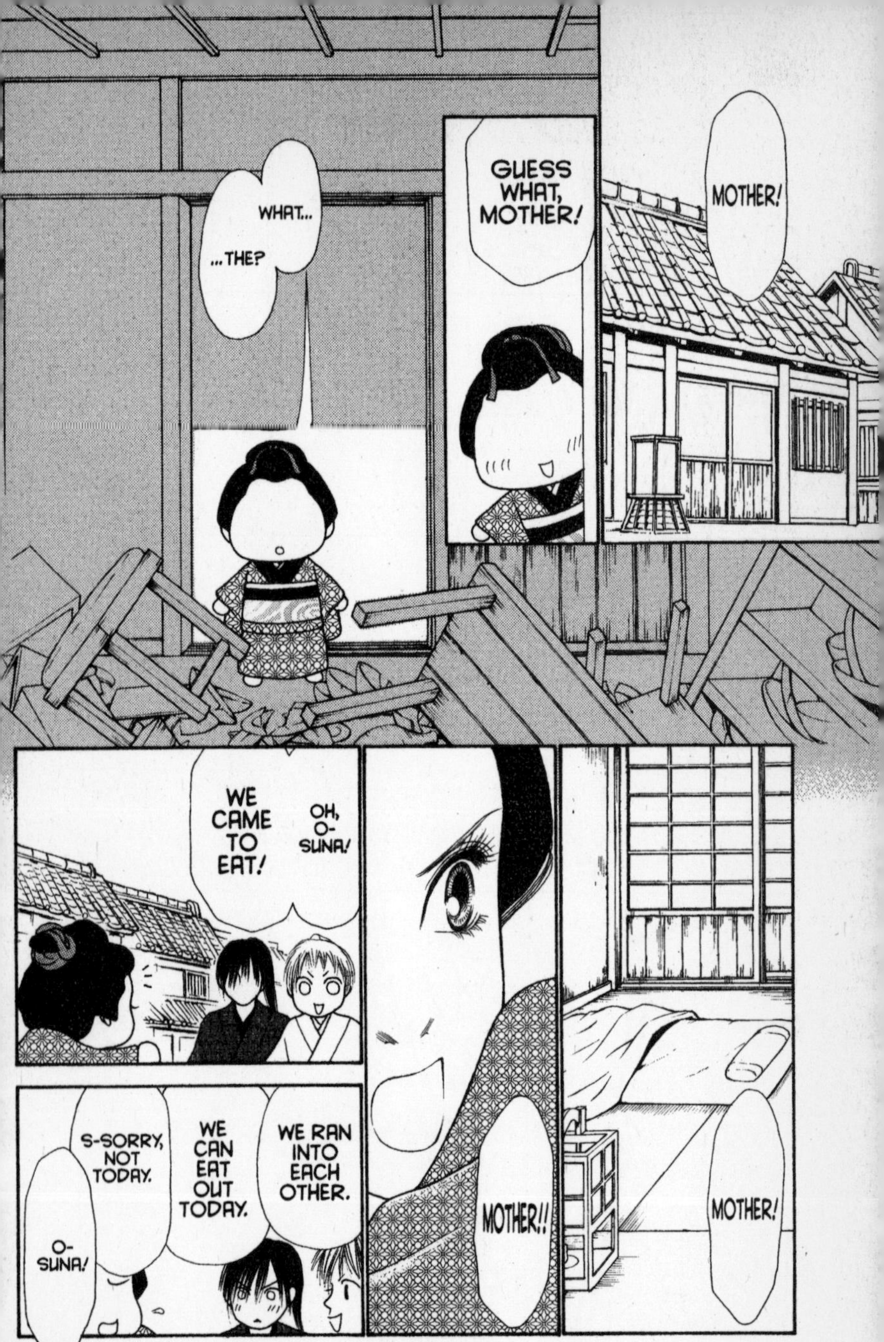
MOTHER!
GUESS WHAT, MOTHER!
WHAT...
...THE?
MOTHER!
MOTHER!!
OH, O-SUNA!
WE CAME TO EAT!
WE RAN INTO EACH OTHER.
WE CAN EAT OUT TODAY.
S-SORRY, NOT TODAY.
O-SUNA!

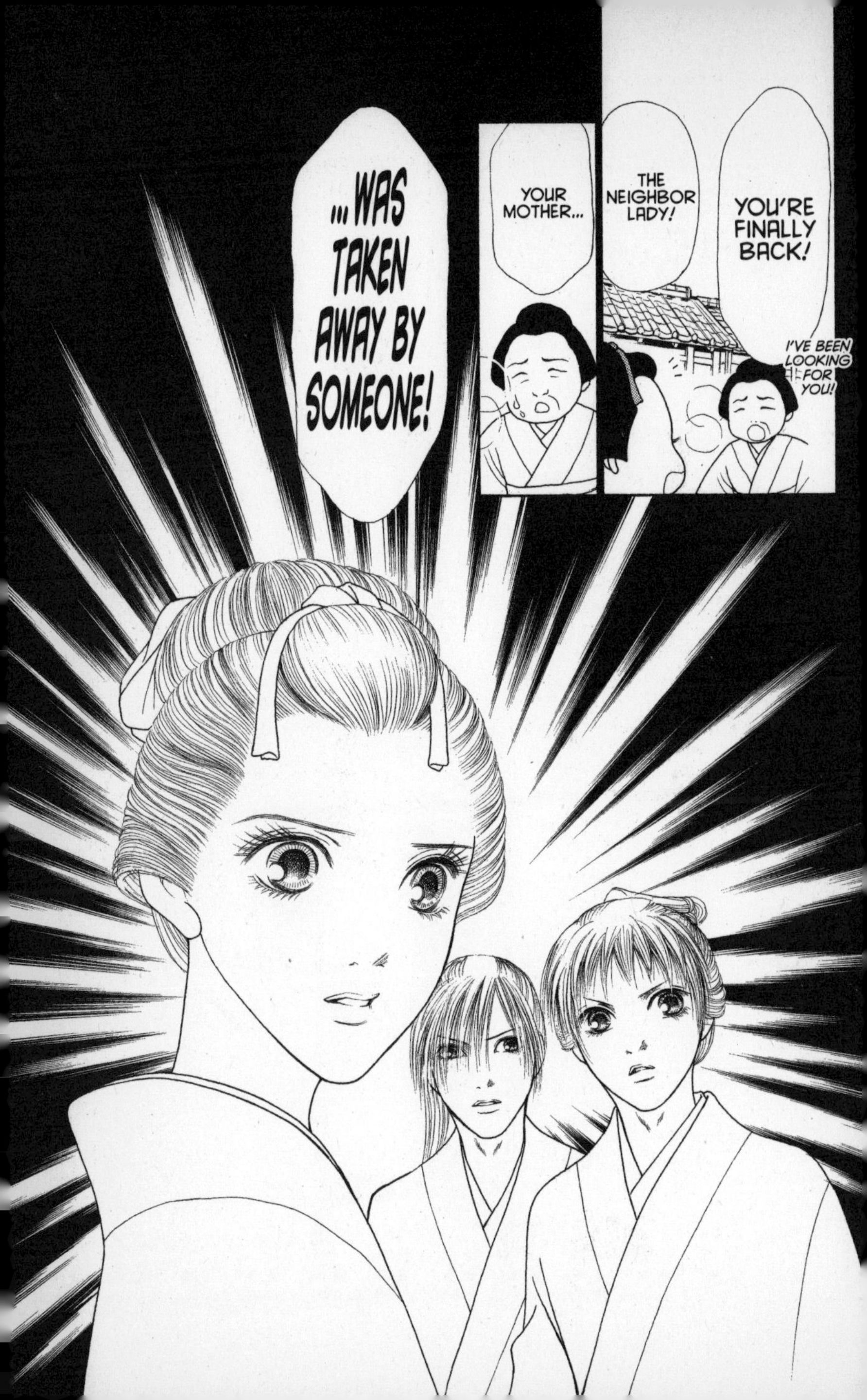
YOU'RE FINALLY BACK!
I'VE BEEN LOOKING FOR YOU!
THE NEIGHBOR LADY!
YOUR MOTHER...
...WAS TAKEN AWAY BY SOMEONE!

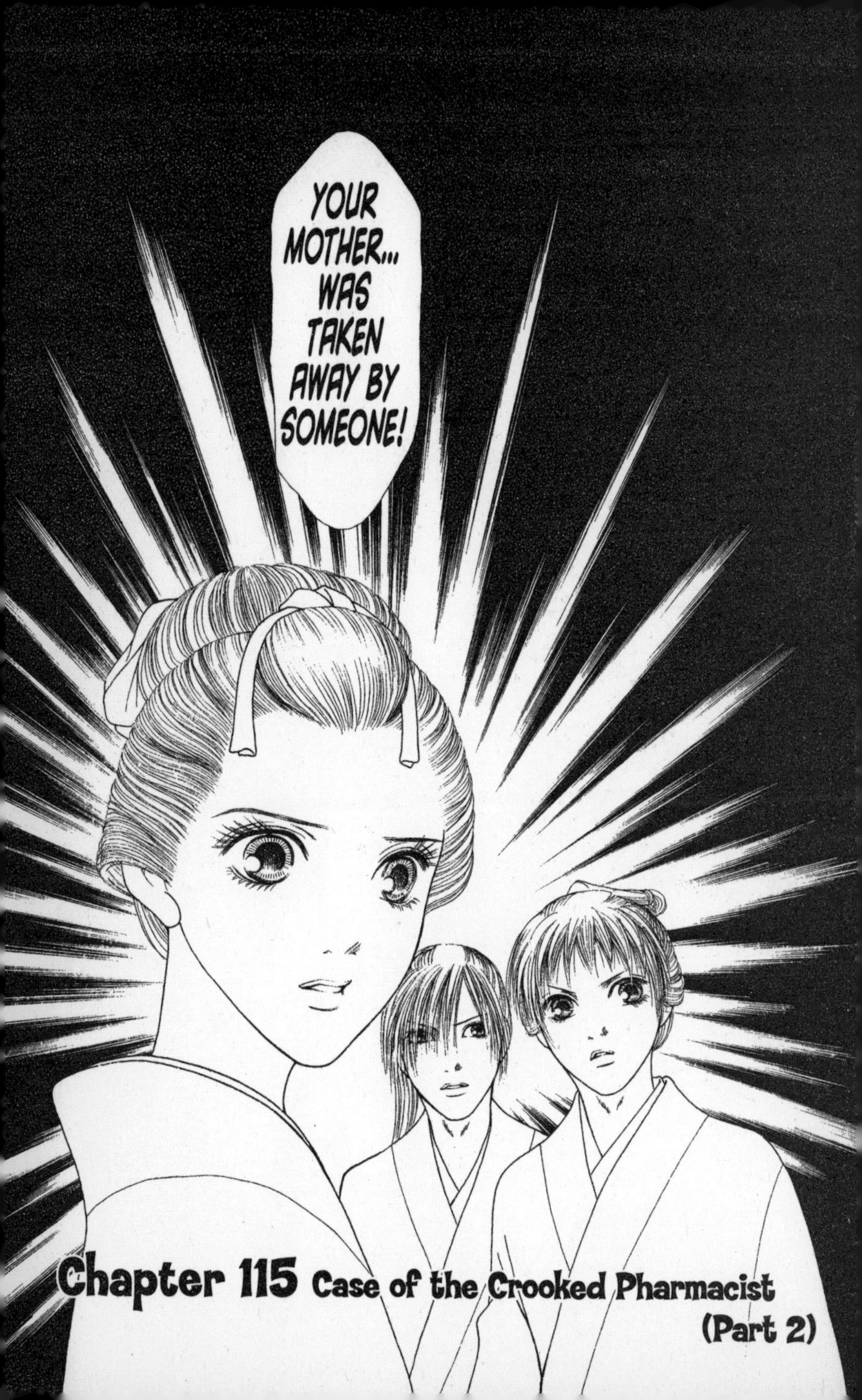
YOUR MOTHER... WAS TAKEN AWAY BY SOMEONE!

Chapter 115 Case of the Crooked Pharmacist (Part 2)

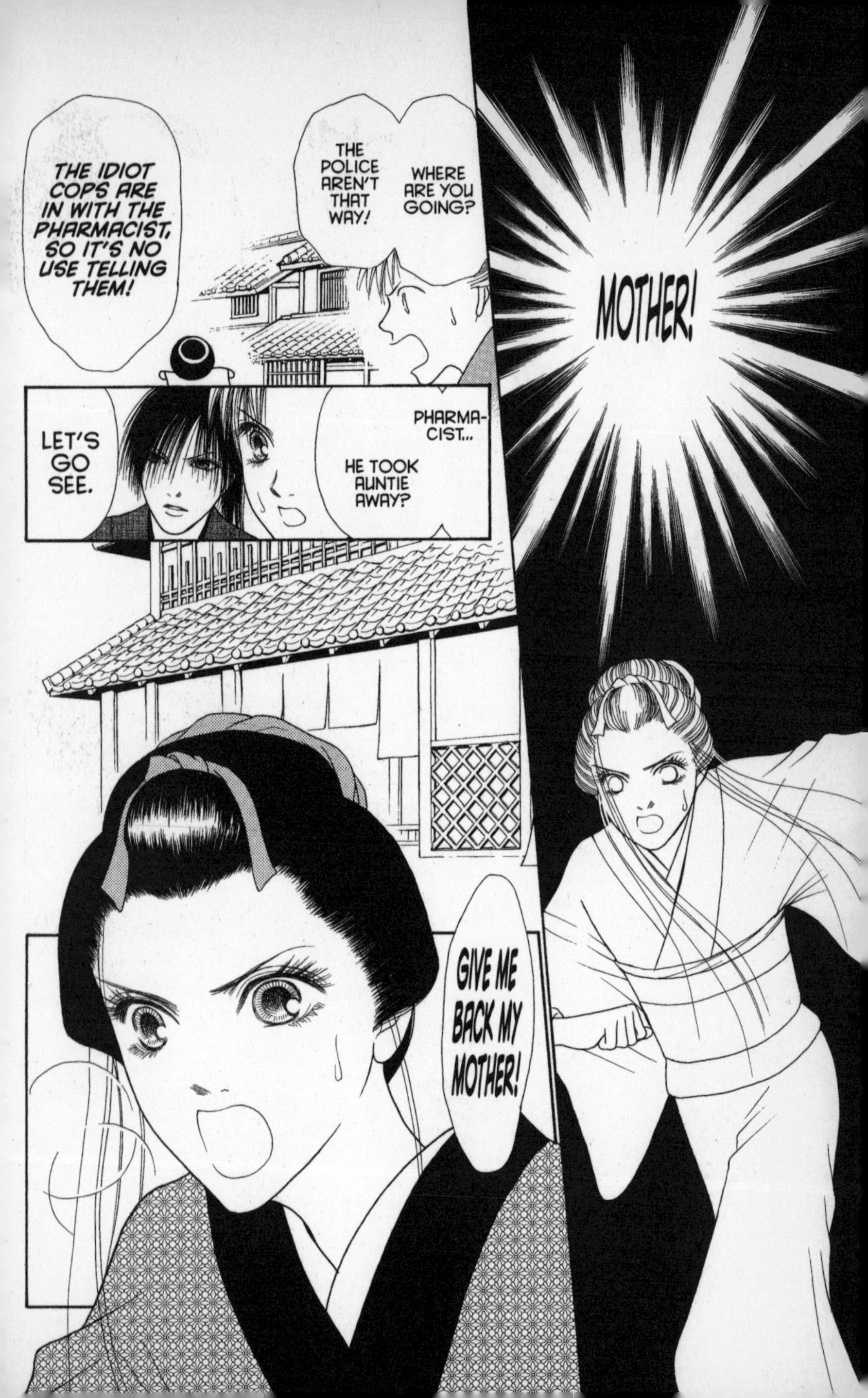
MOTHER!
WHERE ARE YOU GOING?
THE POLICE AREN'T THAT WAY!
THE IDIOT COPS ARE IN WITH THE PHARMACIST, SO IT'S NO USE TELLING THEM!
PHARMA-CIST...
HE TOOK AUNTIE AWAY?
LET'S GO SEE.
GIVE ME BACK MY MOTHER!

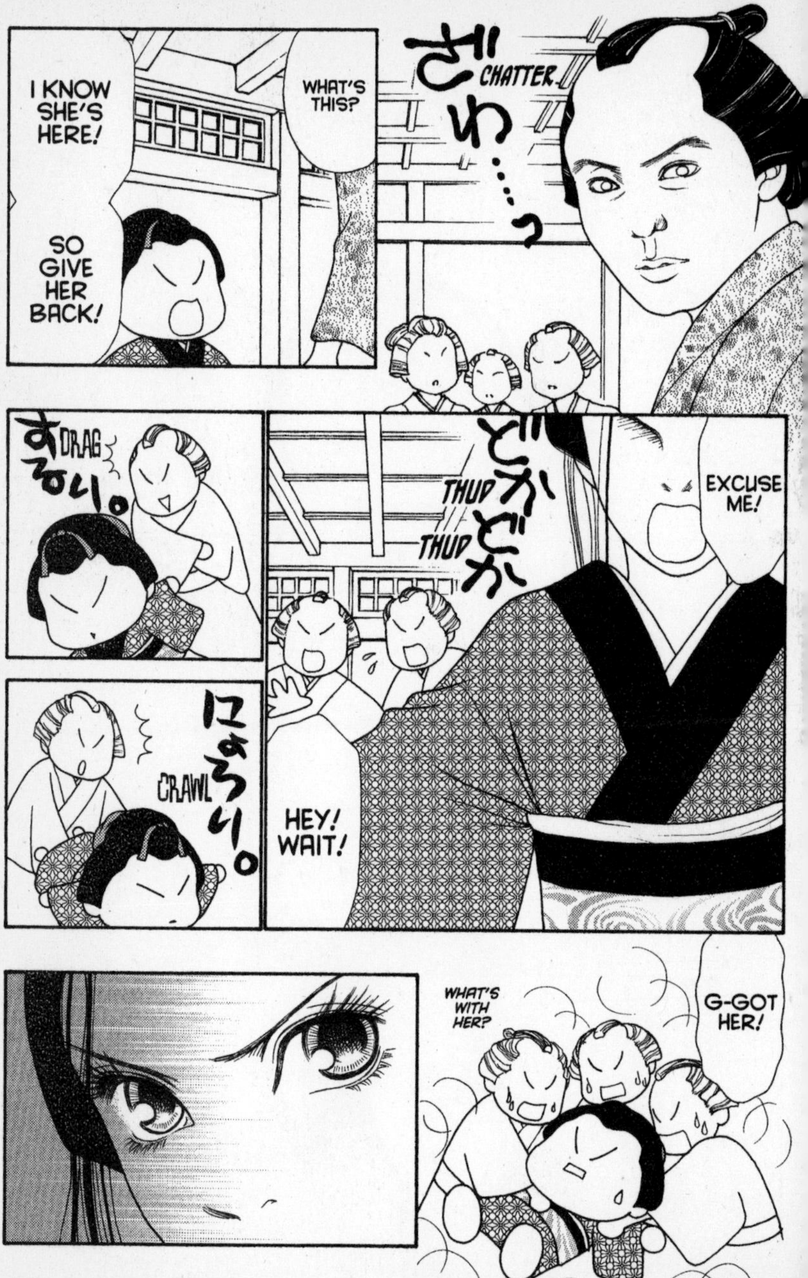
ざわ…っ
CHATTER
WHAT'S THIS?
I KNOW SHE'S HERE!
SO GIVE HER BACK!
EXCUSE ME!
どかどか
THUD THUD
HEY! WAIT!
するり。
DRAG
にょろり。
CRAWL
G-GOT HER!
WHAT'S WITH HER?

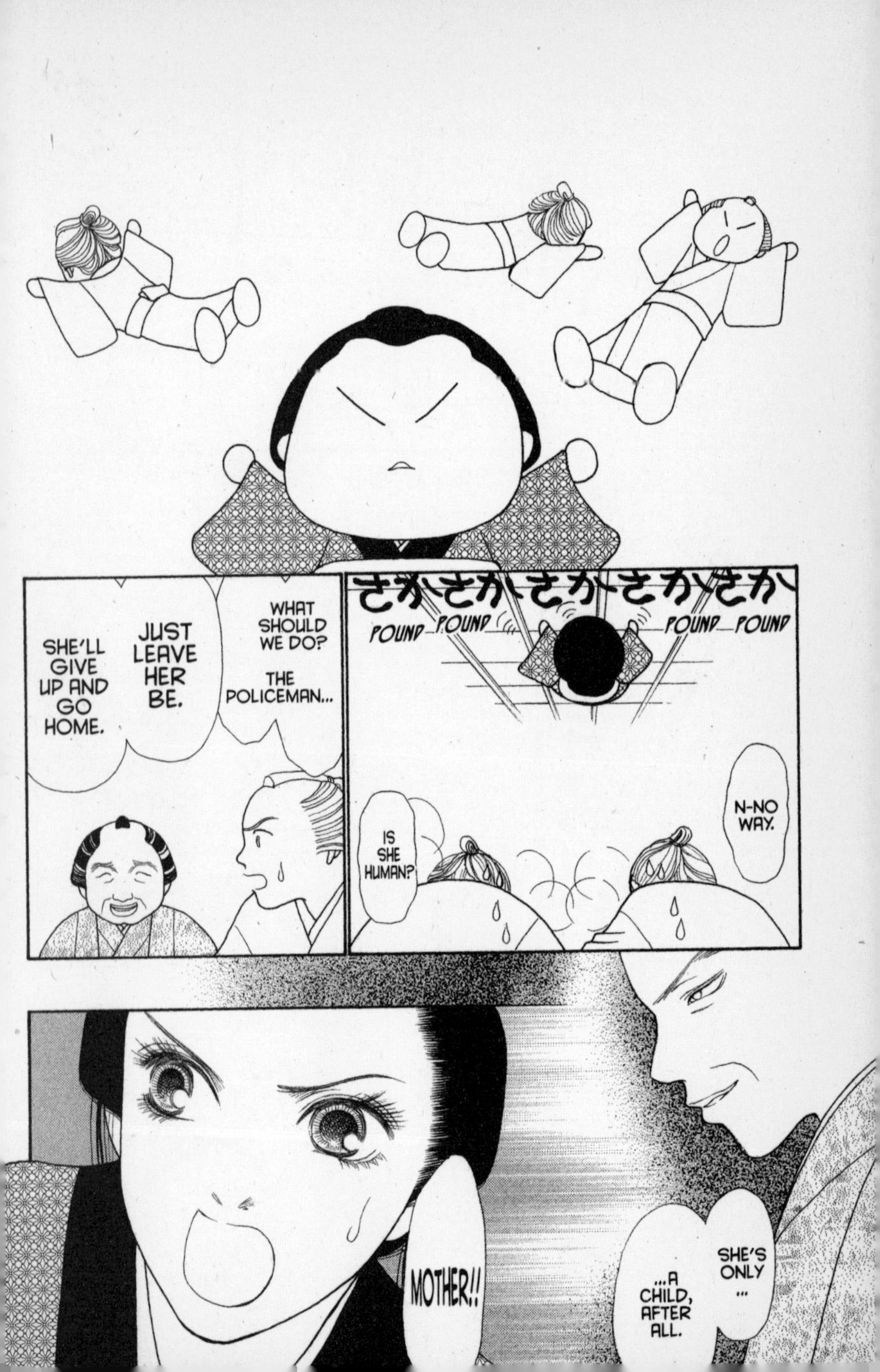
さかさかさかさかさか
POUND POUND POUND POUND
N-NO WAY.
IS SHE HUMAN?
WHAT SHOULD WE DO? THE POLICEMAN...
JUST LEAVE HER BE.
SHE'LL GIVE UP AND GO HOME.
SHE'S ONLY ...
...A CHILD, AFTER ALL.
MOTHER!!

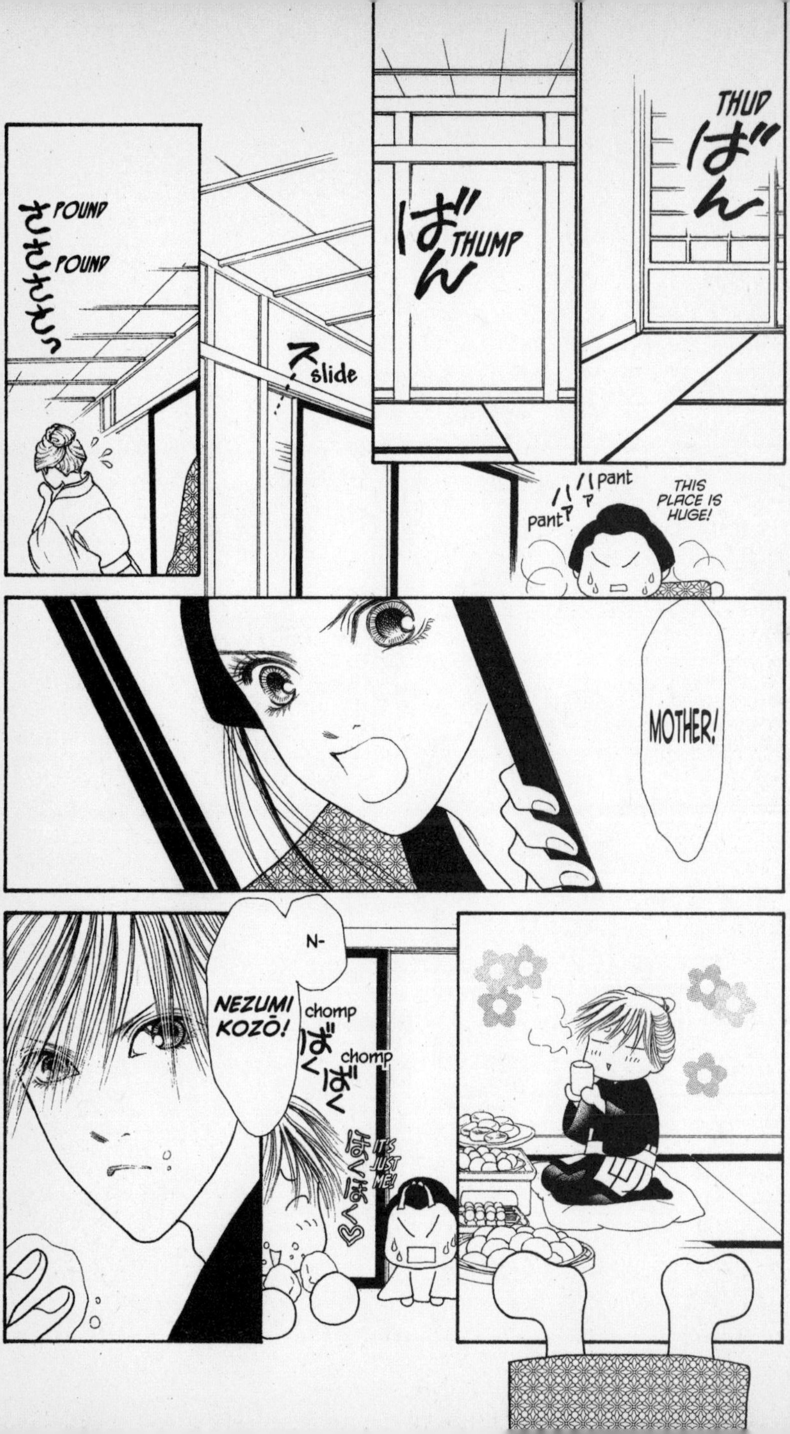
THUD
ばん
ばん
THUMP
ス
slide
さささとっ
POUND
POUND
ハァハァ
pant
pant
THIS PLACE IS HUGE!
MOTHER!
N-
NEZUMI KOZŌ!
ぱくぱく
chomp
chomp
ほくほく♡
IT'S JUST ME!

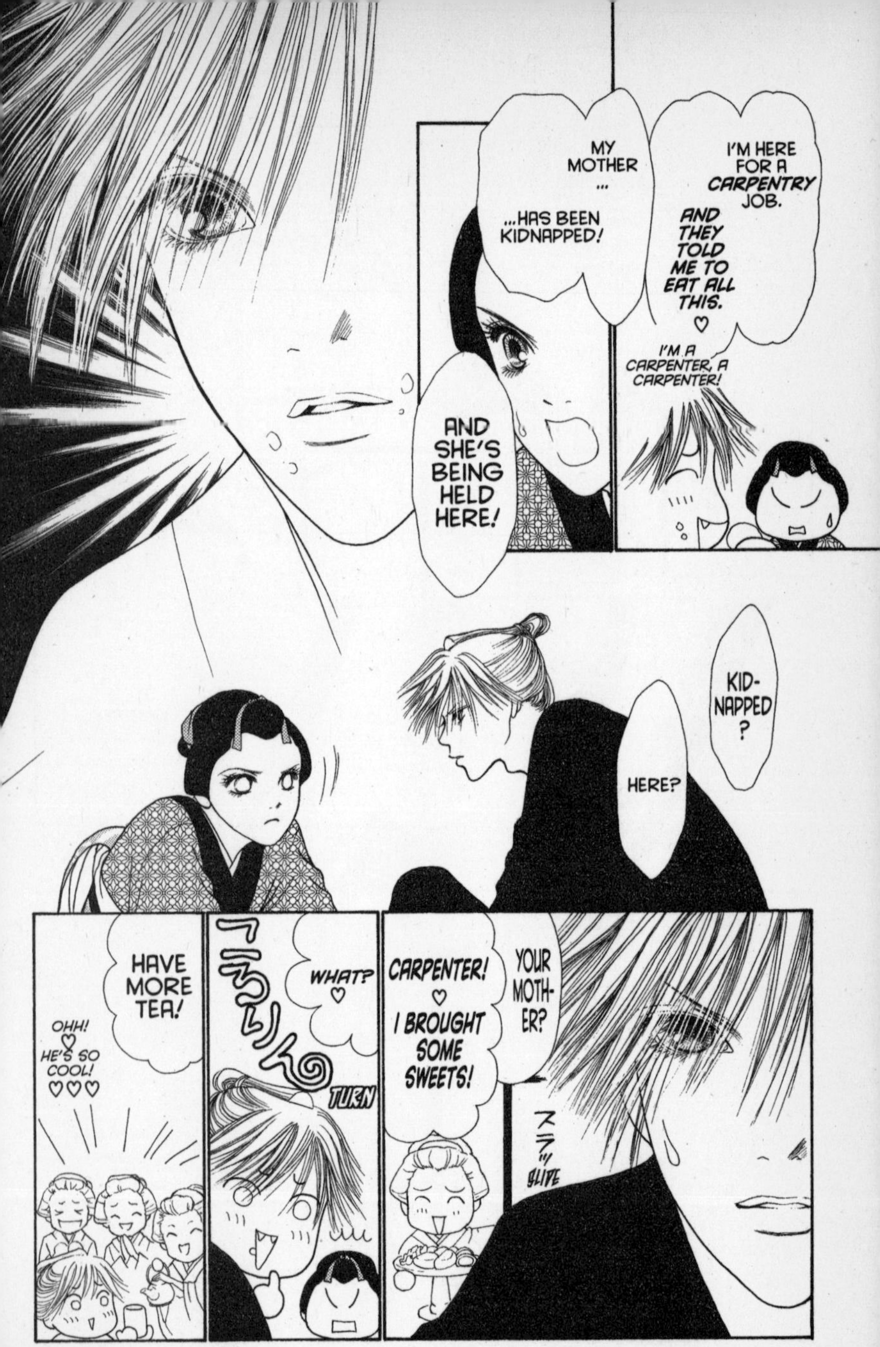

I'M HERE FOR A CARPENTRY JOB.
AND THEY TOLD ME TO EAT ALL THIS. ♡
I'M A CARPENTER, A CARPENTER!
MY MOTHER ...
...HAS BEEN KIDNAPPED!
AND SHE'S BEING HELD HERE!
KID-NAPPED?
HERE?
YOUR MOTH-ER?
スラッ
GLIDE
CARPENTER! ♡ I BROUGHT SOME SWEETS!
WHAT? ♡
くるりん
TURN
HAVE MORE TEA!
OHH! ♡ HE'S SO COOL! ♡♡♡

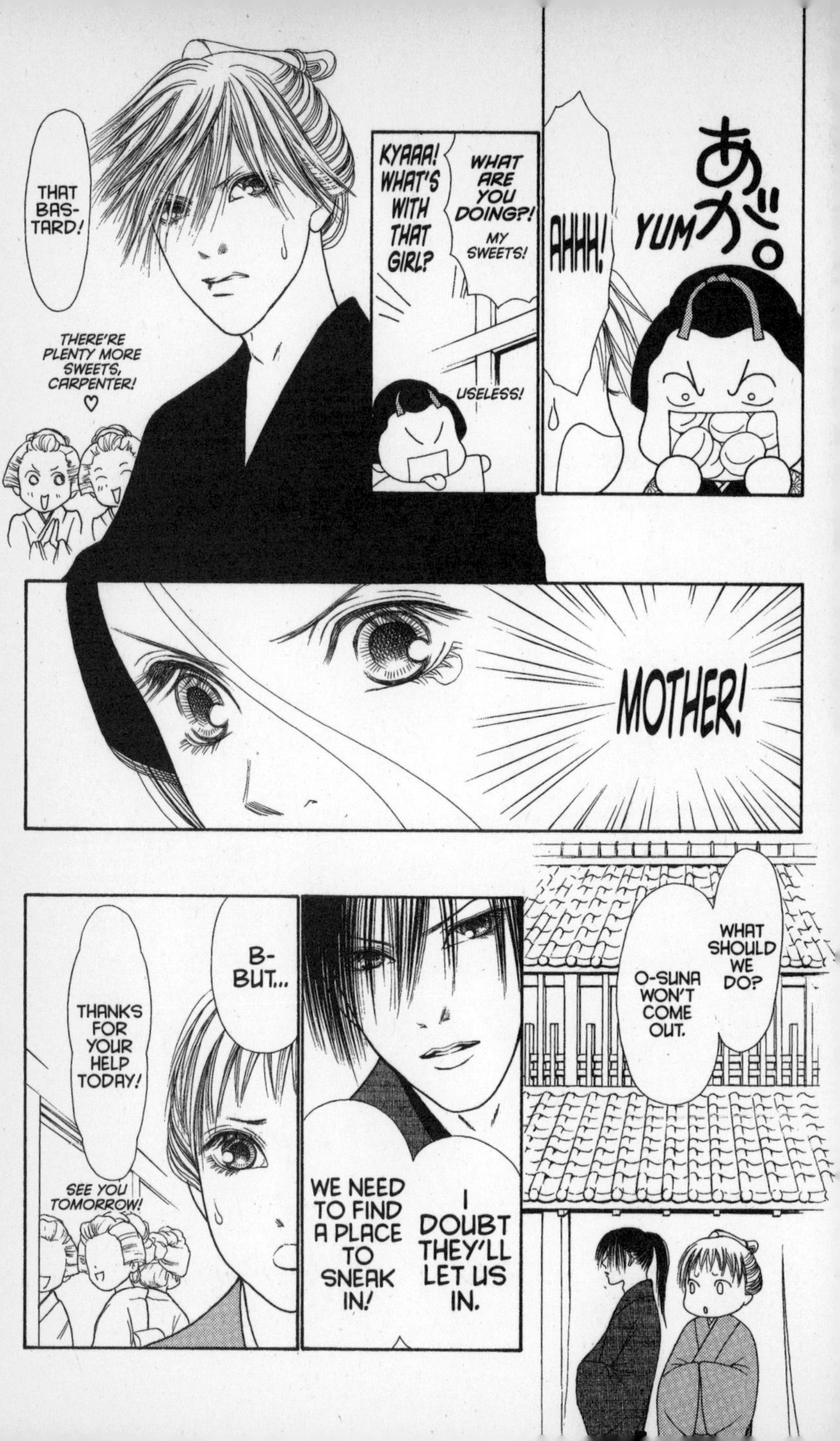

あが。
YUM
AHHH!
WHAT ARE YOU DOING?!
MY SWEETS!
KYAAA! WHAT'S WITH THAT GIRL?
USELESS!
THAT BAS-TARD!
THERE'RE PLENTY MORE SWEETS, CARPENTER! ♡
MOTHER!
WHAT SHOULD WE DO?
O-SUNA WON'T COME OUT.
I DOUBT THEY'LL LET US IN.
WE NEED TO FIND A PLACE TO SNEAK IN!
B-BUT...
THANKS FOR YOUR HELP TODAY!
SEE YOU TOMORROW!

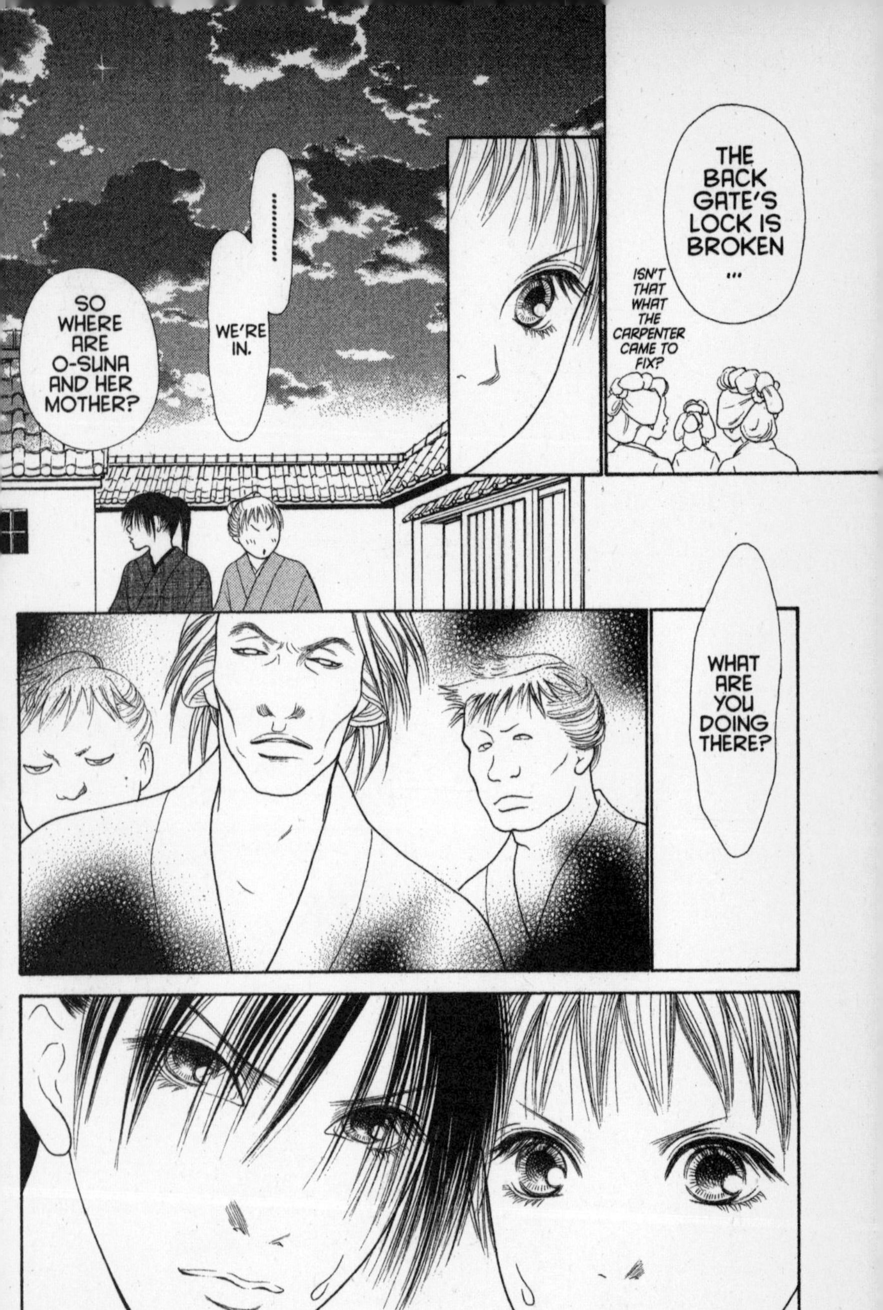
THE BACK GATE'S LOCK IS BROKEN ...
ISN'T THAT WHAT THE CARPENTER CAME TO FIX?
....
WE'RE IN.
SO WHERE ARE O-SUNA AND HER MOTHER?
WHAT ARE YOU DOING THERE?

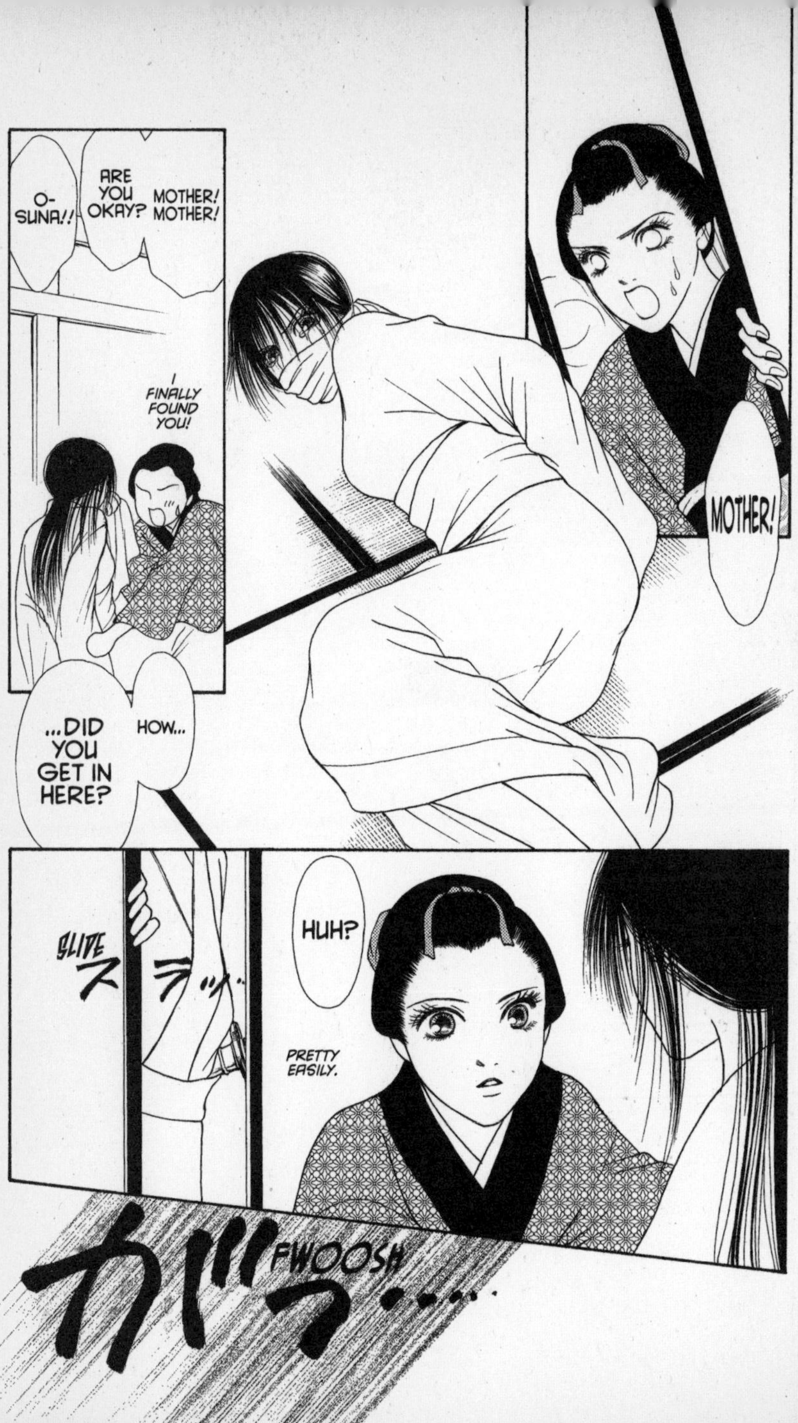
MOTHER!
HOW...
...DID YOU GET IN HERE?
MOTHER! MOTHER!
ARE YOU OKAY?
O-SUNA!!
I FINALLY FOUND YOU!
HUH?
PRETTY EASILY.
SLIDE
FWOOSH

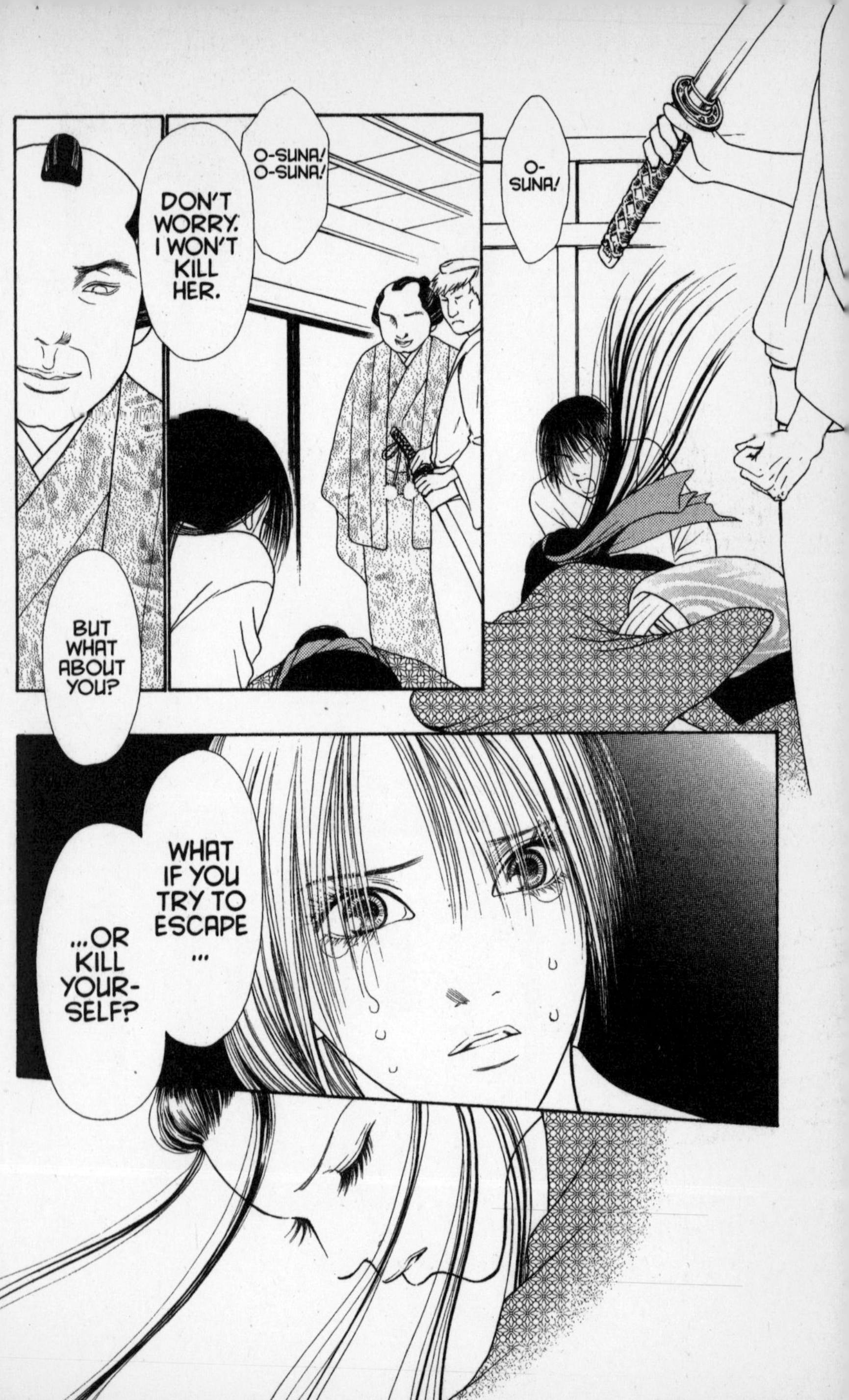
O-SUNA!
O-SUNA! O-SUNA!
DON'T WORRY. I WON'T KILL HER.
BUT WHAT ABOUT YOU?
WHAT IF YOU TRY TO ESCAPE ...
...OR KILL YOUR-SELF?

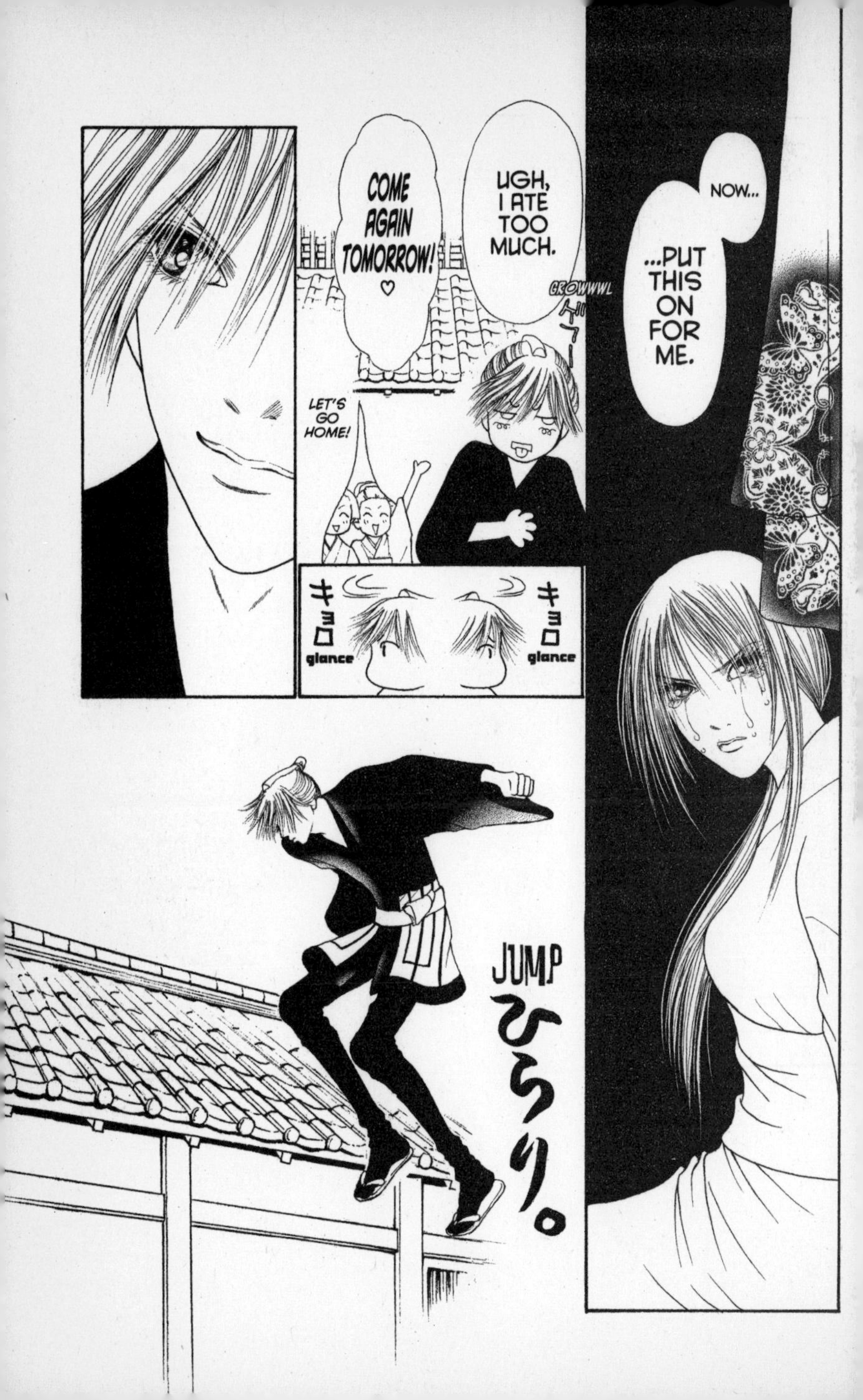
NOW...
...PUT THIS ON FOR ME.
UGH, I ATE TOO MUCH.
GROWWWL
COME AGAIN TOMORROW! ♡
LET'S GO HOME!
キョロ
glance
キョロ
glance
JUMP
ひらり。

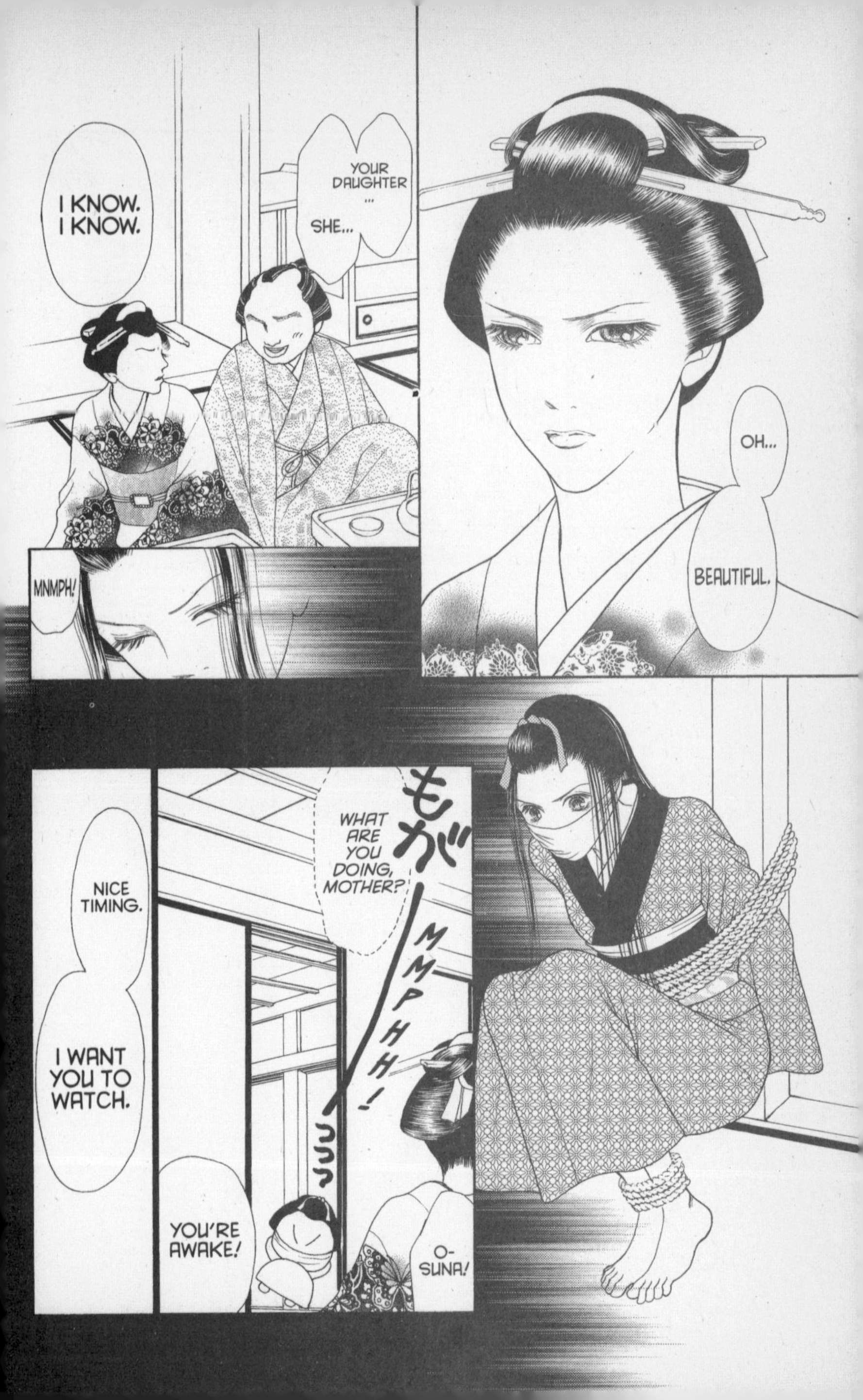
OH...
BEAUTIFUL.
YOUR DAUGHTER ... SHE...
I KNOW. I KNOW.
MNMPH!
もが
WHAT ARE YOU DOING, MOTHER?
MMPHHH!
NICE TIMING.
I WANT YOU TO WATCH.
O-SUNA!
YOU'RE AWAKE!

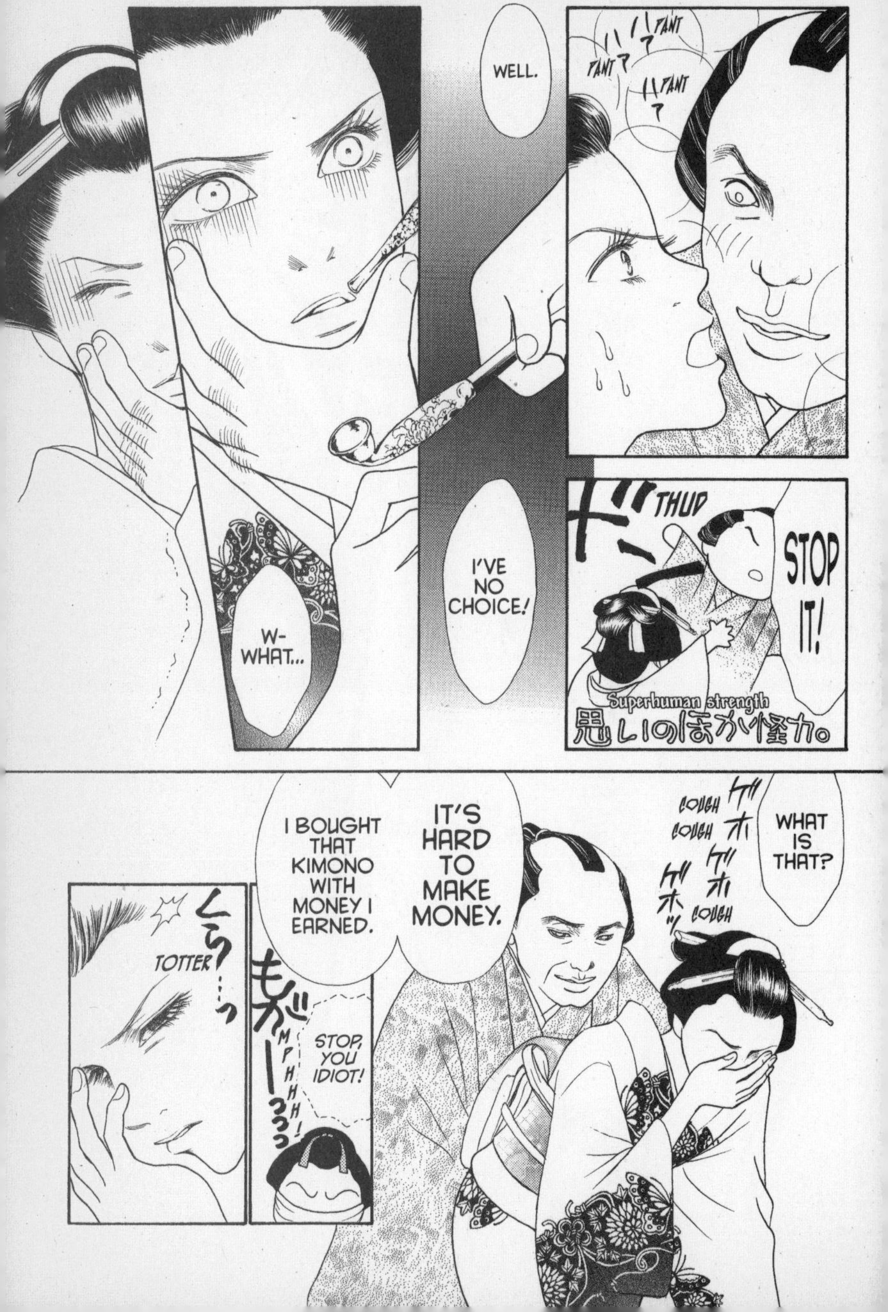

PANT PANT PANT
WELL.
I'VE NO CHOICE!
THUD
STOP IT!
Superhuman strength
W-WHAT...
COUGH COUGH COUGH
WHAT IS THAT?
IT'S HARD TO MAKE MONEY.
I BOUGHT THAT KIMONO WITH MONEY I EARNED.
MPHHH!
STOP, YOU IDIOT!
TOTTER

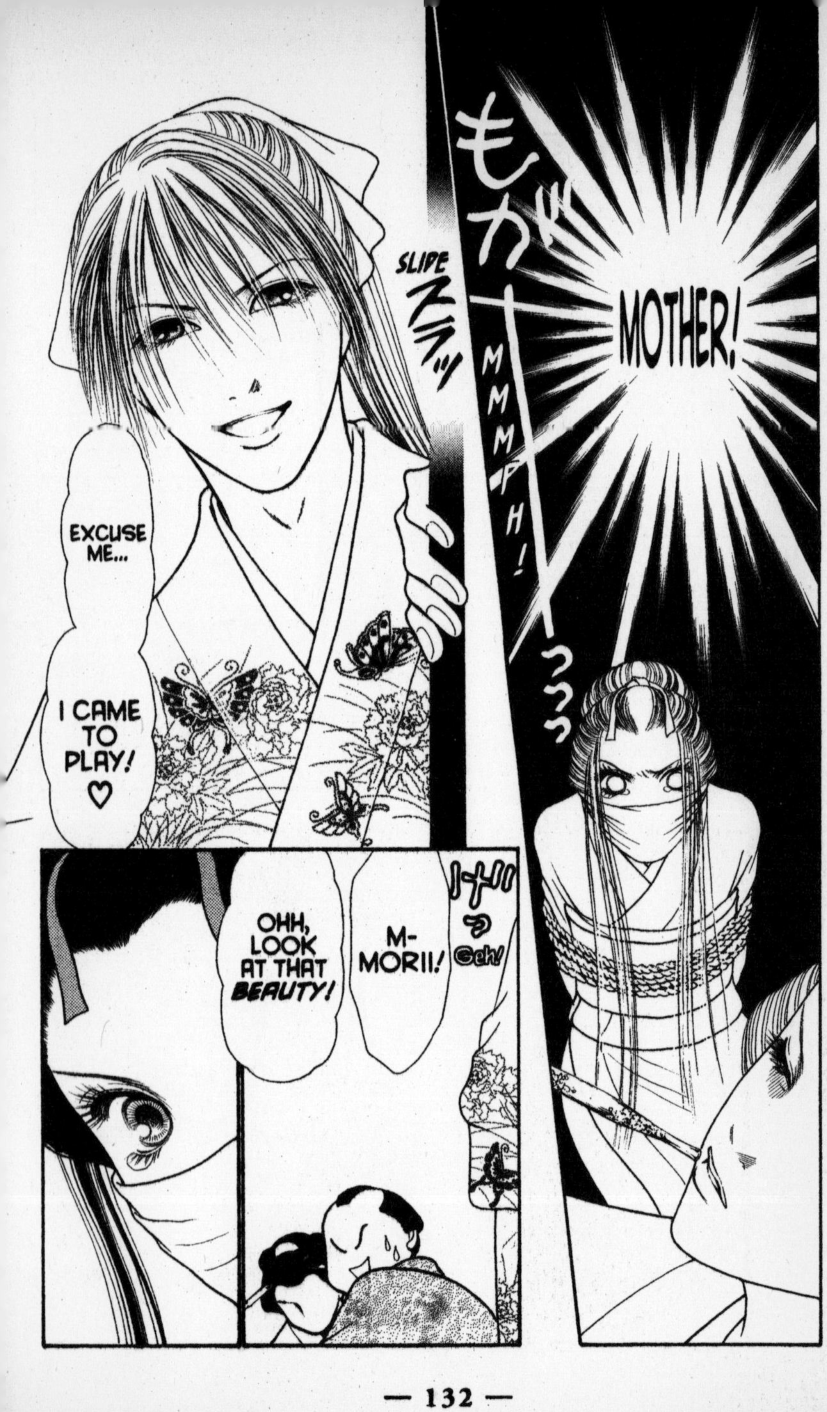

もがーっっっ
MMMMPH!
MOTHER!
SLIDE
スラッ
EXCUSE ME...
I CAME TO PLAY! ♡
ゲッ
Geh!
M-MORII!
OHH, LOOK AT THAT BEAUTY!

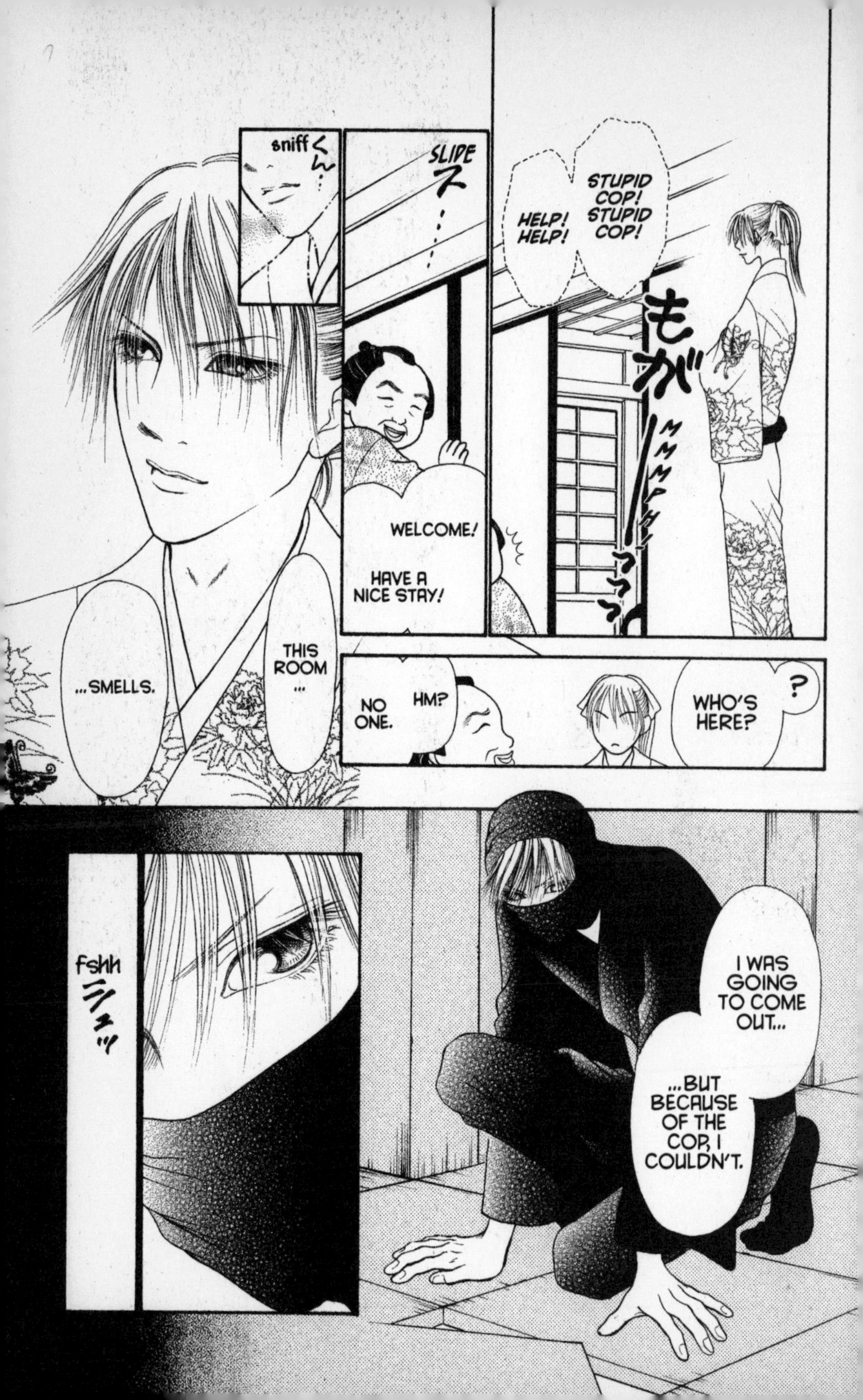
STUPID COP! STUPID COP!
HELP! HELP!
もが
MMMPH!
SLIDE
ス…
WELCOME!
HAVE A NICE STAY!
sniff
くん…
?
WHO'S HERE?
HM?
NO ONE.
THIS ROOM…
…SMELLS.
I WAS GOING TO COME OUT…
…BUT BECAUSE OF THE COP, I COULDN'T.
fshh
シュッ

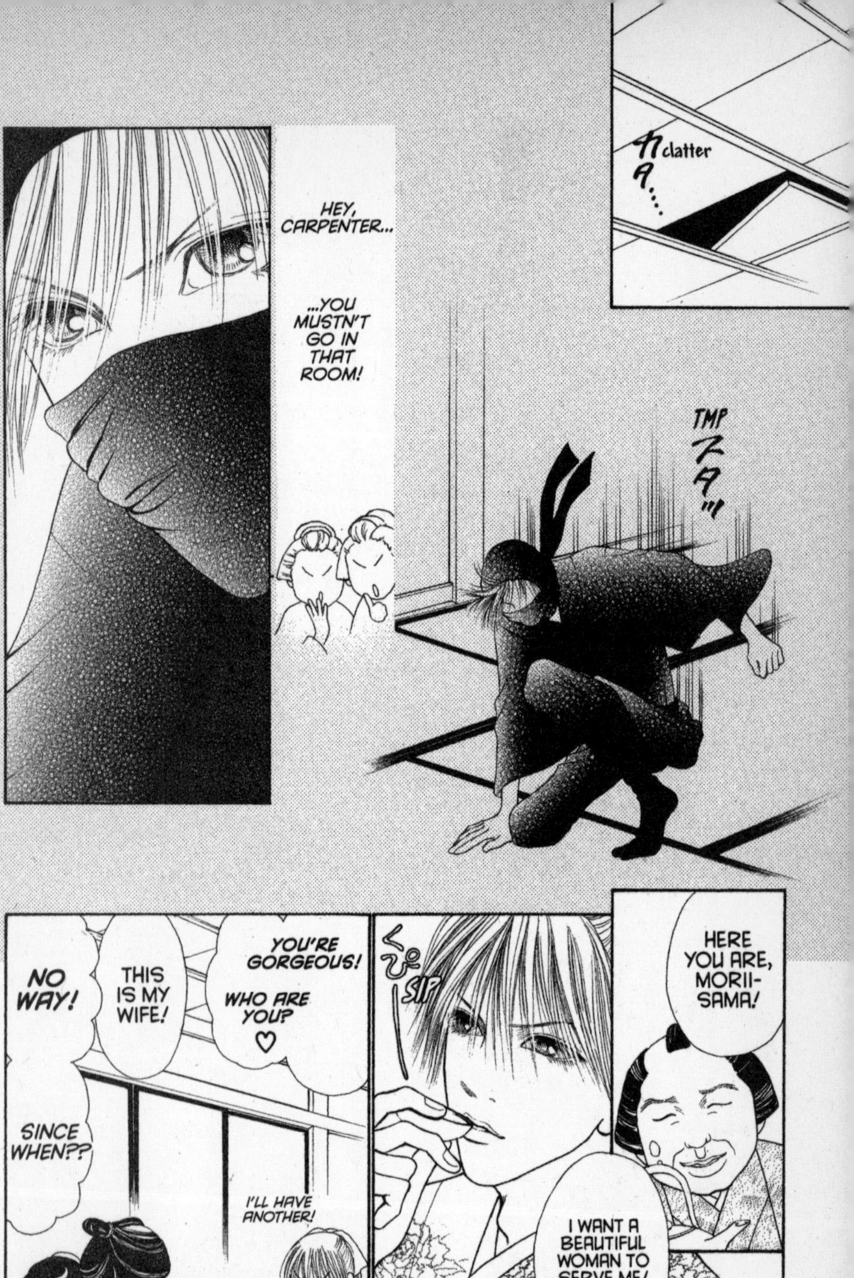
カタ… clatter
TMP スタッ
HEY, CARPENTER...
...YOU MUSTN'T GO IN THAT ROOM!
HERE YOU ARE, MORII-SAMA!
くぴ SIP
I WANT A BEAUTIFUL WOMAN TO SERVE ME!
YOU'RE GORGEOUS!
WHO ARE YOU? ♡
THIS IS MY WIFE!
NO WAY!
SINCE WHEN??
I'LL HAVE ANOTHER!

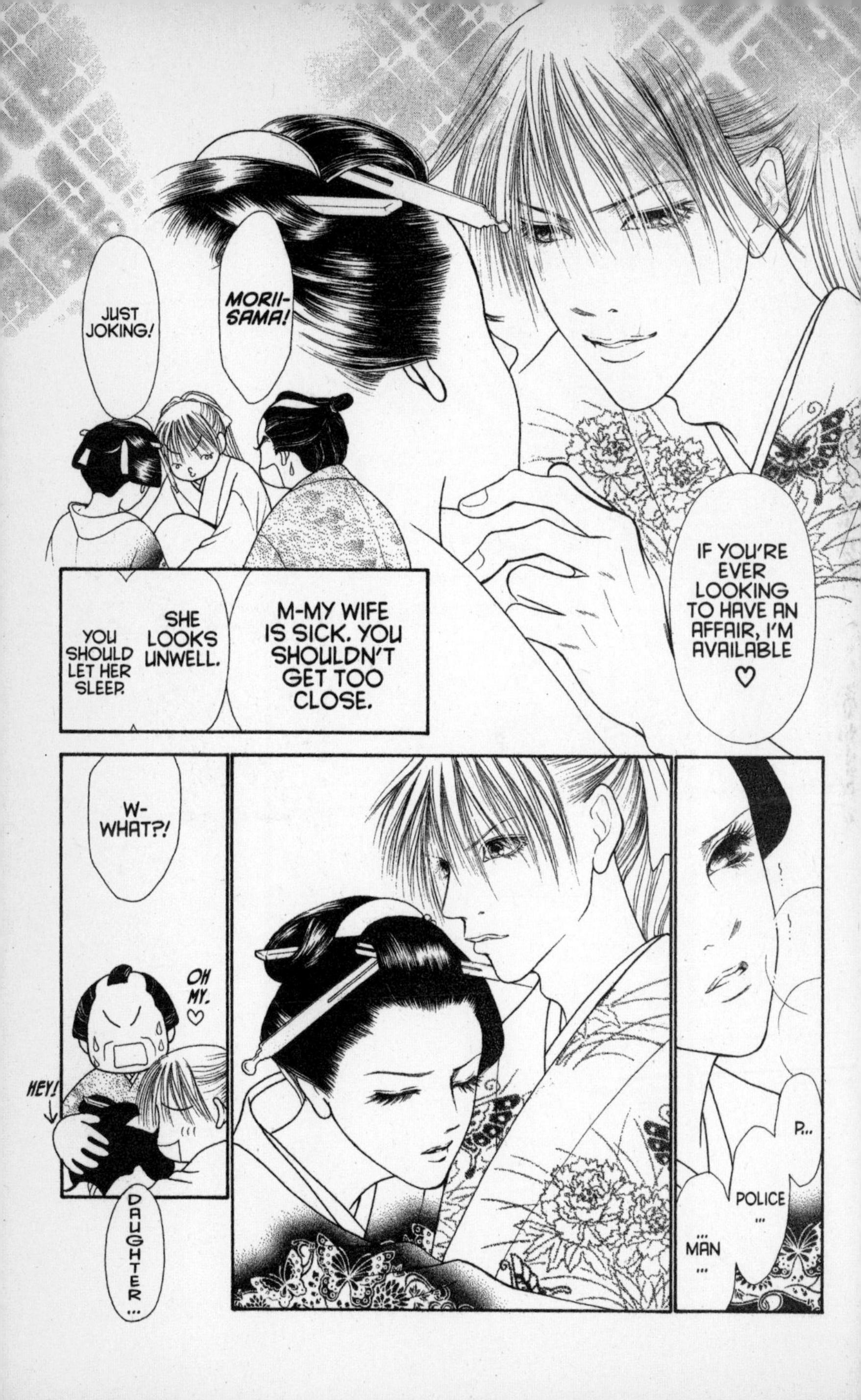
IF YOU'RE EVER LOOKING TO HAVE AN AFFAIR, I'M AVAILABLE ♡
MORII-SAMA!
JUST JOKING!
M-MY WIFE IS SICK. YOU SHOULDN'T GET TOO CLOSE.
SHE LOOKS UNWELL.
YOU SHOULD LET HER SLEEP.
P...
POLICE ...
... MAN ...
W-WHAT?!
OH MY. ♡
HEY!
DAUGHTER ...

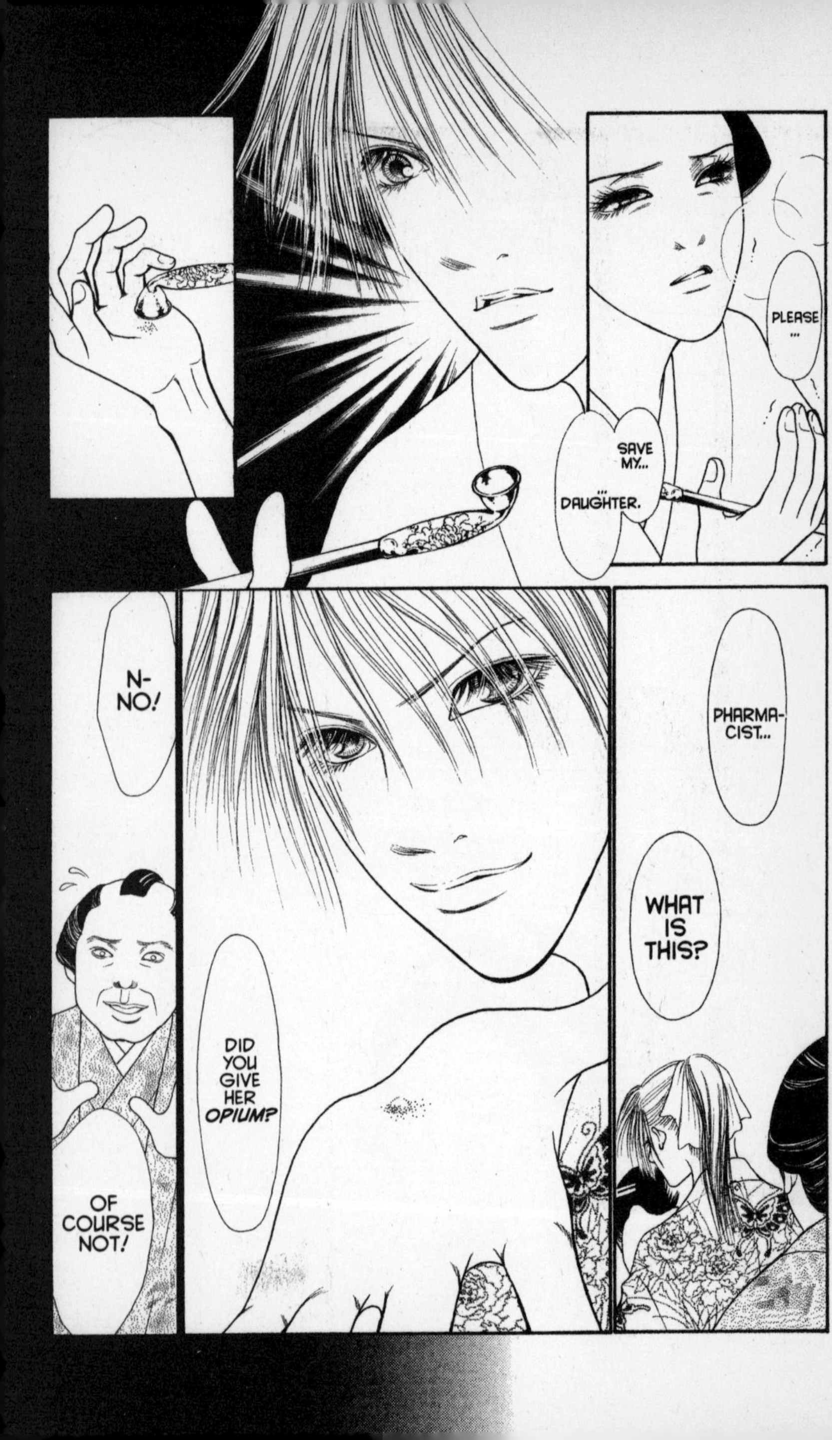
PLEASE ...
SAVE MY... ...DAUGHTER.
PHARMA-CIST...
WHAT IS THIS?
DID YOU GIVE HER *OPIUM?*
N-NO!
OF COURSE NOT!

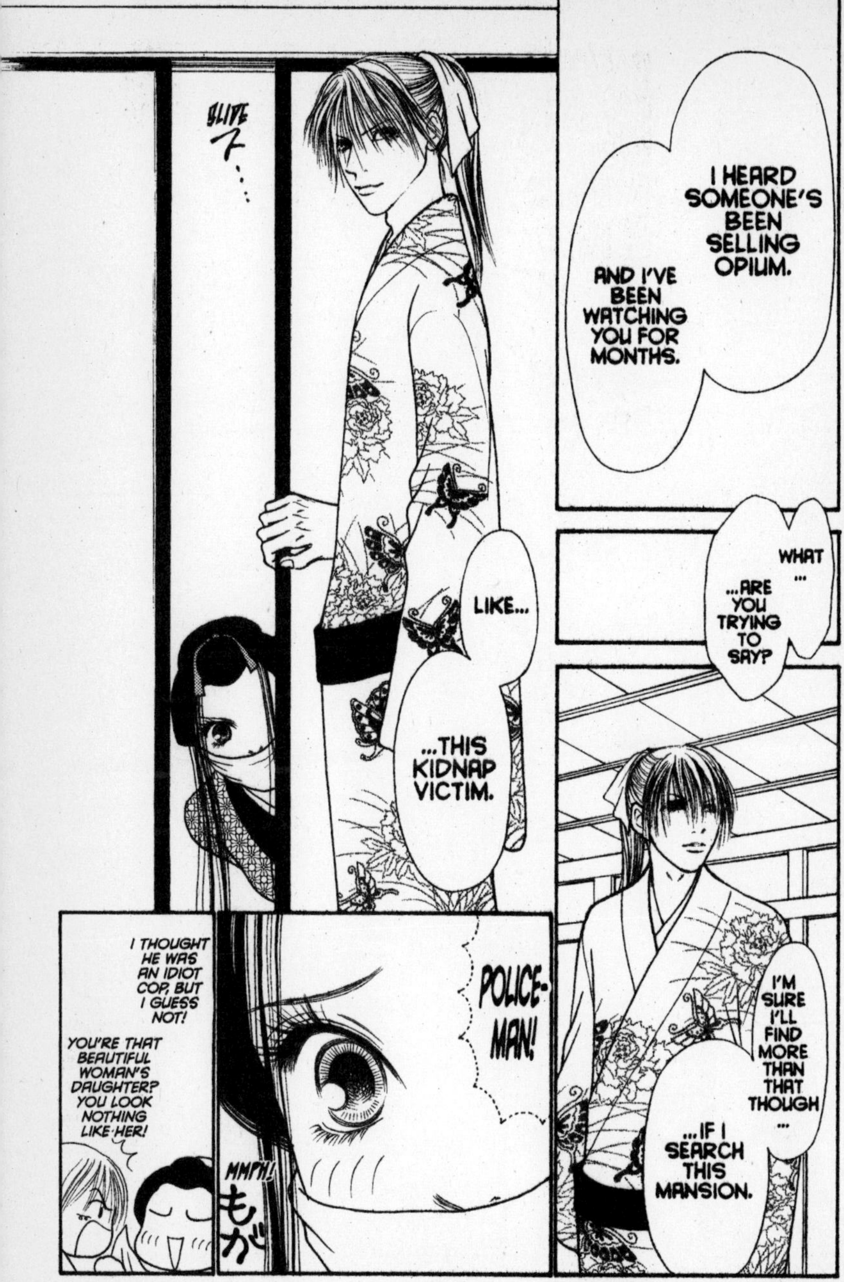
I HEARD SOMEONE'S BEEN SELLING OPIUM.
AND I'VE BEEN WATCHING YOU FOR MONTHS.
WHAT ...
...ARE YOU TRYING TO SAY?
I'M SURE I'LL FIND MORE THAN THAT THOUGH ...
...IF I SEARCH THIS MANSION.
SLIDE
LIKE...
...THIS KIDNAP VICTIM.
POLICE-MAN!
MMPH!
もが
I THOUGHT HE WAS AN IDIOT COP, BUT I GUESS NOT!
YOU'RE THAT BEAUTIFUL WOMAN'S DAUGHTER? YOU LOOK NOTHING LIKE HER!

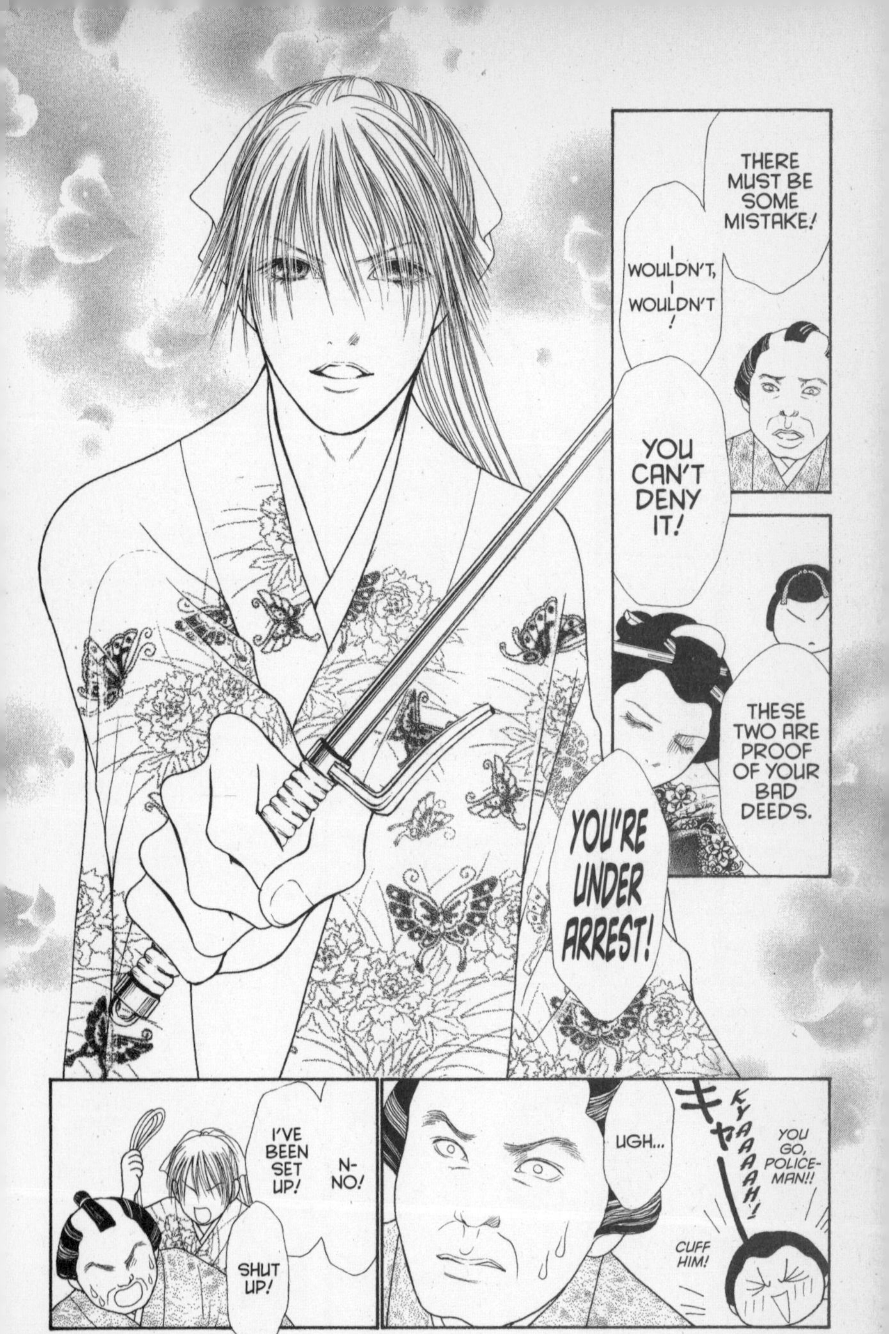
THERE MUST BE SOME MISTAKE!
I WOULDN'T, I WOULDN'T!
YOU CAN'T DENY IT!
THESE TWO ARE PROOF OF YOUR BAD DEEDS.
YOU'RE UNDER ARREST!
YOU GO, POLICE-MAN!!
キャ
KYAAAAH!
UGH...
CUFF HIM!
N-NO!
I'VE BEEN SET UP!
SHUT UP!

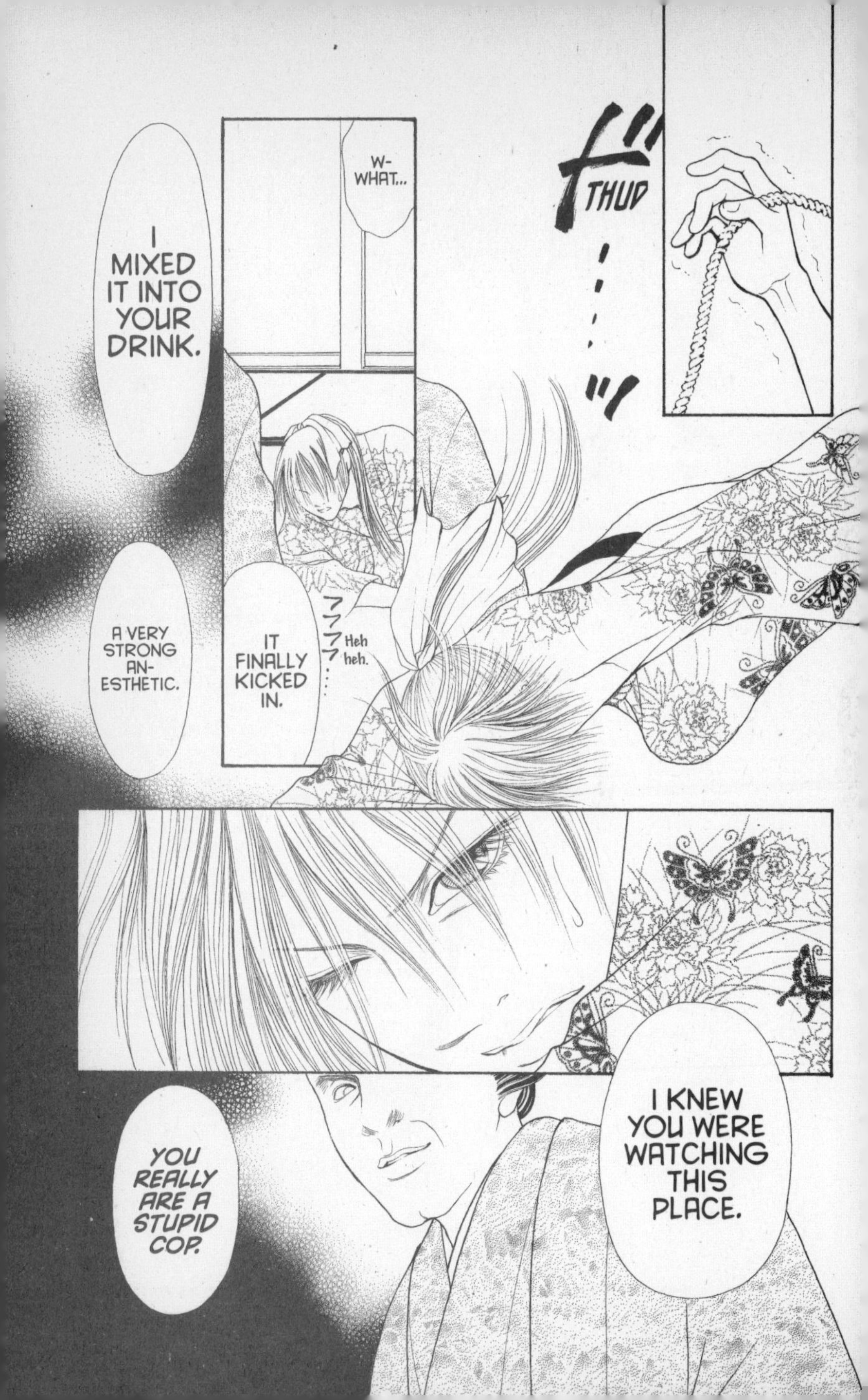
THUD
W-WHAT...
IT FINALLY KICKED IN.
Heh heh.
I MIXED IT INTO YOUR DRINK.
A VERY STRONG AN-ESTHETIC.
I KNEW YOU WERE WATCHING THIS PLACE.
YOU REALLY ARE A STUPID COP.

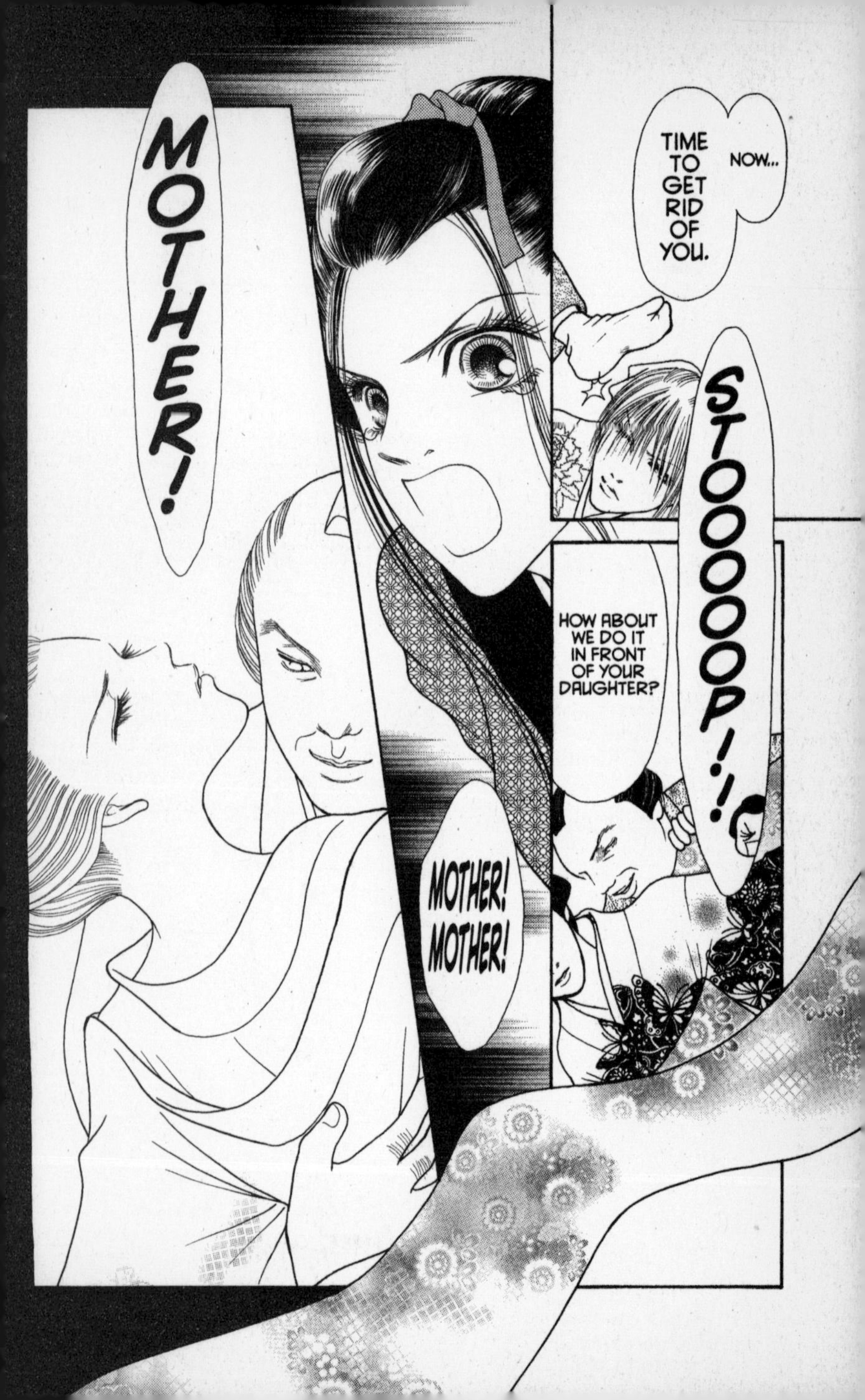
NOW...
TIME TO GET RID OF YOU.
STOOOOOP!!
HOW ABOUT WE DO IT IN FRONT OF YOUR DAUGHTER?
MOTHER! MOTHER!
MOTHER!

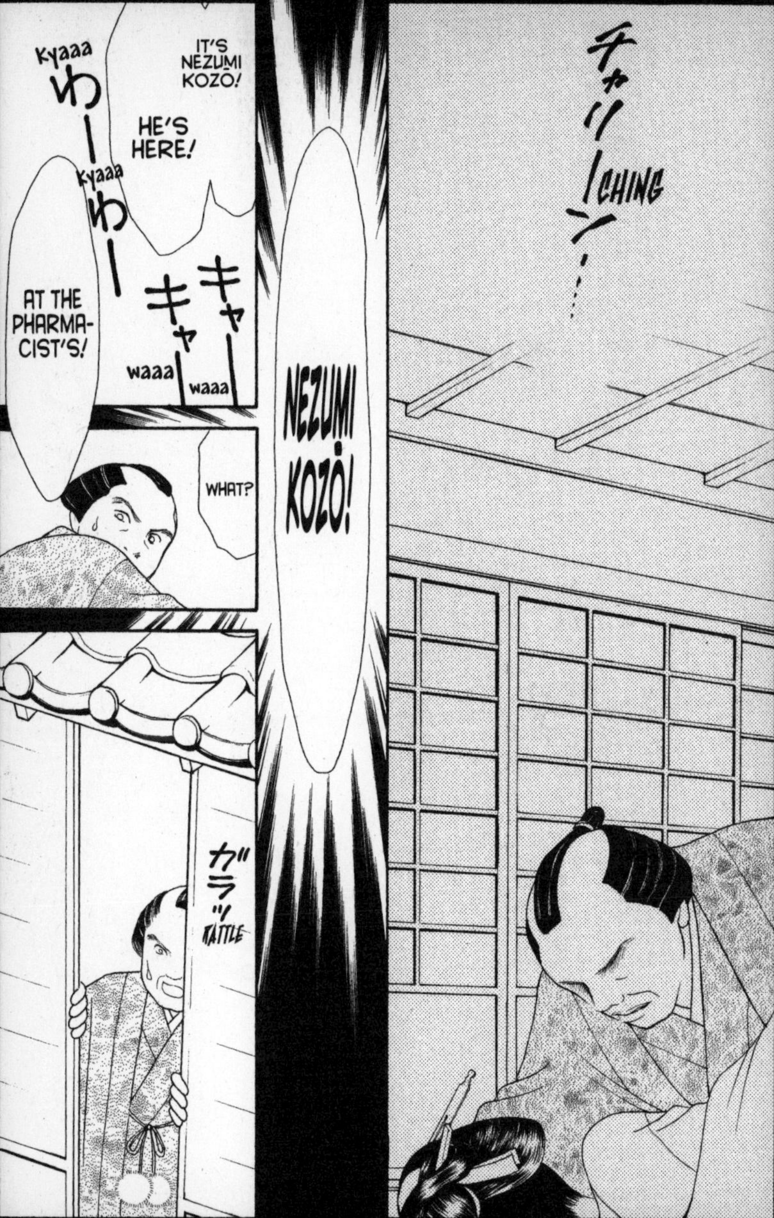

チャリーン
CHING
NEZUMI KOZŌ!
IT'S NEZUMI KOZŌ!
HE'S HERE!
キャー
waaa
キャー
waaa
わー
Kyaaa
わー
Kyaaa
AT THE PHARMA-CIST'S!
WHAT?
ガラッ
RATTLE

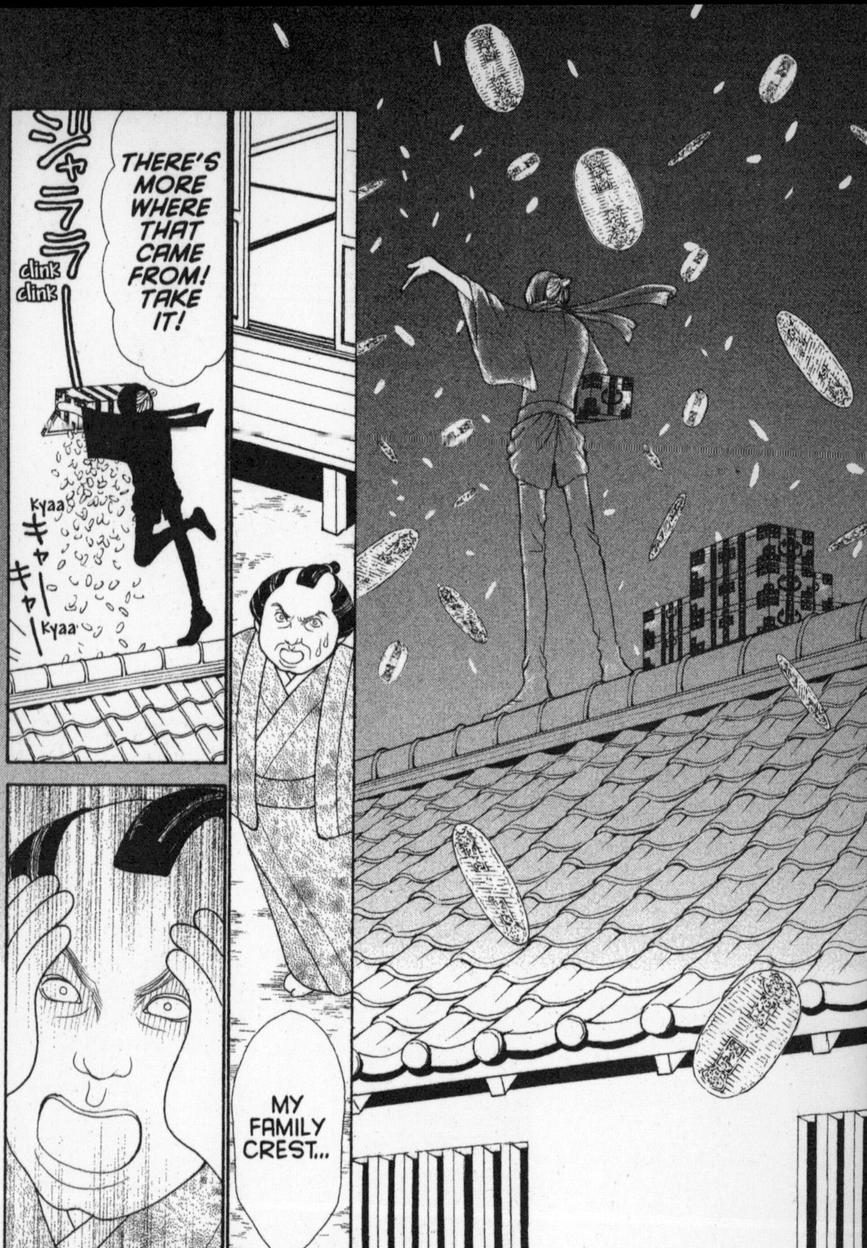
MY FAMILY CREST...
THERE'S MORE WHERE THAT CAME FROM! TAKE IT!
シャラ
clink clink
キャーキャー
kyaa kyaa

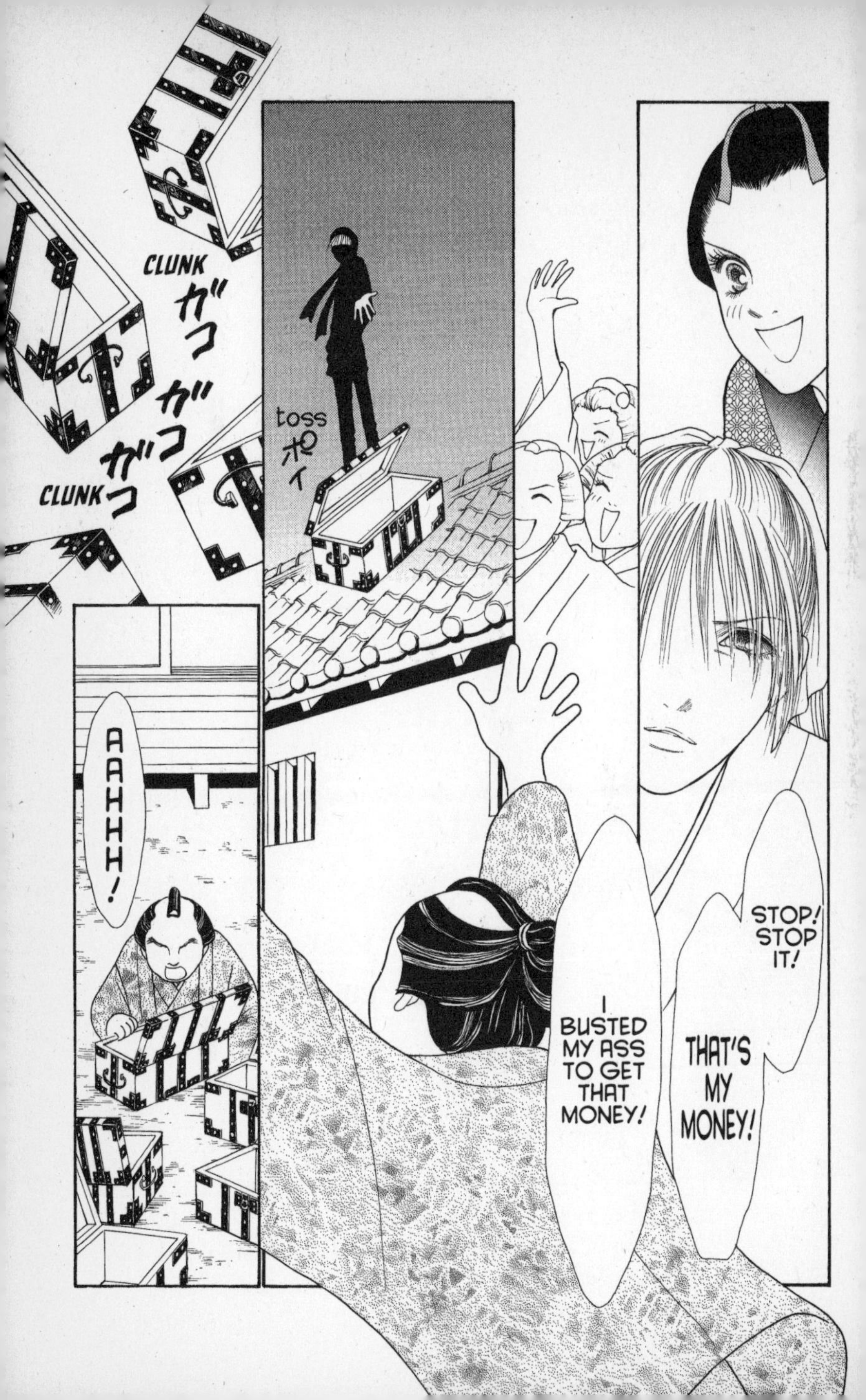
STOP! STOP IT!
THAT'S MY MONEY!
I BUSTED MY ASS TO GET THAT MONEY!
toss
ポイ
CLUNK
ガコ
ガコ
ガコ
CLUNK
AAHHHH!

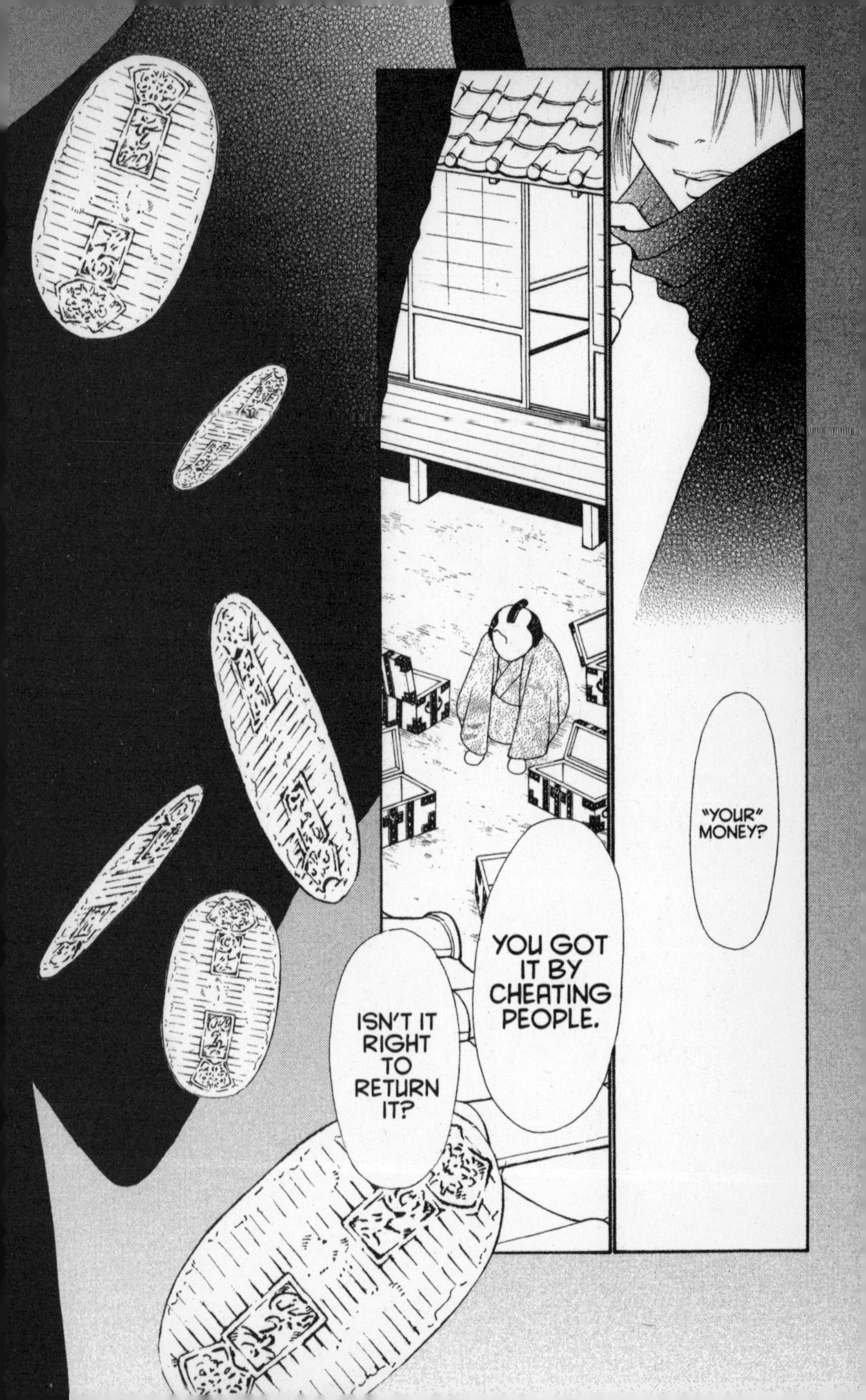
"YOUR" MONEY?
YOU GOT IT BY CHEATING PEOPLE.
ISN'T IT RIGHT TO RETURN IT?

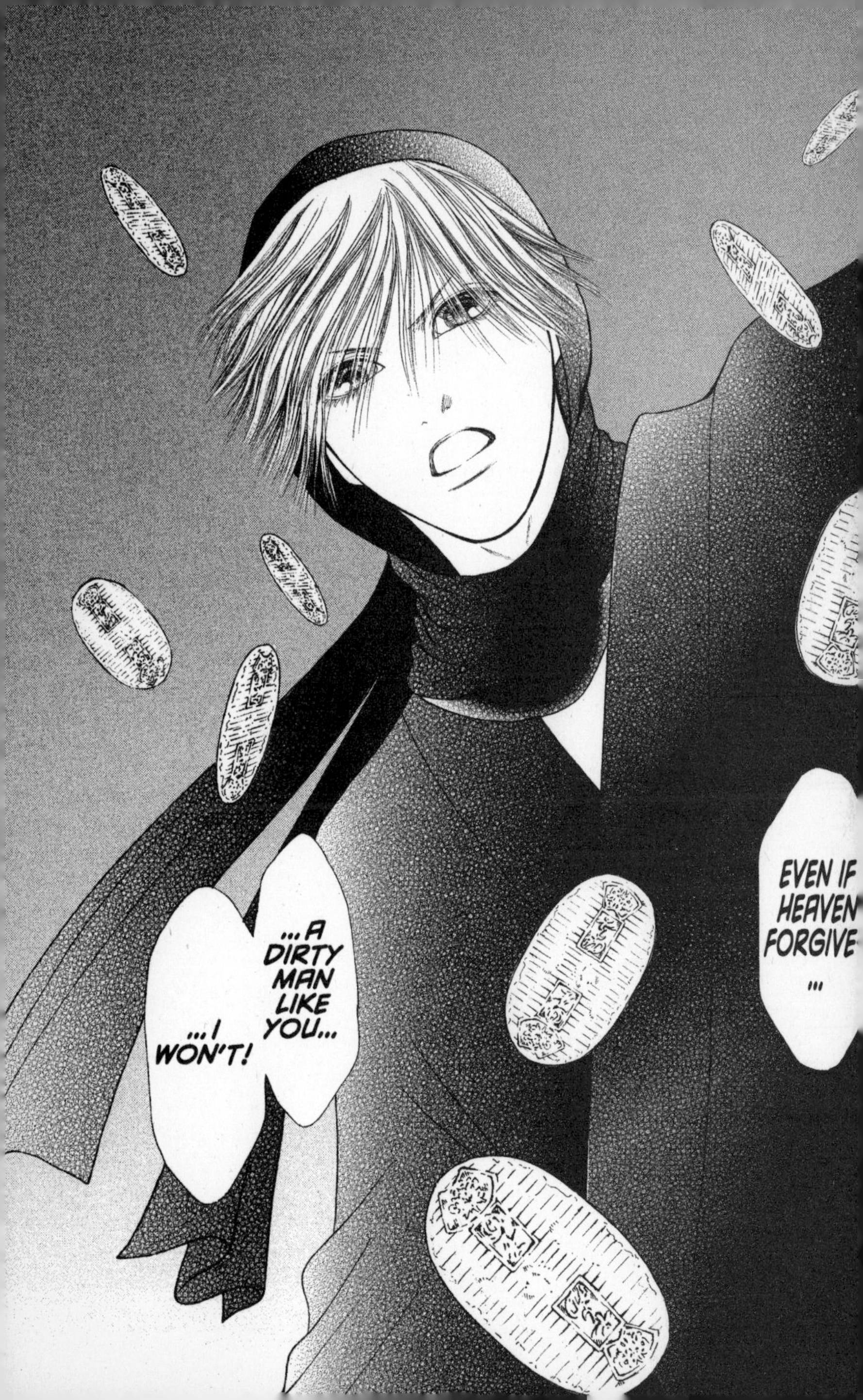
EVEN IF HEAVEN FORGIVE ...
...A DIRTY MAN LIKE YOU...
...I WON'T!

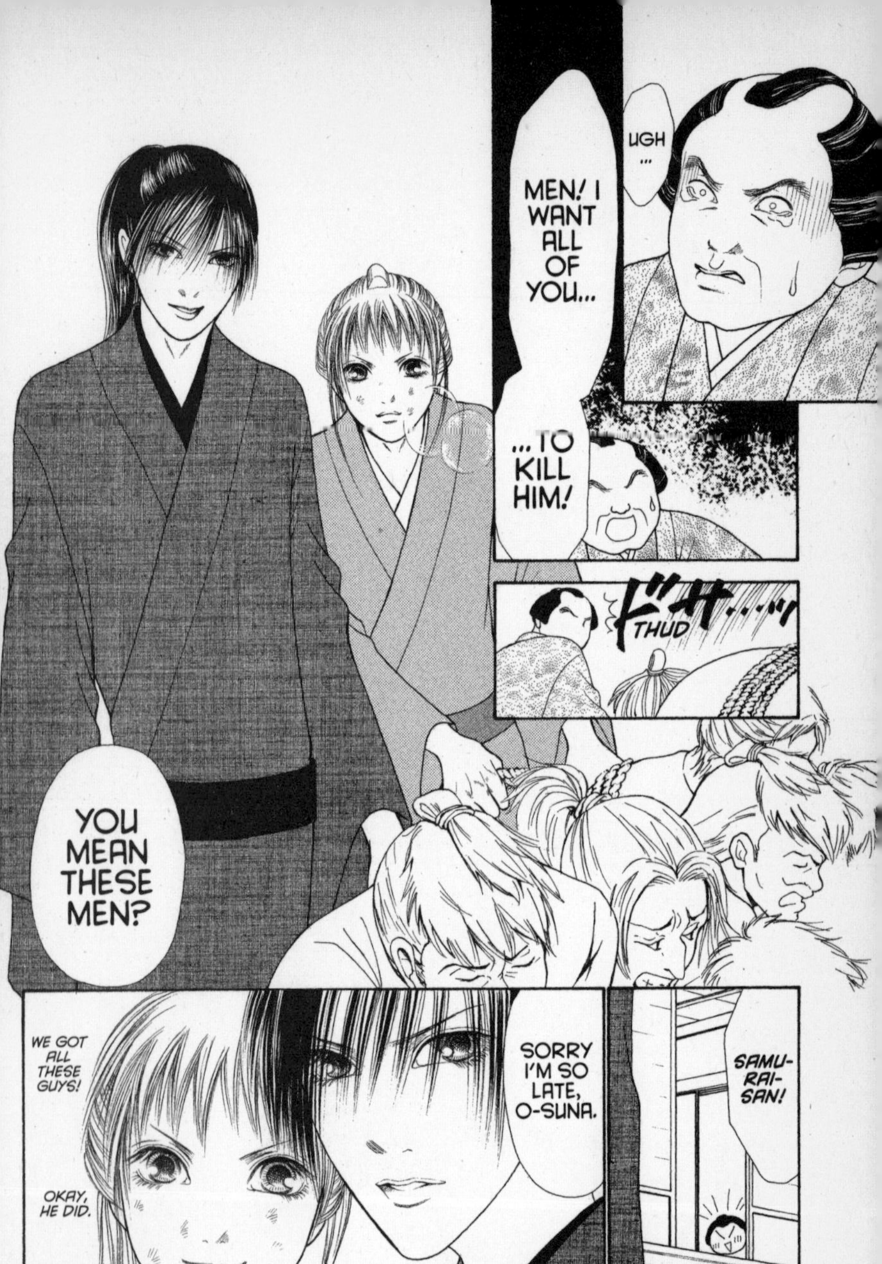

UGH...
MEN! I WANT ALL OF YOU...
...TO KILL HIM!
THUD
YOU MEAN THESE MEN?
SAMURAI-SAN!
SORRY I'M SO LATE, O-SUNA.
WE GOT ALL THESE GUYS!
OKAY, HE DID.

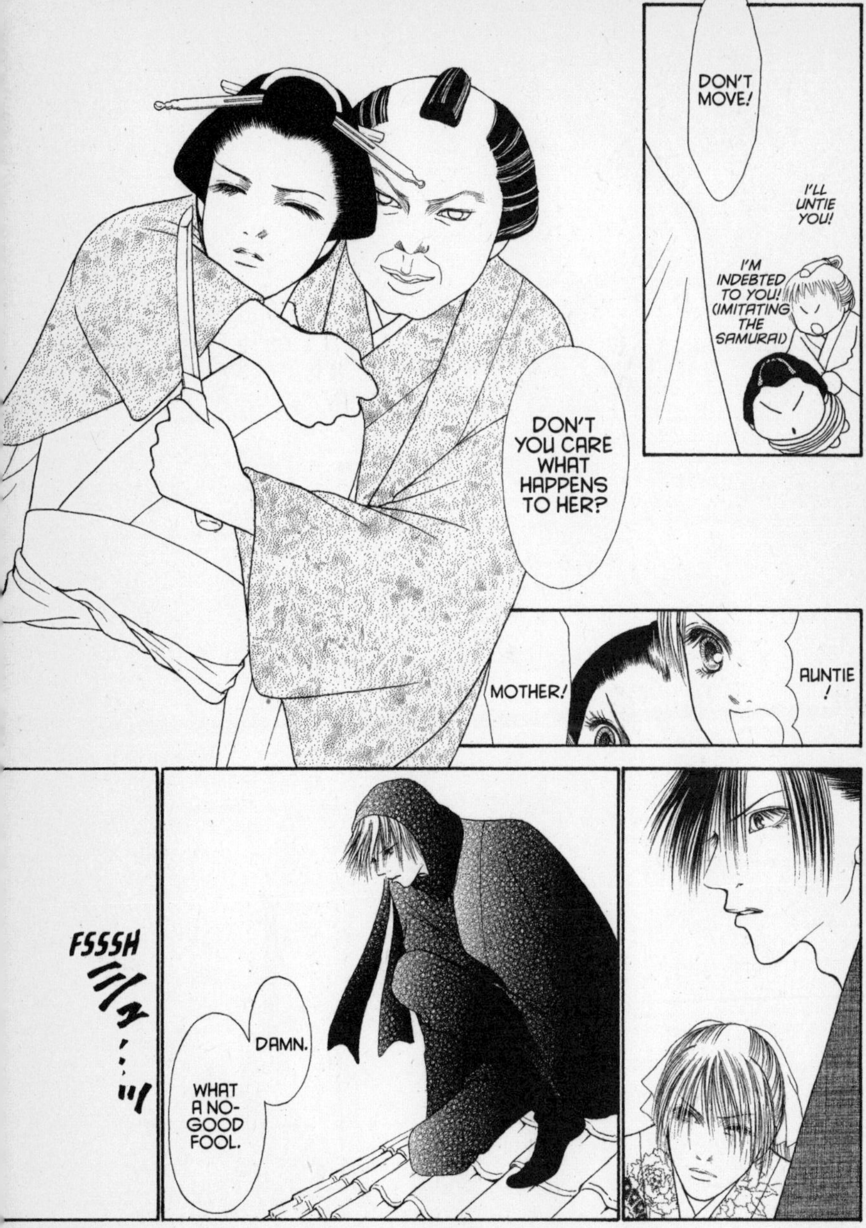
DON'T MOVE!
I'LL UNTIE YOU!
I'M INDEBTED TO YOU! (IMITATING THE SAMURAI)
AUNTIE!
MOTHER!
DON'T YOU CARE WHAT HAPPENS TO HER?
DAMN.
WHAT A NO-GOOD FOOL.
FSSSH

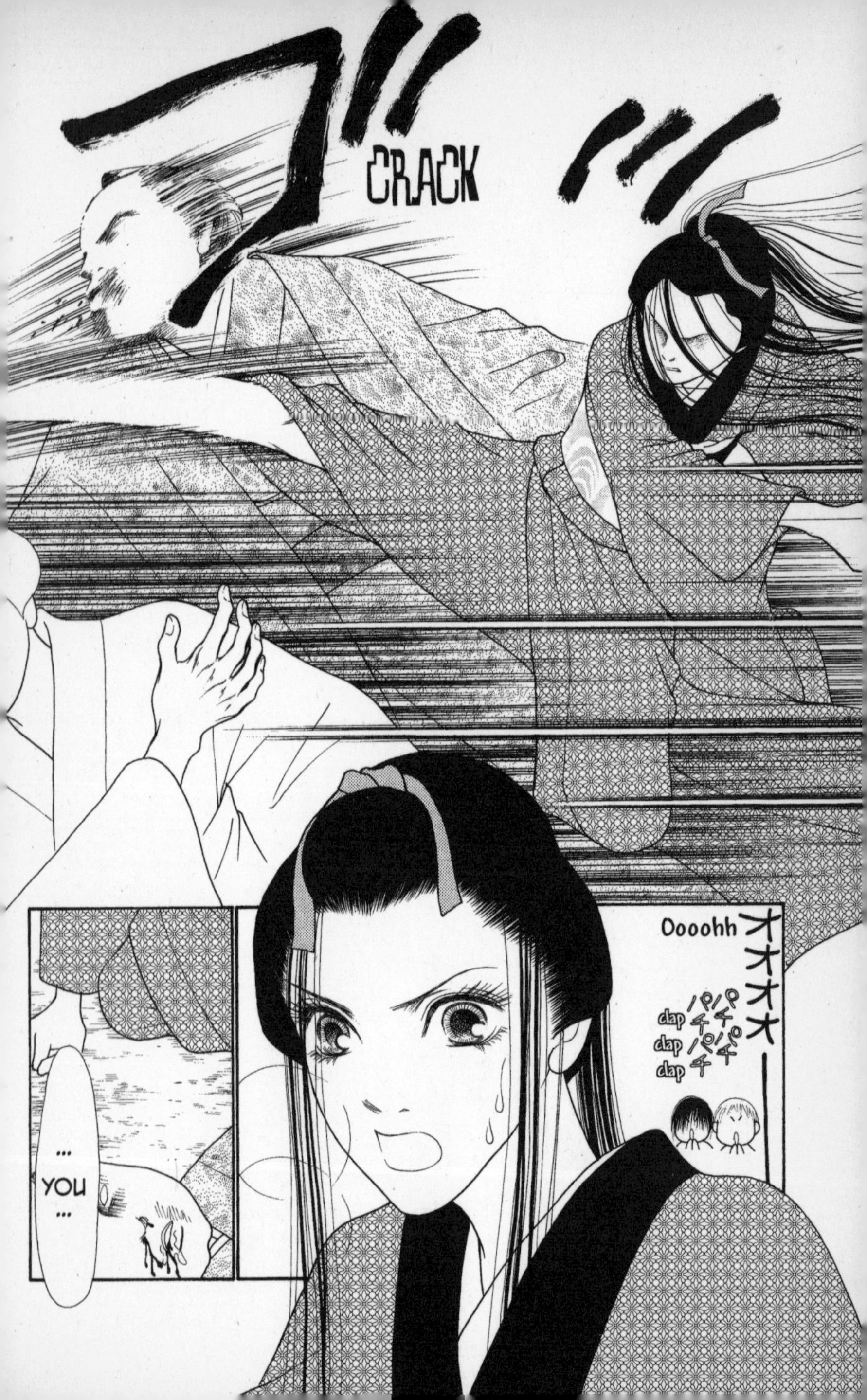
CRACK
Oooohh
オオオオ
パチパチパチ
clap clap clap
... YOU ...

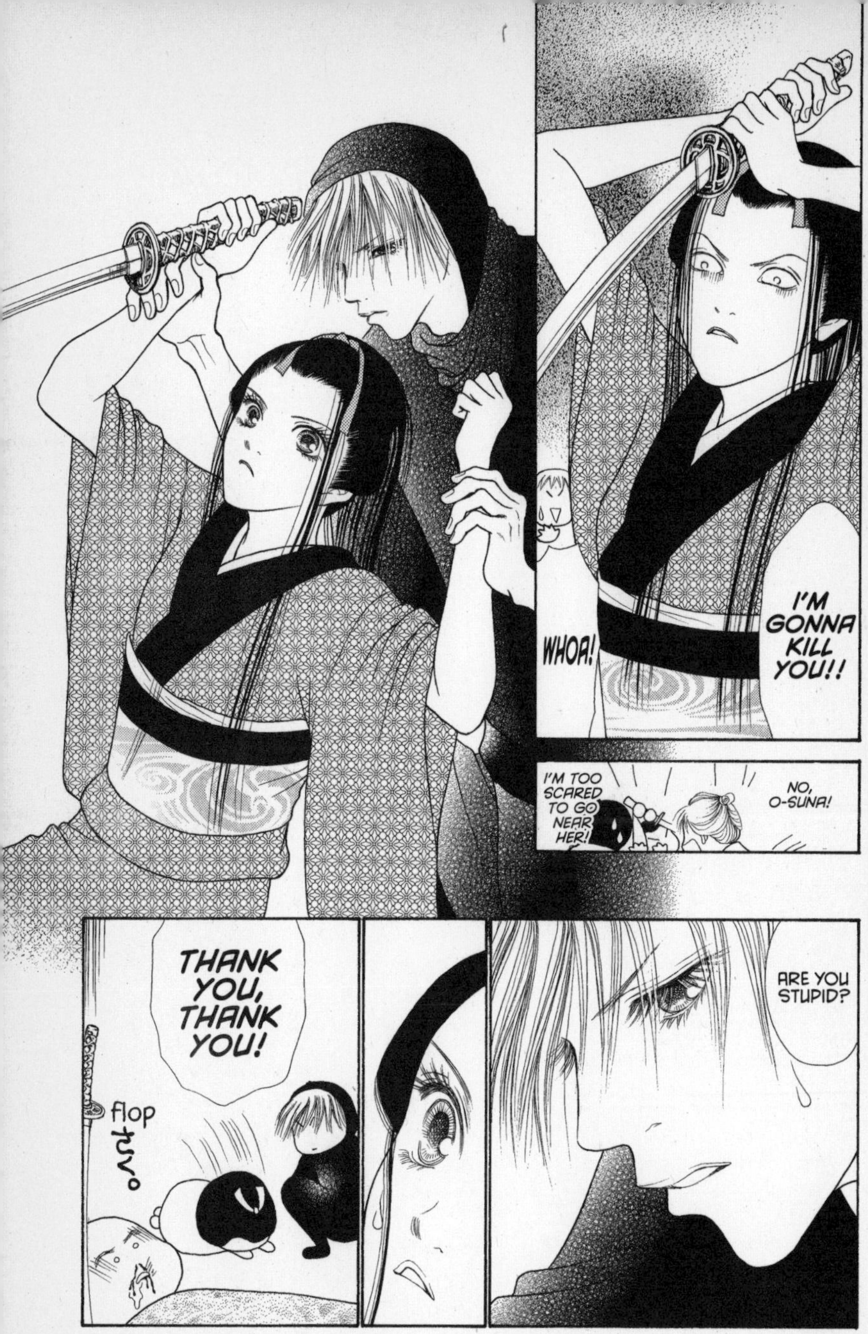
I'M GONNA KILL YOU!!
WHOA!
NO, O-SUNA!
I'M TOO SCARED TO GO NEAR HER!
ARE YOU STUPID?
THANK YOU, THANK YOU!
flop

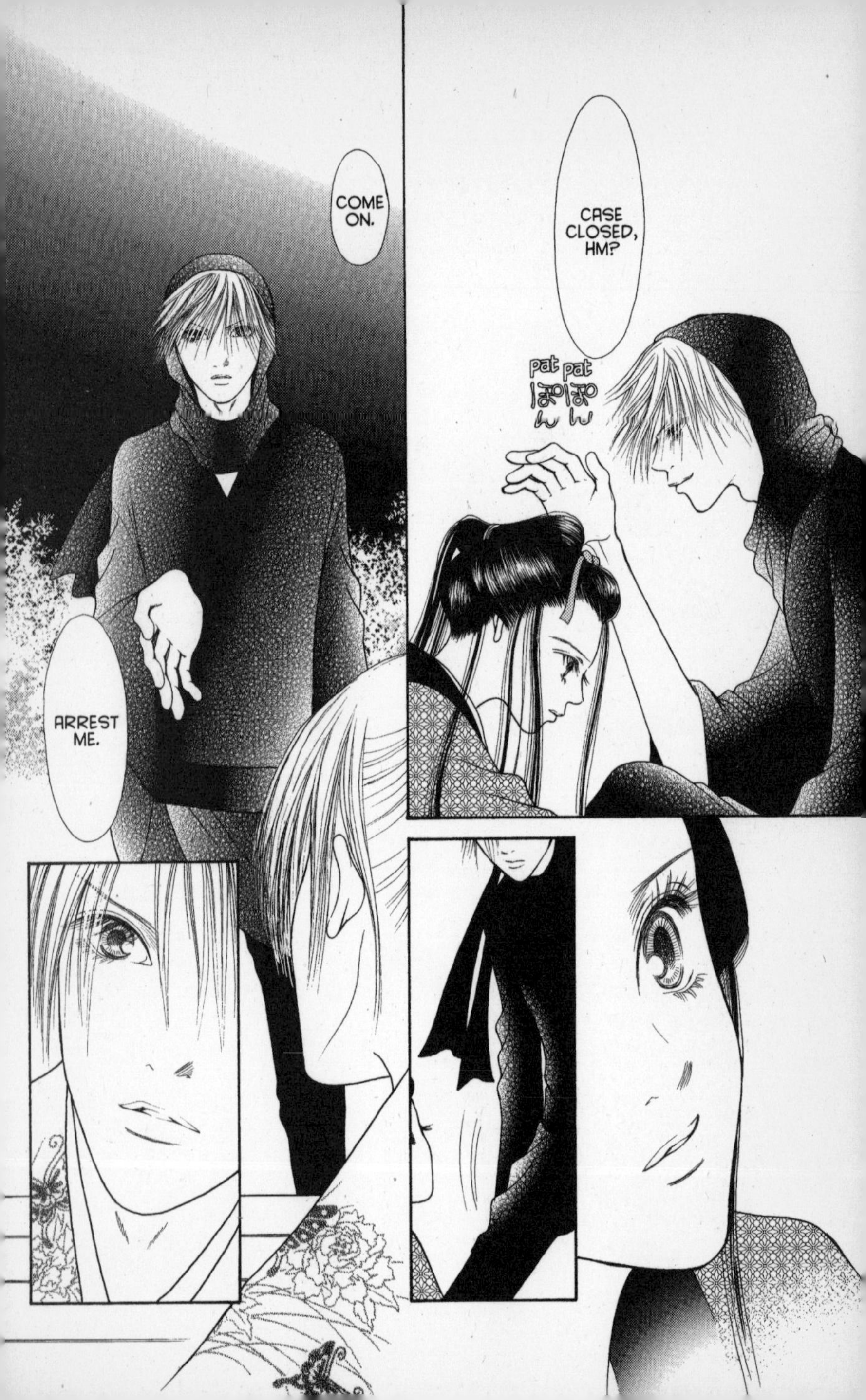
CASE CLOSED, HM?
pat pat
ぽんぽん
COME ON.
ARREST ME.

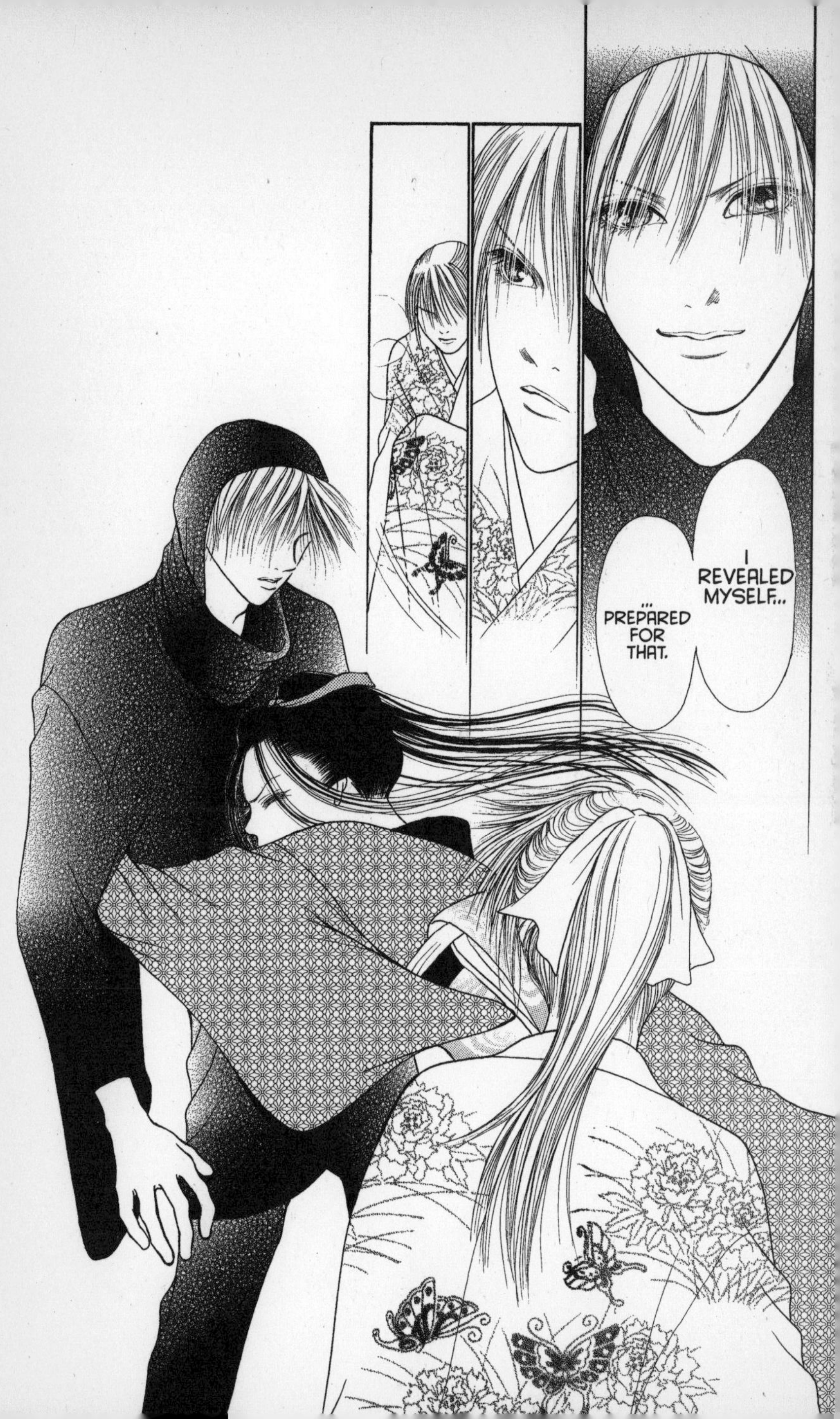
I REVEALED MYSELF...
...PREPARED FOR THAT.

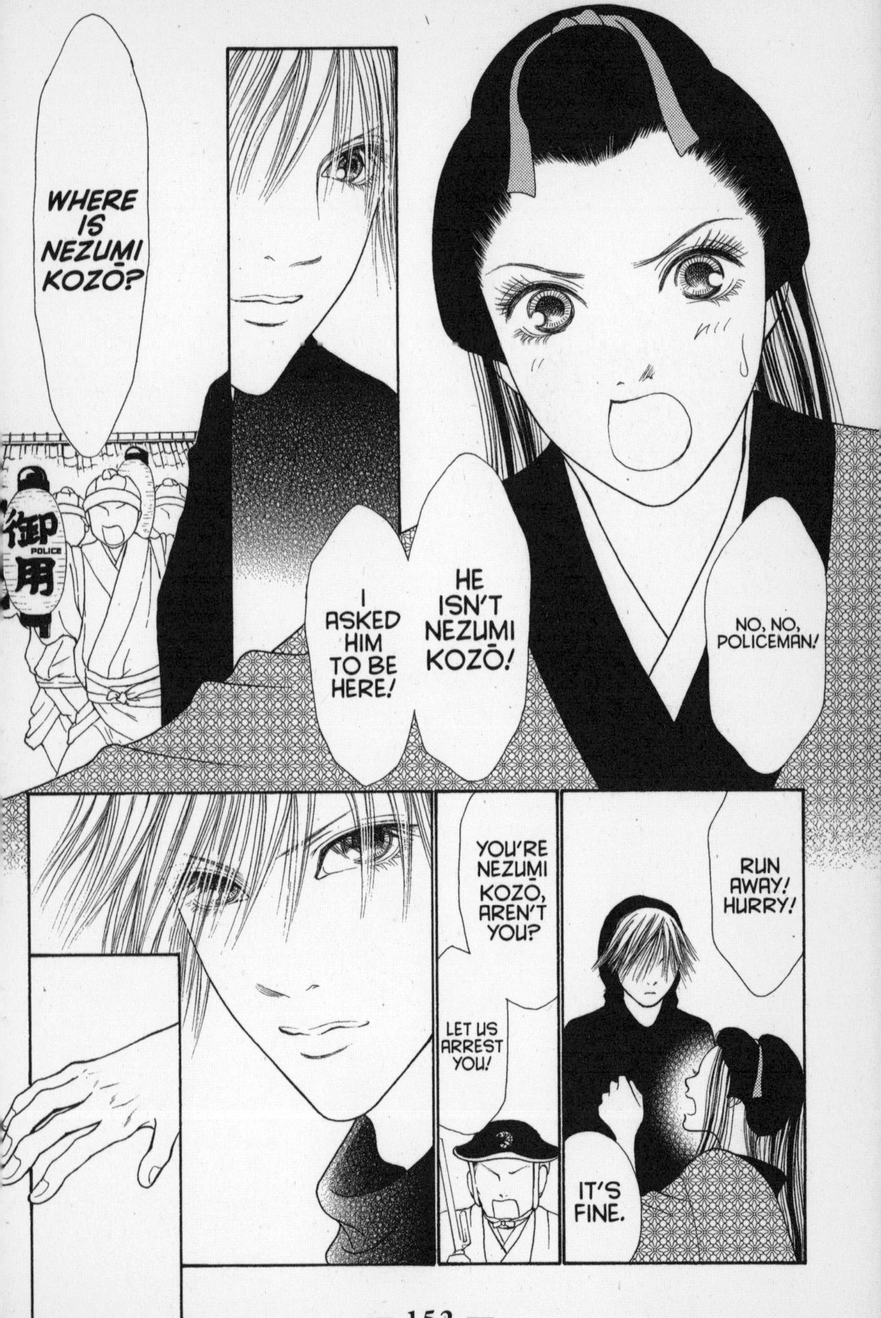
NO, NO, POLICEMAN!
HE ISN'T NEZUMI KOZŌ!
I ASKED HIM TO BE HERE!
WHERE IS NEZUMI KOZŌ?
御用
POLICE
RUN AWAY! HURRY!
IT'S FINE.
YOU'RE NEZUMI KOZŌ, AREN'T YOU?
LET US ARREST YOU!

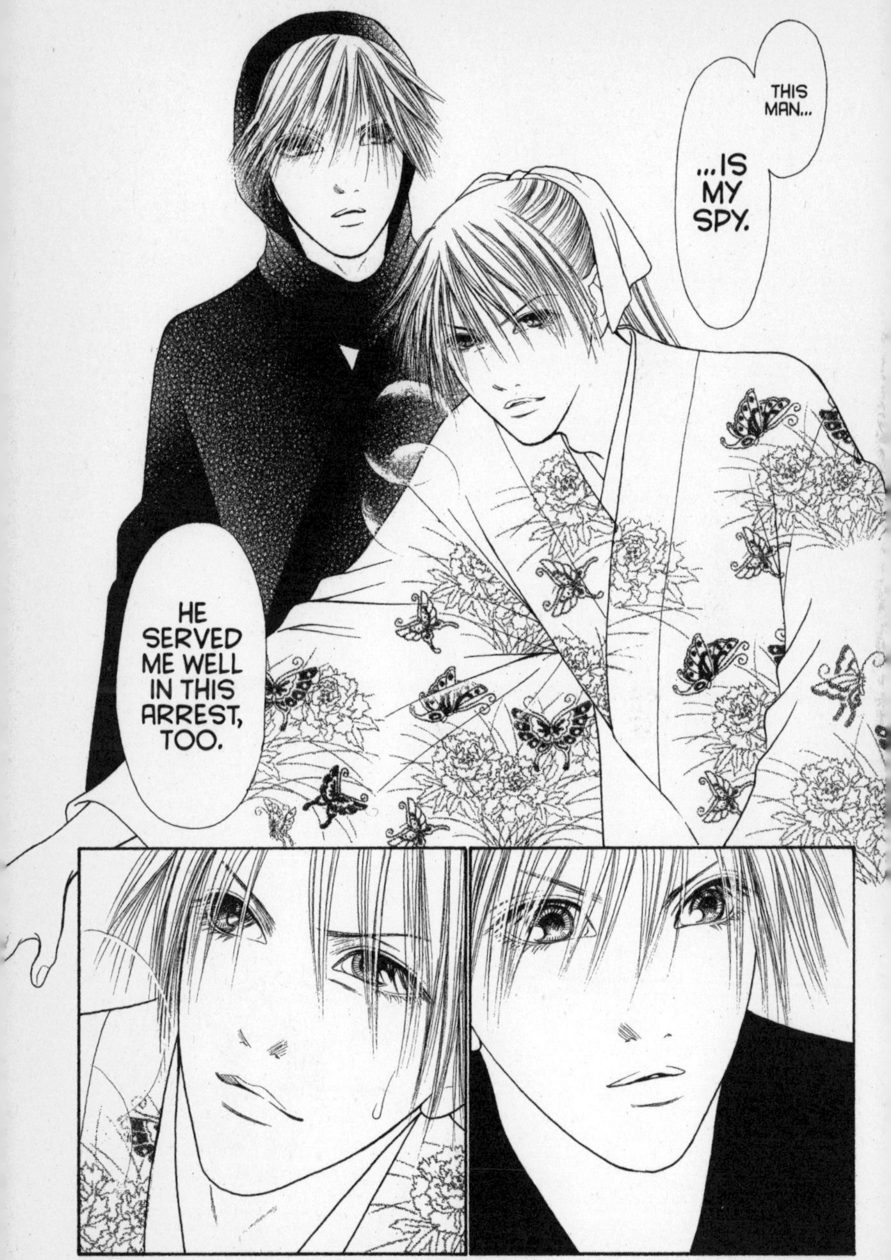
THIS MAN...
...IS MY SPY.
HE SERVED ME WELL IN THIS ARREST, TOO.

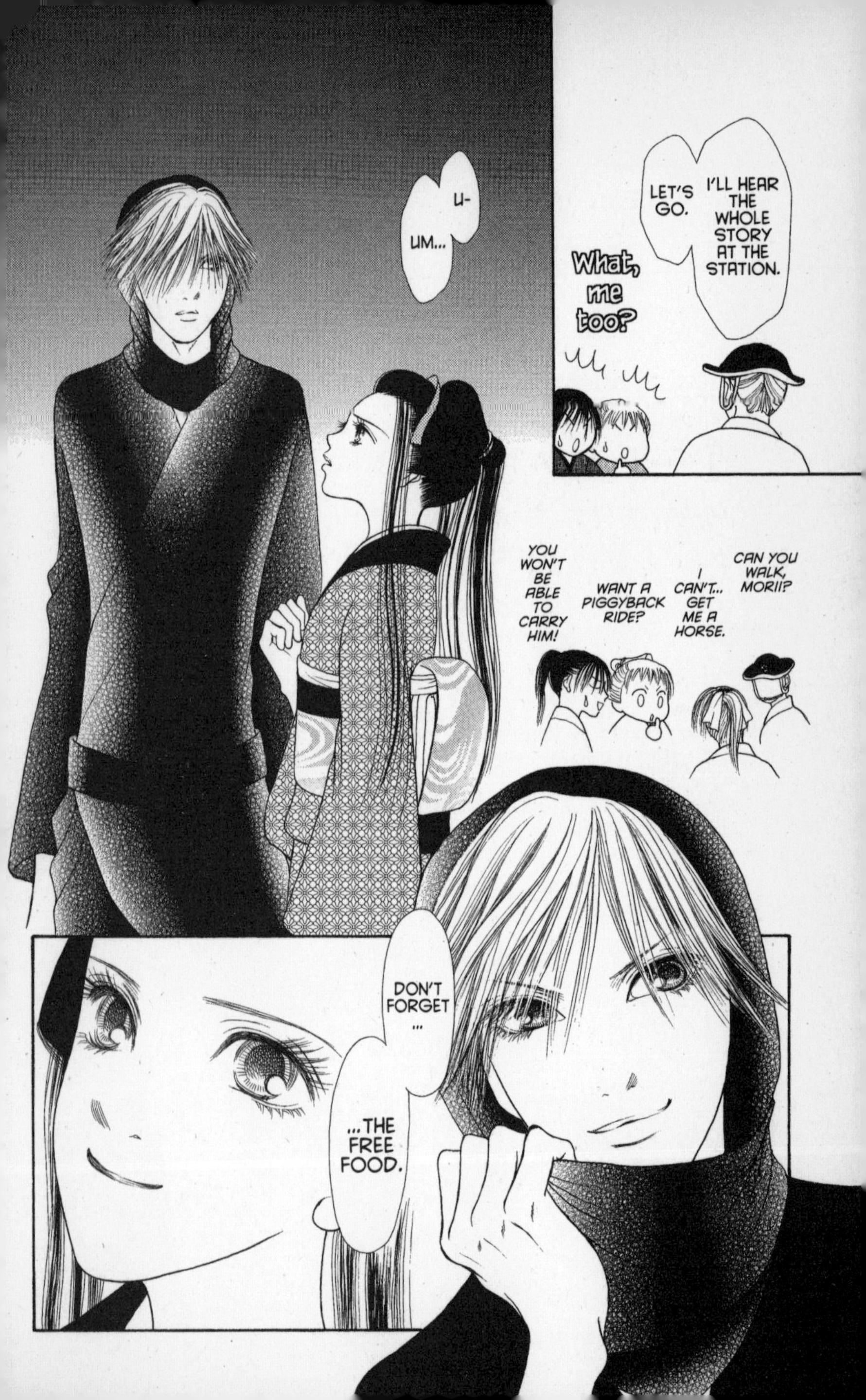
I'LL HEAR THE WHOLE STORY AT THE STATION.
LET'S GO.
What, me too?
CAN YOU WALK, MORII?
I CAN'T... GET ME A HORSE.
WANT A PIGGYBACK RIDE?
YOU WON'T BE ABLE TO CARRY HIM!
U-UM...
DON'T FORGET...
...THE FREE FOOD.

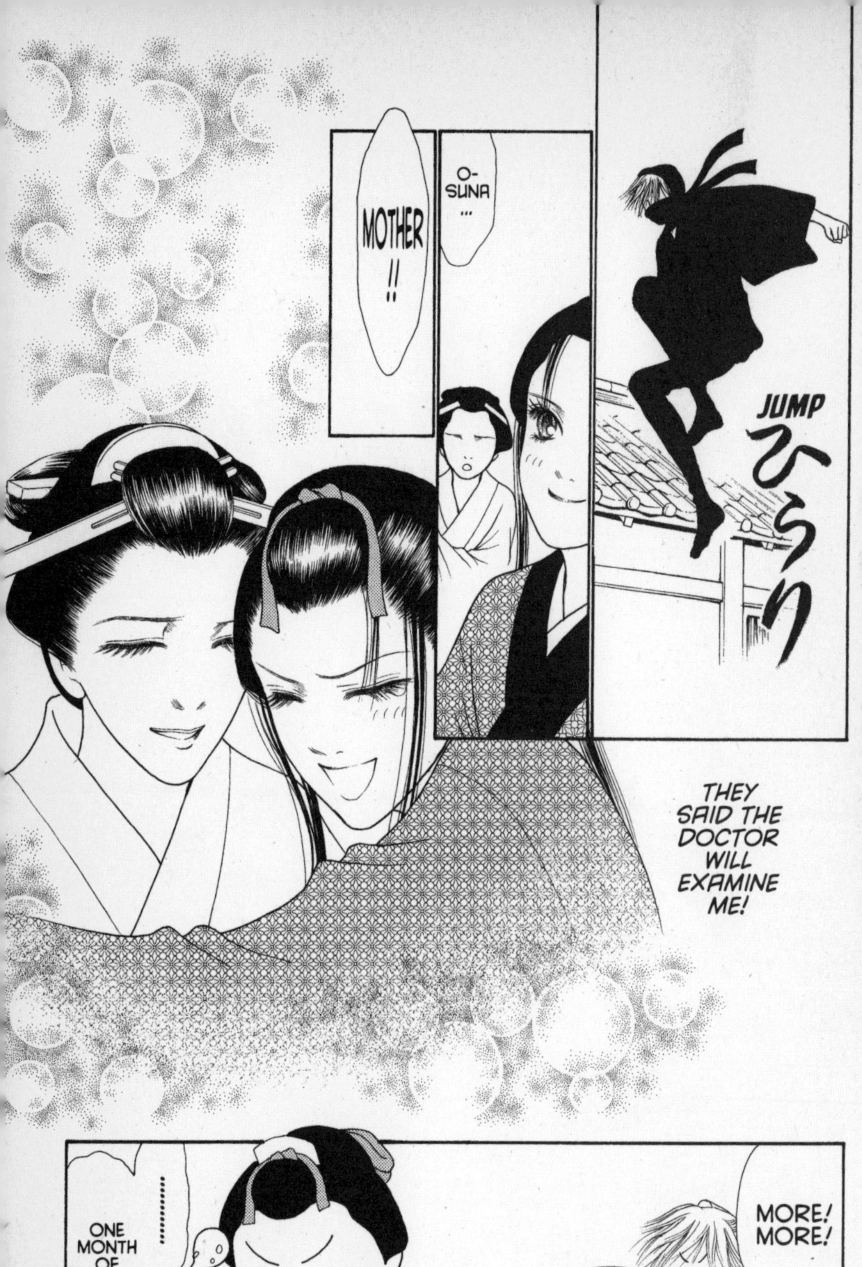
JUMP
ひらり
O-SUNA...
MOTHER!!
THEY SAID THE DOCTOR WILL EXAMINE ME!
MORE! MORE!
....
ONE MONTH OF THIS...

TO BE CONTINUED IN WALLFLOWER 29...

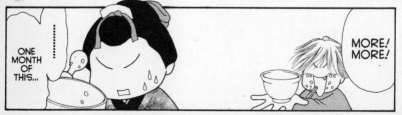

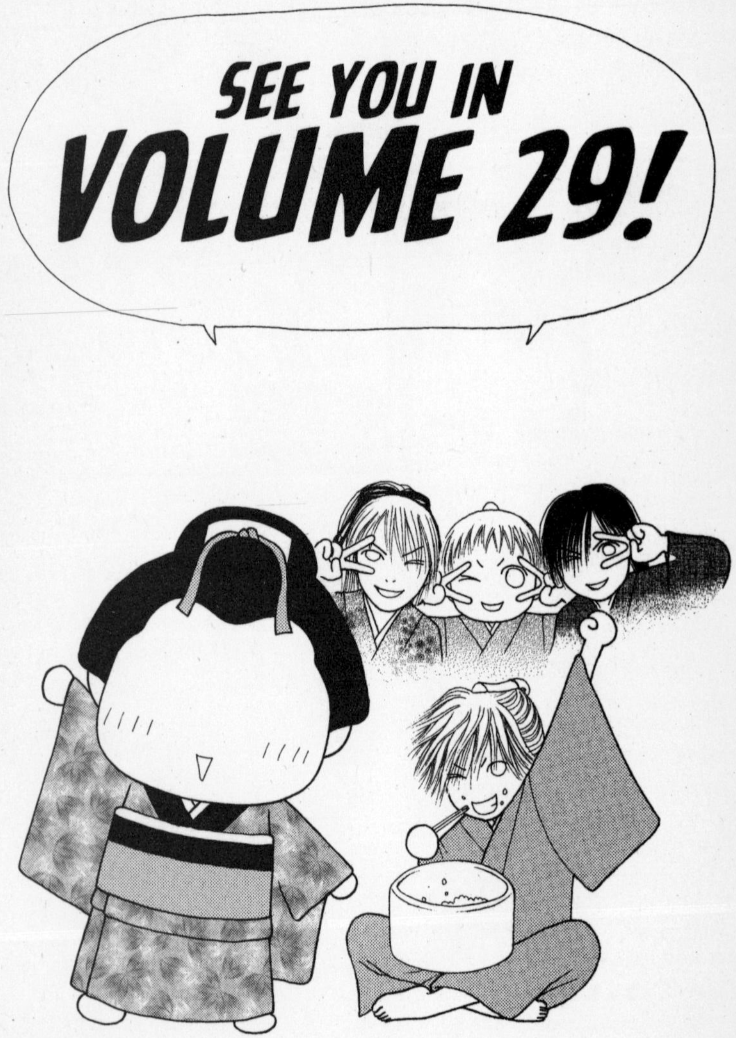
SEE YOU IN VOLUME 29!

Translation Notes

Japanese is a tricky language for most Westerners, and translation is often more art than science. For your edification and reading pleasure, here are notes on some of the places where we could have gone in a different direction in our translation of the work, or where a Japanese cultural reference is used.

Nerimono, page 13.3

A term used for any food that is made from cooked ground fish and spices, such as the white and pink fish cakes one might find in ramen.

Daikon, page 25.3

A large Japanese radish.

Kōmon-sama page 26.3

The boys and Sunako are listing characters from Mito Komon, the longest running period drama in Japan. First aired in 1969, the story is about a retired vice-shogun who, disguised as a retired crepe merchant, travels Japan righting wrongs with his two faithful samurai retainers Suke-san and Kaku-san.

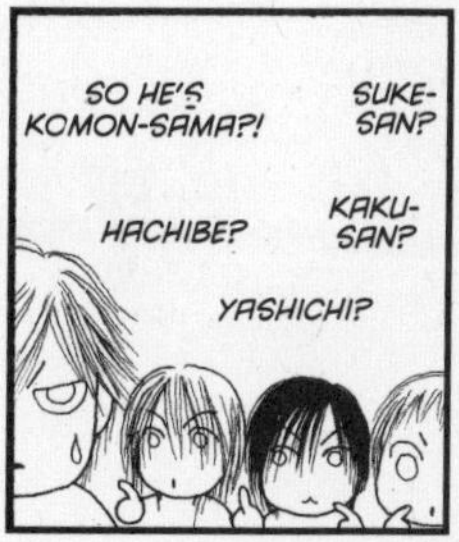
SUKE-SAN?
SO HE'S KOMON-SAMA?!
KAKU-SAN?
HACHIBE?
YASHICHI?

Punch perm, page 56.8

A favorite hairstyle of thugs and gang members in which the hair is tightly permed. Named after its resemblance to needle-punch carpets.

Nezumi Kozō, last two chapters

Based on the real-life Japanese thief and folk hero Nakamura Jirokichi, who, much like Robin Hood, stole from the rich and gave to the poor. His nickname was Nezumi Kozō, roughly meaning "mouse boy," referring to his agility as a thief.

Preview of

THE WALLFLOWER

YAMATONADESHIKO SHICHIHENGE

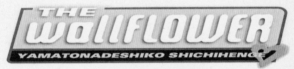

VOLUME 29

We're pleased to present you a preview from *THE WALLFLOWER*, volume 29. Please check our website (www.kodanshacomics.com) to see when this volume will be available in English.

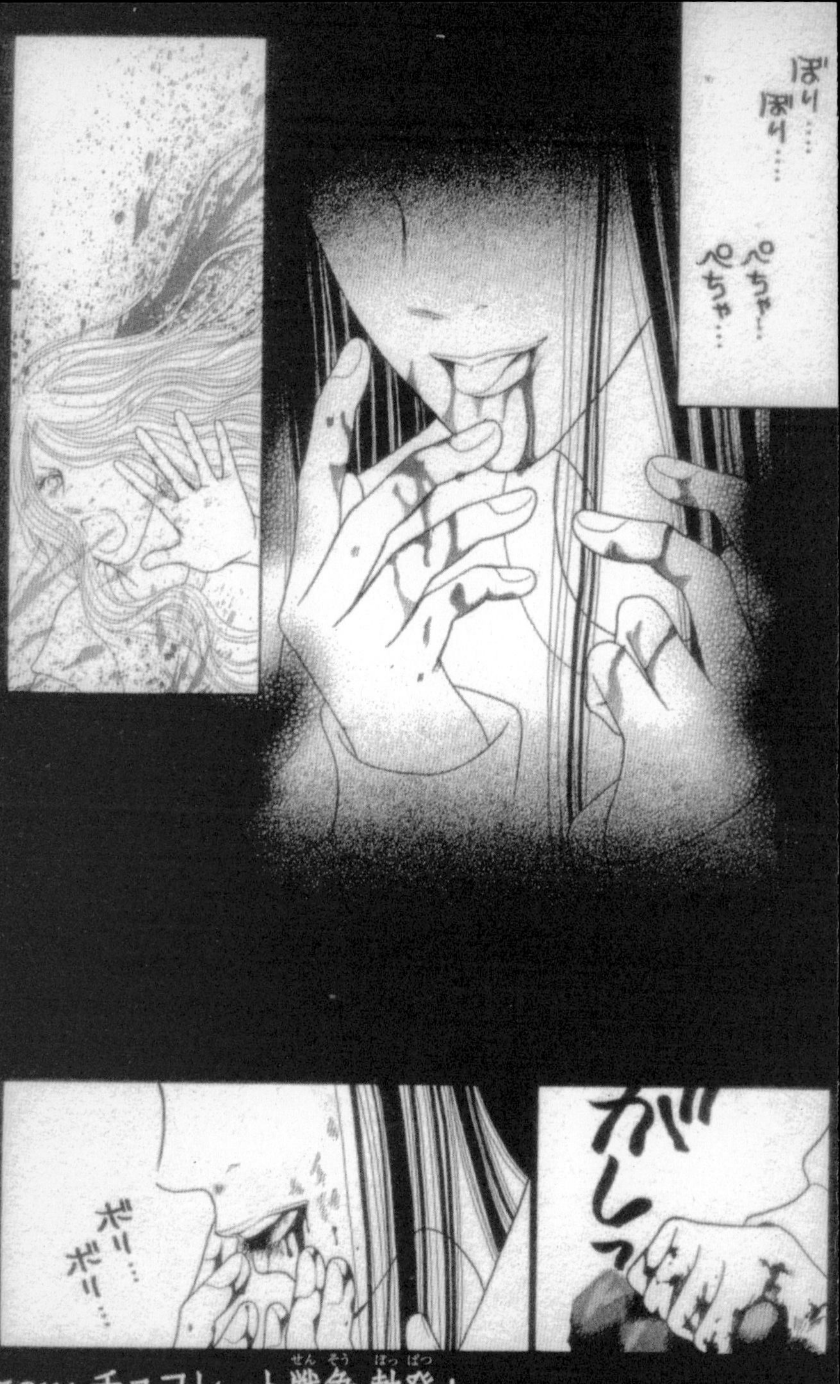
ぽり
ぽり……
ぺちゃ…
ぺちゃ…
がしっ
ボリ…
ボリ…

その116. チョコレート戦争、勃発！

その116. チョコレート戦争、勃発！

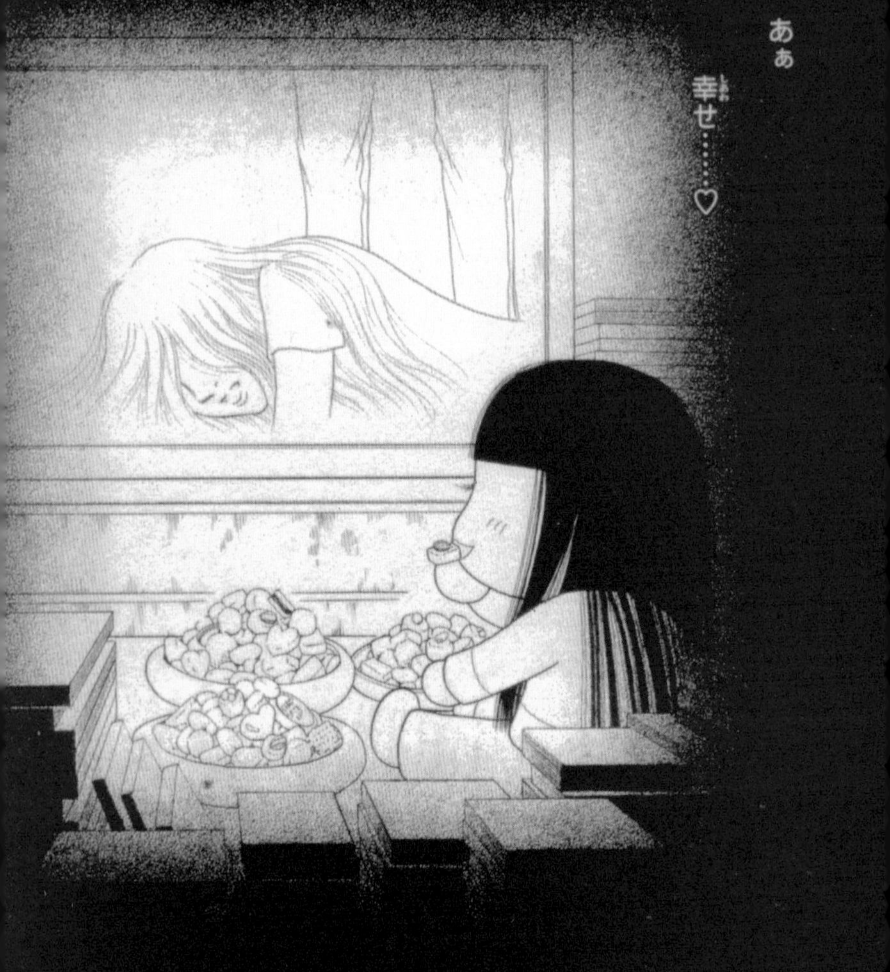
ああ
幸せ……♡

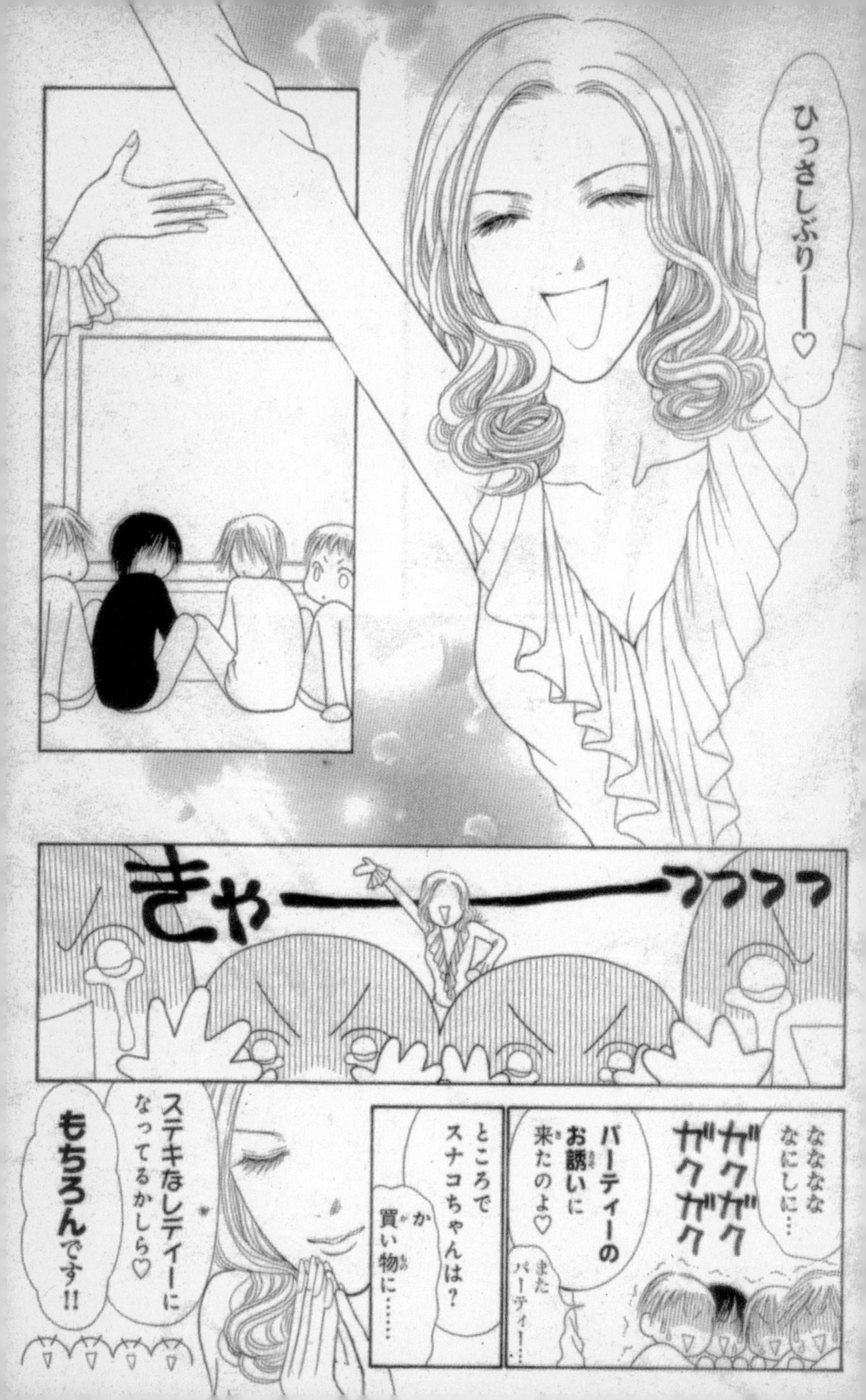
ひっさしぶりーー♡
きゃーーーーっっっっ
なななななにしに…
ガクガク ガクガク
パーティーのお誘いに来たのよ♡
また パーティー…
ところでスナコちゃんは？
買い物に……
ステキなレディーになってるかしら♡
もちろんです!!

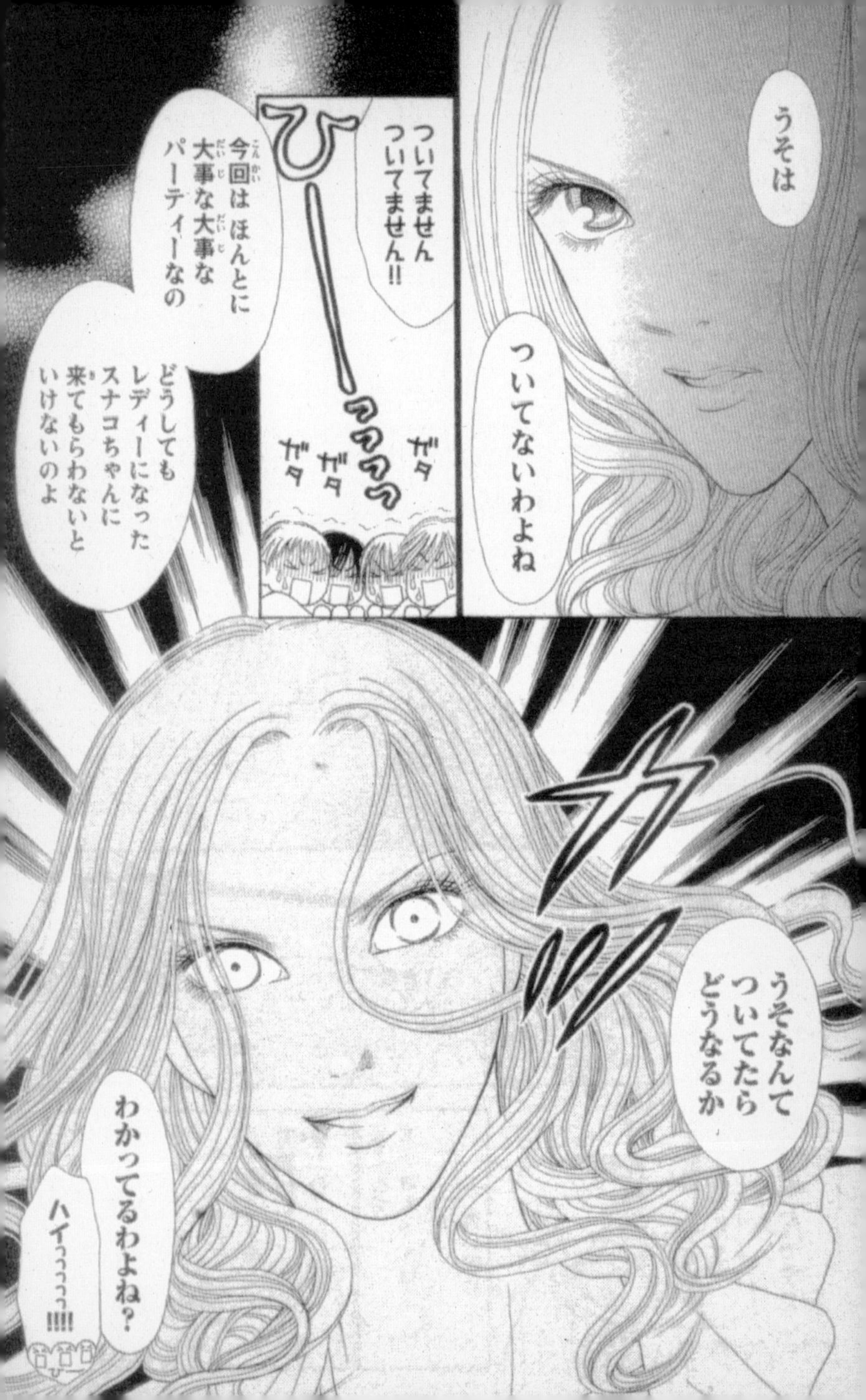
うそは
ついてないわよね
ついてません
ついてません!!
ひーーーっっっ
ガタ
ガタ
ガタ
今回は ほんとに
大事な大事な
パーティーなの
どうしても
レディーになった
スナコちゃんに
来てもらわないと
いけないのよ
ガッ
うそなんて
ついてたら
どうなるか
わかってるわよね?
ハイっっっっっ!!!!

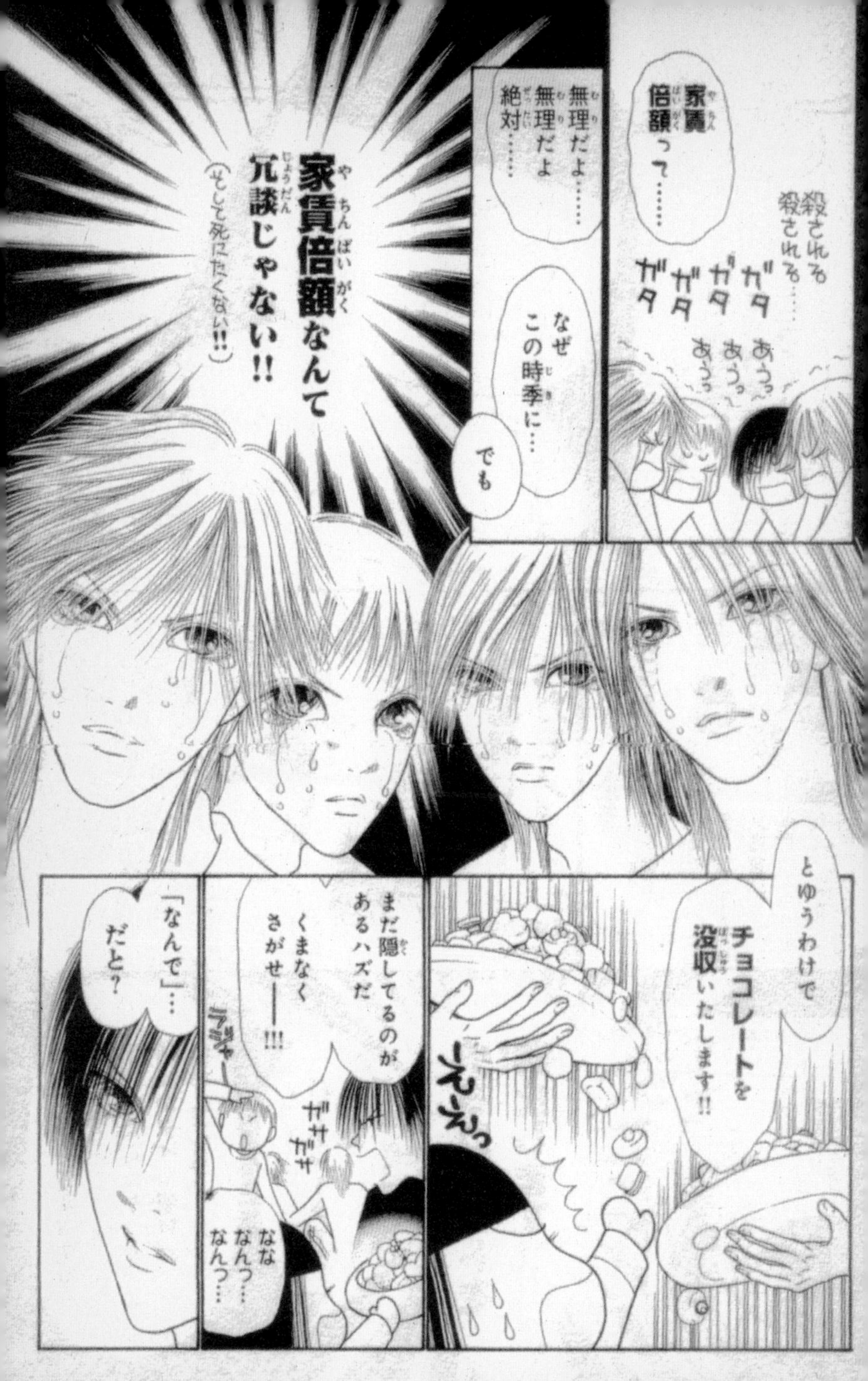

殺されるぞ
殺されるぞ……
ガタガタガタガタ
あうっあうっあうっ
家賃倍額って……
無理だよ…… 無理だよ 絶対……
なぜ この時季に… でも
家賃倍額なんて冗談じゃない!!
(そして死にたくない!!)
とゆうわけで チョコレートを没収いたします!!
えぇっ
まだ隠してるのがあるハズだ くまなくさがせーー!!!
ラジャ
ガサガサ
ななんっ… なんっ…
「なんで」…だと?

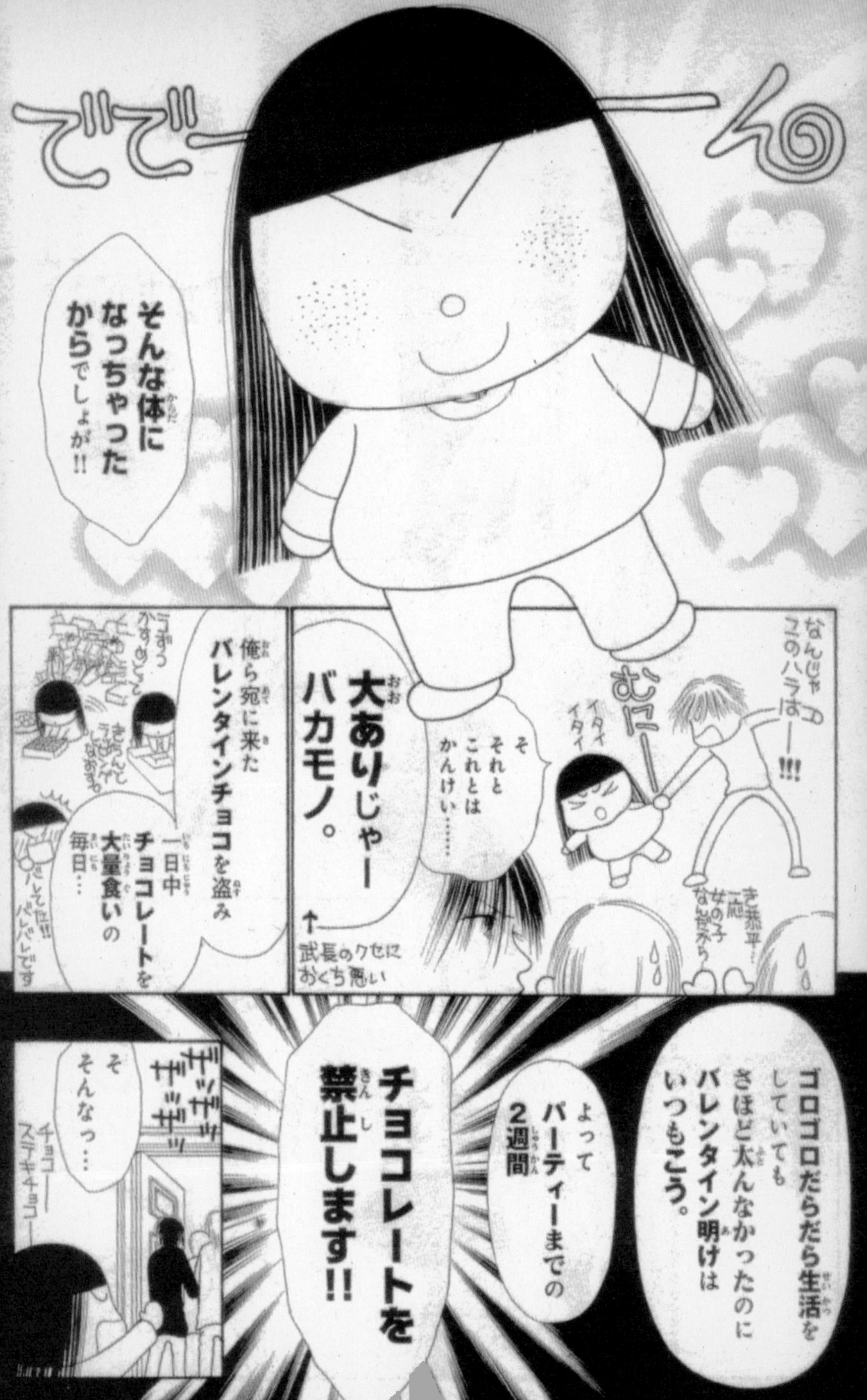
でででーーーん
そんな体になっちゃったからでしょが!!
なんじゃコのハラはコーー!!!
むにーー
イタイイタイ
そ それとこれとはかんけい……
大ありじゃーバカモノ。
きょ恭平… 一応女の子なんだから…
↑武長のクセにおくち悪い
俺ら宛に来たバレンタインチョコを盗み
一日中チョコレートを大量食いの毎日…
バレてた!! バレバレです
ゴロゴロだらだら生活をしていてもさほど太んなかったのにバレンタイン明けはいつもこう。
よってパーティーまでの2週間
チョコレートを禁止します!!
ザッザッザッ
そ そんなっ…
チョコーステキチョコー

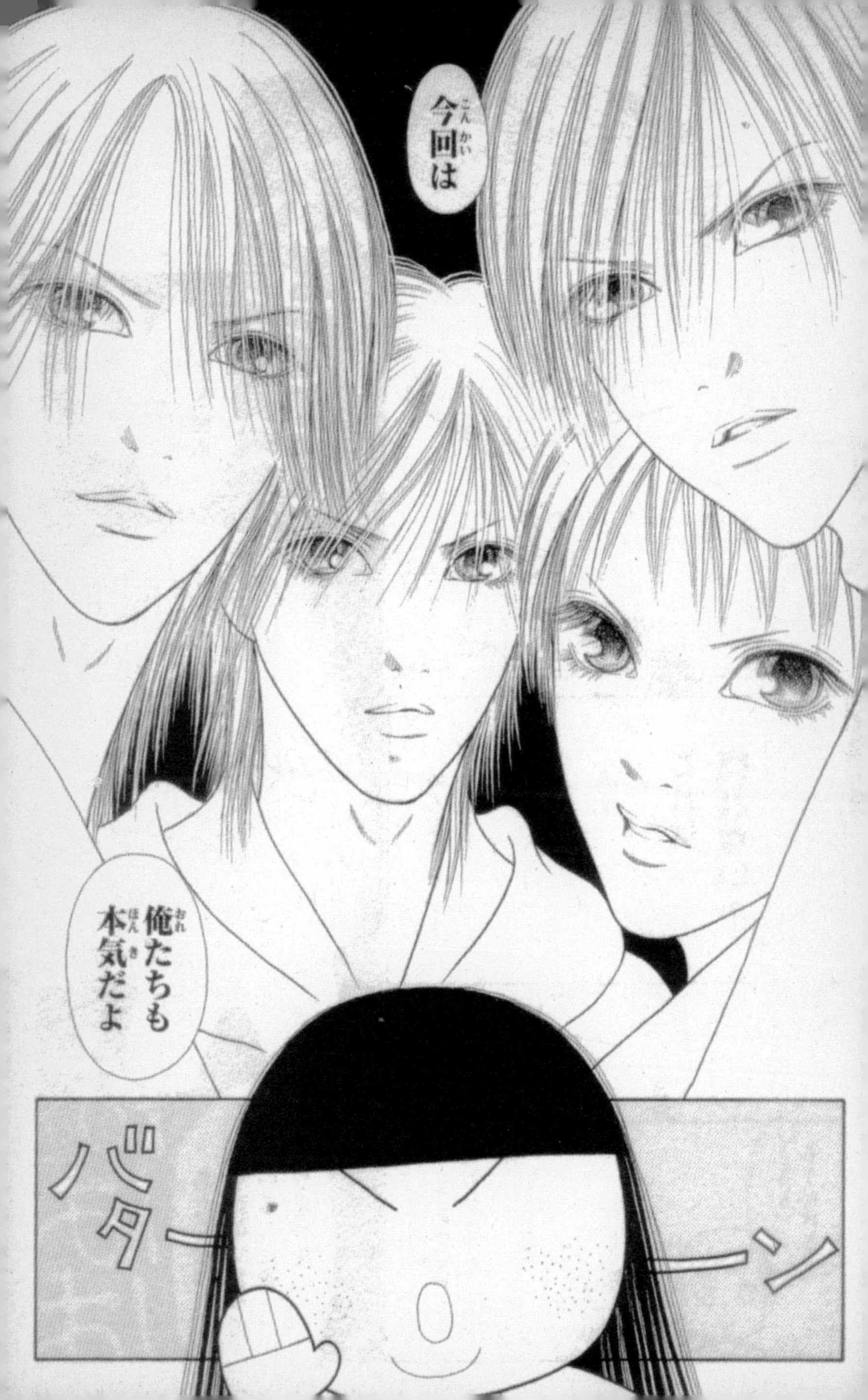
今回は
俺たちも本気だよ
バターーン

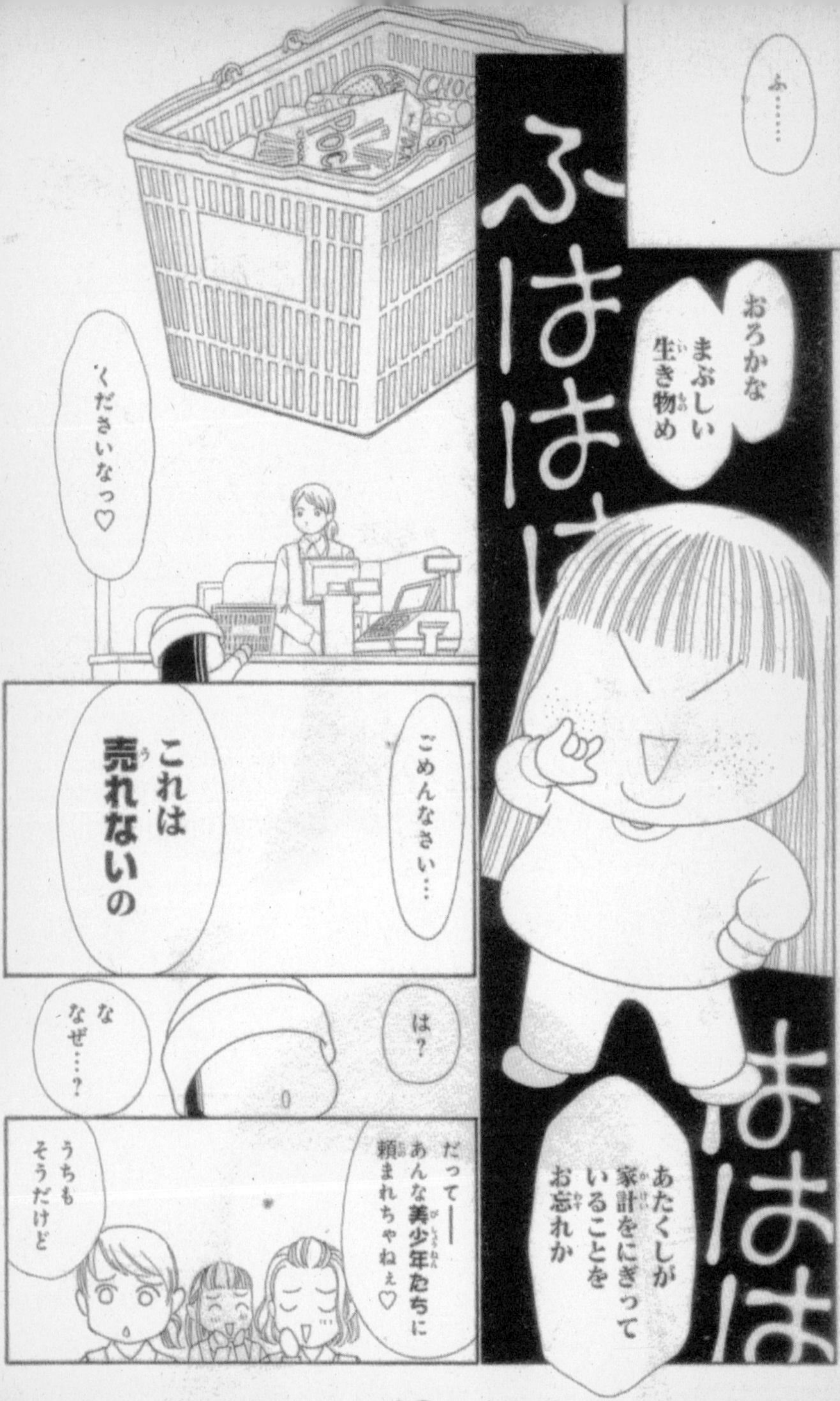
ふ……
おろかなまぶしい生き物め
あたくしが家計をにぎっていることをお忘れか
くださいなっ♡
ごめんなさい…
これは売れないの
は？
なぜ…？
だって——あんな美少年たちに頼まれちゃねぇ♡
うちもそうだけど

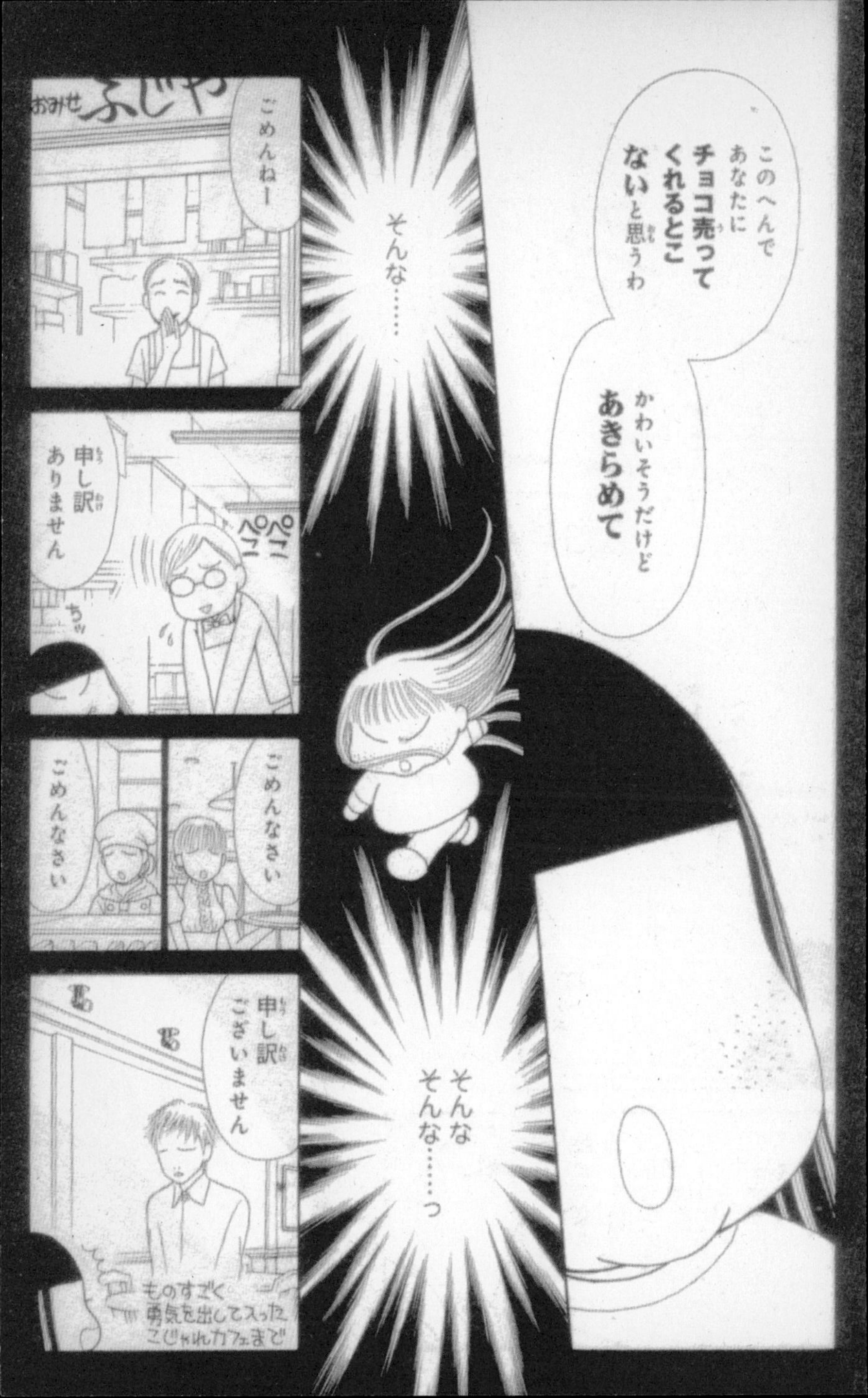
このへんで あなたに チョコ売ってくれるとこ ないと思うわ
かわいそうだけど あきらめて
そんな……
そんな そんな……っ
おみせ ふじや
ごめんねー
申し訳ありません
ペコペコ
ちッ
ごめんなさい
ごめんなさい
申し訳ございません
ものすごく勇気を出して入ったこじゃれカフェまで

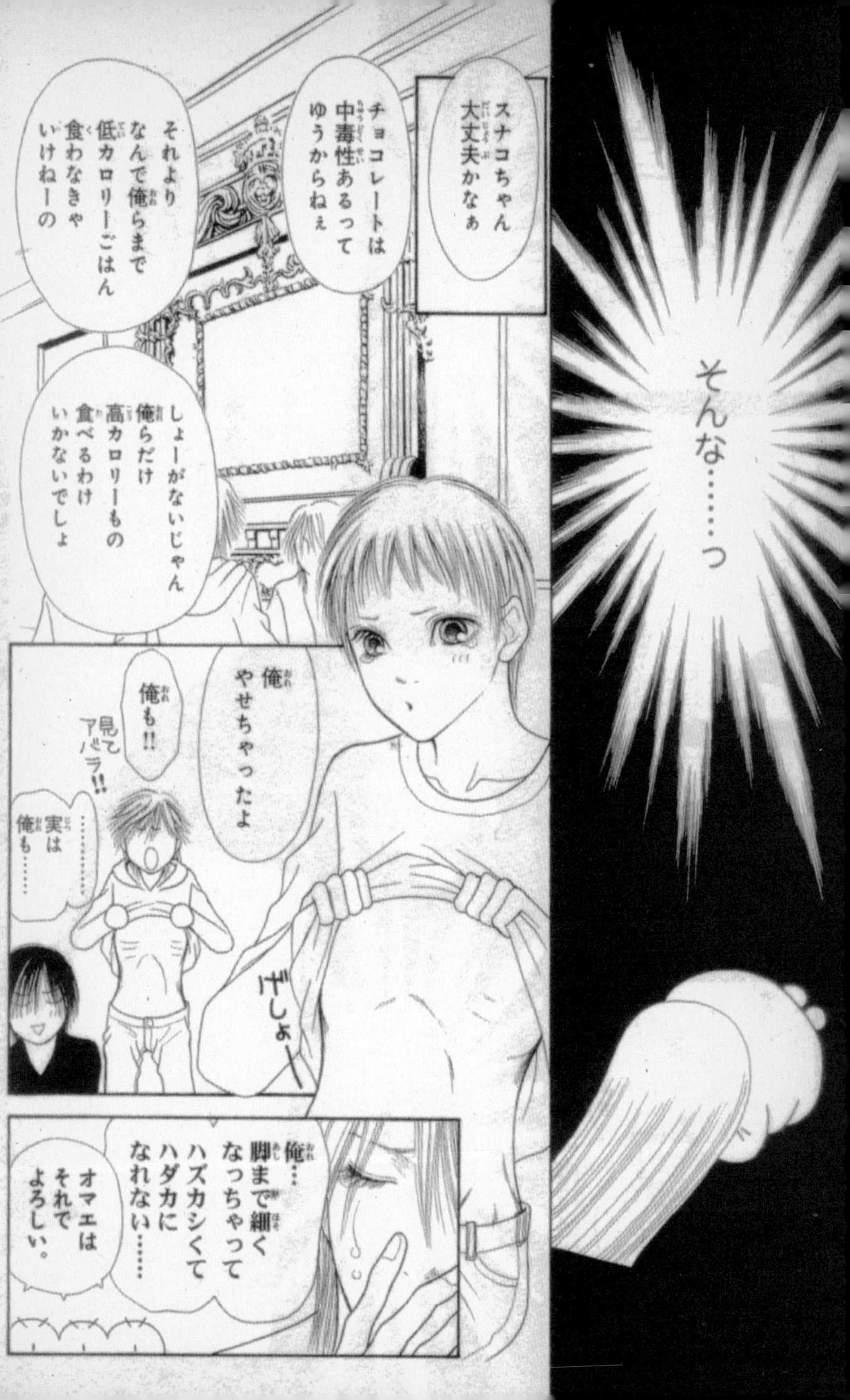
そんな……っ
スナコちゃん大丈夫かなぁ
チョコレートは中毒性あるってゆうからねぇ
それよりなんで俺らまで低カロリーごはん食わなきゃいけねーの
しょーがないじゃん俺らだけ高カロリーもの食べるわけいかないでしょ
俺やせちゃったよ
俺も!!
見てアバラ!!
……実は俺も……
げしょー
俺…脚まで細くなっちゃってハズカシくてハダカになれない……
オマエはそれでよろしい。

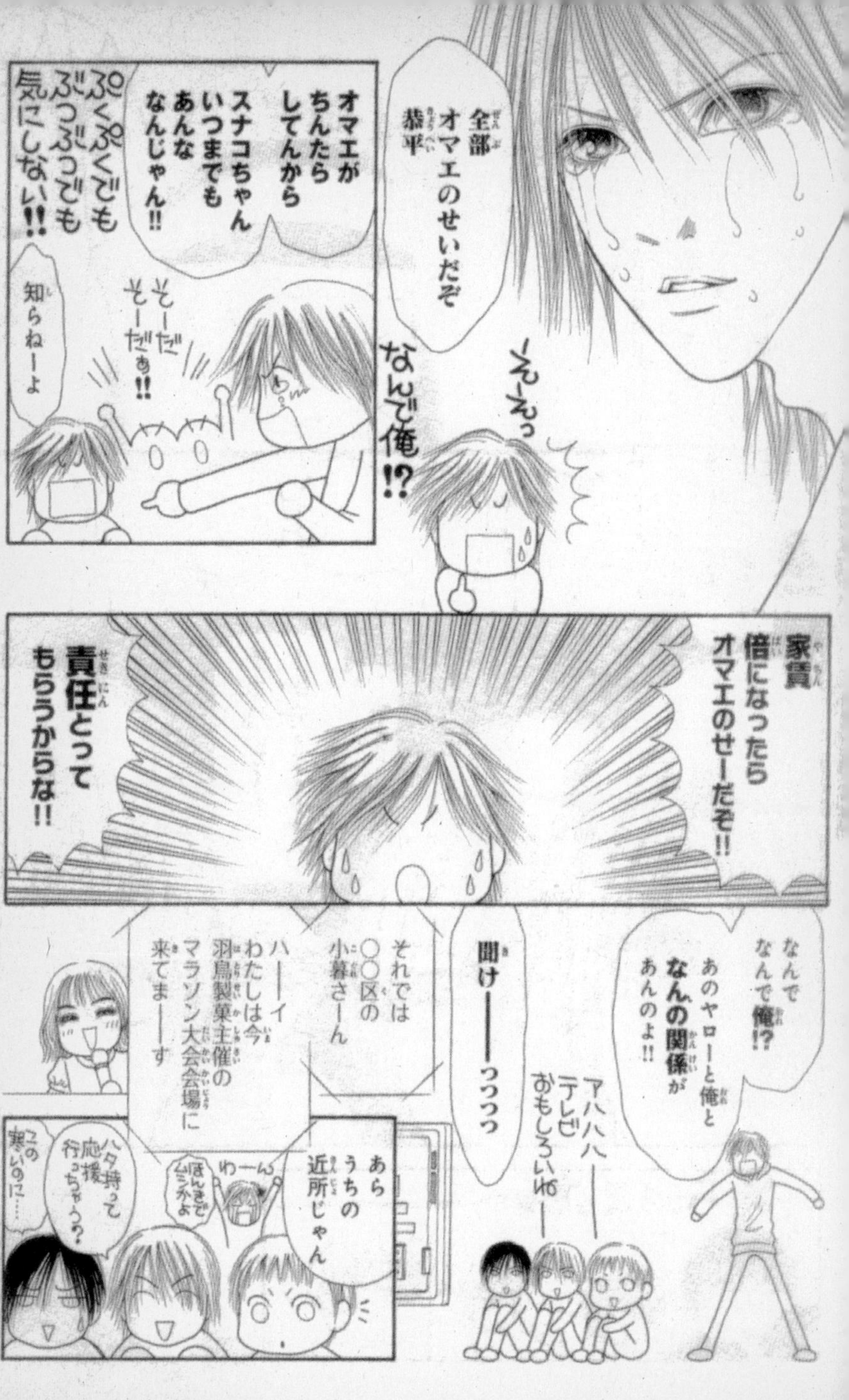
全部オマエのせいだぞ恭平
えーえっ
なんで俺!?
オマエがちんたらしてんからスナコちゃんいつまでもあんななんじゃん!!
そーだそーだぁ!!
ぷくぷくでもぶつぶつでも気にしない!!
知らねーよ
家賃倍になったらオマエのせーだぞ!!
責任とってもらうからな!!
なんでなんで俺!? あのヤローと俺となんの関係があんのよ!!
アハハハーテレビおもしろいねー
聞けーーーっっっ
それでは○○区の小暮さーん
ハーーイわたしは今羽鳥製菓主催のマラソン大会会場に来てまーーす
あらうちの近所じゃん
わーん
ほんきでムシかよ
ハタ持って応援行っちゃう?
この寒いのに……

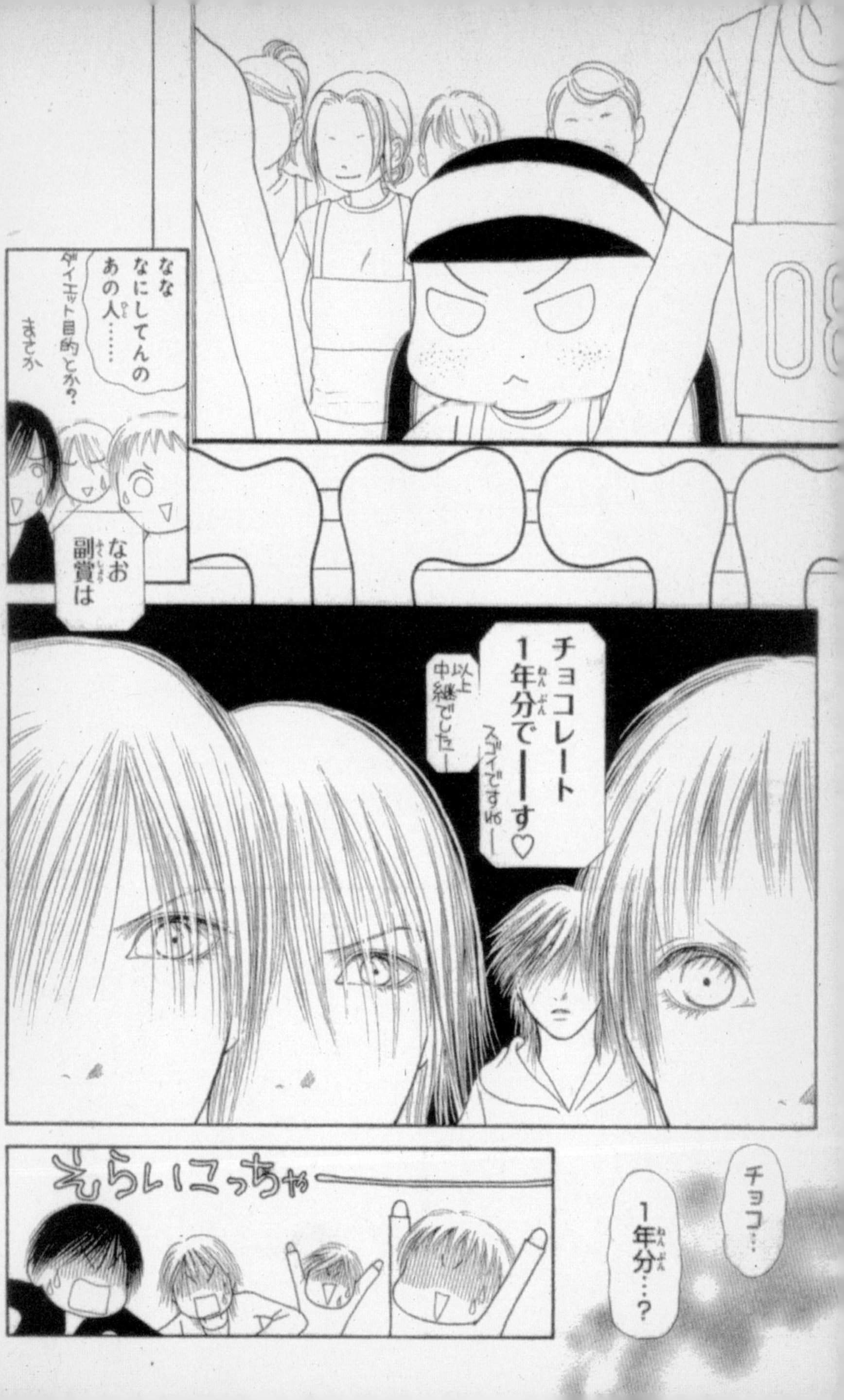
なな
なにしてんの
あの人……
ダイエット目的とか？
まさか
なお副賞は
チョコレート1年分でーーす♡
スゴイですねー
以上中継でしたー
チョコ…
1年分…？
えらいこっちゃーー

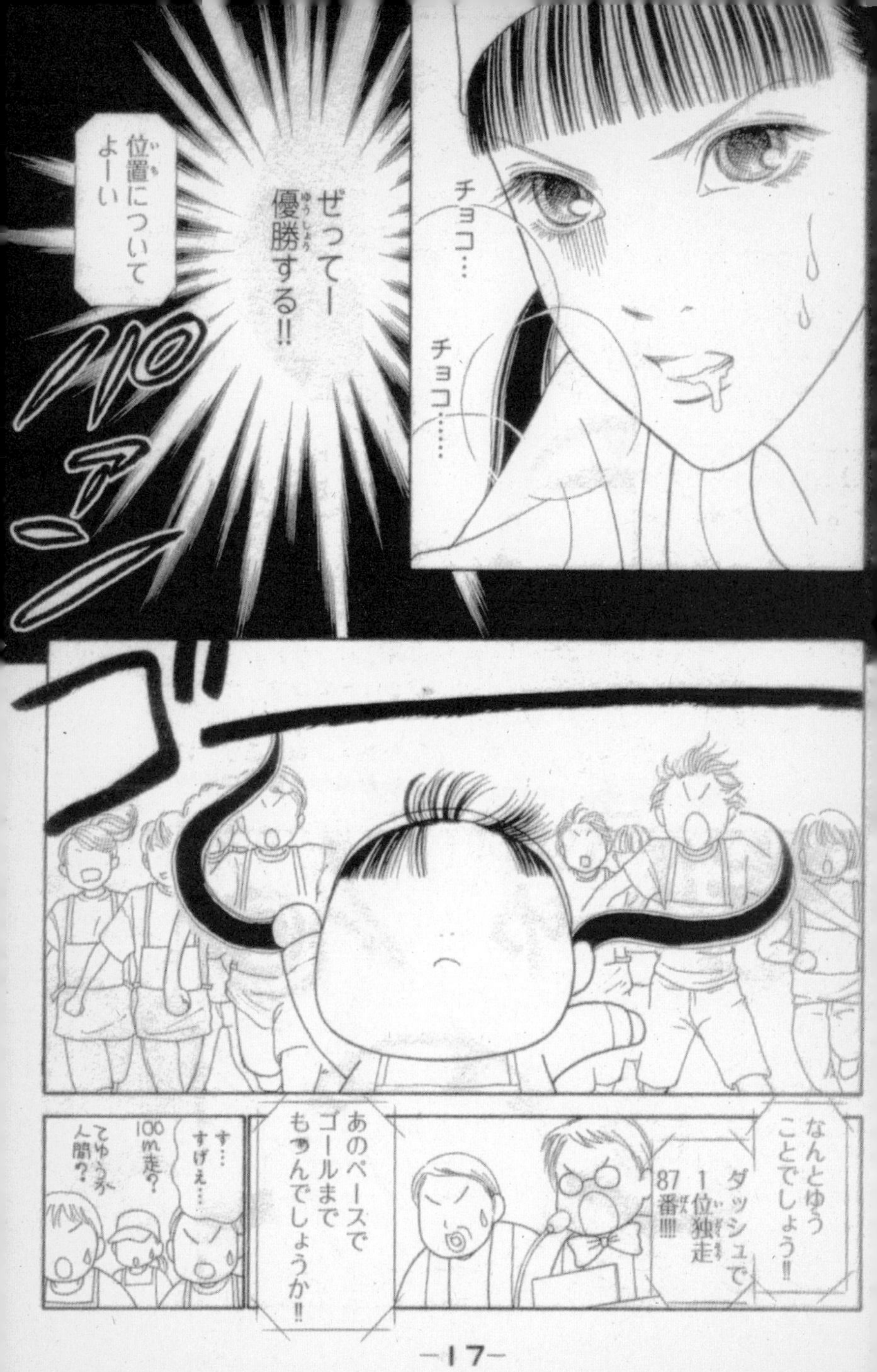
チョコ…
チョコ……
ぜってー優勝する!!
位置についてよーい
パァーン
ゴー
なんとゆうことでしょう!!
ダッシュで1位独走87番!!!!
あのペースでゴールまでもつんでしょうか!!
す…すげえ…
100m走?
てゆうか人間?

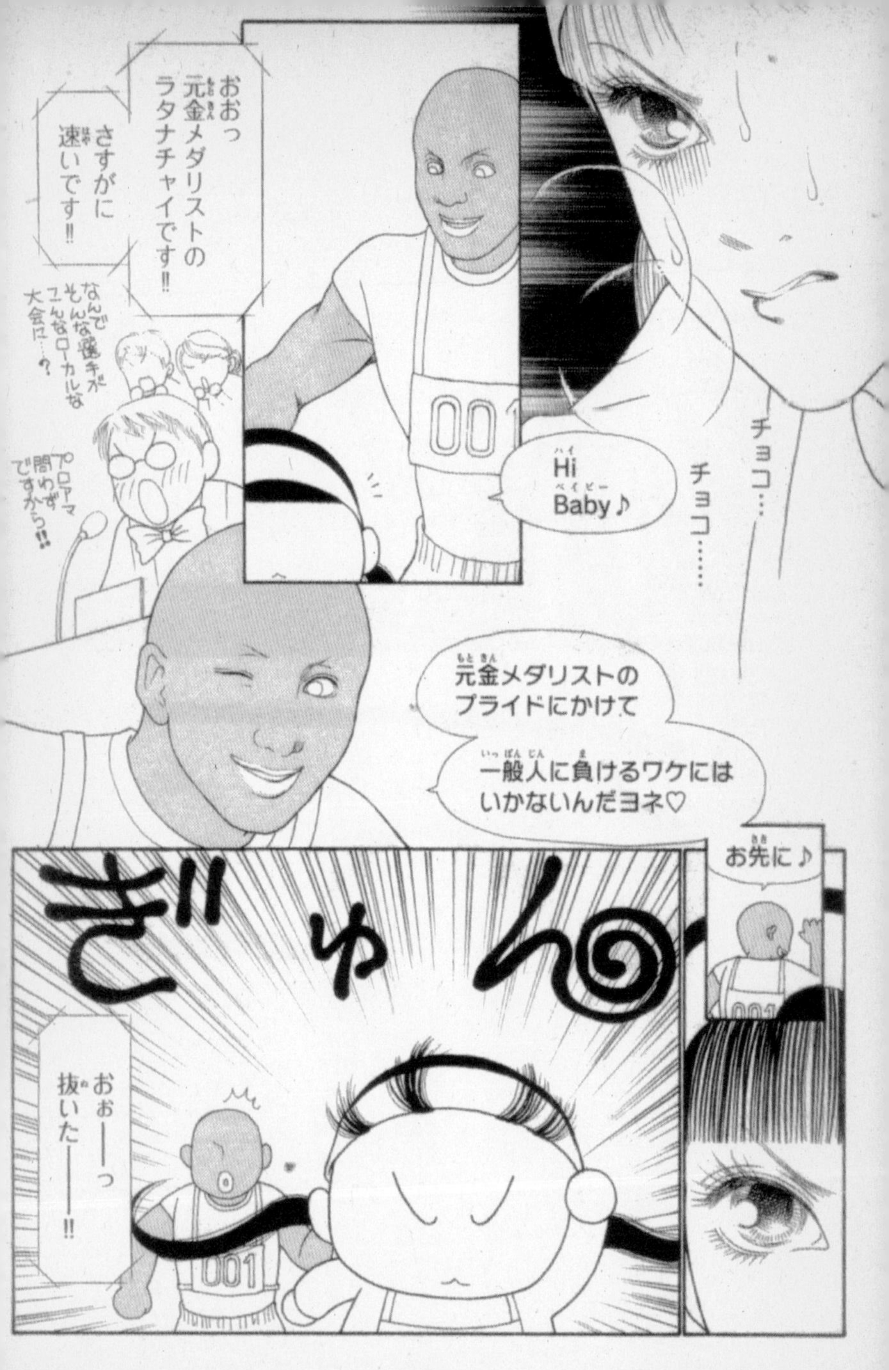
チョコ…
チョコ……
Hi Baby♪
おおっ元金メダリストのラタナチャイです!!
さすがに速いです!!
なんでそんな選手がこんなローカルな大会に…?
プロアマ問わずですから!!
元金メダリストのプライドにかけて
一般人に負けるワケにはいかないんだヨネ♡
お先に♪
ぎゅん
おぉーーっ抜いたーーー!!

The Wallflower volume 28 is a work of fiction. Names, characters, places, and incidents are the products of the author's imagination or are used fictitiously. Any resemblance to actual events, locales, or persons, living or dead, is entirely coincidental.

A Kodansha Comics Trade Paperback Original

Published in the United States by Kodansha Comics, an imprint of Kodansha USA Publishing, LLC., New York.

Publication rights for this English edition arranged through Kodansha Ltd., Tokyo.

First published in Japan in 2011 by Kodansha Ltd., Tokyo, as *Yamatonedeshiko Shichihenge,* volume 28.

ISBN 978-1-61262-118-0

Printed in the United States of America

www.kodanshacomics.com

9 8 7 6 5 4 3 2 1

Translator/Adapter—Andria Cheng
Lettering—Karl Felton

TOMARE!

You're going the wrong way!

Manga is a completely different type of reading experience.

To start at the *beginning,* go to the *end!*

That's right! Authentic manga is read the traditional Japanese way—from right to left. Exactly the *opposite* of how American books are read. It's easy to follow: Just go to the other end of the book, and read each page—and each panel—from right side to left side, starting at the top right. Now you're experiencing manga as it was meant to be!

ATTACK ON TITAN

"A Manga To Look Forward to in 2012" – MTV

FOR THE LAST CENTURY, A GIANT, THREE-WALLED CITY WAS THE ONLY THING STANDING BETWEEN MANKIND AND THE SAVAGE TITANS. BUT WHEN A NEW BREED OF THESE COLOSSAL MONSTERS THREATEN HUMANITY'S HIDDEN FORTRESS, THE REMAINING SURVIVORS MUST BAND TOGETHER...OR FACE TOTAL ANNIHILATION!

ATTACK on TITAN

1

SMASHING INTO BOOKSTORES JUNE 2012

ATTACK on TITAN

BY **HAJIME ISAYAMA**

KODANSHA COMICS

VISIT KODANSHACOMICS.COM TO:
- View release date calendars for upcoming volumes
- Find out the latest news about new Kodansha Comics series